Child Sexual Abuse in Black and Minoritised Communities

"This collection addresses some extremely important chasms in our understanding of child sexual abuse, which have real consequences for child protection strategies, both overarching and in individual cases. Deploying cross-disciplinary analyses of different communities across the globe, the contributors bring to bear empirical and analytical techniques from law, social work, criminology, and sociology to address some profound questions. This rich, thoughtful approach demonstrates that child sexual abuse is not a one-dimensional, homogenous cultural problem in these communities, but instead must be understood within an intersectional framework, often featuring multiple overlapping structural inequalities, which the book assays to construct. The book could help to displace practitioners' trepidation about such cases, informing their professional approaches, especially in considering the investigation and prosecution of such offences, and in weighing the implications for protection of children and other vulnerable family members in the family courts. It deserves a wide audience."

—Laura Hoyano, *Emeritus Professor of Law, University of Oxford, UK and Emeritus Fellow, Wadham College Oxford, UK, Barrister, Red Lion Chambers*

"Childhood sexual abuse (CSA) is an often silent global pandemic that impacts millions of children and families. *Child Sexual Abuse in Black and Minoritised Communities: Improving Legal, Policy, and Practical Responses* features profound intersectional insights into CSA from leading researchers and practitioners. Their work develops more nuanced understandings of CSA in global communities of colour and proposes holistic ways to respond to this form of violence. Professor Aisha K. Gill's and Dr. Hannah Begum's edited collection is a timely and critically needed resource for those engaged in breaking unspeakable silences and ending sexual violence committed against children."

—Aishah Shahidah Simmons, *editor,* Love WITHAccountability: Digging Up the Roots of Child Sexual Abuse, *and producer/director, NO! The Rape Documentary*

"The outstanding quality of this book is that it engages with the contextual features of racially minoritised communities for understanding the scale and nature of child sexual abuse in Black, Asian and minority ethnic communities."
—Claudia Barnard, *Goldsmiths, University of London, UK*

Aisha K. Gill · Hannah Begum
Editors

Child Sexual Abuse in Black and Minoritised Communities

Improving Legal, Policy and Practical Responses

Editors
Aisha K. Gill
The Faculty of Social Sciences and Law
School for Policy Studies
Bristol, UK

Hannah Begum
The Centre of expertise on child sexual abuse
Barnardo House
London, UK

ISBN 978-3-031-06336-7   ISBN 978-3-031-06337-4 (eBook)
https://doi.org/10.1007/978-3-031-06337-4

© The Editor(s) (if applicable) and The Author(s), under exclusive license to Springer Nature Switzerland AG 2022
Chapter 7 is licensed under the terms of the Creative Commons Attribution 4.0 International License (http://creativecommons.org/licenses/by/4.0/). For further details see license information in the chapter.
This work is subject to copyright. All rights are solely and exclusively licensed by the Publisher, whether the whole or part of the material is concerned, specifically the rights of translation, reprinting, reuse of illustrations, recitation, broadcasting, reproduction on microfilms or in any other physical way, and transmission or information storage and retrieval, electronic adaptation, computer software, or by similar or dissimilar methodology now known or hereafter developed.
The use of general descriptive names, registered names, trademarks, service marks, etc. in this publication does not imply, even in the absence of a specific statement, that such names are exempt from the relevant protective laws and regulations and therefore free for general use.
The publisher, the authors, and the editors are safe to assume that the advice and information in this book are believed to be true and accurate at the date of publication. Neither the publisher nor the authors or the editors give a warranty, expressed or implied, with respect to the material contained herein or for any errors or omissions that may have been made. The publisher remains neutral with regard to jurisdictional claims in published maps and institutional affiliations.

This Palgrave Macmillan imprint is published by the registered company Springer Nature Switzerland AG
The registered company address is: Gewerbestrasse 11, 6330 Cham, Switzerland

Foreword

In *Child Sexual Abuse in Black and Minoritised Communities: Improving Legal, Policy and Practical Responses,* Gill and Begum offer a breath of material so that the experiences of victims and survivors who are racially diverse can be better understood. This innovative book deploys intersectional thinking, values and knowledge to take account of the complex and wide-ranging factors framing how child sexual abuse is theorised and understood across disciplinary boundaries. This volume is especially important, as childhood sexual abuse, particularly intrafamilial sexual abuse, is understood and responded to differently depending on the definitions used. The authors bring home the point that in the multi-racial, multi-cultural and multi-faith contexts of contemporary Britain, different cultural beliefs and attitudes towards child sexual abuse are brought into sharp focus because there is not a shared definition of what constitutes harmful sexual behaviour (Bernard 2019). Most notably, the hidden nature of sexual abuse means that it is shrouded in shame, denial, secrecy and silence and the authors paint a vivid picture of how those victimised experience and disclose sexual abuse in a context of systemic racism. Deeply embedded ideas about race, culture and religion that relate to gender-based violence mean that responding to sexual abuse in some minoritised communities is made more complex, as victims and survivors have a deep distrust of institutions such as the police and social services, and fear betraying families (Bernard 2019).

It is also clear that with the increased attention being given to racial justice, because of the re-energised anti-racist activism currently being advanced in the UK, that *Child Sexual Abuse in Black and Minoritised Communities* is to be welcomed because of the need to disrupt the predominant discourses in the sexual abuse field that advance ethnocentric and gender-neutral approaches to the topic. The outstanding quality of this book is that it engages with the contextual features of racially minoritised communities for understanding the scale and nature of child sexual abuse in Black, Asian and minority ethnic communities. In doing so, we are introduced to a diverse group of scholars from different disciplines, who address themes including intrafamilial and extrafamilial abuse; the sexual abuse of males; online facilitated and non-contact sexual abuse; cultural norms, beliefs and attitudes, rights-based approaches, and social justice, to name but a few of the topics tackled. Each chapter offers a rich source of knowledge that weaves together the factors that create the conditions for gendered-oppression risks for children from racially minoritised backgrounds.

It is certainly the case that by foregrounding debates on child sexual abuse through an intersectional lens, the scholars in this collection spotlight the dominant construction of gender in child sexual abuse for understanding the causes, scope and impact of this phenomenon. Indeed, an important feature of *Child Sexual Abuse in Black and Minoritised Communities* is that it encourages us to interrogate the deeply embedded cultural and racialised assumptions that still predominate in much of the literature on child sexual abuse in minoritised communities. An important component of Gill and Begum's objective for the book is to disrupt dominant thinking about racialised and gendered norms, beliefs and assumptions that prevail about child sexual abuse, for developing interventions that are better able to bring about good outcomes for racially minoritised children. Additionally, this collection not only addresses how socio-cultural factors operate at different levels in child sexual abuse, the book also provides a foundation to examine the engrained gendered assumptions that underlie child sexual abuse discourses. Furthermore, the book challenges us to attend to the ways that interventions into child sexual abuse can entrench, rather than challenging, the dominant oppressive discourses about sexual abuse that fuel the mother-blaming that prevails in interventions into intrafamilial sexual abuse. Thus, this book will facilitate important conversations to enable safeguarding professionals and criminal justice advocates to challenge such entrenched ideas about intrafamilial and extrafamilial sexual abuse.

Contemporary debates about child sexual abuse have only just started to pay attention to the specific aspects of Black and minority ethnic children's experiences for a more nuanced appreciation of the intersectional dynamics of intrafamilial sexual abuse in contexts of systemic racism (Bernard 2016). Put simply, we need a good deal more intersectional inquiry in child sexual abuse research as more remains to be understood. In this way, *Child Sexual Abuse in Black and Minoritised Communities* fills a critical gap in the literature and will undoubtedly play an essential role in expanding intersectional research in child sexual abuse. Indeed, the book offers important new insights into multiple intersecting oppressions that impact the experiences of those who suffer sexual abuse within various forms of victimisation, such as domestic violence, forced marriage, child marriage, to name but a few topics. The scholars in this collection have thus provided a compelling guide to help us see the ways in which Black, Asian and minority ethnic children experience multiple forms of oppression that are not reducible to race, and which significantly impact the situational context of sexual abuse. It is from this angle that we need to interrogate the norms and assumptions that underlie much thinking about child sexual abuse in racially minoritised communities for grounding understandings of the enduring consequence and to eschew replicating cultural stereotypes. In essence, this book's main contribution is the relevance of intersectional approaches for understanding the interacting factors that create unique barriers to the disclosure of sexual abuse for children who are intersectionally marginalised.

Professor Claudia Bernard
Goldsmiths, University of London
London, UK

References

Bernard, C. (2016). Child sexual abuse in the lives of black children. In C. Bernard and P. Harris (Eds.), *Safeguarding Black Children: Good Practice in Child Protection*. Jessica Kingsley Publishers.

Bernard, C. (2019). Working with cultural and religious diversity, In J. Howarth and D. Platt (Eds.), *The Child's World: The Essential Guide to Assessing Vulnerable Children, Young People and Their Families*. (3rd ed.). Jessica Kingsley Publishers.

Professor Claudia Bernard is a Professor of Social Work and Head of Postgraduate Research in the Department of Social, Therapeutic and Community Studies. She is a qualified social worker, has worked in local authority children and families social work and has retained this interest in her research and teaching. She joined Goldsmiths in 1994 and previously held a lectureship at the University of Portsmouth. Her general interests lie in the areas of social work with children and families, gender-based violence, critical race theory, equalities and social justice. She has also developed an interest in research ethics. She teaches on courses at undergraduate and postgraduate levels and also leads the Ph.D. programme in the department. As an educator and researcher, her primary interests are in delivering the highest quality of social work education and in developing students' research-mindedness for research-informed practice. She has published widely in child abuse and neglect and in equality and diversity issues in social work education.

Acknowledgements

This edited collection brings together leading researchers and practitioners from criminology, social work, law, philosophy, psychology, social policy and sociology to enrich the existing knowledge base by illuminating the experiences of child sexual abuse (CSA) survivors across the world. This depth of understanding can only be achieved by locating CSA within an intersectional framework, thus enabling effective examination of the dominant paradigms that, in some instances, reduce this form of violence to a cultural problem. The book's central aim is to challenge such widely held but problematic beliefs about CSA by reviewing existing multidisciplinary knowledge and presenting new research in a theoretically informed, practice-oriented and context-specific manner. With this approach, the editors hope to promote a more nuanced perspective on CSA that addresses both the commonalities and particularities of these crimes across and within societies around the globe.

We acknowledge the lives and experiences of all the victims of child sexual abuse and sexual violence who are represented in our project. We recognise the individual stories of courage, hope and resilience that form the basis of continued research in this area. Various individuals have helped us, in different ways, put this body of work together. Whilst it is not possible to thank everyone by name, we would like to single out a number of people who believed in this project and provided logistical support. We wish to thank the wonderful staff of Palgrave Macmillan for their help, support and attention to detail. We especially wish to thank Josie Taylor for her enthusiasm and for providing the platform that allowed this unique collection of papers to be published as a single volume. This publication was also made possible by the cooperation and expertise of the contributors, who generously worked to the project's tight deadlines and who were unfailingly generous with their time and knowledge.

To thank all the people who have helped me, directly and indirectly, with the writing and editing of this special collection would significantly add to its length. My loved ones, my colleagues and my fellow violence against women activists and practitioners have always been so kind and generous in offering me support, information and advice throughout my years of working in this sector. Most importantly, I am indebted to all the victims/survivors of child sexual abuse whose lives have touched mine. You know who you are—thank you! It is in the memory of my mother, *Surinder Kaur*, that I perform this kind of work. Finally, this book is for *Maya, Dharam, Karam and Jude*, who bring me endless joy and love. I hope that one day they will live in a world where a subject like this does not need to be written about

[Aisha K. Gill]

The completion of this book would not have been possible without the support and cooperation of the contributors—thank you. I would like to extend a special thanks to my loved ones, for their continued support and encouragement in all of my endeavours. I also owe a debt of gratitude to Aisha K. Gill for her commitment to this collection, and whose tireless work and efforts in campaigning for the rights of victims are nothing short of inspirational. Finally, this book is dedicated to all victims and survivors of child abuse worldwide.

[Hannah Begum]

Contents

1   **Introduction**   1
    Aisha K. Gill and Hannah Begum

2   **Epistemic Injustice: Racially Marginalised Adult Survivors of Child Sexual Abuse**   31
    Geetanjali Gangoli and Marianne Hester

3   **Understanding the Experiences of British South Asian Male Survivors of Child Sexual Abuse**   59
    Hannah Begum and Aisha K. Gill

4   **Maternal Mimesis: The Impact of Intersectional Abuse on African-Caribbean British Maternal Responses to 'Tellings' of Child Sexual Abuse by Daughters**   115
    Joanne Wilson

5   **'Preserving What for Whom?' Female Victim/Survivor Perspectives on the Silence Behind Child Sexual Abuse in Britain's South Asian Communities**   155
    Vanisha Jassal

6   Survivors Speak Up: Improving Police Responses
    to Sexual Abuse Cases in Black and Racially
    Minoritised Communities   185
    Aisha K. Gill and Yasmin Khan

7   Institutional Responses to Child Sexual Abuse
    in Ethnic Minority Communities   217
    *Rachel Hurcombe, Theresa Redmond, Holly Rodger,
    and Sophia King*

8   Addressing Harmful Sexual Behaviours Among
    Children and Young People: Definitional
    and Regulatory Tensions   249
    Elizabeth Agnew and Anne-Marie McAlinden

9   He Didn't Want Any of That: Considerations
    in the Study and Theorization of Black Boys' Sexual
    Victimization in the United States   273
    Tommy J. Curry

10 Child Sexual Abuse in Latinx Populations
    in the United States: An Examination of Cultural
    Influences   303
    *Maureen C. Kenny, Claire Helpingstine,
    and Maheshi Pathirana*

11 Truth, Trauma and Healing: Stories of Aboriginal
    Survivors of Child Sexual Abuse in Out-of-Home
    Care   341
    Carlina Black, Muriel Bamblett, and Margarita Frederico

12 The Blurred Line: Balancing the Treatment
    of Personality Disorders, Personal Trauma,
    and Cultural Trauma Among Individuals Who Have
    Sexually Offended   371
    Michael P. Lasher

13 "Pussy Power"? Reflecting on Research Practice with Aboriginal and/or Torres Strait Islander Men Who Have Offended Sexually 401
Jodi Death and Kelly Richards

Index 431

Notes on Contributors

Dr. Agnew Elizabeth is an ESRC Postdoctoral Research Fellow in the School of Law at Queen's University Belfast. Her doctoral research explored the emergence, nature and impact of cyberbullying and sexting behaviours among young people in Northern Ireland. More broadly, her research interests include children's rights, youth justice, online harmful sexual behaviours and issues of consent. To date, she has published work in the *International Journal of Children's Rights* and is currently working on her monograph 'Cyberbullying and Sexting: Regulatory Challenges in the Digital Age,' due to be published by Hart.

Adjunct Professor Bamblett Muriel, AO is a proud Yorta Yorta and Dja Dja Wurrung woman who is a determined and tireless advocate for Aboriginal children, families and communities. She has been the CEO of the Victorian Aboriginal Child Care Agency (VACCA) since 1999, and under her leadership, VACCA has grown exponentially and is the leading organisation of its type in Australia. She is also the Chairperson of SNAICC, the national peak body representing Aboriginal and Torres Strait Islander child and family services. She is active on over 30 advisory groups, committees and boards concerning the Aboriginal community and is an Adjunct Professor at La Trobe University.

Dr. Begum Hannah is currently a Researcher based at Barnardos, centre of expertise on child sexual abuse. She is also part of a research team at Birmingham City University working on an ESRC-funded project exploring the impact of COVID-19 on minority Muslim communities in Birmingham. She completed her Ph.D. in 2019 with a thesis that focused on the experiences of British Asian survivors of childhood sexual abuse. Her research interests lie broadly in the fields of victimology, child sexual abuse and the experiences of Black and minoritised communities in the criminal justice system. She is a Fellow of the Higher Education Academy and has previously taught at the Universities of Coventry, De Montfort, Newman, Birmingham Staffordshire, and London Metropolitan and at both undergraduate and postgraduate levels.

Black Carlina is a Ph.D. candidate in Social Work and Social Policy at La Trobe University, exploring cultural healing in the context of complex childhood trauma and collective trauma: Amplifying the voice of Aboriginal expertise. She was awarded the Robin Clark Berry Street Postgraduate Scholarship for research excellence in childhood trauma to undertake this research. She has worked in the areas of evidence-informed and translational research in child welfare for 20 years. For the last seven years, she has worked in Indigenous child welfare, specifically senior research, evaluation and policy roles at the Victorian Aboriginal Child Care Agency (VACCA).

Professor Curry Tommy J. joined the Philosophy Department at the University of Edinburgh in the Fall of 2019. His research interests are in Africana Philosophy and the Black Radical Tradition. His areas of specialisation are: nineteenth-century ethnology, critical race theory, social political theory, and Black male studies. He is the author of *The Man-Not: Race, Class, Genre, and the Dilemmas of Black Manhood* (Temple University Press 2017), which won the 2018 American Book Award. He is the author of *Another white Man's Burden: Josiah Royce's Quest for a Philosophy of Racial Empire* (SUNY Press 2018).

Dr. Death Jodi is a criminologist specialising in victimology and sexual violence, particularly institutional child sexual abuse. She has received research funding as part of interdisciplinary teams, including grants from the Royal Commission into Institutional Responses to Child sexual abuse, ANROWS, and a Criminological Research Grant (CRG). These projects have included survivors' perspectives on sex offender reintegration, children's perspectives of safety in institutions and children and young people's perspectives on safety in out-of-home-care. She has partnered with both government and non-government organisations including Bravehearts Foundation, Queensland Corrective Services, Department of Health and Human Services (Victoria), Family and Community Services (New South Wales), the now Department of Children, Youth Justice and Multicultural Affairs (Queensland), CREATE Foundation and the Clergy Abused Network (CAN).

Professor Frederico Margarita, AM is an internationally recognised leader and expert in child and family welfare. She is the Graduate Research Coordinator in Social Work and Social Policy at La Trobe University and Principal Research Consultant of Victoria, Australia's Berry Street Take Two program. She teaches and researches in child protection and child and family welfare and leadership. She was awarded life membership of the Australian Association of Social Workers and of Berry Street. She is also a Director of Jesuit Social Services and Odyssey House Victoria.

Dr. Gangoli Geetanjali is Associate Professor, Department of Sociology, Durham University, and Co-Editor of the *Journal of Gender Based Violence*. She works in the field of gender-based violence, and her particular specialism is in looking at the intersecting roles of class, ethnicity, gender, sexuality and disability in terms of the perpetuation, the experience of and the prevention of gender-based violence and abuse. She is concerned with the implications for practice, and the intersections between policy and practice; particularly around issues concerning BME communities, female genital mutilation and honour-based violence.

Professor Gill Aisha K., Ph.D. CBE is Professor of Criminology at University of Bristol, UK. Her main areas of interest and research focus on health and criminal justice responses to violence against Black, minority ethnic and refugee women in the UK, Afghanistan,

Georgia, Iraqi Kurdistan, India, Libya, Pakistan and Yemen. She has been involved in addressing the problem of violence against women and girls/, 'honour' crimes and forced marriage at the grassroots/activist level for the past 23 years. Her recent publications include articles on crimes related to the murder of women/femicide, 'honour' killings, coercion and forced marriage, child sexual exploitation and sexual abuse in South Asian/Kurdish and Somali communities, female genital mutilation, sex selective abortions, intersectionality and women who kill. 100+ peer-reviewed publications including in *British Journal of Criminology, Criminal Justice Policy Review, Feminist Criminology*, and *Journal of Gender-Based Violence, Violence against Women Journal*. She is editorial member of the British Journal of Criminology. In 2019, appointed Co-Chair of End Violence Against Women Coalition. Since 2020, she has been involved in Nuffield funded research on the effectiveness of forced marriage protection orders in collaboration with University of Lincoln. During the coronavirus pandemic, she has also been hands-on at the grassroots level in terms of raising emergency COVID-19 funds for abused migrant women and children—who have no recourse to public funds. In April 2021, she was appointed to the CEDAW People's Tribunal hearings into women's human rights in the United Kingdom.

Professor Hester Marianne Ph.D. OBE FAcSS is Head of the Centre for Gender and Violence Research, University of Bristol, and Editor-in-Chief of the international *Journal of Gender Based Violence*. She has written about many aspects of violence and abuse including domestic and sexual violence, child contact, domestic abuse in LGBT+ communities and forced marriage, and is researching approaches to domestic abuse perpetrators and meaning of justice. She works closely with NGOs tackling gender-based violence in the UK and Europe, and frequently acts as advisor to government departments. She is Affiliated Professor at the University of Gothenburg.

Helpingstine Claire is a doctoral student in the Department of Psychology at Florida International University (FIU). Her research focuses on the role of culture, context and intersectionality in women and girl's experiences of CSE entry and exit in the US and globally.

Hurcombe Rachel has over ten year's research experience in the fields of child sexual abuse, homelessness and health. As a Senior Research Officer at the Independent Inquiry into Child Sexual Abuse, she led the quantitative analysis of victims and survivors' accounts of child sexual abuse, and worked on projects exploring child sexual abuse in ethnic minority communities and the impacts of child sexual abuse. Her other published works include studies on drinking cultures among young people and alcohol use among people from different ethnicities. She has an M.Sc. in Criminology from the London School of Economics.

Jassal Vanisha (SFHEA) has been with the Centre for Child Protection since 2012. She is Senior Lecturer and Director of Studies for the M.A. in Advanced Child Protection programme, a popular interprofessional online and distance learning programme. She is a Senior Fellow with the Higher Education Academy. The M.A. attracts students from a variety of child protection agencies from across the world. She also manages the Centre's standalone M.A. modules, creating opportunities for students to achieve qualifications through pathways which are not exclusively based on the M.A. route. She is currently studying for a Ph.D. in managing child sexual abuse in the British South Asian communities.

Professor Kenny Maureen C. is a Professor of Counselor Education in the Department of Counseling, Research and School Psychology at Florida International University (FIU). FIU is a Hispanic serving institution in Miami, Florida. She has extensive clinical and research experience with child victims of sexual abuse and has published on child sexual abuse and prevention efforts with minority populations.

Dr. King Sophia is a government researcher with a background in cognitive psychology with experience building analytical capability and working on large-scale social surveys. Whilst working as a Principal Research Officer at the Independent Inquiry into Child Sexual Abuse, she designed and led research on child sexual abuse from accounts shared with the Inquiry's Truth Project, and later was responsible for the Inquiry's entire research and analytics programme.

Khan Yasmin, M.Sc. is Founder and Director of the Halo Project, a national charity supporting Black and minoritised victims and survivors of abuse such as forced marriage, honour-based violence and female genital mutilation. She is also a National Adviser to the Welsh Government on Violence against Women, Domestic Abuse and Sexual Violence. Her work includes developing the UK's first Forced Marriage/HBV case scrutiny group, chairing Independent Advisory and Race Scrutiny Groups with the police and Crown Prosecution Service, and launching a super-complaint on police failings in dealing with sexual abuse cases from Black and minoritised communities. The report aims to transform police investigations in England and Wales and bring justice to survivors.

Dr. Lasher Michael P., Ph.D. is a Clinical Psychologist specialising in the evaluation and treatment of adults who have sexually offended. He has worked with this population in outpatient treatment, prison-based treatment and civil commitment across four different states. He currently provides behavioural treatment services in the Virginia Center for Behavioral Rehabilitation. In addition to his clinical practice, he is the co-author of the SOTIPS and VASOR-2, two risk assessment instruments for use with this population. He also published on evaluation and treatment methods for individuals who have sexually offended, prevention issues, and interprofessional engagement, and independently engages in research and consultation on these issues.

Professor McAlinden Anne-Marie is Professor of Law and Criminal Justice in the School of Law at Queen's University Belfast. She is a world-leading expert on sexual offending and the author/editor of over 60 publications including five books. She has been the lead or co-investigator on a number of funded projects including currently 'Apologies, Abuses and Dealing with the Past' (ESRC). She has also acted as a consultant to local criminal justice agencies and gave expert evidence to the Australian Royal Commission into Institutional Responses to Child Sexual Abuse on 'Grooming and Entrapment'. She has been interviewed for and cited in *The New York Times* and *The Economist.*

Pathirana Maheshi is a clinical mental health counselling student in the Department of Counseling, Recreation and School Psychology at Florida International University. She has worked with U.S. war veterans and people in the community who have experienced homelessness and are in sustainable housing.

Dr. Redmond Theresa is a Senior Research Fellow at the Policing Institute for the Eastern Region (PIER). She has extensive research and practitioner experience and expertise in the field of child sexual abuse and exploitation (CSAE) and vulnerabilities. Her interest in researching CSAE, as a specific form of gendered violence, focuses on how it is experienced and made sense of by victims/survivors, as well as developing policy and practice responses. Before joining PIER, she worked at the Independent Inquiry into Child Sexual Abuse researching child sexual abuse in institutional settings, in the context of schools and in ethnic minority communities.

Dr. Richards Kelly is an Associate Professor in the School of Justice at Queensland University of Technology, where her research focuses primarily on sexual offending and the reintegration of those who perpetrate sexual violence. In 2010, she was awarded the ACT Government Office for Women Audrey Fagan Churchill Fellowship to investigate Circles of Support and Accountability in Canada, America and the United Kingdom. She recently finalised a project funded by Australia's National Organisation for Women's Safety (with Dr Jodi Death, QUT and Professor Kieran McCartan, University of the West of England) on community-based approaches to reintegrating those who sexually offend, as well as the views of victim/survivors of sexual violence about offender reintegration. She was recently awarded a Fulbright Senior Scholar Award and will use this to further her research at California State University and the University of Vermont.

Rodger Holly is a Government Social Researcher with extensive experience in generating and using research to drive evidence-informed change in public services. She has worked in research and policy in the fields of child protection and family justice since completing an M.Sc. in Gender Studies at the London School of Economics. Whilst working as a Principal Research Officer at the Independent Inquiry into Child Sexual Abuse, she designed and led the Inquiry's research on child sexual abuse in ethnic minority communities and in schools.

Dr. Wilson Joanne received her doctorate from the Child and Women's Abuse Studies Unit (CWASU) and has worked on several highly sensitive research projects exploring sexual/domestic abuse. She has over 10 years of experience as a social researcher/ research coordinator, on projects promoting race, class and gender equality. More recently, she has been a module leader on MSc Community Psychology at the University of East London and currently lectures in Sociology at Northumbria University. Her research specialisms include: using qualitative lived experiences to illustrate intersectional (racially-classed, gendered) abuse, feelings of belonging/citizenship within marginalised and disempowered groups from a UK perspective.

List of Tables

Table 2.1	Demographic information	40
Table 2.2	Types of abuse experienced	40
Table 3.1	Participants	68
Table 4.1	Participant details: three experts identifying as victim-survivors and the seven victim-survivor participants	127
Table 4.2	Process of telling	140
Table 4.3	Response of parents to disclosures of CSA	144
Table 4.4	Explicit, implicit disclosures by mothers	146
Table 5.1	Key messages and implications for policy, practice and research	174
Table 9.1	Kaplan Meier (KM) estimates for surviving free of sexual debut through 17th birthday, according to race and gender	283
Table 11.1	Demographics of Aboriginal survivors abused in OOHC in Victoria, Australia	348
Table 11.2	Connections between racism, cultural abuse and sexual abuse	351
Table 11.3	Cultural impacts of abuses	355

Table 11.4	An Aboriginal model of Social and Emotional Well-being (SEWB)	358
Table 11.5	Survivors' hopes for self, categorised using Gee's model of Aboriginal SEWB	360
Table 12.1	Six key principles for trauma-informed care	391

1

Introduction

Aisha K. Gill and Hannah Begum

While child sexual abuse (CSA) is acknowledged to be a widespread, global health issue (Russell et al. 2020), quantifying its true extent and defining its exact nature remain problematic for a number of reasons. Firstly, there is no universally agreed upon definition of CSA, nor is there any clear agreement on when childhood ends and the age of majority in terms of sexual consent is reached. Secondly, the existence of varied, wide-ranging and diverse definitions of CSA can yield inconsistent estimates of the incidence of CSA and thus impact understandings of its prevalence (Sanjeevi et al. 2018). Thirdly, the power imbalance between the abuser and the abused, along with the inherently secretive and hidden nature of CSA activities, means that disclosure and self-report rates are

---

A. K. Gill (✉)
The Faculty of Social Sciences and Law, School for Policy Studies, Bristol, UK
e-mail: ak.gill@bristol.ac.uk

H. Begum
The Centre of expertise on child sexual abuse, Barnardo House, London, UK

known to capture only a minority of cases (Rumble et al. 2018). Finally, disclosure and reporting rates for males and females vary and, in many cases, those who do disclose and report their abuse do so only in adulthood rather than at the time when the abuse is actually taking place. Thus, despite a well-established body of research into the causes, impacts and experiences of CSA, much remains to be learnt about its complexity and consequences (Mathews and Collin-Vezina 2019) and how CSA, particularly in the context of Black and racially minoritised communities, can most effectively be researched, detected, prevented, communicated about and treated. In taking an intersectional perspective on current debates and challenges regarding CSA in Black and racially minoritised communities around the world, it is hoped that this book goes some way towards achieving those ends.

Defining Child Sexual Abuse and Its Parameters

Numerous attempts have been made to define CSA and its parameters. The US Centers for Disease Control and Prevention, for example, defines CSA as 'any completed or attempted (non-completed) sexual act, sexual contact with, or exploitation (i.e. non-contact sexual interaction) of a child by a caregiver' (CDC 2008), whereas in England, practitioners and policymakers commonly define CSA as follows:

> [F]orcing or enticing a child or young person to take part in sexual activities, not necessarily involving a high level of violence, whether or not the child is aware of what is happening. The activities may involve physical contact, including assault by penetration (for example, rape or oral sex) or non-penetrative acts such as masturbation, kissing, rubbing and touching outside of clothing. They may also include non-contact activities, such as involving children in looking at, or in the production of, sexual images, watching sexual activities, encouraging children to behave in sexually inappropriate ways, or grooming a child in preparation for

abuse [including via the internet] ... Sexual abuse is not solely perpetrated by adult males. Women can also commit acts of sexual abuse, as can other children.
(HM Government 2018).

This definition of CSA includes both contact and non-contact activities and notes that the recipient of the abuse may not realise that they are being victimised, as the activities constituting CSA may take place 'whether or not the child is aware of what is happening'. The CDC definition simply specifies the term 'caregiver' and so overlooks the possibility of peer-on-peer CSA. Despite their attempts to capture much of the essence of CSA overall, both definitions focus on the many situations in which CSA could occur.

Variation in laws on the age of sexual consent and the parameters of who is a child also exacerbate CSA definitional issues. In the United Kingdom, the legal age of consent to sexual activity is 16 (Lammasniemi 2020); however, under Article 1 of the United Nations Convention on the Rights of the Child (UNCRC), a child is anyone under the age of 18 (UNICEF 2022). In Western societies, sexual activity is often associated with adulthood and maturity. Thus, the age at which one can legally give sexual consent can be seen as an indicator of the end of one's childhood (Dalessandro 2019). Moreover, perceptions of childhood exist along a spectrum and are influenced by the social and cultural norms within a particular society at any given time. The ramifications of operationalising childhood are wide-reaching; in India, for example, CSA law has increased the age of consent for sex from 16 to 18, changing the definition of a child in the process (Pitre and Lingam 2022).

Despite legal definitions for a range of sexual crimes against children, many of which are housed under the Sexual Offences Act 2003 in the UK, inconsistencies exist in terminology for the sexual exploitation and sexual abuse of children. Consequently, these two terms are often incorrectly conflated (Beckett and Walker 2017). This is an important issue because definitional ambiguity creates problems in how legal systems process CSA cases, particularly in terms of prosecutions and outcomes (Mathews and Collin-Vezina, 2019). Furthermore, reflecting the ever-changing nature of crime (Nagy 2020), the ubiquity around online sexual offending brings additional challenges in clearly defining CSA.

Although some global consensus exists regarding conceptions of CSA, for instance incest, sexual touching and exposing a child to pornography (Dubowitz 2017) are all accepted forms of CSA, it is clearly necessary to define the full range of behaviours that constitute CSA in order to better inform prevention, identification and treatment efforts (Simon et al. 2020). Indeed, because cultural differences perpetuate classifications of CSA, Sanjeevi et al. (2018) suggest that definitions that were simply proposed on a regional level would inspire little change on a worldwide scale. Thus, they argue that there is a need for a culturally sensitive 'global reset' around the defining characteristics and priorities around CSA's prevention, identification and treatment.

Child Sexual Abuse Across the Globe: The UK

Between March 2019 and 2020, British police recorded 83,000 CSA offences (including obscene publications), a 267% increase since 2013. Of these cases, around 58,000 would be considered contact offences, showing an increase of 202% in the rate of this offending for the same period. However, these figures do not include certain sexual offences such as rape committed against 16- and 17-year-olds; nor do they include sexual assaults committed against children over the age of 13. In January 2020, the Office for National Statistics published exploratory data on sexual offences which had not been recorded as CSA, despite their involving a child victim/survivor and found that approximately 73,200 such offences had occurred in the year ending March 2019. This figure offers a sense of just how much CSA data is potentially missing, both in scope and in scale. Furthermore, it is widely recognised that crime statistics significantly underestimate the scale of the problem (NSPCC, 2021). Factors such as the secrecy that often surrounds abusive situations, the shame felt by victims, the chance of not being believed and the low likelihood of prosecution (let alone conviction) mean that few victims come forward (Augusti and Myhre 2021). The issue of under-reporting is compounded in British South Asian communities; thus, despite increasing social and professional interest in addressing CSA in Black, Asian and racially minoritised communities, data on prevalence remains limited.

While UK Black and racially minoritised females are just as likely as females from other ethnic groups to be victims of sexual abuse in childhood, prior research (Gill 2013; Patel 2013) shows that Black and racially minoritised victims/survivors face additional issues and pressures that can compound their situation. Located as they are at the intersection of numerous structural inequalities, their experiences of abuse differ from those of their White counterparts in several key ways, and these differences influence the responses of both victims/survivors themselves and service providers. For instance, Black and racially minoritised children are more likely to suffer abuse from multiple family members (Gill et al. 2018). They are also more likely to experience inappropriate professional responses from statutory and voluntary agencies, including failures in multi-agency cooperation and coordination, high levels of stereotyping and racism, and even a reluctance of support services to engage for fear of appearing racist (Gill and Day 2020; Izzidien 2008).

Professionals can pathologise, misunderstand or essentialise cultural norms, traditions and values when they work with Black, Asian and racially minoritised families. While this has been an ongoing issue of discussion in social care literature, little has changed regarding how the issue is dealt with on the ground (Qureshi et al. 2012). Indeed, professionals widely report that problems in effective service delivery in these communities often result from their inadequate understandings of cultural features (Qureshi et al. 2012).

Community attitudes co-exist alongside these structural problems, compounding the culture of silence around CSA—for example, the belief in some UK Black and racially minoritised communities that CSA 'doesn't happen' in their midst. Such a belief suggests the need to link these attitudes, understandings of identity and everyday forms of violence (Gill and Harrison 2019). Thus, a key question for this edited collection is to determine whether acknowledging CSA in Black and racially minoritised communities would result in a seismic shift in how these communities view themselves and their respective cultures and what other factors might have a significant impact on increasing engagement with preventive efforts.

Ethnicity, class and sex form the basis of many systems of power and inequality, affecting not only individual lives and group interactions, but also the ability of oppressed groups to enjoy the same fulfilment of their human rights as that accorded to more privileged groups and how they affect females (Anderson and Collins 2006). According to Brah and Phoenix (2004), a person's multiple identities—are inseparable: each identity has its own unique, related form of oppression or dominance that alters when it intersects with another identity. For example, racially minoritised females face the differing oppressions that stem from being women and being part of an ethnic minority. Ignoring intersectionality by emphasising only one particular identity (e.g. ethnicity) or neglecting some identities altogether does not offer a holistic understanding of people's lived realities. Such partial understandings also assume that groups are homogeneous: adopting a universal approach to understanding multiple forms of discrimination assumes 'sameness or equivalence of the social categories connected to inequalities' (Verloo 2006: 211). This simplistic approach is problematic because it masks the diversity of individuals and experiences, as this edited collection shows.

Feminism has always recognised the role of different forms of power and, importantly, the interplay between them, although it has further still to go on exploring the role of racial inequalities. A critical element of progress achieved by feminism is the unpacking both of the notion of heteronormativity, which is often inherent in discourses on gender and how socio-economic status can be not only a source of oppression for females but also a privilege reserved for certain women at the expense of others (Anderson and Collins 2001). However, much feminist scholarship is still rooted in the experiences of White women, and the movement as a whole—both activist and academic—has been slow to respond to long-standing criticisms of its failures to represent the diverse experiences and needs of minoritised women and children. In many contexts and communities, the discourse on violence is 'inextricably intertwined with constructions of sexuality and gender' (Sielke 2009: 11). Representations of violence in these communities are often underpinned by essentialist conceptualisations (Wiper 2012). The problem of violence perpetrated against people in these communities is thus rendered invisible; consequently, there is a pressing need for new work that considers the complex needs of child (and adult) abuse victims/survivors who are situated at the intersections of race, sex, culture, class and also religion.

According to scholars and practitioners, when examining understandings and experiences of CSA disclosure, particular attention must be given to the intersecting socio-cultural forces at play (Anthias, 2013; Patel, 2013). Indeed, culture (Xioa and Smith-Prince 2015), alongside age and gendered inequalities (Alaggia et al. 2019), complicates the dynamics of CSA disclosure, which is often either delayed until adulthood or never occurs at all (Fontes and Plummer, 2010). Disclosure of CSA has been conceptualised as an ongoing, complex process influenced by a spectrum of intrapersonal, interpersonal and contextual factors (Azzopardi et al. 2019). Barriers that impede CSA disclosure include guilt and shame, lack of support systems in the victim's social environment and the perceived negative consequences (for themselves or others) of revealing the abuse (Lemaigre et al. 2017). Tishelman and Geffner assert that 'culture is pertinent to each case of suspected child sexual abuse but only barely (gets) touched on by existing research' (Lemaigre et al. 2017: 487). Culture remains a significant barrier to disclosure for victims from Black and racially minoritised communities.

Child Sexual Abuse Across the Globe: The Global South, Southeast Asia, the Middle East, Africa and Turkey

Despite global recognition of the prevalence and severe harms of CSA (Mathews and Collin-Vézina 2019), few Western studies have focused on CSA in the Global South. However, according to UNICEF, CSA is pervasive in Latin America, where the problem is complicated by weak judicial systems, patriarchal cultures and widespread inequalities within and across social groups (UNICEF, 2022). Empirical research across Latin America has documented both the nature and extent of CSA and its impact on victims, thus providing a unique snapshot of how CSA is conceptualised, understood and responded to in the Global South. For instance, Guerra et al. (2021) study of sex differences in the disclosure of CSA among Chilean adolescents found lower disclosure rates among male victims. The researchers attributed the greater reluctance of males to disclose to Chile's dominant 'macho' culture and that suffering such abuse calls a boy or man's masculinity into question. One consequence of this misconception was that female CSA victims received more support at the time of disclosure than male CSA victims did because of the cultural assumption that more readily categorised females as victims. Nevertheless, both male and female victims cited guilt and shame as barriers to disclosure. Arredondo et al. (2016) presented similar findings in their study of Chilean children, reporting lower disclosure rates among Chilean boys than girls and longer periods before disclosure among boys.

In Southeast Asia, discourses on sexual violence against children often revolve around child sex tourism and child sexual exploitation (Davy, 2018; Lyneham and Facchini, 2019). Since the scale of the child sex trade in the region is significant, it often eclipses the issue of CSA in domestic and familial settings. For example, when Wismayanti et al. (2021) analysed CSA in Indonesia across policy and law, they found that children are perceived as a disempowered group in Indonesian society and that high levels of gendered discrimination and stigmatisation consequently make female victims more vulnerable to CSA. These vulnerabilities are compounded by a lack of consensus on child protection laws and policy and by gaps between policies and implementation in child protection programmes. Similarly, in Malaysia, limited CSA data and research mean that this abuse remains largely hidden (Ahmad and Hamid 2020). Despite Malaysia's implementation of the Sexual Offences Against Children Act 2017, conviction rates for child sex abusers remain low, and public knowledge of CSA is poor (Fernandez et al. 2021).

Research on CSA in the Middle East and North Africa also remains sparse. For example, CSA is understudied and underreported in Saudi Arabia, although exceptions do include recent empirical work by Almuneef (2021) who explored CSA's impact on victims, including its relationship to health outcomes. The study reported an increased incidence of victims developing physical and mental health disorders, including diabetes, coronary heart disease and depression. CSA disclosure rates were higher among boys than girls (12.1% compared with 8.7%), which is largely attributable to the different socialisation patterns in Saudi Arabia where cultural norms and values dictate that girls seldom leave the house unattended. The literature also suggests that CSA disclosure carries greater stigma for females in Arab and Muslim societies, as it may cast doubt on their virginity and risk bringing 'dishonour' to their families. In addition, pervasive walls of silence, taboos, and the forbidding of discussion of sexual matters exacerbate the situation for CSA victims in these contexts (Attrash Najjar et al., 2022; Haboush and Alyan 2013).

In Turkey, problems in conceptualising and responding to CSA have been hampered by the lack of a national CSA perpetrator database and limited empirical research (Koçtürk and Bilge 2018). However, even limited statistical data shows the urgent need for effective prevention strategies, with figures indicating that 12.1% of children in Turkey were subjected to sexual crimes in 2017 (Turkish Statistical Institute 2018). Tunc et al. (2018) recommend a two-pronged prevention strategy: (1) increasing personal knowledge about protections against CSA among young Turkish children and (2) fostering a positive attitude towards discussing sex and sexuality.

Rates of CSA across Africa are believed to grossly underestimate the problem which encompasses harmful practices (such as female genital mutilation and child marriage), alongside a wider epidemic of violence against women and children in large parts of the continent (Badoe 2017). In South Africa, as in other parts of the world, the social context of CSA hinges largely on gendered inequalities, with patriarchal systems reinforcing male dominance and increasing the sexual victimisation of females (Vermeulen and Greeff 2015). Similarly, in terms of CSA against boys, some research suggests that certain social and personal vulnerability factors—including low socio-economic status and a physique that others perceive as weak—may increase the risk of CSA (Richter et al. 2018). Sanchez et al. (2019) applied an intersectional framework to their study of Black/Afro-Latina victims of CSA to understand the barriers and challenges faced by these communities at the nexus of race, culture and gendered inequalities. They argue that the 'double consciousness' of existing as both Black and Latinx exacerbates systemic barriers to help-seeking, while interpersonal barriers to seeking support were primarily rooted in embedded stereotypes of Black girls as hypersexualised. Epstein et al. (2017) support this finding by coining the term 'adultification' to refer to the construction of Black girls as less innocent and more adult than White girls, citing this construct as a reason why they may be less likely to be viewed as 'legitimate' victims of sexual abuse. Sanchez et al.'s work has important implications for practitioners, as it demonstrates the need for racially and culturally informed interventions to ensure equally effective support irrespective of an individual's ethnicity.

More research is needed across the globe to gain a fuller understanding of the phenomenon of CSA in terms of the similarities and differences between groups, countries and socio-cultural contexts and to better prevent it and support CSA victims/survivors. In particular, there is a need for further research that looks beyond CSA in specific countries and cultures and to other contexts in which CSA is known to occur such as in religious organisations and contexts.

Advances in Policy and Practice

Collectively, the chapters in this volume aim to challenge unicausal and essentialist perceptions of CSA by questioning and understanding the context, contours, causes, consequences and continuum of this abuse by interrogating and also analysing wider systems of oppression and exclusion. In the introductory chapter, Gill and Begum consider issues of theory, policy and practice in relation to the book's central themes: CSA, culture, rights, social justice and intersectionality, and criminal justice responses in general. In Chapter 1, Gangoli and Hester draw on interviews with seven Black and minority ethnic women who experienced CSA and also endured multiple forms of victimisation into adulthood. As children, these women's polyvictimisation included sexual abuse, exposure to domestic violence, forced marriage, child marriage, grooming and trafficking for prostitution. As adults, they experienced a range of sexual and domestic violence and abuse, including marital rape.

Gangoli and Hester explore the women's testimonies using the conceptual framework of epistemic injustice and the intersecting factors that shape their experiences.

Most existing research focuses on the experiences of female CSA survivors, leaving male CSA survivors with limited access to evidence-based support services. Chapter 2 explores eight semi-structured, in-depth interviews with British South Asian male survivors. Using interpretative phenomenological analysis, Begum and Gill identify several key themes in these accounts. These include barriers to disclosing CSA, the effect of concepts of masculinity and sexuality on how survivors process their abuse, and the impact of socio-cultural norms that impede discussing and disclosing CSA. A masculinities theory lens illuminates the role of cultural imperatives of shame and honour and how British South Asian men construct and understand their experiences of CSA largely in accordance with cultural and societal expectations of 'being a man'. The narratives illustrate how British South Asian male survivors must try to recover from their trauma while simultaneously being expected to embody the culturally sanctioned ideals that complicated and compounded their abuse in the first place. The research demonstrates that engaging with parents and communities to discuss these sensitive topics is a necessary first step in breaking down barriers to disclosure and recovery.

In Chapter 3, Wilson examines the disclosures or 'tellings' of CSA experiences by seven African-Caribbean British victims/survivors. The chapter uses the concept of 'maternal mimesis' to explain intergenerational (re)productions of the 'strong black woman' racial stereotype as a coping strategy for victims/survivors (Beauboeuf-Lafontant 2009) of CSA. Wilson argues that this historical racial stereotype, created to justify the 'de-gendering' of African womanhood for the purposes of additional slave labour, continues to be a template of resilience *used by* African and African-Caribbean British women to cope with their CSA experiences (Crenshaw 1991). The participants' 'tellings' (1998, p. Opcit; Alaggia 2004), and the maternal responses to them, are located within Taussig's (1993) theory of alterity and mimesis. Participants expressed how their mothers implicitly/explicitly outlined their own histories of sexual abuse, thus demonstrating the commonness of the experience.

Participants further recalled being fearful of their mothers because of their harsh responses to their daughters' abuse disclosures, which often involved extensive physical abuse (beatings) to coerce their daughters into silence. Mothers offered their own histories of CSA and intersectional abuse as a template their daughters could replicate in order to live with their own experiences of sexual and racial abuse. The chapter interweaves an analysis of the television series *How to Get Away with Murder* with the study participants' accounts as a way to illustrate how intersectional abuse both informs and conflates CSA experiences for women of African descent in Western societies.

Family and community relations matter to individuals—they are what makes us feel wanted and needed and they preoccupy much of our time, attention and energy. In some communities, this interconnectivity can be particularly intense; in South Asian communities, it can also be governed by influential constructs of shame and honour. In the context of CSA, this interconnectivity, twinned with embedded constructs of shame and honour, can lead to victims' existing in a vacuum of secrecy, shame and solitude. Through individual guided conversations with 15 female survivors of CSA from Britain's Bangladeshi, Indian and Pakistani communities, Jassal in Chapter 4 provides insights into the experiences of this group of survivors.

Chapter 5 explores the work of the Halo Project that supports victims of honour-based violence, forced marriages and female genital mutilation. Halo has criticised policing responses to CSA and sexual violence (SV) in Black and racially minoritised communities. This chapter focuses on cases the project has supported over the last decade in which recourse (and complaints about failures to provide appropriate support and redress) has been pursued through formal processes. Worryingly, none of these cases has elicited a satisfactory response from the criminal justice system. Therefore, Chapter 5 documents Halo's super-complaint which is intended to raise awareness of these systemic failures. Gill and Khan discuss the multiple barriers that prevent victims and those at risk of CSA from reporting their situation to the police as well as the alarming fact that, in many instances, the police's handling of previous sexual abuse reports has deterred further reporting, causing some victims to suffer serious consequences for going to the police, including physical retribution from family and/or community members. The chapter also addresses how fear of shaming or dishonouring the family name is a significant barrier to reporting in some minority groups because it directly threatens collectivist family values which are considered more important than the needs of the individual. Halo's super-complaint prioritises the experiences of Black and minoritised survivors, demonstrating the importance of centring these voices and changing the current 'postcode lottery' that governs police responses and frequently deters Black and minoritised survivors from reporting.

Chapter 6 continues the focus on barriers to victim and survivor disclosure and support in ethnic minority communities. Prior research has indicated institutions' systemic failures to protect ethnic minority children from CSA (Webb et al. 2002) and has identified intra-cultural barriers to disclosure such as gendered norms and shame (Gill and Harrison 2019). This chapter by Hurcombe, Redmond, Rodger and King examines how ethnicity, community and culture have contributed to shaping victims/survivors' experiences. It draws on the voices of 82 participants from ethnic minority communities across England and Wales, revealing how they encountered cultural stereotypes and racism that prevented them from receiving appropriate recognition and help from support services. Crucially, this research reveals that some of the professionals to whom these participants spoke when they were seeking support for CSA saw only their ethnicity and thus failed to fully grasp their lived experiences as victims/survivors within their particular cultures and communities. This chapter helps improve our understanding of the cultural specificities and institutional barriers that impede CSA disclosures and identifies the need to improve prevention and support when victims/survivors have spoken out about their abuse.

As noted earlier in this Introduction, 16- to 17-year-old adolescents and children over the age of 13 also commit child sexual abuse offences against other children. Hence, harmful sexual behaviour (HSB) among children and young people is another area of CSA that requires deeper understanding and research. In recent years, concerns associated with HSB have featured prominently in child protection and safeguarding policy and debates. Drawing on two empirical projects they conducted, in Chapter 7, McAlinden and Agnew critically examine a range of definitional and regulatory tensions associated with HSB among young people in Chapter 8. There the authors argue that antiquated legal and policy frameworks fail to account for the diverse range of peer-based HSBs with which young people are presented. In particular, McAlinden and Agnew note how prevailing socio-cultural pressures result in blurred boundaries around 'normal' or 'healthy' sexual behaviour and 'harmful' and potentially 'abusive' sexual behaviour among peers. Therefore, this chapter (1) explores how emerging forms of peer-based HSB, including digital forms of HSB, are challenging how CSA is defined and classified within social, legal and professional discourses and (2) reveals some of the challenges and practical implications associated with investigating and managing HSB among young people, including the risk of overcriminalisation within certain contexts (e.g. sexting). Furthermore, given the complexity and range of HSBs, this chapter also considers the significant challenges facing professionals seeking to identify young people as either the 'person being harmed' or the 'person inflicting the harm'. Indeed, HSB among young people can often obfuscate traditional conceptions of 'victim' and 'offender'. The chapter concludes by briefly exploring the need for broader, prevention-based educative responses that can more effectively address the nuances and complexities of peer-based HSB.

Traditional notions of 'victim' and 'offender' are also often obscured in the context of CSA committed against Black men and boys, who are not recognised as vulnerable in the current literature concerning CSA or rape. In Chapter 8, Curry aims to understand the public health implications of SV committed against racialised males, specifically the role trauma plays in their lives. Such a perspective requires a marriage between epidemiology and theory, such that scholars interested in Black men and boys can better articulate more general theories of Black maleness that recognise the sexual vulnerability of this group. For example, in the United States, Black males reported higher levels of contact SV (6.5%, including rape, being made to penetrate, sexual coercion and unwanted sexual contact) than Black women (5.8%) and White women (3.6%) over a 12-month period. The Optimus Study in South Africa similarly found that, unlike in some European countries, sexual assault of Black South African boys was higher than that of their female counterparts. How and why these young Black men and boys are ignored consistently by gender theory is of major theoretical and policymaking concern. This chapter thus argues that recognising the sexual vulnerability of young Black boys is key to understanding women as perpetrators in the sexual abuse and rape of racialised males and how it affects our definition of rape.

Few studies have investigated the intersection of culture and trauma. Chapter 9 summarises the current literature on CSA in Latinx populations, focusing on risk factors and cultural norms surrounding the issue. In the United States, the Latinx community is large and includes individuals from numerous countries with their own ethnic identities, languages and cultural values. While Kenny and Helpingstine recognise this, the chapter's goal is to present the existing literature in order to illuminate the potential, unique influences of Latinx cultures on the trauma of sexual abuse. The role of culture in sexual abuse is relevant in terms of how cultural beliefs may contribute to family environments in which children are abused, hinder disclosure of abuse and shape how sexual abuse is discussed. Most existing literature on CSA features contradictions and inconsistencies regarding the occurrence of and characteristics related to CSA in Latinx groups. This chapter examines these contradictions and inconsistencies and the effect of culture on incidence and disclosure as well as family, victim and perpetrator characteristics. It also critiques the current weaknesses in the literature and makes recommendations for future research.

Chapter 10 by Black, Bamblett and Frederico also addresses the role of collective trauma in CSA. Shifting to an institutional context, it highlights the voices and expertise belonging to Aboriginal survivors of institutional CSA. The chapter presents a thematic analysis of 51 narratives from adult Aboriginal CSA survivors who were abused in out-of-home care between the 1940s and the 1990s—these survivors provided their narratives to the 2013 Australian Royal Commission into Institutional Responses to Child Sexual Abuse. The Commission found that all children in institutions between the 1940s and 1990s were vulnerable to CSA but that Aboriginal children experienced increased vulnerability due to a range of historical and contemporary factors. Findings indicate that institutional CSA occurred in the context of cultural abuse and collective trauma. The narratives provided evidence that the avenues Aboriginal survivors accessed for healing included mainstream services, Aboriginal-specific programmes, non-professional support, and engagement in art and creative pursuits, culture and relationships. The chapter presents survivors' experiences of abuse and trauma, the lifelong and intergenerational impacts of those experiences, and their hopes and ideas for policy and practice that can create a safer society and child welfare system.

Offenders' own experiences of CSA are also integral to shaping effective policy and practice. This is highlighted in Chapter 11 by Lasher, which addresses the need for trauma-informed care for individuals who have sexually offended (ISOs) and who have also experienced CSA. In recent years, early childhood abuse has manifested as a major concern among ISOs. This is often discussed in the context of adverse childhood experiences, including one's history of CSA. For example, men who were sexually abused as children are approximately three times more likely to engage in future sexual offending, particularly against children. While this is often considered in the context of preventing children from engaging in further abusive behaviours, the dynamics of an adult's history of abuse is an important factor in the individual's responsivity to behavioural treatment. While in treatment, ISOs may confront their own history of abuse as well as the parallels between that abuse and the harm they have caused others. This chapter highlights the importance of trauma-informed care when working with ISOs. Accordingly, it discusses the current research on trauma-informed interventions and forensic treatment of ISOs who have experienced sexual abuse or other forms of trauma. Evaluators and treatment providers face a major challenge of differentiating between trauma-reaction behaviours and behavioural manifestations of personality disorders. Behavioural management of cluster B personality disorders, such as antisocial personality disorder and borderline personality disorder, is hallmark of forensic behavioural treatment, particularly for ISOs. Lasher's work addresses the interaction between post-traumatic reactions and personality disorders and, using case examples, offers suggestions for balancing the treatment of these two psychological needs in order to improve outcomes for ISOs.

Finally, Chapter 12 explores the epistemological and methodological questions encountered when undertaking research on a perpetrator intervention programme for Aboriginal and/or Torres Strait Islander men convicted of serious sexual offending (including against children) in Queensland, Australia. The chapter documents the work of Indigenous Elders in providing cultural and spiritual support and mentorship to Aboriginal and/or Torres Strait Islander individuals who have been released from prison following a period of incarceration for serious sexual offending. Here, Death and Kelly draw on semi-structured qualitative interviews with a range of local stakeholders and service providers who contributed to the research. The chapter critically interrogates White feminist researchers' views on the intricacies of working with mandated clients in ways that reflect culturally safe practices. The authors also discuss questions raised for them as non-Indigenous women researching a programme that responds to Indigenous men. They explore the ways in which they navigate intersections of culturally sensitive practice when considering constructions of gender that challenged their own perspectives as White feminist researchers.

Conclusion: Devising Inclusive and Intersectional Interventions for Change

The impetus to produce this book was to offer practitioners and policymakers an intersectional perspective on current debates and challenges regarding CSA in Black and racially minoritised communities. The result is a rich collection that explores the implications of this perspective for policy and practice, where issues of difference, diversity and complexity across the spectrum of CSA abound. The authors have interwoven a number of arguments about the contours, contexts and consequences of CSA; debated a range of definitional issues; and considered various ways of understanding socio-cultural factors, including how abusers gain access to their victims, responses to abuse disclosures from family, community and state; and the importance of creating safe spaces for therapeutic interventions. Key themes include the multifaceted nature of CSA, its intersections with race, ethnicity, age, class and Indigenous issues, and other structural factors, such as poverty and entrenched historical forms of systemic discrimination. The chapters in this book provide an overview of the issues of power and responsibility at play in CSA experiences and of who is heard and who is not.

As argued by Gangoli and Hester in Chapter 1, racially minoritised victims/survivors of CSA experience testimonial and hermeneutic forms of injustice that emerge in their interactions with structural (law, criminal, justice, immigration) and cultural (familial and/or religious norms and codes) systems. The importance of inclusive intersectional interventions is thus central to supporting victims/survivors and ensuring that they receive the responses they deserve from the criminal justice system. These responses must be shaped by cultural awareness training that can enable police forces to develop a deeper understanding of the contexts in which Black and racially minoritised victims/survivors of CSA live.

Little research has addressed the specific problem of CSA from a multidisciplinary perspective (Gill 2021). One reason for this lacuna is that the recent foregrounding in media and policy discourses of CSA in racially minoritised communities has taken place through the lens of cultural essentialism, occluding the causes of CSA by focusing on racialised elements, such as the role of traditional cultural practices. As Black and racially minoritised children are located at the intersection of multiple, overlapping structural inequalities (Gill 2013), their specific experiences of victimisation are still largely overlooked in the criminological literature, even though solid progress has been made during the last decade in understanding CSA in British Asian communities. For instance, Gill and Harrison (2019) have highlighted the role of cultural factors in concealing CSA, including how notions of 'honour' often act as barriers to disclosure. Although honour and its inverse, shame, have been explored in many scholarly discussions of gendered violence in Asian communities (Cowburn et al. 2015; Gilbert et al. 2004; Gill and Brah 2014), more work could enable culturally competent responses to CSA cases, in particular through recognition of the unique barriers and difficulties that racially minoritised victims face.

As many of the chapters point out, identifying factors that inhibit and facilitate disclosure would strengthen preventive strategies and improve treatment, support and understanding for all victims (Kellogg et al. 2020). Shame, fear of being disbelieved, and self-blame are key barriers to disclosure across all cultures, countries and religions (Collin-Vézina et al.

2015). However, how these barriers operate in specific contexts remains opaque (Alaggia et al. 2019) and so inhibits efforts to help and encourage children to disclose swiftly, thus preventing further abuse (Alaggia and Wang 2020).

While culture and racism do affect both how victims/survivors make sense of CSA, their opportunities for recognition as victims, and the support they receive, overlooking the commonalities between different forms of CSA can result in racialising forms of abuse that are more common in minority communities than in other communities and so reduce the effectiveness of interventions (Gill and Harrison 2019). Furthermore, a tendency to stereotype individuals based on their culture/ethnicity/gender also helps to explicate why some professionals may be less likely to recognise victims from ethnic minority communities as victims and to elucidate why, for example, Black boys are rarely believed to be victims of sexual violence. As Chapter 3 notes, Black feminists have therefore called for specificity and accountability in the sphere of safeguarding in relation to Black and racially minoritised communities' experiences of CSA. However, victims'/survivors' decisions in relation to disclosure are shaped not only by their gender but also by culture, racialisation, political Blackness and the myriad intersectional forms of discrimination and oppression that conspire to marginalise them and their experiences. Thus, support services need to embed their awareness of the issue of increased vulnerabilities to abuse among some groups of children (Jassal 2020) (because of their ethnicity, disability, gender and sexual orientation) and design actions and services to address their particular needs.

As Chapter 5 explains, yet another of the obstacles to responding to CSA in diverse communities is the allocation of adequate resources and concerns on the part of victims/survivors about confidentiality and the competence of institutions to manage cases involving this type of abuse. The varying needs and experiences of victims/survivors, coupled with the lack of consensus among professionals on issues such as support services and on how to effectively respond to instances of CSA in Black and racially minoritised communities, clearly highlight how victims/survivors in these communities would benefit from flexible and multifaceted institutional responses that ensure that, irrespective of their culture, ethnicity and gender, all CSA victims/survivors receive the support to which they are entitled.

In the light of these issues, safeguarding must be prioritised and designed in such a way that it does not reconfigure or compound the abusive contexts of CSA. Doing so requires substantial resourcing to deconstruct taken-for-granted assumptions about the operation of socio-cultural social/political power/knowledge frameworks that challenge existing structures of abuse and future formations of CSA. Safeguarding will also require developing policies and practices that recognise the complexity and diversity of the lives of those who experience CSA, including the importance of acknowledging both the harm that has been inflicted by systemic racism and discrimination against Aboriginal communities and of challenging oppressive practices. As Chapters 10 and 12 note, the impacts of invasion, colonisation, and systematic racism and discrimination need to inform models of healing for Aboriginal survivors. Forms of individual, collective and intergenerational trauma are interrelated and must all be addressed in healing processes for Aboriginal survivors. Listening to and learning from lived experience experts can shape healing models that are culturally informed and culturally safe. This approach is critical to developing a culturally responsive service system, because it also requires attention to what is defined as gendered and sexualised violence (including CSA) and how it ought to be responded to. Finally, there is a need to acknowledge that some forms of CSA may not be value-neutral, but that they may instead be shaped by the ongoing effects of the colonial project.

It is also important to further invest in measures to understand consensual and non-consensual sexual behaviour and how they influence popular understandings of 'healthy' and 'explorative' sexual activity compared with 'exploitative' and 'abusive' activity, as was done in Chapter 8. Achieving this end will involve devising more comprehensive education programmes for young people, parents and practitioners that address the complexity of sexual behaviours in which young people are engaging. Assisting parents in overcoming barriers to sexual discussion and raising awareness about the prevalence of CSA are also paramount in helping our youth. Within this education framework, prevailing socio-cultural myths and stereotypes, particularly in relation to gender roles and sexual norms, must be challenged. Professionals need to recognise culture when planning prevention and education programmes about CSA. Devising culturally informed programmes that are accessible across diverse communities is a necessity. As noted in Chapter 11, skilled treatment providers are aware of their own countertransference as a result of both individual experiences and societal dynamics—in a therapeutic relationship, intersectionality is relevant for both the treatment provider and the treatment recipient. Thus, irrespective of whether a skilled treatment provider working with the victims of sexual abuse or those who have sexually abused others (or in many cases both) is dealing with a discrete event, repeated occurrences or a cultural context, considering trauma is an ongoing process. Employing a trauma-informed perspective is integral to this process—and with the extant opportunities for training and continuing education today—there is little reason to avoid its use.

This edited collection addresses all these future possibilities and directions. In bringing together leading researchers and practitioners from criminal justice, criminology, forensic psychology social work, sociology and law, it enriches the existing knowledge base by illuminating the experiences of CSA survivors across the world. This depth of understanding can only be achieved by locating CSA within an intersectional framework that allows for effective examination of the dominant paradigms that, in some instances, reduce this form of violence to a cultural or religious problem. The book's central aim is to challenge widely held but problematic beliefs about CSA by reviewing existing multidisciplinary knowledge and presenting new research in a theoretically informed, practice-oriented and context-specific manner. Through this approach, the editors hope to promote a more nuanced understanding of CSA that addresses both the commonalities and particularities of these crimes across and within societies around the world.

References

Ahmad, Y., and Hamid, S. (2020). Monster in the family, young victims and issues across border: Future outlook of child sexual abuse in Malaysia. *Journal of Critical Reviews*, 7(8), 1713–1718.

Alaggia, R. (2004). Many ways of telling: expanding conceptualizations of child sexual abuse disclosure. *Child Abuse and Neglect*, 28(11), 1213–1227.

Alaggia, R., Collin-Vézina, D., and Lateef, R. (2019). Facilitators and barriers to child sexual abuse (CSA) disclosures: A research update (2000–2016). *Trauma, Violence and Abuse*, 20(2), 260–283.

Alaggia, R., and Wang, S. (2020). "I never told anyone until the #metoo movement": What can we learn from sexual abuse and sexual assault disclosures made through social media? *Child Abuse and Neglect*, 103.

Almuneef, M. (2021). Long term consequences of child sexual abuse in Saudi Arabia: A report from national study. *Child Abuse and Neglect*, 116, 1.

Anderson, M., and Collins, P. (2001). Introduction. In M. Anderson, and P. Collins (Eds.), *Race, class and gender: An anthology*. Wadsworth.

Anthias, F. (2013). Cultural difference. In M. Evans, and C. H. Williams (Eds.), *Gender: Key concepts*. Routledge.

Arredondo, V., Saavedra, C., Troncoso, C., and Guerra, C. (2016). Develación del abuso sexual en niños y niñas atendidos en la Corporación Paicabi. *Revista Latinoamericana de Ciencias Sociales, Niñez y Juventud*, 14(1), 385–399.

Attrash Najjar, A., Tener, D., and Katz, C. (2022). "The most shocking thing was that I didn't respond to the abuse": The peritraumatic responses and transitions as conveyed by survivors of continuous child sexual abuse. *Child Abuse and Neglect*, 132, 105818.

Augusti, E. M., and Myhre, C. M. (2021). The barriers and facilitators to abuse disclosure and psychosocial support needs in children and adolescents around the time of disclosure. *Child Care in Practice*.

Azzopardi, C., Eirich, R., Rash, C. L., MacDonald, S., & Madigan, S. (2019). A meta-analysis of the prevalence of child sexual abuse disclosure in forensic settings. *Child Abuse & Neglect*, 93, 291–304.

Badoe, E. (2017). A critical review of child abuse and its management in Africa. *African Journal of Emergency Medicine*, 7, 32–35.

Beauboeuf-Lafontant, T. (2009). *Behind the mask of the strong black woman: Voice and the embodiment of a costly performance*. Temple University Press.

Beckett, H., and Walker, J. (2017). Words matter: reconceptualising the conceptualisation of child sexual exploitation. In H. Beckett, and J. Pearce (Eds.), *Understanding and responding to child sexual exploitation* (pp. 9–23). Routledge.

Bedihi, M. (2008). Characteristics, etiology and therapy for sexual offenses in the Haredi world. In H. Mahe, M. Hovava, and M. Golan (Eds.), *Addictions, violence and sexual offenses: Treatment in light of the law* (pp. 458–477). Carmel.

Blakemore, T., Herbert, J. L., Arney, F., and Parkinson, S. (2017). The impacts of institutional child sexual abuse: A rapid review of the evidence. *Child Abuse and Neglect*, 74, 35–48.

Boakye, K.E. (2009). Culture and nondisclosure of child sexual abuse in Ghana: A theoretical and empirical exploration. *Law and Social Inquiry*, 34(4), 951–979.

Brah, A., and Phoenix, A. (2004). Ain't I a woman? Revisiting intersectionality. *Journal of International Women's Studies*, 5(3), 74-87.

Buchbinder, E. and Schoob, T. (2013). Essential partnership: Child welfare officers' perceptions of cooperation with Rabbis in the Ultra-Orthodox Jewish community in Israel. *Journal of Social Service Research*, 39(2), 204–217.

Centres for Disease Control and Prevention. (2008). *Child maltreatment surveillance: Uniform definitions for public health and recommended data elements*. http://www.cdc.gov/violenceprevention/pdf/cm_surveillance-a.pdf. Accessed 2 November 2021.

Collin-Vézina, D., De La Sablonnière-Griffin, M., Palmer, A. M., and Milne, L. (2015). A preliminary mapping of individual, relational, and social factors that impede disclosure of childhood sexual abuse. *Child Abuse and Neglect*, 43, 123–134.

Cowburn, M., Harrison, K., and Gill, A. K. (2015). Speaking about sexual abuse in British South Asian communities: Offenders, victims and the challenges of shame and reintegration. *Journal of Sexual Aggression*, 21(1), 4–15.

Crenshaw, K. (1991). Mapping the margins: Intersectionality, identity politics, and violence against women of color. *Stanford Law Review*, 43, 1241–1299.

Dalessandro, C. (2019). Manifesting maturity: Gendered sexual intimacy and becoming an adult. *Sexualities*, 22(1–2), 165–181.

Davis, J. D., Miles, G. M. and Quinley III, J. H. (2019). "Same same, but different": A baseline study on the vulnerabilities of transgender sex workers in the sex industry in Bangkok, Thailand. *International Journal of Sociology and Social Policy*, 39(7–8), 550–573.

Davy, D. (2018). Trafficking of Vulnerable Children in Southeast Asia. In J. Szente (ed.), *Assisting young children caught in disasters. educating the young child—advances in theory and research, implications for practice.* Springer.

Dubowitz H. (2017). Child sexual abuse and exploitation-A global glimpse. *Child abuse and Neglect*, 66, 2–8.

Epstein, R., Blake, J. J., and Gonzalez, T. (2017). *Girlhood interrupted: The erasure of black girls' childhood.* http://www.law.georgetown.edu/academics/centers-institutes/poverty-inequality/upload/girlhood-interrupted.pdf. Accessed 9 November 2021.

Fernandez, J. A., Fernandez, J. A. and Jaladin, R. A. M. (2021). Beware of the menacing monsters around us: protecting Malaysian children from sexual abuse. *British Journal of Guidance and Counselling*.

Fontes, L. A. and Plummer, C. (2010). Cultural issues in disclosures of child sexual abuse. *Journal of Child Sexual Abuse*, 19(5), 491–518

Frame, J. (2017). Exploring the approaches to care of faith-based and secular NGOs in Cambodia that serve victims of trafficking, exploitation, and those involved in sex work. *International Journal of Sociology and Social Policy*, 37(5–6), 311–326.

Gilbert, P., Gilbert, J., and Sanghera, J. (2004). A focus group exploration of the impact of izzat, shame, subordination and entrapment on mental health and service use in South Asian women living in Derby. *Mental Health, Religion and Culture*, 7(2), 109–130

Gill, A. K. (2013). Feminist reflections on researching so-called "Honour" killings. *Feminist Legal Studies*, 21, 241–61.

Gill, A. K., and Brah, A. (2014). 'Interrogating cultural narratives about 'honour'—based violence'. *European Journal of Women's Studies*, 21(1), 72–86.

Gill, A. K., Cox, P., and Weir, R. (2018). Shaping Priority Services for UK Victims of Honour-based Violence/Abuse, Forced Marriage and Female Genital Mutilation. *Howard Journal of Criminal Justice*, 57(4).

Gill, A. K. and Harrison, K. (2019). 'I am talking about it because I want to stop it': Child sexual abuse and sexual violence against women in British South Asian communities. *The British Journal of Criminology*, 59(3), 511–529.

Gill, A. K., and Day, A. S. (2020). Applying intersectionality to partnerships between women's organizations and the criminal justice system in relation to domestic violence. *The British Journal of Criminology*, 60(4), 830–850.

Gill, A. K. (2021) Improving police responses to sexual abuse offences in British South Asian communities. In: Monk, H, Atkinson, K., Barr, U., Tucker. K. (eds). *Feminist responses to injustices of the State and its institutions: Politics, intervention, resistance*, Bristol: Bristol University Press.

Guerra, C., Arredondo, V., Saavedra, C., Pinto-Cortez, C., Benguria, A. and Orrego, A. (2021). Gender differences in the disclosure of sexual abuse in Chilean adolescents. *Child Abuse Review*, 30(3), 210–225.

Haboush, K. L and Alyan, H. (2013). "Who Can You Tell?" Features of Arab Culture That Influence Conceptualization and Treatment of Childhood Sexual Abuse. *Journal of Child Sexual Abuse*, 22(5), 499–518.

HM Government. (2018). *Working together to safeguard children: A guide to inter-agency working to safeguard and promote the welfare of children*. https://assets.publishing.service.gov.uk/government/uploads/system/uploads/attachment_data/file/942454/Working_together_to_safeguard_children_inter_agency_guidance.pdf. Accessed 3 November 2021.

IICSA. (2021). *Child protection in religious organisations and settings: Investigation report*. https://www.iicsa.org.uk/key-documents/26895/view/child-protection-religious-organisations-settings-investigation-report-september-2021.pdf. Accessed 8 November 2021.

Izzidien, S. (2008). 'I can't tell people what is happening at home': Domestic Abuse within South Asian Communities—The Specific Needs of Women, Children and Young People. https://ecald.com/assets/Resources/Assets/Domestic-Abuse-South-Asian-Communities.pdf. Accessed 10 January 2021.

Jassal, V. (2020). Sexual abuse of South Asian children: what social workers need to know. Community Care. https://www.communitycare.co.uk/2020/08/20/sexual-abuse-south-asian-children-social-workers-need-know/

Katzenstein, D. and Fontes, L. A. (2017). Twice silenced: The underreporting of child sexual abuse in Orthodox Jewish communities. *Journal of Child Sexual Abuse*, 26(6), 752–767.

Keenan, M. (2013). *Child sexual abuse and the Catholic Church: Gender, power and organizational culture*. Oxford University Press.

Kellogg, N. D., Koek, W., and Nienow, S. M. (2020). Factors that prevent, prompt, and delay disclosures in female victims of child sexual abuse. *Child Abuse and Neglect*, 101.

Koçtürk, N. and Bilge, F. (2018). Social Support of Adolescent Survivors of Child Sexual Abuse and Sexual Revictimization in Turkey. *Journal of Child Sexual Abuse*, 27(1), 38–52.

Lammasniemi, L. (2020). "Precocious Girls": Age of consent, class and family in late nineteenth-century England. *Law and History Review*, 38(1), 241–266.

Lemaigre, C., Taylor, E. P., and Gittoes, C. (2017). Barriers and facilitators to disclosing sexual abuse in childhood and adolescence: A systematic review. *Child Abuse and Neglect*, 70, 39–52.

Lueger-Schuster, B., Weindl, D., Kantor, V., Knefel, M., Gluck, T., Moy, Y. and Butollo, A. (2014). Resilience and mental health in adult survivors of child abuse associated with the institution of the Austrian Catholic church. *Journal of Traumatic Stress*, 27(5), 568–557.

Lusky-Weisrose, E., Marmor, A., and Tener, D. (2020). Sexual abuse in the Orthodox Jewish community: A literature review. *Trauma, Violence, and Abuse*, 22(5):1086–1103.

Lyneham, S., and Facchini, L. (2019). Benevolent harm: Orphanages, voluntourism and child sexual exploitation in South-East Asia. *Trends and Issues in Crime and Criminal Justice*, 574, 1–16.

Mathews, B., and Collin-Vézina, D. (2019). Child sexual abuse: Toward a conceptual model and definition. *Trauma, Violence, and Abuse*, 20(2), 131–148.

Nagy, V. M. (2020). Women, Old Age, and Imprisonment in Victoria, Australia. *Women and Criminal Justice*, 30(3), 155–171.

Namy, S., Carlson, C., O'Hara, K., Nakuti, J., Bukuluki, P., Lwanyaaga, J., Namakula, S., Nanyunja, B., Wainberg, M. L., Naker, D., and Michau, L. (2017). Towards a feminist understanding of intersecting violence against women and children in the family. *Social Science and Medicine*, 184, 40–48.

NSPCC. (2021). Child sexual abuse: statistics briefing. https://learning.nspcc.org.uk/research-resources/statistics-briefings/child-sexual-abuse. Accessed 1 March 2022.

Otterman, S., and Rivera, R. (2012). *Ultra-Orthodox shun their own for reporting child sexual abuse*. http://www.nytimes.com/2012/05/10/nyregion/ultra-orthodox-jews-shun-their-own-for-reporting-child-sexual-abuse.html?_r=3. Accessed 1 November 2021.

Patel, P. (2013). Multi-faithism and the gender question: Implications of government policy on the struggle for equality and human rights for minority women in the UK. In Y. Rehman, L. Kelly, and H. Siddiqi (Eds.), *Moving in the shadows: Violence in the lives of minority women and children*. Ashgate.

Persian, J. (2015). *Jehovah's Witness hierarchy means child sex abuse goes unreported. The conversation.* https://theconversation.com/jehovahs-witness-hierarchy-means-child-sex-abuse-goes-unreported-45651. Accessed 6 November 2021.

Pitre, A., and Lingam, L. (2022). Age of consent: challenges and contradictions of sexual violence laws in India. *Sexual and Reproductive Health Matters,* 29(2).

Quayle, E. (2020). Prevention, disruption and deterrence of online child sexual exploitation and abuse. *ERA forum,* 21, 429–447.

Qureshi, K., Charsley, K., and Shaw, A. (2012). Marital instability among British Pakistanis: Transnationality, changing conjugalities and Islam. *Ethnic and Racial Studies,* 37 (2), 261–279.

Rashid, F., and Barron, I. (2019). Why the focus of clerical child sexual abuse has largely remained on the Catholic Church amongst other non-Catholic Christian denominations and religions. *Journal of Child Sexual Abuse,* 28(5), 564–585.

Richter, L. M., Mathews, S., Nonterah, E., and Masilela, L. (2018). A longitudinal perspective on boys as victims of childhood sexual abuse in South Africa: Consequences for adult mental health. *Child Abuse and Neglect,* 84, 1–10.

Rosmarin, D. H., Pirutinsky, S., Appel, M., Kaplan, T. and Pelcovitz, D. (2018). Childhood sexual abuse, mental health, and religion across the Jewish community. *Child Abuse and Neglect,* 81, 21–28.

Rumble, L., Febrianto, R. F., Larasati, M. N., Hamilton, C., Mathews, B. and Dunne, M. P. (2018). Childhood sexual violence in Indonesia: A systematic review. *Trauma, Violence and Abuse,* 21(2), 284–299.

Russell, D., Higgins, D., and Posso, A. (2020). Preventing child sexual abuse: A systematic review of interventions and their efficacy in developing countries. *Child Abuse and Neglect,* 102.

Sanchez, D., Benbow, L. M., Hernández-Martínez, M. and Serrata, J. V. (2019). Invisible bruises: Theoretical and practical considerations for Black/Afro-Latina survivors of childhood sexual abuse. *Women and Therapy,* 42(3–4), 406–429.

Sanjeevi, J., Houlihan, D., Bergstrom, K. A., Langley, M. M., and Judkins, J. (2018). A review of child sexual abuse: Impact, risk, and resilience in the context of culture. *Journal of Child Sexual Abuse,* 27(6), 622–641.

Sawrikar, P. and Katz, I. (2017). Barriers to disclosing child sexual abuse (CSA) in ethnic minority communities: A review of the literature and implications for practice in Australia. *Children and Youth Services Review,* 83, 302–315.

Schein, M., Biderman, A., Baras, M., Bennett, L., Bisharat, B., Borkan, J., Fogelman, Y., Gordon, L., Steinmetz, D., & Kitai, E. (2000). The prevalence of a history of child sexual abuse among adults visiting family practitioners in Israel. *Child Abuse and Neglect*, 24(5), 667–675.

Sielke, S. (2009). *Reading rape: The rhetoric of sexual violence in American literature and culture*. Princeton University Press.

Simon, J., Luetzow, A., and Conte, J. R. (2020). Thirty years of the convention on the rights of the child: Developments in child sexual abuse and exploitation. *Child Abuse and Neglect*, 110 (1).

Spröber, N., Schneider, T., Rassenhofer, M., Seitz, A., Liebhardt, H., König, L. and Fegert, J. F. (2014). Child sexual abuse in religiously affiliated and secular institutions: A retrospective descriptive analysis of data provided by victims in a government-sponsored reappraisal program in Germany. *BMC Public Health*, 14, 282–294.

Stevens, J. M., Arzoumanian, M. A., Greenbaum, B., Schwab, B. M., and Dalenberg, C. J. (2019). Relationship of abuse by religious authorities to depression, religiosity, and child physical abuse history in a college sample. *Psychological Trauma: Theory, Research, Practice, and Policy*, 11(3), 292–299.

Taussig, M. (1993). *Mimesis and alterity: A particular history of the senses*. Routledge.

Terry, K. J., Smith, M. L., Schuth, K., Kelly, J., Vollman, B., and Massey, C. (2011). *Causes and context of the sexual abuse crisis in the Catholic Church*. https://www.usccb.org/sites/default/files/issues-and-action/child-and-youth-protection/upload/The-Causes-and-Context-of-Sexual-Abuse-of-Minors-by-Catholic-Priests-in-the-United-States-1950-2010.pdf. Accessed 3 November 2021.

Terry, K. J. (2015). Child sexual abuse within the Catholic Church: A review of global perspectives. *International Journal of Comparative and Applied Criminal Justice*, 39(2), 139–154.

Tishelman, A. C. and Geffner, R. (2010). Forensic, cultural, and systems issues in child sexual abuse cases-Part 1: An introduction. *Journal of Child Sexual Abuse*, 19(5), 485–490.

Tunc, G. T., Gorak, G., Ozyazicioglu, N., Ak, B., Isil, B. and Vural, P. (2018). Determining the appropriateness of the "what if" situations test (WIST) with Turkish pre-schoolers. *Journal of Child Sexual Abuse*, 27(3), 292–304.

Turkish Statistical Institute. (2018). *Results of address-based census*. http://www.tuik.gov.tr/PdfGetir.do?id=27587. Accessed 5 November 2021.

UNICEF. (2010). *The United Nations Convention on the Rights of the Child*. https://www.unicef.org.uk/what-we-do/un-convention-child-rights/. Accessed 2 November 2021.

UNICEF. (2014). *Hidden in plain sight: A statistical analysis of violence against children*. https://www.unicef.org/documents/hidden-plain-sight-statistical-analysis-violence-against-children. Accessed 4 November 2021.

UNICEF. (2022). *UNICEF annual report 2021*. London: UNICEF.

Verloo, M. (2006). Multiple inequalities, intersectionality and the European Union. *European Journal of Women's Studies*, 13(3), 211–228.

Vermeulen, T., and Greeff, A. P. (2015). Family resilience resources in coping with child sexual abuse in South Africa. *Journal of Child Sexual Abuse*, 24(5), 555–571.

Warner, S. (2009). *Understanding the effects of child sexual abuse: Feminist revolutions in theory, research and practice*. Routledge.

Webb, E., Maddocks, A., and Bongilli, J. (2002). Effectively protecting black and minority ethnic children from harm: overcoming barriers to the child protection process. *Child Abuse Review*, 11(6), 394–410.

Wiper, C. (2012). Responding to violence against South Asian women in the British domestic violence movement. *Graduate Journal of Social Science*.

Wismayanti, Y. F., O'Leary, P., Tilbury, C., and Tjoe, Y. (2021). The problematization of child sexual abuse in policy and law: The Indonesian example. *Child Abuse and Neglect*, 118.

World Health Organization. (2020). *Violence against children factsheet*. https://www.who.int/news-room/fact-sheets/detail/violence-against-children. Accessed 1 September 2021.

Xiao, H., and Smith-Prince, J. (2015). Disclosure of child sexual abuse: The case of Pacific Islanders. *Journal of Child Sexual Abuse*, 24(4), 369–384.

Zalcberg, S. (2017). The place of culture and religion in patterns of disclosure and reporting sexual abuse of males: A case study of Ultra-Orthodox male victims. *Journal of Child Sexual Abuse*, 26(5), 590–607.

2

Epistemic Injustice: Racially Marginalised Adult Survivors of Child Sexual Abuse

Geetanjali Gangoli and Marianne Hester

Introduction

This chapter will explore how intersectional disadvantage impacts on racially minoritised women's experiences of child sexual abuse (henceforth CSA), and further experiences of abuse, and discuss the ways in which these experiences shaped their experience of justice, in particular how epistemic injustice related to their sexual and other abuse. The

---

G. Gangoli (✉)
Centre for Research in Violence and Abuse, Department of Sociology, Durham University, Durham, UK
e-mail: geetanjali.gangoli@durham.ac.uk

M. Hester
Centre for Gender & Violence Research, School for Policy Studies, University of Bristol, Bristol, UK
e-mail: marianne.hester@bristol.ac.uk

paper draws on interviews with seven adult women from racially minoritised, mainly South Asian, communities[1] who experienced sexual abuse as children but also experienced multiple forms of victimisation and abuse from childhood to adulthood. As children, they experienced sexual abuse, exposure to domestic violence, forced marriage, child marriage, grooming and trafficking for prostitution, and marital rape; and as adults, they experienced a range of sexual and domestic violence and abuse.

There is a general lack of literature regarding sexual abuse of children in Black and minoritised communities in the UK (Independent Inquiry into Child Sexual Abuse 2018), and the small number of studies that do exist has tended to focus on sexual abuse in South Asian communities. The Independent Inquiry into Child Sexual Abuse in the UK has included specific research with a wider group of Black and minoritised communities, including 89 individuals from Black African, Caribbean or other Black ethnic groups (49%), Asian ethnicities (33%) or 'mixed' ethnicities (10%) who were victim-survivors or linked to organisations working with survivors. While the prevalence of CSA in racially minoritised communities is no different to that in the population more generally, it tends to be underreported or not identified in minoritised communities (Gill and Harrison 2019). However, the patterns of abuse may vary within Black and minoritised communities as the contexts and opportunities for abuse can vary. For instance, Gill and Harrison (2019) indicate there are disproportionately more family and community abusers at least in relation to CSA in South Asian communities.

Victims-survivors from racially minoritised communities have been found to face particular barriers to help-seeking and accessing support for sexual violence and abuse, shaped especially by perceptions that statutory services such as the police, social care or children's mental health services will lack understanding of the communities concerned, and may apply inappropriate and racist approaches (Allnock et al. 2009; Bradby et al. 2007; Gill and Harrison 2019; Jay et al. 2021). For instance, the report from the Independent Inquiry to Child Sexual Abuse (Rodger et al. 2020), on CSA in relation to children from Black and minoritised communities, concludes that cultural stereotypes and racism by professionals lead to failures in practice as well as greater difficulties for individuals to disclose:

> Cultural stereotypes and racism can lead to failures on the part of institutions and professionals to identify and respond appropriately to child sexual abuse. They can also make it more difficult for individuals in ethnic minority communities to disclose and speak up about child sexual abuse.
> (Rodger et al. 2020: 22)

Such cultural stereotypes and racism can also lead to professionals erroneously seeing sexual abuse as merely part of racially minoritised cultures, and this is evident not only in this report (Rodger et al. 2020), but in earlier work on a range of gender-based abuse in these communities (see, for example, Burman et al. 2004; Thiara and Gill 2009).

In one particularly telling response to the Inquiry (Rodger et al. 2020: 22), a survivor reports that *'The social worker was white, okay, and she said to me, 'This is not sexual abuse. This is your culture'. Even today, I'm so traumatised by this'*. At the same time, concerns about racism may place further barriers on disclosure as victims-survivors have concerns about how their communities will be perceived if they disclose, and also of bringing shame on their families and communities. The studies that exist thus tend to show that victims-survivors will disclose to family or friends, if at all, rather than to agencies and institutions.

Cases such as the child sexual exploitation in Rotherham have at the same time shown up the reluctance of the police and other statutory agencies to intervene in minoritised communities for fear of being perceived as racist, leaving victims without routes to safety or well-being (Peach 2015). In Rotherham, between 1997 and 2003, at least 1,400 girls were systematically abused and sexually exploited by groups of men mainly from the Asian (Pakistani heritage) community. More than a third of the children were known by local services to be vulnerable. The report commissioned into the failure to deal with the Rotherham situation outlines how the children:

> ... were raped by multiple perpetrators, trafficked to other towns and cities in the north of England, abducted, beaten, and intimidated. ... Girls as young as 11 were raped by large numbers of male perpetrators.
>
> (Jay 2014: 1)

But the extensive abuse they experienced was ignored and minimised by agencies who blamed the girls for engaging in 'prostitution' and also due to concerns about being seen as racist. As Jay notes:

> ...there was a reluctance to engage...councillors did not engage directly with the Pakistani-heritage community to discuss how best they could jointly address the issue... Several staff described their nervousness about identifying the ethnic origins of perpetrators for fear of being thought racist; others remembered clear direction from their managers not to do so.
>
> (Jay 2014: 2)

A super-complaint against the police in 2020 resulted from these contradictory problems regarding the response to Black and minoritised victims of sexual abuse. The super-complaint was raised (Tees Valley Inclusion Project and Halo 2020) and included concerns about excessive focus on both community impact and failure by the police to consider family reprisals when abuse was reported to them.

Abusers may also exploit contexts where discourses of family and community 'honour' are prevalent thus shielding their abusive behaviour from being seen or disclosed. While child sexual abuse in racially minoritised communities may be overrepresented in the media and policy as gang-based/peer child sexual exploitation, echoing the Rotherham case (Child Exploitation and Online Protection Centre 2011; Office of Children's Commissioner 2012; Kelly and Karsna 2018), as Gill and Harrison (2019) point out, in South Asian communities abuse is more often perpetrated by family and community members than in the wider population. The experiences of the women in our sample below also reflected this pattern of largely familial and community abuse, with cousins, uncles, fathers, husbands and religious leaders perpetrating the abuse. Our interviewees, who were from different ethnic and faith communities, talked about not only experiencing sexual abuse as children, but also about further abuse from family members, members of their various minoritised and religious communities as well as from partners or husbands.

The multiple instances and forms of abuse experienced by our respondents as children and young people may seem akin to the concept of 'polyvictimisation' (Finkelhor et al. 2009, 2015) which Finkelhor and colleagues deem as children who experience very high levels of victimisations of different types. The model, which Finkelhor and team have developed and honed over the years, has focused largely on identifying individual risk factors and individualised characterisations, so-called adverse childhood experiences or ACEs (e.g. Finkelhor et al. 2015). In their earlier work, Finkelhor and colleagues (2009) found that there may be particular 'pathways' to becoming a polyvictim, which they describe as '(a) residing in a dangerous community, (b) living in a dangerous family, (c) having a chaotic, multi-problem family environment, or (d) having emotional problems that increase risk behaviour, engender antagonism, and compromise the capacity to protect oneself' (p 316). However, they found that race did not feature as a specific risk feature in this regard. In contrast, as we show later, the specific experiences of the women from the racially minoritised communities that we interviewed indicated that where 'race' was an important aspect that created specific risks of abuse and shaped their experiences. If we were to apply the Finkelhor 'pathways' characterisation of polyvictimisation to the multiple experiences of abuse in racially minoritised communities that our respondents talked about, this might thus further demonise such communities as 'dangerous' or inadequate.

In further exploration of the adverse circumstances (ACEs) that may impact especially on children's development, and consideration of how these may differ over time, Finkelhor and colleagues (2015) indicate the importance of both CSA and living in contexts where mothers are subject to domestic abuse for detrimental impacts on children's development and well-being. Our sample participants also talked specifically of experiencing CSA and witnessing mothers being abused by partners.

In a more recent study exploring the notion of polyvictimisation and longer-term outcomes on adults, Nguyen and colleagues (Nguyen et al.

2019) found that experiencing victimisation across multiple developmental stages of childhood, especially when this involves polyvictimisation, is a strong indicator of poor well-being during adulthood. This has greater resonance with our sample who experienced both CSA and lived in contexts of domestic abuse at ages 6 and 8, abuse as teenagers, or experienced continuous CSA victimisation from an early age to when they were teenagers, and consequently suffered from depression or other mental health effects, as well as further abuse, as adults.

The literature on polyvictimisation begins to provide a backdrop and patterning that resonates with the experiences of our small sample. However, such an approach, based largely on identifying risk factors, remains individualised and focused on the victims, while lacking explanatory power to take into account the particular opportunities for abusers who live in a structurally racist society with institutionally racist agencies and services. Instead, we need frameworks for understanding the multiple instances of abuse experienced by the women in our sample, that move beyond a merely psychologically and individually informed approach to abuse, to understanding such abuse within family, community and intimate relationships shaped by community and wider societal beliefs about women, ethnicity and age.

In what follows, we therefore explore the testimonies of the women in our small sample, by looking at the contextually situated intersecting factors that shape their experiences and using the conceptual frameworks of epistemic injustice and intersectionality. We will also explore how survivors may resist these forms of injustice, particularly in the context of giving meaning to their words, and seek to understand connections between child and adult abuse, where these may exist.

Conceptual Frameworks

We understand epistemic injustice as injustice related to knowledge and the ability to articulate that knowledge (Fricker 2007). Fricker defines epistemic injustice as the unfair discrimination against some actors in their capacity as knowers, based on prejudices linked to people's social identities and attributes, including gender, social background, ethnicity, race, sexuality, accent, and class, and argues that there are two distinct forms of epistemic injustice, namely *testimonial injustice* and *hermeneutical injustice*. *Testimonial injustice* can take place when the testimonies of some speakers are seen as less credible than others, and this refers back to prejudices about the speaker (Fricker 2007) and gives an unfair advantage to those who are not subject to these prejudices.

Testimonial injustice can lead to *hermeneutical injustice* (Fricker 2007: 162), where due to systematic underrepresentation of the experiences of marginalised individuals and groups, members of these groups are not able to make sense of their experiences, including lacking the language to articulate these experiences. The lack of conceptual frameworks to make sense of one's experiences is an injustice, according to Fricker (2007), because it unfairly advantages those who are able to have their experiences represented in the collective body of knowledge to be able to successfully communicate their experiences to other people: 'the powerful have an unfair advantage in structuring collective social understandings (Fricker 2007: 147)'. We look briefly at the application of these conceptualisations to explore the ways in which women resist their forms of injustice, through both individual and collective speech and actions.

Children from all ethnic communities, including White communities, suffer from epistemic injustice, because their testimonies of suffering are not articulated in the language of adults, or in forms that adults deem to understand (Burroughs and Tollefsen 2016), and are more generally deemed to be unreliable. This is particularly the case in CSA, where the testimony of the child challenges adult authority, and in cases of male perpetrators, hegemonic masculinity. However, the specific complexities of epistemic injustice for children from racially minoritised communities need further exploration. There is some research that relates to epistemic injustice in the context of Black and minoritised communities, including asylum-seeking communities, particularly in the context of their experiences with the asylum-seeking process (Cabot 2016; Sertler 2018). For example, the majority of asylum application outcomes appear predetermined and rest on hierarchies of eligibility established in relation to nationality, gender, sexual orientation and other factors (cf. Cabot 2016), and the testimonies of asylum seekers are often (mis)represented in arbitrary ways in order to reach conclusions that may be aligned to wider immigration policies in certain countries and regarding social groups (Sertler 2018). We seek to explore and expand these frameworks with regard to the testimonies of racially minoritised adult women who have experienced sexual abuse as children.

We also draw on the conceptual framework of intersectionality, which we understand as 'the notion that subjectivity is constituted by mutually reinforcing vectors of race, gender, class and sexuality' (Nash 2008: 2). Kimberle' Crenshaw (1991) is credited with introducing the term 'intersectionality' to the feminist lexicon in the late 1980s as part of antiracist struggles, and especially a focus on structural intersectionality in the context of violence against Black women. She interrogated the law's penchant in fixing identities and therefore not paying enough attention to how Black women may suffer from both race and gender inequalities. Nash has argued that the notion of intersectionality is under-theorised, suggesting that it has focussed so far on how marginalised people are (adversely) affected by their identities, rather than how those in power are able to use intersectional identities to their advantage. We believe that it is impossible to discuss the complexities of gender-based violence, including CSA without due attention to multiple sites of oppression and privilege that impact victims/survivors, and this is also what we aim to explore in this chapter.

Methods

This chapter draws from the interviews conducted as part of the Justice, Inequality and Gender-Based Violence project.[2] As part of the wider project, we conducted interviews with 251 victims/survivors of GBV, and we draw on seven of the interviews here. The project obtained research ethics approval from the University of Bristol ethics committee. With regard to the interviews, the research design was phenomenological, as the intention of the research was to understand the meanings of justice from the perspectives of survivors of gender-based violence and abuse (Williamson et al. 2021). Following this design, participants were recruited by asking partner agencies and other agencies working in the field of gender-based violence prevention to send information about the project to their service users. We offered language interpretation or other support for the interviews. In total, we recruited participants through more than 80 different organisations, and these organisations supported the survivors. The interviews were conducted in person, over the phone or using online software, and included some specific demographic and experience-related questions which we aimed to ask all participants that included age, income, employment and education. We asked questions about their experiences of gender-based violence and tried to explore what justice meant to them both abstractly and in the context of their own experience. Interviews lasted between an hour and two hours, with the average interview just over an hour. All the interviews were recorded and transcribed verbatim either by a team member or a professional transcriber, and pseudonyms were allotted to each participant.

Sample

This chapter examines a sub-sample of racially minoritised women, who had experienced CSA. Seven women from the overall sample met these criteria and the paper is based on the analysis of these seven interviews. Six of our respondents were South Asian, and one was mixed race (White and African). Four identified as middle class, two as working class and one did not disclose her class identity. All but one of the middle-class women were university educated. There were three Muslims, two Sikhs and one Christian in the sample. All but one were heterosexual, with one woman identifying as lesbian. Three respondents alluded to depression or other mental health issues. Four of the respondents did not seek any redress or justice for their experience of CSA; one approached the police and the NSPCC in adulthood; one disclosed to her husband; and one approached their community religious temple. While the sample is small, we believe that the rich data from the interviews offers an insight into the issue of CSA within racially minoritised, particularly South Asian, communities.

See Tables 2.1 and 2.2 for demographic information on each case, as well as age of CSA, the other form(s) of GBV experienced, and help/justice routes sought in the context of the CSA.

Table 2.1 Demographic information

Name	Social class	Education	Disability	Religion	Ethnicity	Sexuality
Cathy	Middle class	University	Depression	Christian	Mixed – White and Black	Heterosexual
Maliha	Middle class	University	Depression	Muslim	Bangladeshi	Heterosexual
Jaspreet	Working class	NVQ	Missing	Sikh	British Asian	Heterosexual
Amina	Middle class	University	None	Muslim	British Asian	Lesbian
Ruksana	Working class	GCSE	Mental health	Muslim	British Pakistani	Heterosexual
Simran	Middle class	Not known	None	Sikh	British Indian	Heterosexual
Vikki	Not known	Not known	None	Asian	British Asian	Heterosexual

Table 2.2 Types of abuse experienced

Name	CSA age	Perpetrator of CSA	Justice type	GBV as child	GBV as adult
Cathy	Not known	Uncle	None	Witnessed DV	DV, SV
Maliha	8, 15	Uncle, husband	None	None	DV, SV
Jaspreet	Not known	Priest in Sikh temple	Told ex-husband and friends	Witnessed DV	DV, SV
Amina	6 to 17	Two uncles	NSPCC, police	Witnessed DV	DV, SV
Ruksana	15–16	Cousin	None	Witnessed DV	DV, SV
Simran	15	Family member	Told Sikh temple	None	DV, SV
Vikki	Not known	Family member	None	Witnessed DV	DV

For the purpose of the chapter, we used a grounded theory approach, where we developed the theoretical models from the interview data. The interview data was analysed, coded and compared to yield the themes relating to the data. The two key themes that emerged from the data were intersectionality (in terms of how class, religion/faith, immigration, ethnicity and gender intersected in the experiences of abuse) and epistemic injustice (in terms of how the testimonies of racially minoritised women with experiences of CSA were represented and/or used in formal and informal routes to justice). We also obtained valuable data on how some women tried to challenge and resist epistemic injustice. The interview data has been collected, recorded and transcribed within strict ethical guidelines as described above. The analysis has resulted in theoretical frameworks emerging from the data itself, to ensure that the data analysis is credible. We use extended quotes from of our participants to give them voice, convey rich detail and illustrate the themes.

Findings and Analysis

All our respondents had experience of CSA and multiple other forms of gender-based violence and abuse as children and as adults. These forms of abuse included witnessing domestic abuse as children and experiencing sexual and domestic violence as adults. In all but one case, the perpetrator of the CSA was a family member. In the seventh case, the abuse was perpetrated by a priest. We also found that intersectional disadvantage was implicit in the ways in which these minority ethnic women were treated, and these disadvantages were in respect to religion/culture, age and gender. The impact of social class is not always clear in the testimonies, but we have included it in Table 2.1 to provide a full picture.

Testimonial Injustice

The framework of testimonial injustice includes the extent to which credibility is compromised because of the deflated significance credited to their narratives vis-à-vis other sources of knowledge and other speakers.

The intersections of age, gender and community/religious norms served to silence victims/survivors of CSA in our sample. In only two cases did the survivors speak out about the abuse while it was taking place, and in both cases, they were not believed:

> I think my mum ... again she slapped me a few times. She slapped me ... the guy who abused me showed me a porn magazine and I tried telling my mum about it, and she slapped me [saying] 'That is ridiculous!'
>
> (Amina)

There has been some research on the role of religion in perpetration of coercive control and domestic abuse (Aghtaie et al. 2020), and crimes in the name of honour, including female genital mutilation (Gangoli et al. 2018), and this is further articulated in the testimonies of some of our respondents. Jaspreet who was abused as a child by a priest talked about how she knew that the abuse was wrong, but was not able to speak out because of her age, and the power that her abuser enjoyed within the community:

> He wants me to take my top off. From there, that's when I knew it wasn't right, but because I was so young I didn't know what to do.
>
> (Jaspreet)

Jaspreet was aware, even as a child, that no one would believe her if she spoke out:

> No, no, because I couldn't tell anybody because my parents didn't believe me and if I'd have said anything in school, it's like shame. Like it's the girl that gets blamed for it
>
> (Jaspreet)

She went on to explain that there was a culture of collusion because of the religious authority that the priest enjoyed:

> Then I tried to avoid him, but then he'd just come up and just give me a hug, but it wasn't a hug; it was a grope. Because everybody knew him and he's known to like hug you, hug you, give kids sweets, nobody said anything, but I used to try to avoid him.
>
> (Jaspreet)

When survivors did speak out as adults (as in 4 cases), their earlier child sexual abuse was used against them to revictimise and perpetrate further abuse. As Jaspreet expressed:

> So my ex knew everything, that I was abused and what sort of life I had. I don't know if he used that against me because he forced sex, saying, you know, "That's what you like. You're a slag. You're this." Yes, so I was beaten up by him regularly. He was possessive. I wasn't allowed to go out the house.
>
> (Jaspreet)

Maliha, a Muslim woman, who was forced to marry at the age of 15 in her country of origin, was sexually abused as a child by her uncle before her marriage and her husband after the marriage. The intersections in her positioning by ethnicity, immigration status, cultural context and age meant that she lacked any ability to speak out and was discouraged from doing so by her peers:

> I only had like a few cousins [in country of origin] that I could talk to. But they would be like 'If you don't do this you're going to get battered, you're going to get …' cos they'd apparently seen it with other people and they were like 'You just need to do this'. They were like trying to make me aware of what consequences there were … not in a malicious way, cos they were my age and they were like 'Oh my God, you know, if you don't do this, this and this will happen' you know you need to really comply with what they want. And I was like 'Really?' and it shocked me.
>
> (Maliha)

Maliha felt that victims of sexual abuse were therefore not able to talk about the impact of the abuse on their lives.

> …the perpetrator gets away with everything. Or gets away with the majority of what they've done…I think it's really unfair when the emotional side is not attached to it and … because I feel victims suffer a lot more than the perpetrators.
>
> (Maliha)

Maliha left her husband at 17 for another man, but her community in the UK did not recognise her second relationship as legal or valid:

> And cos I was still like in the eyes of religion I was still married to the other person, it was shameful.
>
> (Maliha)

Previous work on victims/survivors of different forms of gender-based violence of abuse has found procedural injustice to be implicit within the policing and judicial system, particularly in the case of racially minoritised women and girls (Gangoli et al. 2020; Mulvihill et al. 2018). Our respondents, including those who did not approach the police, also spoke of the criminal justice system, as implicitly unjust. Respondents believed that in a courtroom, and criminal justice system more generally, decisions were made by people who were not involved, and that the victim-survivor's words were never believed. For example, Amina, who experienced sexual abuse at the hands of her uncles, and reported this as an adult to the National Society for the Prevention of Cruelty to Children (NSPCC) and the police, had this to say:

> so justice is basically where if somebody perpetrates a crime against you then they are … I use the word 'tried' – they go to a tribunal or a court, and there's a discussion by people who are not involved and there's a decision that if the evidence is there to show that this was done. And you know that it's happened, but actually it is for the jury or whoever to decide that yes this person needs to be punished for what they've done.
>
> (Amina)

Cathy, a mixed-race woman, who was sexually abused by her uncle as a child, talked about her decision not to report to the police when she was an adult:

> (Friends asked me) to take him to court and prosecute him so that it doesn't happen to anyone else. But at the same time at that moment in time you don't want to see that person again, you don't want to put yourself through that. You know even when they're talking about that they can do it on the video link and stuff, it still wasn't convincing to me

that you know ... it wasn't convincing enough to me that I was going to be fully safe.

(Cathy)

Amina talked about how victim blaming was common in cases of sexual abuse and rape, particularly in the criminal justice system:

> So yeah, so an injustice may be where that happens basically that somebody ... for example in sexual abuse, or even in rape cases ... but that someone tells you 'Oh you shouldn't be wearing that dress ... that you're asking for something because you are wearing this.

(Amina)

Hermeneutic Injustice

Hermeneutic injustice occurs as a process of cultural and structural collusion, where marginalised groups find that they lack the language and resources to speak out, including an ability to fully process their experience (Fricker 2006; 2007). This creates particular barriers to disclosure involving language and reaction from family and community. In the context of child sexual abuse, the women in our sample found that they were being gaslit by norms both within their own communities and within wider structures of racism.

In the context of general disbelief and abuse, women were not able to make sense of their experiences, whether they were of CSA or other forms of parental control, and this socialised them to be silenced further. For example, Amina, who was forced to wear a hijab at an early age, disliked it and found it 'embarrassing', but finally gave up at age sixteen.

Further in the interview, Amina stated that she was not able to articulate her embarrassment to her family, 'because they wouldn't understand what there was to be embarrassed about' fed into the process of hermeneutic injustice, as she 'just gave up'. Consequently, women did not have the language or space to articulate the abuse because of gendered and community norms:

> I just couldn't do anything because obviously being a girl you couldn't tell your parent anything.
>
> (Jaspreet)

Our respondents articulated this in the context of how they saw older women in their family also being controlled, and silenced, and this created an atmosphere of fear:

> Every time we broke the rules my mum would always get punished, even if it was subtle. There was a lot of pressure, especially as we got older, as we became teenagers, that's when it really really became apparent...We weren't allowed to go out, we weren't allowed to listen to music. We hated it, but it wasn't violence or shouting or screaming, it was just the rules were there.
>
> (Ruksana)

Some respondents talked about how they felt split between what was 'normal' and not. When Amina was being forced into marriage as a teenager, she could not speak out against it:

> No, I didn't talk to my parents about it either because ... I just thought it was normal, but it didn't seem normal to me. That's what they did but it wasn't normal to me.
>
> (Amina)

Amina and the other interviewees felt a sense of cognitive dissonance between what they were told was 'normal' by their families/communities and what they actually felt *was* normal behaviour. We suggest that if girls and women constantly and repeatedly experience this dissonance, it is very likely that they would not be able to articulate it.

Ruksana, a Muslim woman, who was sexually abused by a cousin as a young teenager, explained that she did not report it to anyone because of her previous experience as a child, when her school colluded with her family to deny her equal access to educational activities:

> [in] schools where my voice didn't seem to count – that was injustice. So it was not just that everything happened ... I felt like I tried to explain

to [teachers] that this is how our life is – why is my life different, why aren't you doing anything about it, why am I not allowed to go on school trips. And [they] said that's the way it is in your culture. So why is that allowed, you know … that to me was that whole injustice, the unfairness of it all … and all because I was a girl, you know.

(Ruksana)

First generation women found that their previous experiences in their country of origin did not equip them to articulate their abuse and also created barriers to disclosure due to shame:

But I come from India and come from the Sikh family, never had problem there, so we weren't trained for that – if you need help, where do you have to go? Plus, those days, you think it's shame to the family if you do something, if police come to your door, or in the house there's loud noise, fighting, arguing and all that.

(Simran)

Our participants found that their experiences of child sexual abuse had led to a sense of normalisation of the abuse, and their adult relationship with the perpetrator complicated their ability to recognise what was happening to them as abuse (Middletoet al. 2017; Stark 2007):

That is just emotionally, financially, and all aspects that he damaged … he damaged my way of life, thinking [this is] how life should be.

(Maliha)

When women tried to speak out, they found that they lacked the language and knowledge to articulate the abuse, and ended up blaming themselves and internalised the abuse:

I think I went to the GP once when I was being abused and I said 'I think I'm pregnant' and the GP said 'Have you had sex?' and I kind of knew what sex was and I thought 'No, but I'm not sure if it's through clothes' but I couldn't say I was being abused, because I didn't want to then have to deal with that. So I thought it would be my fault because I told everyone.

(Amina)

Resisting Epistemic Injustice by Voicing the Abuse

This section will look at the efforts made by women to resist these forms of epistemic injustice. As we have seen in previous sections, women and girls find it difficult to articulate what is happening to them as abuse. Resistance comes from a recognition of the problem and naming what has happened as abuse (Rich, 1979). Like many other victims of child sexual abuse (Frazer and Hutchings 2020), Jaspreet talked about how as an adult she wanted to work towards a space where girls and women are believed and the abuse they experienced acknowledged:

> Okay. Justice is, for me, oh, God, how do I explain it? For me it would be like, say, for women, it's to stand up for women's rights, that's justice, to acknowledge that what happened to these victims, it's the knowledge they were abused and, you know, these women shouldn't have gone through this because of like being female. So for me it's like to stand up just to see someone admitting that they did wrong to these women.
>
> (Jaspreet)

Some of our participants spoke of different ways that as children, they tried to resist the gendered norms that prepared them for accepting abuse. Amina recounted how her mother was conditioning her to be a good South Asian woman from a young age, but explained that she found ways to resist her:

> Yeah so that was something that I kind of noticed from the age of about 10, that my mum … I felt she was preparing me in some way. I kind of remember being in the kitchen from a young age, that I had to learn to cook, and I had to clean. And at that age I remember [wanting to join my brother in] …climbing trees and playing and learning to ride a bicycle… I wasn't allowed to ride a bicycle because girls didn't ride bicycles. But I did it secretly, my brother and I learnt on a bicycle that didn't actually have a chain on it. So we lived on a hill so we'd ride down the hill, then we'd have to walk it back up.
>
> (Amina)

One of our participants found ways to stop the abuse temporarily, by cutting herself in her genitals so that she could pretend that she was menstruating. She did this as a way to stop the perpetrator from raping her:

> Myself I mutilated myself I suppose, just … I'm not saying I cut myself to the extent that I gave myself significant harm, I don't think I did that, but … just enough you know to be bleeding, so I could stop him having sex.
>
> (Ruksana)

Ruksana drew on Islamic religious norms that menstruating women are unclean, and that men are prohibited to have sex with them (Mazuz 2020). While these norms have been seen as discriminatory to women (Poureslami and Osati-Ashtiani 2002), Ruksana was able to use them to prevent abuse, albeit with injury to herself.

One of our respondents eventually reported her childhood experiences of abuse to the police as an adult only when she felt that other children were in danger from the perpetrator:

> And I reported it for the first time last year … well I talked to the NSPCC and they filed a report to the police, because there are children still in the house, so they had to go and let them know that there had been a report … they didn't say it was from me … so they were investigating … but they were just made aware that there was something. I told my mum about it for the first time last year.
>
> (Amina)

Making the report to the NSPCC empowered Amina to the extent that she was able to then speak to her mother about the abuse.

Jaspreet reported to the temple when she was an adult, that she had been abused there as a child, and found the experience difficult:

> It was, I'm not going to lie. It was one of the hardest times of my life, and being disowned as well by everyone. Everything you know, you've been going to that temple since you were young. I even wrote a letter to this priest, I'll say it now, I wrote a letter of my abuse. I wanted them

to know who abused me in the temple, what goes on. They called me and they ripped the letter up and said to me, they said, "Nobody should know about this.

(Jaspreet)

However, Jaspreet went on to state that she did not regret speaking out, '*even if it made no difference*'. This is a testament to the power of speaking out for victims of child sexual abuse.

For some respondents, their sense of resisting years of epistemic injustice came simply by moving on mentally and physically from the abuse:

I am both a victim and a survivor, because whatever happened it was too much to handle at the time, I just moved from there. Now I'm all right, I'm happy, and God has given me everything. My children are happy, I'm happy. I'm living my life. I eat what I want to eat, I go where I want to go, I wear what I want to wear.

(Simran)

Discussion and Conclusion

As the previous sections illustrate, racially minoritised women and girls may experience multiple forms of abuse that may constitute 'polyvictimisation' and can have detrimental long-term impacts on their mental health. Moreover, racially minoritised women and girls experience epistemic injustice in the context of child sexual abuse and further abuse. This is complicated by different intersections, and these will be explored here. We also found that racially minoritised women and girls resist the silencing of their voices. The key intersecting factors that inhibited women and girls' ability to be heard and believed were intersections of religion, gender and age; and within these the discourses of shame and honour that particularly impacts some racially minoritised women, particularly from South Asian communities (Gill 2004; 2009).

Our respondents experienced the restrictions of shame and honour from a young age, and this was further complicated by gendered norms. As earlier studies indicate (Kandiyoti 1988), older women in the family, particularly mothers, were often complicit in perpetuating these forms of testimonial and hermeneutic injustice by ignoring and/or punishing their daughters when they speak out. Several respondents (Ruksana, Amina, Jaspreet) in our sample spoke about the role of their mothers by creating a context within which speaking out was impossible, or speech was punished. In one case (Ruksana), implicit threats against the mother by the father were used to silence her. In all cases, respondents felt trapped into silence, because children, particularly girls, are not believed when they speak out.

Another intersecting factor is religion. Religious coercion in these cases can be seen as coercive control, as ways of manipulating women's behaviour by using religious justification; for example, there is evidence some religious practitioners talked about the role of scripture and religious teaching in constraining justice for victims of violence and abuse (Mulvihill, et al. 2018) and therefore trapping women further in what Stark (2007) has called the 'cage of male domination'.

In line with earlier theoretical (Menon 2004) and empirical (Baxi 2017) studies on gender-based violence and justice that point to a fundamental lack of fit between justice and law, none of our respondents had any faith in the criminal justice system, and they pointed to the systematic failures within these systems that did not prioritise victim/survivor voices and testimonies. Epistemic injustice was also implicit in our participants dealing with other structures, including education (Ruksana); immigration (Simran); and religion (Simran, Jaspreet, Cathy).

In this context of general epistemic injustice, what enabled women to speak out and be heard? We suggest that women's and girls' resistance was sometimes implicitly dependent on their ability to escape the hermeneutic injustice they experienced and being able to recognise their experience as abuse. In other words, they were often able to name their abuse when they were older and were in a safe space (Maliha, Amina and Jaspreet) either professionally or in their personal life. In two cases (Amina, Ruksana), there was resistance at the time of the abuse, even if they were not able to fully articulate their abuse as such. Even where their resistance appeared unsuccessful (Simran) or a form of self-harm (Ruksana), the very act of resistance was responsible for *restoring a sense of self* (Draucker et al. 2009) that has been lost to them through their abuser (Maliha).

In conclusion, our chapter demonstrates that racially minoritised victims/survivors of CSA experience testimonial and hermeneutic injustice, and these forms of injustice are reflected and explicit in their interactions with structural (law, criminal, justice, immigration) and cultural (familial and/or religious norms and codes) systems. However, it was evident in their testimony that women were able to resist these forms of injustice, particularly when they were enabled to do. The power of speaking out as a form of resistance cannot be underestimated as a form of healing for women and girls who have experienced child sexual abuse.

Summary

This chapter draws on interviews with seven adult women from racially minoritised communities who experienced sexual abuse as children and multiple other forms of abuse both as children and as adults. The theoretical frameworks used to explore the women's testimonies were epistemic injustice and intersectionality. We found that racially minoritised women who are survivors of child sexual abuse face particular vulnerabilities to both testimonial and hermeneutic forms of epistemic injustice, both as children and also as adults. These included: faith-based/religious restrictions and community and family enabled gendered norms; wider structural issues, and as children, age-related restrictions. Some of the respondents were not able to articulate the abuse, even to themselves, particularly as children. However, a few were able to both articulate and find ways to resist the abuse as children, but mostly commonly, from a space of safety, as adults. We argue that racially minoritised girls are particularly vulnerable to epistemic injustice when subjected to child sexual abuse, and recommend that policy and practice be better adapted to reflect this in order to support them, and co-create safe spaces with them to enable them to voice and resist the abuse.

Notes

1. In the light of recent concerns about the acronym *BAME* used to describe Black and Ethnic Minority Communities, we will be using the term racially minoritised instead (Milner and Jumble 2020).
2. (ESRC grant ES/MO10090/1, Universities of Bristol, Cardiff and West of England with Women's Aid and Welsh Women's Aid). The project addressed the knowledge gap that exists regarding justice, inequality and gender-based violence (GBV), and explored how 'justice' (in its wider sense) is understood, sought and experienced by victims/survivors of GBV and key practitioners.

References

Aghtaie, N., Mulvihill, N., Abrahams, H. and Hester, M. (2020). Defining and Enabling 'Justice' for Victims/Survivors of Domestic Violence and Abuse, *Religion and Gender*, 10(2), 155–181. https://doi.org/10.1163/18785417-20200001

Allnock, D, Bunting, L, Price, A, Morgan-Klein, N, Ellis, J, Radford, L and Stafford, A. (2009). *Sexual abuse and therapeutic services for children and young people: The gap between provision and need (Full report)*. NSPCC: London.

Thiara, R. and Gill., A. K. (2009). *Violence against women in South Asian communities: Issues for policy and practice*. Jessica Kingsley Publishers.

Baxi, P. (2017). *Public secrets of law: Rape trials in India*. Oxford: Oxford University Press.

Burman, E., Smailes, S. L., and Chantler, K. (2004). 'Culture' as a barrier to service provision and delivery: domestic violence services for minoritized women. *Critical Social Policy*, 24(3), 332–357.

Burrough, M. and Tollefsen, D. (2016). Learning to listen: Epistemic injustice and the child, *Episteme*, 13(3), 359–377. https://doi.org/10.1017/epi.2015.64

Bradby, H., Varyani, M., Oglethorpe, R., Raine, W., White, I. and Minnis, H. (2007). British Asian families and the use of child and adolescent mental health services: A qualitative study of a hard to reach group, *Social Science and Medicine*, 65(12), 2413–2424.

Cabot, H. (2016). "Refugee Voices": Tragedy, Ghosts, and the Anthropology of Not Knowing. *Journal of Contemporary Ethnography*, 1–28. https://doi.org/10.1177/0891241615625567

Child Exploitation and Online Protection Centre. (2011). *Out of mind, out of sight: breaking down the barriers to child sexual exploitation: Executive summary*. Out of mind, Out of sight. www.basw.co.uk. Accessed 11 November 2021.

Crenshaw, K. (1991). Mapping the margins: Intersectionality, identity politics, and violence against women of Color. *Stanford Law Review*, 43(6), 1241–1299. https://doi.org/10.2307/1229039

Draucker, C. B., Martsolf, D. S., Ross, R., Cook, C. B., Stidham, A. W. and Mweemba, P. (2009). The essence of healing from sexual violence: A qualitative metasynthesis. *Research in Nursing & Health*, 32(4), 366–378. https://doi.org/10.1002/nur.20333

Finkelhor, D., Ormrod, R. Turner, R. and Holt, M. (2009). Pathways to Poly-Victimization. *Child Maltreatment*, 14(4), 316–329. https://doi.org/10.1177/1077559509347012

Finkelhor, D., Shattuck, A., Turner, H., & Hamby, S. (2015). A revised inventory of Adverse Childhood Experiences. *Child Abuse & Neglect*, 48, 13–21. https://doi.org/10.1016/j.chiabu.2015.07.011

Frazer, E. and Hutchings, K. (2020). The feminist politics of naming violence. *Feminist Theory*, 21(2), 199–216. https://doi.org/10.1177/1464700119859759

Fricker, M. (2006). Powerlessness and social interpretation. *Episteme: A Journal of Social Epistemology*, 3(1), 96–108. https://doi.org/10.1353/epi.0.0004

Fricker, M. (2007). *Epistemic injustice and the ethics of knowledge*. Oxford: Oxford University Press.

Gangoli, G. Gill, A., Mulvihill, N. and Hester, M. (2018). Perception and barriers: Reporting female genital mutilation, *Journal of Aggression, Conflict and Peace Research*, 10(4), 251–260. https://doi.org/10.1108/JACPR-09-2017-0323

Gangoli, G.; Bates L. and Hester, M. (2020). What does justice mean to black and minority ethnic (BME) victims/survivors of gender-based violence? *Journal of Ethnic and Migration Studies*, 46(15), 3119–3135. https://doi.org/10.1080/1369183X.2019.1650010

Gill, A. K. (2004). Voicing the silent fear: South Asian women and experiences of domestic violence. *The Howard Journal of Criminal Justice*, 43(5), 465–483. https://doi.org/10.1111/j.1468-2311.2004.00343.x

Gill, A. K. (2009). Honor Killings and the quest for justice in black and minority ethnic communities in the United Kingdom. *Criminal Justice Policy Review*, 20(4), 475–494. https://doi.org/10.1177/0887403408329604

Gill, A. K. and Harrison, G. (2019). I am talking about it because I want to stop it: child sexual abuse and sexual violence against women in Bristish South Asian communities. *Bristish Journal of Criminology*, 59 (3), 511–529

Independent Inquiry into Child Sexual Abuse. (2018). *INQ001769*. [Online]. Available at: https://www.iicsa.org.uk/key-documents/5554/view/INQ001 769.pdf, Accessed 8 November 2021.

Jay, A. (2014). Independent inquiry into child sexual exploitation in rotherham. [Online]. Available at: https://www.rotherham.gov.uk/dow nloads/file/279/independent-inquiry-into-child-sexual-exploitation-in-rot herham, Accessed 10 November 2021.

Jay, A., Evans, M., Frank, I. and Sharpling, D. (2021) Institutional responses to allegations of child sexual abuse involving the late Lord Janner of Braunstone QC investigation report. A report of the Inquiry Panel. London: House of Commons.

Kandiyoti, D. (1988). Bargaining with patriarchy. *Gender and Society*, 2(3), 274–290. http://www.jstor.org/stable/190357

Kelly, L and Karsna, K. (2018). *Measuring the scale and changing nature of child sexual abuse and child sexual exploitation Scoping report.* London Metropolitan University. 18871_CSA_Scoping_paper_web_FA.pdf (cwasu.org). Accessed 11 November2021

Mazuz, H. A. G. G. A. I. (2020). Revisiting Islamic laws of Istihāḍa. *Journal of the Royal Asiatic Society*, 30(2), 223–229. Cambridge University Press.

Menon, N. (2004). *Recovering subversion: Feminist politics beyond the law.* Urbana and Chicago: University of Illinois Press.

Middleton, W. Sachs, A. and Dorahy, M. J. (2017). The abused and the abuser: Victim–perpetrator dynamics. *Journal of Trauma & Dissociation*, 18(3), 249–258. https://doi.org/10.1080/15299732.2017.1295373

Milner, A. and Jumble, S. (2020). Using the right words to address racial disparities in Covid-19. *Lancet*, 58, 419–420. https://doi.org/10.1016/S2468-2667(20)30162-6

Mulvihill, N. Gangoli, G. Gill, A. K. and Hester, M. (2018). The experience of interactional justice for victims of 'honour'-based violence and abuse reporting to the police in England and Wales, *Policing and Society*, 29(6), 640–656. https://doi.org/10.1080/10439463.2018.1427745

Nash, J. C. (2008). Re-thinking intersectionality. *Feminist Review*, 89(1), 1–15. https://doi.org/10.1057/fr.2008.4

Nguyen, K. H., Kegler, S. R., Chiang, L. and Kress, H. (2019). Effects of polyvictimization before age 18 on health outcomes in Young Kenyan adults: Violence against children survey. *Violence and Victims*, 34(2), 229–242. https://doi.org/10.1891/0886-6708.VV-D-17-00182

Office of the Children's Commissioner. (2012). *'I thought I was the only one. The only one in the world'. The office of the children's commissioner's inquiry into child sexual exploitation in gangs and groups.* Interim report. England, https://www.csepoliceandprevention.org.uk/sites/default/files/cse_guidance_bame.pdf, Accessed 11 November 2021.

Peach, D., Allen, D., Brown, P., Sanghera, K., Sharif, R., Lees, J. and Senior, J. (2015). *Needs analysis report following the sexual exploitation of children in Rotherham.* University of Salford. APPROVED FINAL RMBC CSE Needs Analysis report—Salford.pdf (rotherham.gov.uk), Accessed 12 November 2021.

Poureslami, M. and Osati-Ashtiani, F. (2002). Assessing knowledge, attitudes, and behavior of adolescent girls in Suburban districts of Tehran about Dysmenorrhea and menstrual hygiene. *Journal of International Women's Studies*, 3(2), 51–61. http://vc.bridgew.edu/jiws/vol3/iss2/4

Rich, A. (1979). *On lies, secrets and silence: Selected prose 1966–1978.* New York City: W. W. Norton & Company.

Rodger, H., Hurcombe, R. Redmond, T. and George, R. (2020) "People don't talk about it": Child sexual abuse in ethnic minority communities. Independent inquiry to child sexual abuse. IICSA Independent Inquiry into Child Sexual Abuse, Accessed 12 November 2021.

Sertler, E. (2018). The institution of gender-based asylum and epistemic injustice: A structural limit. *Feminist Philosophy Quarterly*, 4(3). https://doi.org/10.5206/fpq/2018.3.5775

Stark, E. (2007). *Coercive control: The entrapment of women in personal life.* Oxford: Oxford University Press.

Tees Valley Inclusion Project and Halo (2020) Invisible Survivors. The Long Wait for Justice, available online: Invisible_survivors___The_long_wait_for_justice.pdf (publishing.service.gov.uk), Accessed 5 November 2021.

Williamson, E., Aghtaie, N., Bates, L., Eisenstadt, N., Gangoli, G., Hester, M., Matolcsi, A., McCarthy, L., Mulvihill, N., Robinson, A., and Walker, S.-J. (2021). *The justice, inequalities and gender based violence*

(GBV) project: A description of the methodological and analytic approach to phase 3 qualitative interviews with victim-survivors (v-s). University of Bristol: Bristol. https://research-information.bris.ac.uk/en/projects/justice-inequality-and-gender-based-violence, Accessed 11 November 2021.

3

Understanding the Experiences of British South Asian Male Survivors of Child Sexual Abuse

Hannah Begum and Aisha K. Gill

Introduction

Despite South Asian communities having long been settled in Britain, most of the limited, extant research on child sexual abuse (CSA) in these communities only considers the experiences of female CSA survivors. Consequently, male CSA survivors have reduced access to support services—a situation that is further compounded by institutionalised racism. This chapter aims to explore the phenomenon of CSA among British South Asian male survivors and to understand how

H. Begum
The Centre of expertise on child sexual abuse, Barnardo House, London, UK
e-mail: hannah.begum@csacentre.org.uk

A. K. Gill (✉)
The Faculty of Social Sciences and Law, School for Policy Studies, Bristol, UK
e-mail: ak.gill@bristol.ac.uk

© The Author(s), under exclusive license to Springer Nature Switzerland AG 2022
A. K. Gill and H. Begum (eds.), *Child Sexual Abuse in Black and Minoritised Communities*, https://doi.org/10.1007/978-3-031-06337-4_3

they make sense of their experiences. Themes to emerge from interviews with male survivors from these communities include the barriers to disclosing CSA, the effect of concepts of masculinity and sexuality on how survivors process their abuse, and the impact of sociocultural norms that impede discussing and disclosing CSA. Through the lens of masculinities theory, the chapter finds that the way British South Asian men construct and understand their experiences of CSA is largely determined by cultural and societal expectations of 'being a man'. When contextualised within the masculinities framework, the cultural imperatives of shame and honour are revealed as crucial to South Asian men's experiences of this abuse. The survivor narratives illustrate the complex interplay between culture and masculinity—two factors that place British South Asian male CSA survivors in the difficult position of trying to recover from their trauma while also grappling with culturally sanctioned ideals of masculinity and being expected to live up to or embody these ideals. The research finds that engaging with parents and communities to discuss these sensitive topics is a necessary first step in breaking down the conversational barriers identified in this study.

British South Asian male CSA survivors face a twofold problem: lack of research on this phenomenon and limited service provision. First, male CSA survivors have traditionally been marginalised in favour of female CSA survivors, a group that forms the basis of most academic research and to whom the majority of counselling and support services currently operating in the UK cater (Gagnier and Collin-Vézina 2016). The centrality of these female experiences, although crucial to understanding the experiences of CSA survivors in general, has eclipsed the specific narratives of male survivors. Second, despite the UK's incredibly multicultural population, people from minoritised backgrounds still experience institutional forms of racism that are entrenched in service provision and research and that lead to racialised and Eurocentric perspectives and practices (Singh 2019; Dominelli 2017). This chapter thus seeks to contribute to and expand on the existing body of literature on male CSA in minoritised groups. It illuminates the experiences of male survivors from British South Asian communities, creating space for the much-needed voices of a critically under-researched group.

Child Sexual Abuse Within South Asian Communities

To date, no studies have examined the experiences of South Asian male CSA survivors, which raises the question of why. Black and minoritised communities have often been labelled 'hard to reach', a highly ambiguous and contested term used by various agencies to describe communities that they have difficulty accessing (Darko 2021). Ironically, when this term is used in an attempt to tackle inequality across the board—including in health care, education and academic research—it actually perpetuates stereotypes of minoritised groups as problematic and reluctant to be reached (Hardy and Chakraborti 2019). Therefore, this chapter attempts to uncover the hidden victims of CSA—in this case, British South Asian men—and to illuminate their lived experiences of this form of abuse.

Two pertinent constructs play a large part in how South Asian communities operate: *izzat* and *sharam*, which broadly correspond to 'honour' and 'shame', respectively, in Western understanding (Sangar and Howe 2021). These social and cultural constructs emerged from the traditionally patriarchal structure of South Asian families and often pertain to the women of the household, who bear the responsibility of upholding honour and avoiding shame (Tonsing and Barn 2017). However, there is increasing evidence that men are also affected by izzat and sharam (Jaspal 2020). One of the ways in which sharam can be brought upon a South Asian family is through acts that are considered taboo and break with tradition—in families who adhere strictly to religion, such acts can also be regarded as 'sinful'. They include marrying outside of caste/ethnicity/religion, dating, having sexual relations before marriage and disclosing issues such as domestic violence and abuse outside of the family or community (Couture-Carron 2020; Begum et al. 2020). These issues have traditionally been considered off limits for discussion with external actors, with the ability to contain such information reflecting an individual's, their family's and the wider community's izzat (Kaur and Kaur 2020; Mucina and Jamal 2021).

When izzat and sharam have a ripple effect on an individual's family and community, it creates what is known as 'reflected' shame and honour

(Gilbert et al. 2004; Mucina and Jamal 2021). That consequence places pressure on individuals to recognise the importance of maintaining family izzat and how it is linked to one's personal sharam. Mesquita (2001; Sahota 2019) argues that this view of communal honour and shame relates to the collectivist nature of South Asian communities, in which emotions are connected to how behaviour reflects on others; conversely, in more individualistic communities, emotions such as honour and shame reflect more on the self. In the context of sexual abuse, izzat and sharam can be understood to operate beyond cultural boundaries, with research indicating that these constructs resonate with many South Asian survivors of abuse (Reavey et al. 2006). Though it is widely acknowledged that shame is a universal emotion and a common outcome for CSA survivors (Goffnett et al. 2020; MacGinley et al. 2019), South Asian people can face the added pressure to remain silent in order to not compromise the izzat of their family unit by bringing sharam upon it (Gilbert et al. 2004; Jaspal 2014; Peart 2013). This means they still conceptualise their shame in a way that is external to their experience as a survivor.

Reavey et al. (2006) gained access to South Asian female sexual abuse survivors who struggled with 'cultured selves'. This term refers to problems in transferring Westernised notions of selfhood to situations where help for sexual abuse is needed; such problems are rooted in a wide range of cultural differences and practices. In South Asian communities, traditional conceptualisations of culture would consider selfhood a largely redundant notion, with individuals instead measuring their actions according to the standard that is accepted at a community level rather than for one's own benefit. Gilbert et al (2004; Jaspal 2014; Peart 2013) illustrate this point by arguing that shame can not only be internal, related to negative self-perceptions and feelings, but can also relate to how one thinks others feel and think about one. Gilbert et al. (2004) emphasise that South Asians grapple with decontextualising their personal schema of self and others, as this schema has evolved from cultural dispositions and personal histories. This view is reinforced by Dey et al. (2017), who assert that British South Asians possess dual/multiple cultural identities and that their daily lives and sociocultural interactions are influenced by the dichotomies and complexities that emanate from their bicultural/multicultural heritage.

Gilligan and Akhtar (2006) explored some of the cultural barriers to CSA disclosure in South Asian communities across Bradford. They found that although many people within these communities shared the view that abuse must be responded to, numerous factors prevented those who knew about the abuse of others from responding in any impactful way. Focus groups and consultations with (mostly) South Asian women across Bradford revealed that the cultural imperatives of sharam and izzat were powerful enough to hamper CSA disclosure. In addition, there was a lack of basic knowledge about CSA, a fear of public exposure if the abuse was disclosed, a lack of awareness regarding the provisions available following disclosure and a fear of culturally insensitive responses from service providers. Gilligan and Akhtar (2005) call for more culturally competent professional responses to CSA in minoritised communities and recommend avoiding support service practice that is based on generalised assumptions of a particular ethnic/cultural/religious group.

While Gill and Harrison (2017) acknowledge that the full range of barriers to sexual abuse disclosure is multidimensional and universal and that these barriers exist in some form within all communities of all ethnic backgrounds, their study of 13 British South Asian CSA survivors identified the following significant barriers to disclosure: honour and consequential shame (including repercussions or consequences arising from the disclosure), compromised modesty, fear of being disbelieved, language barriers and not recognising that the abuse they had experienced was sexual. Gill and Harrison recognised that the most influential barrier for British South Asian women was honour and consequential shame. Although shame is recognised as a barrier for survivors more generally, its translation and conceptualisation within the South Asian communities in this particular study appeared more powerful because it produced a ripple effect for the survivor's entire family.

Given the majority of CSA studies are based on female experiences of disclosure, little is known about male experiences of disclosure (Sivagurunathan et al. 2019). Even when male participants are included with females in CSA study samples, their numbers are often so small that their experiences are overlooked compared with those of female survivors (Hohendorff et al. 2017). Although the literature in this area is growing and service provision is increasingly catering to the needs of male CSA survivors, significant progress still needs to be made in attempting to understand the complexities of male CSA.

Male Child Sexual Abuse and Masculinities Theory

Male CSA survivors face the same social pressures to live up to the ideals of masculinity as other men do (Kia-Keating et al. 2005). However, they must also deal with cultural definitions of 'manhood' and the conflicting experience of sexual victimisation, which involves violation within an interpersonal context (Kia-Keating et al. 2010). This chapter thus draws on masculinities theory to analyse the experiences of British South Asian men who were sexually abused in childhood and to explore how such abusive experiences infringe on a male survivor's sense of masculinity.

Many men with histories of CSA struggle with issues of masculinity and face gender-role conflicts (Gagnier et al. 2017). For example, Spataro et al. (2001; Soni 2013; Robertson et al. 2016) report that male survivors feel it is 'unmasculine' to be labelled a victim, particularly in cases of sexual violence. These feelings are exacerbated when the abuser is male, as male survivors then contend with issues of shame, stigma and homophobia (Easton et al. 2014). Stereotypes of 'ideal' men—as aggressive, stoic and dominant—are conveyed by a hegemonic construct that is, in turn, underpinned by heterosexuality. Further, culturally sanctioned expectations that men must reject 'feminine' characteristics, be economic providers and have a preoccupation with sex (Kia-Keating et al. 2005) point towards an overarching system of heteropatriarchy that favours heterosexuality and cisgender males. Traditional conceptualisations of masculinity oppose feminine-associated behaviours, equating femininity with helplessness and passivity, while homophobia and dominance prove one's masculinity (Eisen and Yamashita 2019). Moreover, Kia-Keating et al. (2010) emphasise how gender-role socialisation encourages men to avoid emotions and vulnerabilities. Consequently, male CSA survivors are up against a direct contradiction of masculinity's core expectations: to be strong and invulnerable.

Depraetere et al. (2020) assert that the underrepresentation of male victims of sexual violence in academic research is rooted in prevailing gender roles and stereotypical rape scripts. Kia-Keating et al. (2010) too acknowledge a 'societal disinclination' to accept men in a role of sexual victimisation rather than sexual prowess. Eriksson (2009) discusses this positioning of men and women into two very distinct categories of perpetrator and victim in the context of a constructivist notion of 'ideal victims'. The 'ideal victim' is perceived as dependent, passive and helpless, conforming to cultural constructions of 'childlike' and 'feminine' behaviour; conversely, characteristics associated with perpetrators include agency, dominance, control and violence and align with constructions of 'adultlike' and 'masculine' behaviour. An adult male disclosing a history of CSA thus presents a direct contradiction of the 'ideal victim' construct, which can become an instant barrier to disclosure. Research has also found that male survivors of sexual violence are less likely to be recognised as 'legitimate' victims (Hlavka 2017), thus demonstrating the power of gendered social constructs. The perpetuation of these stereotypes has fuelled perceptions of how men and women should behave, indoctrinating these ideas internally through the external force of societal expectation.

The concept of masculinity within minoritised communities is underexplored, particularly in the UK (Jaspal 2019). However, slowly emerging studies in the US have examined masculinities in relation to Southeast Asian American (such as Chinese and Korean), African American and Hispanic men (Kyler-Yano and Mankowski 2020; Walters and Valenzuela 2020). Purkayastha (2000) is a notable example: this study explored how masculinities are embodied within South Asian American communities. Purkayastha found that the parental expectations of Asian youths—that these youths should be respectful, reserved and accommodating—contrasted with the parental expectations of their White peers. The aforementioned traits were considered effeminate by those outside these South Asian American communities, as American norms of youth masculinity prioritise competitiveness, physical prowess and aggression over politeness and compassion. Young Asian men may then seek respect through behaviours that conform to these masculine norms, yet find that these lead to their further exclusion from mainstream society (Balzani 2010). This is an example of 'protest masculinity' (Connell and Messerschmidt 2005), which usually affects men who are marginalised and disempowered in particular societies. Archer's (2001) work with young British South Asian Muslim men found elements of protest masculinity in their behaviour and identified how the men used this specific model of hegemonic masculinity ('powerful patriarchal') to assert their position among White and African-Caribbean men and Muslim women.

Kia-Keating et al. (2005) argue that racial and cultural expectations serve to perpetuate masculine norms, resulting in hypermasculinity. Hypermasculinity is the exaggeration of male stereotypical behaviour, with those classed as hypermasculine embracing physical and behavioural traits such as aggression or developing a more muscular physique (Balani 2019; Szto 2020). Kalra (2009) highlights how racialised minorities, such as British South Asians, are often conceived as problematic in the context of the broader sociocultural discourse, which then shapes how South Asian masculinities are conceptualised and presented in mainstream media and in political and academic discourse. For example, Kalra (2009) points to the media coverage of young Asian men rioting in Northern England in 2001, which resulted in a narrative that presented these men as hypermasculine. British South Asian men have very often been viewed as embodying an 'assertive and deviant masculinity', which again feeds into the hypermasculinised perception of this group (Kalra 2009: 115). More recently, Gill and Day (2020) explored negative media representations of British South Asian men following the Rochdale sexual exploitation case (and similar cases that followed). They argue that negative media portrayals of the alleged perpetrators in these cases reinforced culturally specific misconceptions of British South Asian masculinity. Hesse (2000) contends that there are two dominant discourses around the masculinities of young Muslim men: one emphasises patriarchy and aggression and the other effeminacy and academicism. Hesse (2000: 337) calls for an empirical effort to 'disrupt these dichotomised stereotypes by exploring the complex, multiple and multi-faceted nature of youthful Muslim masculinities'.

The discourses and stereotypes that currently prevail leave little space for alternative representations of Asian masculinity outside of the dominant framework of deviance (Gill 2020). They also leave little space for male CSA survivors: Javaid (2017) contends that male victims of sexual violence are relegated in the gender hierarchy, as they are perceived to embody subordinate masculinities and are thus marginalised as a result. This goes some way to explaining low disclosure rates among male victims of sexual violence, as this form of abuse largely challenges and inverts overall norms of hegemonic masculinity and sexuality (Javaid 2017).

Some researchers have attributed the paucity of research into male CSA survivors to a social belief that men are the perpetrators of abuse and not the victims (Yancey and Hansen 2010). According to Stanko and Hobdell (1993), criminology fails to acknowledge male experiences of victimisation, and this lacuna, in turn, is ascribed to men's reluctance to speak out and expose their own 'vulnerability'. In patriarchal societies, men may feel further pressure to conceal or suppress feelings associated with victimisation because they fear denigration and social stigmatisation, particularly in cases of rape and sexual violence (Begum 2018; Elkins et al. 2017). This returns us to masculinities theory, which suggests that normative heterosexuality underpins society's expectations of male behaviour and that behaviours that do not adhere to heterosexual ideals are to be rejected (Balani 2019; Kukreja 2021; Walklate 2007).

Methodology

The overall aim of this research was to examine how male British South Asian CSA survivors make sense of their experiences. This aim was split into several discrete sub-aims:

- to understand the complexities around the disclosure process;
- to explore how men's sense of masculinity is impacted by abuse;
- to explore the significance of culture and community in relation to CSA disclosure;

- to explore men's experiences of help-seeking and the implications of this for service provision.

All participants were adults, and the decision to interview adult rather than child survivors was made for two reasons. First, there are significant ethical issues to consider when working with children in trauma research (Crane and Broome 2017). Randall et al. (2016) point out that disclosure of abuse from children needs to be met with caution, and researchers have a duty to report a revelation of ongoing abuse to authorities. Second, the age at which survivors tend to disclose abuse and the symptoms that arise in adulthood as a consequence of that abuse justified the adults-only sample. Many studies concur that the majority of survivors confide in people about abuse during adulthood (Tener and Murphy 2015). McTavish et al. (2019) highlight post-traumatic stress disorder and other psychological problems that can manifest in adult survivors as a direct result of CSA, including suicidal tendencies, depression, anxiety, and drug and alcohol abuse. Purposive sampling was adopted to recruit participants.

Demographics of the Sample

Eight South Asian male survivors volunteered to take part in the study. The youngest was 20 years old and the oldest was 41. The details of the participants are presented in Table 3.1.

Table 3.1 Participants

Pseudonym of survivor	Age	Ethnic background
Nathan	20	South Indian (Tamil)
Gurdeep	26	Indian Punjabi
Mahmud	34	Pakistani
Ayaan	24	Bengali
Dev	41	Indian Gujarati
Suleman	29	Bengali
Sanjay	31	Indian
Aman	33	Indian Punjabi

The Interview Process

Research with sexual abuse survivors has increased over the past 30 years, resulting in a distinct, parallel body of literature on how participating in research affects survivors (Kirkner et al. 2019). Though much of this literature indicates that survivors generally report little to no distress after participating in research (Jaffe et al. 2015; Legerski and Bunnell 2010), there is evidence that survivors with histories of CSA have reported negative reactions to participation (Edwards et al. 2013; Massey and Widom 2013). One way of mitigating participants' distress is to ensure the research actively seeks to empower them, in line with the principles of emancipatory research (Noel 2016; Biggeri and Ciani 2019). This was incorporated during the research design phase of this study: Butler (2002) code of ethics, which endorses emancipatory research with disempowered communities and individuals, was heavily drawn upon.

Emancipatory research also stipulates that researchers should enter interviews with the overall aim of the study in mind and should possess self-awareness and reflexivity, traits that will encourage them to constantly question their motivations, values and actions and ensure that these promote participant well-being (Dodgson 2019). Smith et al. (2009) advise researchers to monitor the effect of the interview on the participant and to look for verbal and non-verbal cues that indicate how participants feel. These cues should guide researchers throughout the interview and determine what direction they can take with the questions. In this study, most of the interviews had a similar trajectory: each individual interview situation was met with an individualised response, and the survivor's welfare was the primary concern. None of the participants wished to end their interview and demonstrated great courage when narrating their experiences. A debrief was carried out between the interviewer and participant after the interviews had taken place and participants were offered a chance to see their transcripts and make any changes.

The next section introduces the eight survivors and their individual life stories. It includes a timeline that documents significant events and stages in each survivor's life.

Nathan[1]

Nathan was 20 years old at the time of the interview. He had a South Indian Hindu background and was born and raised in England. He came from a single-parent family, as his parents divorced when he was six years old. He lived alone with his dog and was a university student at the time of the interview. Over a two-year period, beginning when Nathan was eight years old, his abuser, a male family friend, abused him during family gatherings and occasionally during religious events where community members would come together. As Nathan came to associate the abuse with his religion, he could no longer bring himself to practise it. He therefore classified himself as an atheist.

In the aftermath of the abuse, at around 17 years old, Nathan began exhibiting symptoms of post-traumatic stress disorder. He tried to push the abuse flashbacks he was experiencing to the back of his mind, but in his first year of university, Nathan felt that he could no longer cope. He confided the abuse to his personal tutor, who then referred to him to the university counselling service. The counsellor helped Nathan work through his trauma and discussed the possibility of reporting the abuse to the police. Nathan then confided in his university flatmates, who attended the police station with him when he reported the abuse and provided details of the abuser, who was still in contact with Nathan's family.

The police began their investigation and arrested the abuser; following the arrest, a female member of Nathan's extended family confessed that she had also been subjected to sexual abuse by the same man. The fact that there were now two survivors was of significant help in bringing charges against the abuser, who then stood trial for CSA. He received a sentence of 11 years, which Nathan was not fully satisfied with. However, Nathan said he was grateful that the abuser had been imprisoned for his crimes, as he acknowledged that many survivors did not see any justice with their own cases of abuse.

Nathan disclosed the abuse to his mother after he had confided in his tutor, counsellor and university flatmates. He revealed that his mother did not have the reaction he anticipated; despite being upset by the disclosure, she did not want the abuse dealt with by the police as she feared that the issue would become public in the community. Nathan was upset, angry and disappointed by this response, as he believed that public knowledge of the abuse should not be a deterrent to justice. He went to the police without his mother's approval and, after the trial, cut ties with his mother and his community. He still had contact with his siblings. His support network comprised the university friends he lived with before acquiring his own flat, and he described his dog as a huge comfort and a loyal companion both during and after the trial. Nathan was receiving counselling at the time of the interview and felt that it was having a positive impact on his healing.

Gurdeep

Gurdeep was 26 years old at the time of the interview. He was a British-born Indian with roots in the Punjab, India; he classified himself as Sikh. Gurdeep lived with his family: his parents, grandmother and two siblings. He had a business degree and was working in a sales-based role at the time of the interview. When he was nine, he was abused by an older male relative. The abuse carried on for five years, until the abuser moved abroad, at which point Gurdeep described feeling helpless. Gurdeep tried to carry on with his life but had frequent panic attacks, nightmares and debilitating anxiety that started to affect his schoolwork. He said he felt disappointed that nobody noticed his poor high school grades compared with his good performance at primary school and that nobody questioned why he seemed unhappy.

Gurdeep attended a different school to complete his A Levels. He felt this move was a new start, as no bad memories were attached to this environment; he also made a new group of male and female friends, which boosted his confidence. He performed well, completing his A Levels and gaining a place at his chosen university, which was in a different city to his family home. Gurdeep moved into student accommodation, where he thrived, although he still suffered nightmares and panic attacks. He eventually went to see a GP close to campus. This GP was from a White English background, and Gurdeep stated that he felt comfortable in her presence and confident that she would not know Gurdeep's family or community. Gurdeep confided the abuse to his GP, who referred him to a local counselling service. Gurdeep then saw a counsellor for 12 weeks. He had mixed feelings about this—on the one hand, it helped him accept what had happened to him; on the other, it brought up difficult emotions and increased his nightmares and panic attacks.

Around three months after these initial counselling sessions, Gurdeep found another counselling service a few miles from his university. He felt that this second round of counselling continued helping him in his recovery, as he felt that the previous counsellor he spoke to had helped him start to accept what had happened to him. At this point, Gurdeep had not confided in anyone other than his GP and counsellors. He tried to keep his university and family life separate from his private life, feeling that this compartmentalisation would give him a sense of control over everything. After his second round of counselling, Gurdeep's nightmares and panic attacks were less frequent; he began enjoying the social side of university and also kept busy with his studies. He then graduated with honours and moved back to his family home. After starting employment, Gurdeep occasionally used counselling helplines when he needed support; eventually, he began to receive regular in-person counselling again and was doing so at the time of the interview.

Gurdeep felt more comfortable disclosing the abuse to counsellors and his GP than to his family. He cited the main reason for not wishing to disclose to his family as a fear of being disbelieved and because, as the only son in his household, he would be perceived as a failure. Gurdeep felt he had familial expectations to fulfil and did not want to compromise the respect and high esteem in which he was held by his relatives.

Mahmud

Mahmud was 34 years old at the time of the interview. He was a Pakistani-born male who settled in England at the age of 16. He identified as a practising Muslim and was part of a 'joint' family arrangement, living with his parents, his wife and his two children. Mahmud was 12 years old when he started being abused by a male family member.

Mahmud was living in Pakistan at the time. The abuse occurred sporadically, as the abuser was not a frequent visitor to Mahmud's family home, and took place over a period of roughly two years. Mahmud referred to the abuser as an 'opportunist', as he would carry out the abuse on random visits. At the age of 16, Mahmud, his parents and his siblings moved to England. Mahmud described blocking out the abuse for many years and continuing his college education in England while holding down part-time jobs. Mahmud lived in a densely populated city with his family and was surrounded by a large Muslim community. He met his future wife at university and married her after graduating. He acquired a graduate job in finance and had two children. Living in a joint family made him feel secure, particularly as he had a close bond with his parents.

Mahmud did not disclose the abuse to anybody in his family but instead confided in an imam at his local mosque that he frequented for his daily prayers. The imam encouraged Mahmud to seek help through a counsellor. Mahmud was initially reluctant, so a few years passed before he sought help from a counselling service. During his initial counselling sessions, Mahmud stated that he felt very uncomfortable, as the prospect of telling a stranger what had happened to him was particularly difficult. Mahmud said that he would have preferred an Asian counsellor who may have related to him better, but he was eventually assigned a White female counsellor with whom he developed a good relationship. He felt the abuse was not something he could discuss with his wife and family, as he did not want to burden anybody with an issue he felt was his to deal with. He also stressed that his elderly parents were not in a good enough state of health to be able to handle such a disclosure.

For Mahmud, religion was a major source of help and acted as a calming influence. He also stated that various aspects of his faith helped him come to terms with the abuse, particularly the idea that everything in an individual's life is predestined and the will of God. His faith combined with counselling was an important part of Mahmud's healing process.

Ayaan

Ayaan was 24 years old at the time of the interview. He was a British-born Bangladeshi male who identified as a Muslim, although he stressed that his religious beliefs were moderate. He lived with his girlfriend. For around seven years, starting when he was nine, Ayaan was abused by an uncle in his extended family. The abuse was frequent until Ayaan reached adolescence; as he got older, Ayaan began feeling suicidal and increasingly depressed. When he could no longer cope, he confronted the abuser and threatened to expose him to the rest of the family, but the abuser denied all knowledge of the abuse. Consequently, Ayaan moved out of the family home and worked as a waiter, living above the premises with other staff. After a few years, Ayaan completed a vocational course at college and started working as an apprentice electrician. During his time at college, Ayaan met his non-Muslim girlfriend and stated that he felt, for the first time in his life, happy and content and that he had a sense of control over his life.

Ayaan and his girlfriend began renting their own flat; at this point, Ayaan confided in his girlfriend about the abuse. Her reaction was understanding, and Ayaan said he felt she was the only person he could trust. His girlfriend recommended that he seek counselling, found two local counselling organisations and attended the first session with Ayaan. He enjoyed his first session and continued the counselling for the maximum period the organisation allowed due to waiting-list demands. Ayaan liked the talking element of therapy and felt as though he could discuss all aspects of his life and relationships with his counsellor, not just the abuse, as he did not want the abuse to be a central aspect of his existence.

Ayaan remained in contact with his parents and siblings. He did not feel as though he could tell them about the abuse due to the abuser's relationship to his family and the shame and heartache the disclosure would bring them. The abuser was still in regular contact with Ayaan's family and occasionally visited their home with his wife and children, although Ayaan maintained that he was a much more frequent visitor when Ayaan was younger. Ayaan felt as though he could not face bumping into his abuser, as it would bring up bad memories and send him back into depression. His relationship with the abuser had ended the day Ayaan confronted him, and Ayaan felt as though the abuser had not taken the threat of exposure seriously. The abuser had a lingering impact on Ayaan's life, and Ayaan did not want to risk letting him back in. Ayaan also kept his relationship with his girlfriend hidden from his family, as his parents would not have approved on cultural and religious grounds—it was not deemed correct to live together out of wedlock, nor was it acceptable to be with a non-Muslim partner.

Dev

Dev was 41 years old at the time of the interview. He was a British-born male of Indian heritage who was raised Hindu but, as he had not practised Hinduism since his teens, classified himself as a non-religious Hindu. Dev identified as gay and lived with his partner. Dev's abuse began when he was 14 years old. It was carried out by a young male in Dev's extended family who was not a blood relative. It carried on for around one year and occurred in Dev's family home, usually during family gatherings. Dev described how he did not fight off the abuser as, at the time of the abuse, he was unaware that what was happening was wrong. Dev said that he felt a lot of self-blame for not fighting off the abuser and could not make peace with this. The abuser stopped visiting Dev's family home around the time the abuse stopped, although Dev was unaware of why these visits ceased. He found out many years later that a feud had occurred between the two families and ended their relationship.

Dev described how, in the aftermath of the abuse, he blocked out what had happened and continued to excel in school. He described himself as an overachiever and an avid reader, using fiction as a way of escaping reality. Dev attended university, where again he excelled. At around this time, Dev began to question his sexuality, which he had been unable to explore while living in his family home. He began frequenting gay bars and embarked on his first long-term relationship, which ended when Dev graduated from university and moved to a different city to begin his graduate job. This had been Dev's first serious relationship and marked a significant point in his life, as it was when he came to identify his sexuality. Dev did not tell his family that he was gay, as he did not wish to complicate matters with them—particularly not with his parents, who had very traditional views of marriage and relationships. As Dev entered adulthood, his family placed huge pressure on him to marry somebody from the same ethnic, religious and caste background. As a result of this pressure, and because of his secular and more Western perspectives, Dev lived independently and tried to maintain a distance from his family, keeping contact via phone and visiting only when a family wedding took place.

Dev met his current partner through a work event and described him as his soulmate. His partner is White, and Dev found that their personalities and views were much more compatible than they would have been with an Indian partner. Dev kept this relationship hidden from his family and stated that he felt as though he lived a double life at times. He recalled one occasion when he decided to talk about his past to his partner and, upon doing so, began to cry. Dev believed that he had somehow retrieved 'lost' memories that he had blocked out and, after disclosing the abuse to his partner, sought counselling. Because of Dev's financial position, he was able to begin private counselling sessions and continued these weekly for around three months, until a disagreement with his counsellor made him question their motives—when Dev had to cancel a session because of a work emergency, the counsellor attempted to charge him the hourly rate for this missed session, which Dev disputed. Dev subsequently took a break from counselling until he found that free counselling sessions were available for male abuse survivors. Dev took up these sessions and felt that he benefitted from them, developing a trusting relationship with his female counsellor.

Suleman

Suleman was 29 years old at the time of the interview. He was a British-born Bangladeshi male who identified as a Muslim and lived with his wife and daughter. Suleman was abused for three years from the age of seven. His abuser was an imam who was around the same age as Suleman's father. The imam would abuse Suleman in his private office at the back of the mosque. He would take other boys into the office

3 Understanding the Experiences of British South Asian ...

at different times, and Suleman suspected they were being taken there for the same reasons he was. Suleman reported going numb during the abuse and having an 'out-of-body' feeling. He described this as his coping mechanism. When Suleman was around 10 years old, a complaint was lodged against the imam, the details of which were not told to the children at the mosque. The imam did not return after that, and rumours established that a young girl had reported the imam to the police for inappropriately touching her.

When Suleman was around 12 years old, he told his mother what the imam had done to him; her response was to tell Suleman to keep quiet and not disclose what had happened to anyone else. Suleman was told that saying such things was 'shameful', and this notion of shame stayed with him until he was around 18, when he began to resent his mother for her response (Harrison and Gill 2018; Romo 2013; Sivagurunathan et al. 2019). Suleman questioned why she had told him to hide what had happened to him and, as a result, blamed himself for his abuse for many years. Shortly after Suleman turned 18, his father suddenly passed away from a heart attack, which deeply affected Suleman. He spiralled into a depression and began smoking marijuana, a habit that eventually progressed into a heroin addiction. Suleman was working in an Asian grocery store at the time and used his wages to fund his growing drug habit. At his lowest point, Suleman stole his mother's gold jewellery and sold it to a pawnbroker; Suleman's mother was devastated when she found out what Suleman had done, as the jewellery held sentimental value. Suleman's older brother cast him out from the family, and Suleman temporarily moved in with his mother's sister.

Suleman's drug habit continued for around five years, with his family intervening at many points to offer rehabilitation and help. He continually broke their trust by stealing from them, and his brother and mother eventually took him to Bangladesh. He was told he would be entering an arranged marriage to 'fix' his behaviour and give him a sense of responsibility. For the six weeks he was in Bangladesh, Suleman was drug-free, and he stated that the withdrawal symptoms severely affected him. After spending time with his new bride, he booked an early ticket home and obtained a drug supply within hours of landing. He overdosed and was taken to hospital; his family arrived and Suleman then agreed to attend rehabilitation.

After about two years, Suleman was clean of drugs and had confided in his support counsellor about the sexual abuse. The support worker referred him to a specialist counselling service that dealt with sexual assault and Suleman was assigned a female counsellor. At around this time, Suleman's wife gained a visa to enter the UK. He continued his counselling sessions but did not inform his wife—he felt that since she had a different country of birth, she would not grasp what abuse was. Further, his confidence had been knocked by his mother's response to his disclosure, and he could not face disclosing to another family member.

Sanjay

Sanjay was 31 years old at the time of the interview. He was a British-born Indian male who identified as Hindu and lived with his mother. He was abused by his father and later discovered that his father also abused his older sister. Sanjay was unaware of how old he was when his abuse began, but his earliest memory of it was when he was around four years old. Sanjay's mother was subjected to physical abuse by his father, who would consume alcohol and violently beat her in the presence of Sanjay and his sister. After a particularly bad beating, Sanjay's sister called an ambulance and their mother was taken to hospital, where she stayed for a few days. During this time, social services began investigating Sanjay's family situation; Sanjay and his sister did not reveal that they had been sexually abused, but did report that their mother was frequently beaten by their father. Their father was arrested but subsequently released, as Sanjay's mother did not wish to press charges. They then separated and their father remarried and moved out.

During Sanjay's teenage years, his sister moved out to attend university; Sanjay attended high school and worked part-time at a fast-food chain to help his mother financially. Sanjay had a close bond with his mother and, when he was around 15 years old, confided in her about the abuse. When he told her, she had a nervous breakdown and went into a depression, racked with guilt that she had not been aware of the abuse. When Sanjay's sister came to visit, his mother did not reveal that Sanjay had disclosed the abuse to her, and Sanjay also refrained from telling his sister. However, Sanjay stated that he knew in the back of his mind that she had also been abused because he noted similar traits in their behaviour.

When Sanjay was around 16 years old, he heard through family friends that his father had passed away as a result of his alcoholism. Sanjay recalled feeling nothing when he heard this news—no sadness and no relief. Sanjay's sister had a similarly blank response. When his mother was not present, Sanjay asked his sister whether she had been abused by their father; she admitted that he had abused her frequently from a very young age and that part of the reason she moved away from home for university was to get away from the reminders. She had no idea that Sanjay had also been abused and asked him whether he had told their mother. Sanjay told her that he had and, upon hearing about their mother's reaction, Sanjay's sister decided against telling her, as she did not want to cause her further distress.

Sanjay said he felt as though his life from the age of four had been one big blur and that he had drifted through it with no feelings of happiness. He described feeling as though he was on 'autopilot' until the age of 24, when he met his current girlfriend. She gave him a sense of purpose and was the first person outside of his mother and sister whom he trusted, so he disclosed the abuse to her. She was a trainee nurse at the time and advised him to seek help through a counselling service. Sanjay followed this advice and received counselling for the maximum period of one year the organisation allowed due to waiting-list demands—however, because of the severity of his case, his counsellor continued seeing him for another six months.

Aman

Aman was 33 years old at the time of the interview. He was a British-born Indian male whose family came from the Punjab region of India. He identified as Sikh and lived with his parents, wife and daughter. Aman grew up in a predominantly Asian neighbourhood where 'everybody knew everybody'. He recalled being abused at the age of 11 by a man from the local community. The abuse was a one-time incident and had a long-lasting impact on Aman. The abuser, who was also Sikh Punjabi and lived with his wife and children, was known in the neighbourhood to approach young boys and offer them money to enter his house. Aman was out playing with friends on his street where the abuser lived and wandered away from his friends to walk home. The abuser approached him and offered him £5 to go into his house; as a child, Aman was impressionable and tempted by the offer of £5, which seemed like a lot of money. He entered the house and was taken into the bathroom and abused. The abuser's wife and children were not home at the time of the incident, and after the abuse had taken place, Aman was given the £5 and led out of the house. He walked home and did not tell anybody what had happened until many years later.

Aman completed high school and began working for his father's business alongside his parents and older brother. As he did not perform well academically, the family business was Aman's only career option, but he felt miserable at the prospect of working there permanently. After a few years, Aman started work in a call centre instead and enjoyed being outside the family business, but returned to it after the call centre made him redundant. In his twenties, Aman was given more control over family business decisions. As the business grew, Aman's family bought and moved into a larger home. At around the same time, Aman was approached by his family with a marriage offer for a girl recommended by family friends. Aman met her and agreed to the arranged marriage, as he felt the two of them had clicked. Aman and his wife continued to live in his parents' home, as it was tradition to do so in his family. After a few years, he and his wife had their first baby, and it was around this time that Aman began to have flashbacks of the attack. He had sleeping difficulties and felt as though he could not hide the reason from his wife, whom he trusted deeply. Aman told her about his abuse and she encouraged him to seek professional help. Initially, he did not feel comfortable doing so for numerous reasons, including a fear that his family members might have found out and want to know why. Aman described his family as a 'typical Punjabi family' with traditional views of masculinity and an adherence to many cultural imperatives, including izzat.

Disclosing Abuse

Perhaps one of the biggest challenges for any CSA survivor is trying to disclose their experience of abuse. There are two major categories of CSA disclosure: accidental disclosure and purposeful disclosure, with the former being more common among children and the latter more characteristic of adult survivors. Accidental disclosure occurs when the abuse is observed by someone else or when children exhibit behavioural or physical signs that indicate abuse (Crosson-Tower 2014). Any form of disclosure can be a progressive step towards the healing process, with many survivors reporting that positive changes occur when they take control of their lives, including acceptance from others and feeling a sense of liberation and freedom (Draucker et al. 2011).

'Why Should I Be Scared of Telling My Own Mum?'

For many survivors, the process of disclosing CSA is akin to a journey, a continuum or a process (Collings et al. 2005; Alaggia 2004). All the survivors in this study had disclosed abuse to a family member, peer, partner or health professional, with all but one retrospectively disclosing CSA in their adult years. The exception was Suleman—after experiencing abuse at the hands of an imam in his place of worship, Suleman disclosed to his mother around two years later, after a young girl was rumoured to have reported the imam to the police for a similar offence. For Suleman, trying to tell his mother at the age of 12 was an immense challenge:

> I remember thinking well this is my mum, you know, why should I be scared of telling my own mum? She gave birth to me and up to that point she always kind of treated me like the baby of the family … so yeah I thought I'll just tell her, maybe she'll help me, but no, no. She basically said to me that I have to hide it, don't tell your dad, don't tell your brothers, and at that age you just do what your parents tell you … I was hurt, really hurt. She said we won't tell anyone … and I didn't for a long time. (Suleman)

Suleman's experience of disclosure was tinged with anger, sadness and disappointment. He began his account by describing the difficulty of disclosing and questioning why he feared telling his own mother, particularly since he was the 'baby' of the family, and his expectation was that she would react in a maternal and caring manner. Her blunt response effectively shut down the magnitude of the disclosure and her instinct was to silence him rather than protect and nurture him. Suleman was also silenced by his abuser—in effect, he was wronged in two situations that should each have warranted very different reactions. He was asked not to tell his father or brothers, which reinforced the need to continue keeping the abuse a secret. This first, and arguably most significant, experience of disclosure had an impact on Suleman's decision to not disclose again years later.

According to Allnock and Miller (2013), the average amount of time it takes a survivor to disclose abuse is seven years; the younger the child is when the abuse starts, the longer it takes for them to disclose. Suleman did not fit this profile, deciding to tell his mother in trust and confidence, but he was rebuffed with an unexpected response:

'itha sharam, itha manshoreh koin nah' [it's shameful and we don't tell people that]. (Suleman)

Suleman quoted what his mother told him in Bengali when he disclosed to her. Her justification for keeping the abuse a secret between herself and Suleman was that it would be shameful if other people were to learn of it. This response was steeped in cultural notions of shame being brought upon the family and a desire for Suleman not to tell other people in order to avoid such shame. Gilligan (2005; Kukreja 2021; Jaspal 2019) work with Asian communities across Bradford found that cultural factors had the power to impede individuals' and families' willingness to disclose CSA. These findings are congruent with Suleman's mother's response, which signifies how cultural norms can hamper an individual's ability to sufficiently respond to and deal with sexual abuse disclosure. For Suleman, his mother's response had a debilitating effect later in life in the form of his drug addiction, which he stressed with expletives ('fucked me up later, fucked me up for years'). This statement expressed his anger and frustration at his mother's attitude that the abuse was 'shameful', which placed this shame on Suleman and ultimately made him feel responsible for what had happened to him. Suleman emphasised that this was not an excuse for his drug problems, but an explanation as to why he began using drugs and why his mother's reaction to the disclosure 'fucked [him] up for years' and 'made [him] do all that shit [he] did later'. As a further consequence of his first disclosure experience, Suleman also developed trust issues and did not discuss the abuse again for a long while. In their study of maternal responses to CSA disclosure, McCarthy et al. (2019) found that when disclosure responses conveyed a sense of protection and support, this resulted in improved mental health and social functioning for survivors. They argue that the responses survivors receive from caregivers—and, indeed, from professionals—have the power to either aid their recovery or retraumatise them.

Sanjay's experience of trying to tell his mother about his abuse contrasted with Suleman's. Sanjay was sexually abused by his biological father and was around 14 years old at the time of his disclosure. He lived alone with his mother and felt safe enough to confide in her:

> Telling Mum wasn't easy; I had to keep thinking about what effect it would have on her and whether I was being selfish. I thought I was being selfish by wanting to tell her but I had nothing left. I lost my self-respect early on in my life … I couldn't deal with it anymore and I thought maybe if I tell her, it will get easier for me. So one day I was sitting with her, I think we were watching something … I was waiting, thinking, how do I bring it up? How do I say it? So I thought, just say it … I just said to her, Mum I gotta tell you something, she's like, what, and she didn't know what was coming and I said it's about Kirpal, and she's like, yeah go on, and I just said it … I said he raped me. (Sanjay)

Sanjay's disclosure was blunt and, although rapid in its delivery, extremely powerful. 'He raped me' is abrupt, direct and emotionally charged, suggesting that the abuse was like a pressure cooker inside Sanjay—he was no longer able to keep it a secret. He recalled feeling selfish about his desire to tell his mother, wanting to put her feelings before his own due to the hardships she had also endured at the hands of his father. However, Sanjay expressed having 'nothing left' and being emotionally and physically drained, with no enjoyment in his life and nothing left to lose. He chose a random and mundane moment to reveal the abuse—in the middle of watching television—which demonstrates the urgency he felt to get it off his chest; it was a now-or-never situation. Like Suleman, Sanjay disclosed to his mother because he felt he was able to confide in her—being in a situation where he felt that he and his mother only had each other enabled him to tell her directly what his father had done to him. Sanjay was much more fortunate than Suleman in that his mother's reaction was not to place blame on him or attempt to silence him:

> She was shocked more than anything, I remember her reaction; when I think about it, it makes me wanna cry, she let out this scream, it was such a painful scream like someone had stabbed her in the heart or something, I can't forget that sound and I can't forgive myself for making her hurt like that but ... at the time it really got to her, she got so affected by it, and ... she never blamed me, she never said to me 'you let it happen' or 'why did you tell me or anything', if she did that's what I was scared of, but if she did I would've killed myself, I really, really would've killed myself 'cause I felt like I had nothing at that point and all I wanted was her ... she still loved me and I have nothing but respect for her 'cause she went through all that beating and still she did everything and, see, that's why I didn't respect [my sister] 'cause she never put Mum first when she always put us first.

Sanjay's recollection of his mother's first reaction to his disclosure was one of intense pain and grief—he likened her 'painful scream' to the sound she would make if she were being stabbed in the heart. His choice of analogy indicates the physical and mental anguish his mother's scream caused him, and the impact of this scream was something he could not forget nor forgive himself for. Sanjay's strong sense of protectiveness towards his mother is evident in his account, which indicates a constant need to protect her and place his needs as a survivor aside to ensure that she was okay first. Sanjay was forthcoming about his belief that he would have committed suicide if his mother had blamed him in any way for the abuse and about the fact that the only thing he wanted at that point was his mother's support. His respect for his mother is apparent throughout his account ('I have nothing but respect for her'), and her approval and happiness seemed a core priority for him. This was one of the reasons he expressed unhappiness with his sister, whom he felt had abandoned the family when his mother needed her most. As Sanjay's mother was subjected to domestic violence from his father, it seemed that her reaction to his disclosure of abuse brought them closer together, as they were both survivors of different forms of abuse at the hands of the same person.

Parental reactions to CSA disclosure have been given inconsistent attention in the research. Nevertheless, the studies that have been conducted have yielded similar findings. For example, McElvaney and Nixon (2020) report that parents often grapple with feelings of guilt and struggle with negotiating their parental identity as 'protectors' following such disclosures. Bux et al (2016) emphasise the significant distress that many parents suffer as a result, as was evident in Sanjay's account. According to Allnock (2010), children are most likely to confide in their mother or their peers when disclosing sexual abuse; Wamser-Nanny (2017), Serin (2018), Sawrikar and Katz (2017) and Roberts (2020) corroborate these findings, stating that children are more likely to tell a friend or their mother, as they usually choose the person they think is going to believe them. However, choosing to tell such an individual does not necessarily mean that the survivor will receive a supportive response. This was the case with Nathan, who disclosed to his mother after initially confiding in his university tutor:

> My mum was the main person who raised us, so even though I didn't tell her first for my own reasons, after I told my tutor and other people I thought maybe I have to tell her 'cause at that point I made the decision to go to the police ... her reaction, it was, well, I don't know what I expected really, it's not that she didn't believe me. She got upset, very, very upset, and then said, well, what do you wanna do about it, and I told her, well look I've gone to my tutor and a counsellor and they advised me to go to the police and that's what I want to do ... she couldn't really accept it then and she went into this other mode about, that everyone's gonna find out and [Nathan's abuser] has a family etcetera. (Nathan)

Nathan's decision to disclose the abuse to his mother seemed more of a necessity than something he wanted to do; he had already told his university tutor and a counsellor and at that point had made the decision to go to the police. Disclosing to his mother was the next step, as he was sure it would be only a 'matter of time' until she found out. Nathan picked up on his mother's reluctance to accept what had happened—he stressed that although she believed him, she did not agree with his decision to report the abuse to the police. She was also inclined to consider the impact of the disclosure on the abuser's family and what the community might think if the abuse was to become public knowledge as a result of the police report. Because of her reaction to the disclosure, Nathan ended his relationship with his mother and cut ties with the rest of his family. Only three of this study's eight survivors disclosed their abuse to a close family member, which raises the question of why the other survivors could not confide in a family member about their abusive experiences.

Interestingly, despite Nathan's own construction of his identity as 'not very cultural' *and* non-religious, his mother's consciousness of people finding out about the abuse suggests that culture still played a part in his fractured relationship with her after the disclosure. Further, it demonstrates how, for both Nathan and Suleman, culture contributed to how their relationships with their mothers developed in the light of their abuse disclosure. Their experiences contrast with Sanjay's, whose supportive reaction from his mother brought the two closer together; notably, Sanjay did not mention culture or issues of this nature relating to the disclosure, either for himself or for his mother. On this basis, it can be argued that a cultural consciousness of 'community' finding out—or, in Suleman's case, the notion that the abuse itself and others knowing about it is culturally 'shameful'—reveals how South Asian men's experiences of disclosure are impacted by culture.

'Not Letting Everybody Down'

The majority of the survivors interviewed in this study opted to disclose to non-family members for various reasons. Mahmud, for example, confided his experience of CSA to an Imam; Dev, Ayaan and Aman confided in their partners; and Gurdeep confided in his GP. According to Hunter (2011), the person(s) to whom sexual abuse is disclosed is of great importance and should be included in the construction of theoretical models of disclosure, as the experiences of telling a friend, family member or the police are all very different. These differences were clear in the interviews, and when the analysis of the transcripts commenced, it became clear that certain factors prevented some men from disclosing to family members. One reason for this was the interviewees' feelings that they would be letting their families down in some way if they were to disclose the abuse. Traditional Asian family structures are unique in that first-generation immigrants carry a set of expectations regarding the position of men, women and children within a patriarchal hierarchy. This is characterised by male dominance and patrilineality, or the continuity of the family line through males (Sawrikar and Katz 2017; Pabla 2019). This places an expectation on children to live up to the obligations and ideals of their parents and the wider community (Berrington 2020; Pabla 2019).

> I'm in an Indian family and I hold a certain place, I'm a son, I'm an older brother, a first-born, Asian, so … we have that pressure on us all the time to be not perfect, but it's about pleasing everyone, you know, keeping everyone happy, so 'cause of all that I didn't wanna let them all down. My grandma lives with us and she's a big influence on me, she's like a second mum, but even then she's a hundred billion times more strict than my parents … she's got strong principles, so she's got this thing about her where everything's about what you're looking at, izzat, it's about that, it's just about protecting that and my dad, that's his mum, you have to imagine he's learned everything from her so he has that same thinking … so I can't just one day go up to them and let them all down when I know already I know what they'll say, I know what they think, for me they're everything, I love them and … it isn't their fault and they couldn't have stopped it. (Gurdeep)

Gurdeep listed the many facets of his identity that were obstacles to his disclosing the abuse to his family, including being the first-born Asian male—holding a 'certain place' in this way meant that he had an expectation to live up to that would be shattered if he was to disclose that he was an abuse survivor. He emphasised the importance of pleasing everybody around him because he 'didn't wanna let them all down'. He characterised his paternal grandmother as an important figure in his life and as traditional and strict in her views. Intergenerational dynamics were evident here, with Gurdeep's grandmother and father having shared views on protecting izzat. While Gurdeep himself was not overly supportive of this notion of honour, he exhibited a fear of letting everybody down and, in the process, compromising the family's honour. However, this fear seemed driven primarily by the family pressure that Gurdeep referred to. He demonstrated understanding towards his grandmother and father for their 'strong principles' and maintained that the abuse was not something his family were responsible for, nor could they have prevented it. Gurdeep lived with his family at the time of the interview and did not harbour any ill feeling towards them, instead seeming content that he had disclosed the abuse to his GP and counsellor:

> I had the opportunity to go to my doctor and she was the first person ever who I'd spoke to and she referred me to the counsellor and helped me a lot, I'm grateful to them.

Gurdeep's account of not letting down his family aligns with his view that telling them would be a 'headache', an unnecessary pain that he did not need in his life. He made the decision that he felt was best for himself and his family. Aman articulated a similar view:

> I didn't tell them and I wouldn't tell them and that's not something I think I'll regret because knowing my family the way I do and all of what I've learned growing up, it wouldn't make sense for me to go tell them, especially now at this age, and I don't wanna say it's nothing 'cause for me it was, but people go through worse, I can't say I'm the only person in the world it's happened to … but no I don't regret not telling them. For me, my wife was it for me, she's my rock and she's on a level with me; as soon as I told her she cried and yeah I expected that because she loves me, I'm her husband. (Aman)

Aman tried to downplay the scale of the abuse by stressing that other survivors had endured much worse than him, placing his experience on a comparative scale as a possible way of minimising its severity. He then praised his wife for her support when he disclosed, calling her his 'rock', which signifies how her positive response contributed to the strength of their relationship. Aman shared a number of reasons for his decision not to disclose to his parents; these tended to revolve around cultural factors and a need to not let his family or community down. For Aman and Dev, culture affected their decision not to disclose to their parents. Their belief that their parents' cultural values differed from their own influenced their decisions, with both holding a strong sense that they would be misunderstood. This response indicates a generational clash and difference in worldviews between both men and their parents.

Other survivors, such as Mahmud, expressed concern for their family and a desire to place the family's needs before their own. Mahmud's first disclosure was to an imam whom he had known for a number of years and clearly trusted:

> I just pushed myself in prayer and went to see my imam and it was eating away at me, praying and having patience, it just, as much as it helped, it didn't make me have that release I suppose that I needed ... the imam, he's a good friend of mine too, he's a family man and he's very, very knowledgeable, so it was just instinct for me to trust him really and ... we sat one day and I told him and he was very calm about it and he didn't judge me and that's all I needed ... and because he's not family I wasn't causing him that same pain my mum or dad might feel or even my wife. I couldn't imagine what they would react like especially because [when it] happened it was a good time for my dad ... we had money in Pakistan, my dad had businesses and he's got nothing but good memories from our time there, so for me just to come in and say what happened to me, I think it will destroy all that for everyone ... when we came here to England, we didn't come with a lot and my dad's health was bad and it's gotten worse with age so just all those things put together ... I don't see myself putting [the abuse] on anyone else. (Mahmud)

Mahmud, like many of the interviewed survivors, thought first of the impact the disclosure would have on his family. Juxtaposed against the trauma of his abuse were his cherished memories of life in Pakistan, a time of wealth and stability that his father held dear. Mahmud contrasted this time with the family's life in England, which was characterised by his father's poor health and unstable financial situation. For that reason, Mahmud wished to protect the memory of their former life in Pakistan.

Mahmud seemed motivated by a desire to protect his family from pain. Research has established that many CSA survivors are conscious of the effect their disclosure may have upon other members of the family (McElvaney et al. 2021). Parental reactions to disclosure can have a profound impact on how the survivor ultimately heals from the abuse, with negative reactions aggravating the trauma and positive responses minimising (although not always) the impact of the abuse (Chiaramello et al. 2018).

'They Wouldn't Believe Me'

There are many reasons why survivors choose not to disclose abuse or at least choose to delay disclosure, one of which is a deep-seated fear of being disbelieved (Morrison et al. 2018). Validation of the survivor's experiences is crucial, particularly during their initial disclosure (Stiller and Hellmann 2017). Many survivors who have been sexually assaulted struggle with the fear of being disbelieved or being held accountable for what happened to them and may actually be disbelieved upon disclosing the abuse to someone (Gill and Harrison 2019).

Many survivors feel a sense of uncertainty regarding how family members may react to a disclosure of abuse. Some of the survivors in this study expressed doubts about whether family members would believe their disclosure, and this fear of being disbelieved was a hindrance to them. As Lovett et al. (2018) note, this is a common issue for CSA survivors in general and acts as a huge barrier to disclosure (Harrison and Gill 2018; Roberts 2020). Ayaan was one such survivor who expressed this fear:

> The abuser was a relative so he still goes to see my family and stuff, I can't hack that, I don't wanna see his fucking face 'cause it just takes me back there, so I just stopped going. I talk my mum on the phone still … I don't wanna cut them off … but me telling them about this is different, it's not gonna go down well, they probably wouldn't believe me or they

wouldn't understand it ... he's a cousin of my mum's. They all think he's this nice guy and he's got a wife and kids and ... they wouldn't think someone like that could do that, so I don't see the point of telling them and putting myself through that. (Ayaan)

Ayaan had little faith that his family would believe his account over the abuser, a relative of his mother who was perceived as a 'nice guy' and had a family—for Ayaan, these facts meant that his account of events would not be seen as credible. While it may seem inconceivable that a parent would fail to believe their own child over an extended family member, Ayaan remained adamant that this was the case and that his family 'wouldn't understand' the disclosure. This belief was driven by the fact that the abuser was still in contact with Ayaan's family. Ayaan seemed to have an underlying desire to protect himself emotionally because he anticipated a negative reaction to disclosure, which was his broader reason for choosing not to disclose: 'I don't see the point of telling them and putting myself through that'.

Aman's account echoed Ayaan's in relation to this fear of being disbelieved:

I'm lucky, very lucky [my wife] believed me, it's not something that you talk about in our circles ... our community is very, very close and it's not that easy ... certain things are out of that area, you just can't talk about [them], like White people can say anything to their parents and it's fine but for us it's different. I don't think I could take [my parents] not believing me because for a woman ... we know it happens but for men how many of these cases do you hear about, what would my mum's response be ... she would think I'm mad. (Aman)

Aman attributed his mother's anticipated disbelief to her perhaps not being aware of what CSA is, and he cited the hidden nature of abuse as a contributing factor to this lack of knowledge. Aman felt he was lucky that his wife believed him and noted that sexual abuse was not a topic that could be readily discussed within his community because certain subjects were taboo, whereas he thought White people could discuss anything with their parents. According to Aman, there are cultural differences regarding what discussion is acceptable and what is not. He explained that whereas sexual abuse against women is known to occur, there is less knowledge regarding sexual abuse against men. This lack of knowledge and understanding may also contribute to a survivor being misunderstood or disbelieved, an outcome that Aman did not want to risk.

Of those who chose to disclose to family members, only Sanjay received a sympathetic response—his mother's own experiences of domestic violence at the hands of Sanjay's abuser, his father, possibly led her to believe in and support her son's disclosure. Conversely, Nathan's and Suleman's disclosures to their mothers garnered responses that were loaded with cultural pressures pertaining to shame and the possible loss of community reputation. Those who did not disclose to immediate family members did so for a variety of reasons, with factors that hampered their decisions to disclose to a relative, encompassing undercurrents of cultural shame, a fear of not being believed, a feeling that they were letting everybody down and a fear of causing distress. These survivors reported feeling content and satisfied with disclosing to other people they felt they could trust. Nonetheless, it is important to recognise that disclosure is not a vital step towards recovery from CSA and that these different responses to the issue of disclosure reflect the heterogeneity of survivor experiences (Pabla 2019; Roberts 2020).

Masculinity and Sexuality

A growing body of research points towards the significant impact sexual abuse has on males, and one such impact is the way it influences the development of their masculine identities (Kia-Keating et al. 2005; Pabla 2019). As notions of masculinity are stronger and more prevalent in patriarchal cultures such as those of South Asian communities (Alexander 2004), this research seeks to explore the accumulative effect of this construct on South Asian male CSA survivors. Sexuality is also included in this discussion of masculinity, as there were considerable overlaps in the study findings: masculinity was intertwined with how the survivors' sexuality was perceived by others and their fears of how their sexuality would be construed in the aftermath of abuse. The two subthemes identified and presented below were 'not being manly enough' and 'questioning sexuality after CSA'.

'Not Being Manly Enough'

Research has indicated that many men view sexual abuse as an attack on their masculinity and believe that identifying as a victim of sexual abuse will contribute to the loss of their masculine identity (Corbett 2016; Jaspal 2019; Pabla 2019; Sharma 2020). The men interviewed in this research discussed how they made sense of their own masculinity as CSA survivors:

> I identify as a gay man and for me I'm very secure in my own masculinity; there isn't a lot that could have changed that for me, but thinking back now at the time, yes, it did [confuse me]. I was 14, I was in that growing stage where you're confused and you're still finding yourself, it's hard to figure out what your identity is or what you're sexuality is and I'd never had any other kind of sexual experience prior to that so … it confused me about what kind of person I am. (Dev)

Although Dev's initial response indicates that he was confident in his masculinity and secure in his identity as a gay man, he then stated that the abuse caused him to feel confused—as it occurred during adolescence, his sexual identity had not yet formed, and this negative sexual experience created a sense of uncertainty around the 'kind of person' he was. Aman's response carried a more subtle sense of how he interpreted his masculine identity and how he thought his wife may have perceived him:

> … though you never do in those situations. I thought, what if she thinks less of me, what if she loses respect for me. (Aman)

Aman referred to his first abuse disclosure, which was to his wife, and how he worried that she might have lost respect for him or thought less of him as a result. This example emphasises the fear male survivors possess around disclosing CSA and the gendered expectations to which men are under pressure to conform. Spiegel (2013) explains the process of gender-role socialisation and the ways in which boys are reared to be powerful, resolute and self-reliant. Thus, when a boy is sexually abused, a conflict occurs between two psychosocial processes: the realities of CSA and the mythology of masculinity (Roberts 2020). This conflict affects the ability of many adult survivors to come to terms with and disclose the abuse and to renegotiate their identity in relation to their traumatic experiences. For Sanjay, being abused by his father from a young age made him question his identity as a man and as a son:

> I think I didn't know what was going on; so, for a long time, up till about 11 or 12, when I knew what was happening was wrong, I started getting this feeling of, I don't know [if] it was insecurity. I'd be around other boys at school and I never felt like myself, I can't really explain it. I never felt normal, I never felt like one of them, they used to say things they did with their dad … and I couldn't relate to it so I thought maybe he's [my dad] and I'm a bad son … my mum didn't know so I felt like I betrayed her as well … it was always this feeling I wasn't a normal guy … I still feel it now sometimes. Before I met my girlfriend it was hard for me to approach girls for that kind of thing, like a date or a number, I wouldn't ask, I didn't wanna get close in case they thought I was abnormal or something and [I was] constant[ly] just feeling insecure. (Sanjay)

Sanjay was subtle in his explanation of masculinity, but key pointers in his response indicate that he harboured significant insecurity around his identity as a son, as an adolescent among his peers and as a potential boyfriend. Sanjay referred to multiple dimensions of his masculine identity and the ways in which he felt he could not live up to the expectations of these roles. He was emphatic regarding how insecurity blighted him when he was growing up and referred several times to his sense that he was not 'normal'. He also explained the difficulties he experienced with approaching girls and fear that they would perceive him as 'abnormal'. Crowder (2013; Pabla 2019) argues that many male CSA survivors do not see their relationship difficulties or dysfunctional behaviours as related to the abuse they have experienced; instead, they tend to view themselves as flawed or accept their difficulties as inevitable personality traits. There is evidence of this explanation in Sanjay's response, as he questioned what kind of a son he was to his parents and whether he betrayed his mother by not informing her of the abuse earlier.

Questioning Sexuality After Child Sexual Abuse

Many survivors of male CSA often question their sexuality in the aftermath of abuse (Payne et al. 2014). However, Durham (2003) and Roberts (2020) acknowledge that adolescence is a significant period of change for many young men during which their identity development is evolving—therefore, sexual abuse survivors may attribute confusion around their sexuality to the experience of abuse as opposed to viewing it as a normal part of adolescence. However, what is undoubtable is that such questions and confusion arise for many survivors of abuse and usually intersect with discussions around masculinity, as is apparent in Dev's account:

> As a gay man I've always had people assuming I'm effeminate or camp and there's this added expectation that I'm not manly, which offends me, and that usually comes from other Asians I've encountered, men being the worst. Asian men can be very judgemental towards gay Asians and that just makes me think … they have an insecurity or denial. (Dev)

Dev described the hostility he had received from Asian men and how they had expressed certain attitudes towards his sexuality that questioned or undermined his masculinity, which Dev found offensive. Dev also stressed that Asian men can be judgemental of other Asians who are gay, suggesting that this attitude may indicate 'insecurity or denial' on their part. Homosexuality and same-sex relationships remain taboo within Britain's Asian communities, with religious and cultural pressures to conform to a heterosexual ideal still strong in many Muslim, Sikh and Hindu communities (Mitha et al. 2021). These views shape the way in which homosexuality is conceptualised and negatively perceived within these communities, which is perhaps what Dev had experienced. Alongside the abuse he suffered, Dev kept his sexuality a secret from his family and community:

> My family don't know I'm gay. I've learned to just shut off so when I do see my family on rare occasions I don't divulge personal details, you know, my love life or anything, that's my business ... if somebody isn't willing to accept that side of me, then I have no business in telling them my affairs. (Dev)

McKeown et al. (2010) examined experiences of discrimination and disclosure among Black and South Asian gay men in Britain. Almost all the men interviewed expressed the view that the experiences of gay and bisexual men from minoritised backgrounds were more problematic and challenging than those of White British gay men. Viewed through the lens of intersectionality theory, Dev's ethnic identity as a British Indian man overlapped with his sexuality as a gay man to place him at a disadvantage due to what he perceived as two conflicting identities. Moreover, taking masculinities theory into consideration, powerful heteronormative ideals that are often perpetuated within South Asian communities reinforce the culturally generated silence around homosexuality (Khubchandani 2019; McKeown et al. 2010; Jaspal 2019; Pabla 2019).

Homophobic attitudes in South Asian communities also prevent many survivors from coming forward about abuse, as evidenced by Gurdeep:

> There's always that fear there that maybe they won't understand what you're trying to say, if you turn around and say 'I was abused by a guy' they might say, well, what, you did gay stuff then? I don't think it would register in their head that it's not something you chose ... you had no control over it, but it does make me angry thinking that something that bad can be made into something else ... that's how it is in our community, they don't get it, goreh get it, Indians don't.

Gurdeep expressed anger that his experience of CSA could possibly be misconstrued as a voluntary act of homosexuality, adding that '*goreh*' (which refers to 'White people' in Punjabi/Urdu) would understand it, but his own community would not. This speaks strongly to a cultural ignorance on the part of Asians regarding the phenomenon of male CSA, with a lack of understanding leading to harmful assumptions that could hamper survivor recovery. While it is widely acknowledged that male CSA survivors often experience post-traumatic stress disorder and its associated symptoms, common reactions also include a fear of appearing 'unmasculine', societal, peer or self-questioning of their sexuality and a fear of homophobic reactions (Adams et al. 2018; Petersson and Plantin 2019). Masculinity and homophobia have considerable overlaps in the context of male CSA, as homophobic attitudes towards perceived 'homosexual' acts can call one's masculinity into question. This was a fear expressed by Ayaan:

> You don't want people saying you're gay or something, you'd be surprised how many people say that, I mean we say it as jokes between us like 'oi gay boy you're gay you're gay'.

Ayaan's response offers insight into the humour men use in order to demasculinise other men, which includes equating homosexuality with femininity to ridicule other men into feeling 'weak'. The term 'gay' has long been used as an insult by heterosexuals, usually towards other heterosexuals (Swan 2016). For Ayaan, fears of accusations that he was less masculine or that he was gay were a barrier to disclosing abuse. Roller et al. (2009) discuss how confusion over sexuality is a central issue for many male CSA survivors, who may question whether the abuse 'caused' them to be gay. There is no evidence to suggest that sexually abusive experiences determine one's sexuality, but plenty of research has acknowledged the ambiguity survivors feel about their own sexual identity and their sense of masculinity (O'Leary et al. 2017).

'Not Losing My Honour Within the Family'

Honour, or izzat, was considered a significant subtheme in this research on the basis of the interview findings. Bhanbhro (2021) asserts that izzat is reflected in the way a family (or individual members of that family) conducts itself. There are many interpretations of izzat across the literature and even more interpretations at the individual level (Pabla 2020). The participants in this research discussed what izzat meant to them in relation to their experiences and whether it had any impact on their lives.

> I wouldn't want it to get back to the wrong person and have anything said about my family, I mean I don't care what people say about me … but my family, I wouldn't ever want them spoken about in a bad way, so to protect them, especially my parents … [they're] old and they're vulnerable and they can't really protect themselves, so I see that as my job. (Mahmud)

When asked whether honour had played a part in Mahmud's not disclosing to his family, he acknowledged that it did. However, he was more concerned about protecting his family's izzat than his own. Gurdeep noted that his grandmother and parents placed great emphasis on the concept of honour:

> [My grandmother's] got this thing about her where everything's about what you're looking at, izzat … it's just about protecting that and my dad, that's his mum, you have to imagine he's learned everything from her so he has that same thinking.

While Gurdeep acknowledged that honour played a role in his life because of his parents and his grandmother, he was quick to point out that it was not the sole reason for his decision not to disclose to his family. Gurdeep's position on honour was part of a pattern among some of the other survivors who recognised the importance and existence of honour while also dismissing the standing it had in previous generations (Gill 2021; Pabla 2020). Both Aman and Gurdeep knew how significant honour was for their parents' generation and the integral part it played in their lives. For Aman, living and working with his parents after marriage exemplified this honour, which was all about family image and was experienced within the wider family context (Sodhi 2017). Ayaan offered a slightly different interpretation of honour based on his experiences:

> I've heard about it in Pakistani families like when their daughters run off with a guy or something, it's quite a big thing and they end up killing the girl or the boyfriend, so for them it's bigger than it is for us, I wouldn't say we get that affected by it. (Ayaan)

Ayaan was aware of what honour meant but was not affected by it and stated that the concept did not play a major role within Bengali families. He associated honour with the Pakistani community and used honour killings as an example. However, although izzat is a familiar concept in Pakistani culture (Balani 2019; Chambers 2020), it is not exclusive to this particular community. For Suleman, honour was one of the reasons his mother attempted to silence him after he disclosed his abuse to her. This example puts into perspective the magnitude of honour and how it can outweigh the well-being of one's child. It also demonstrates how individual interpretations of what honour entails differ from person to person, family to family and, indeed, community to community.

> Being told to stay quiet, I'd say that's about honour, that's about izzat and not bringing shame on myself or anyone else. (Suleman)

Social networks are extensive across South Asian communities (Chambers 2020; Giwa 2016; Phillips et al. 2007), and gossip is a powerful tool that can potentially jeopardise the izzat and standing of an individual and their family. A fear that your community will talk about you and subsequently compromise your family izzat is a 'mechanism of social control' that is felt in particular by young British Asians who feel that they are under surveillance from community elders (Gill and Walker 2020).

Notions of guilt and betrayal (of family secrets) can pervade in Asian family structures (Aziz 2017; Chambers 2020), with community and/or family honour being threatened by the admission of 'shameful' secrets. Cowburn et al (2015) list three contributing factors that explain why women from South Asian communities are hesitant about disclosing sexual abuse: a fear that they are somehow betraying the perpetrators of the acts (usually close members of the same family or community), a fear that they will not be believed and a sense that the assault was not violent enough to constitute rape (Gupta 2003; Gill 2008, 2020; Patel

2008). These factors go some way towards demonstrating the complex interplay between the crime of abuse, its impact on the community and the survivor's position in the aftermath of disclosure. Although these findings are from studies of Asian sexual abuse survivors, they are not exclusive to South Asian communities—literature demonstrates that a fear of disbelief and negative consequences in the aftermath of disclosure are common among survivors regardless of ethnicity (Manay and Collin-Vézina 2021). Confidentiality is of paramount importance to abuse survivors across all ethnic groups (Gill and Harrison 2019). However, within South Asian communities, the added layer of exposure to the wider community feeds into their distrust and doubts about whether their confidentiality will be maintained (O'Neill Gutierrez and Chawla 2017).

Research has indicated that in some families, survivors feel so guilty and rejected upon disclosure that their family ties are severed (Alaggia et al. 2019). Many survivors seek resolution and reparation through disclosure, wishing for acceptance, acknowledgement and confirmation in the hope that these will contribute to their healing (Easton and Parchment 2021). Izzidien (2008) reports that in the context of domestic abuse, many South Asian people found it difficult to come forward because they worried that if the community found out, their family would be shunned, made outcasts and exposed to shame. This exposure to shame underpins the fear of community rejection that seems to be prevalent among South Asian abuse survivors. McGregor (2014) reports that many CSA survivors, male and female, fear being cast out of their families for 'airing the family's dirty laundry' or 'dredging up the past for nothing'. This further legitimises ostracism as a very real fear for survivors from all backgrounds. However, what differentiates the experience of Asian survivors, according to the findings of this study, is the added element of community and the way family and community are entwined. These two groups pass a double judgement on the survivor, who may end up being rejected by both. Gagnier and Collin-Vézina (2016) argue that there is a lack of awareness around male CSA that, in turn, leads to a lack of acknowledgement that this form of abuse can impact men as much as it can women. However, it may be that such lack of awareness is driven less by denial and disbelief that such crimes exist than by the socially perpetuated myth of masculinity and manhood, which is incompatible with the traditional image of a 'victim'. When these two phenomena cannot be reconciled, denial is the result.

Conclusion

While CSA can affect children from all communities and ethnicities, it is important to acknowledge the nuances across these experiences and the culturally specific complexities that can present additional challenges for survivors from minoritised communities. With this in mind, the chapter's overall aim was to explore how British South Asian male CSA survivors make sense of their experiences. There is a concerning lack of empirical research on CSA among minoritised men that has left significant gaps in knowledge. Indeed, much existing research on CSA in Asian communities has centralised Asian men as the enforcers of honour and violence—but as this current study demonstrates, Asian women can also perpetuate and maintain harmful cultural practices and attitudes.

Many of the survivors in this research decided not to disclose to family members as a result of fears around unsupportive reactions, ostracisation from family and/or the wider community, and the unprecedented ramifications that survivors often anticipate in the aftermath of disclosure. The tight-knit structure of South Asian communities was recognised as a contributing factor that not only enabled abuse to take place more easily but maintained the silence around it. Hesitancy around disclosure to family members was driven by a fear of ostracism from the family; what distinguished this experience for the South Asian male survivors was the important role of the community and the wider family network within this cultural context. These survivors felt that they had to consider the ramifications of disclosure for their wider family and community, which is why only three out of the eight interviewed had revealed their abuse to immediate family members. This suggests that a significant shift is required to change embedded attitudes around shame, honour and heteronormativity and the ways in which these constructs negatively impinge on healing from trauma.

All eight survivors resisted culturally enforced ideas around izzat, characterising it as a negative construct that acted as a barrier to disclosure. This finding aligned with Ahmed et al's (2009) research into South Asian female survivors of sexual violence, which presents culture as the reason why family and community members in that context held problematic views about sexual violence. Izzat has been conceptualised in the literature as a patriarchal construct created by men to subjugate and control women (Gill 2021). The current study sought to challenge this idea by illustrating the ways in which izzat can also shape the experiences of South Asian men. The findings not only demonstrate how izzat impacts South Asian men but also how it is inextricably linked to men's construction of their own masculinity. Indeed, many of the survivors who did not disclose to family felt they could not because of different culturally driven understandings of, and attitudes towards, masculinity. By contrast, previous research on masculinity in South Asian communities has discussed it in relation to protest masculinity and hypermasculinity (Connell and Messerschmidt 2005; Kalra 2009; Jaspal 2019; Pabla 2020).

The results of this study thus offer insights into how abuse disclosure for British South Asian men would threaten their standing within the family and their (perceived) masculinity. Engaging with parents and communities around these sensitive topics is therefore a necessary first step in breaking down the conversation barriers identified in this research. The secretive nature of CSA means its impact on survivors and society is too easily concealed, and research such as this study can help bring it to light and allow us (survivors and their families, counsellors and others) to understand it better and overcome those communication barriers to progress efforts on identifying, responding to and preventing CSA. Group-based consultations with Asian communities to raise awareness of the harms of CSA and the need to support children and adults who disclose abuse could be one way to mitigate harmful attitudes towards abuse disclosure. This would also open up a dialogue for conversations around subjects that have traditionally been viewed as taboo. These consultations would perhaps be better facilitated by practitioners from a similar ethnic background to prevent exacerbating group-based differences on the basis of ethnicity and any potential power imbalances that may emerge as a result. These consultations could help survivors from Asian communities develop healthier coping mechanisms, disclose abuse earlier and forge a wider support network.

Ultimately, this research has merely scratched the surface of the issue—we still have much to learn regarding the importance of deepening our understanding of South Asian male CSA survivors and how they can be supported. Future research not only needs to recognise and challenge existing assumptions around culture and gender but should also pay greater attention to a critically under-researched group of survivors to ensure their voices and experiences are included in—and can help shape—policy and practice.

Notes

1. All names are pseudonyms.

References

Adams, J., Mrug, S., and Knight, D. C. (2018). Characteristics of child physical and sexual abuse as predictors of psychopathology. *Child Abuse and Neglect*, 86, 167–177.

Ahmed, B., Reavey, P., and Majumdar, A. (2009). Constructions of 'culture' in accounts of South Asian women survivors of sexual violence. *Feminism and Psychology*, 19(1), 7–28.

Alaggia, R. (2004). Many ways of telling: Expanding conceptualization of child sexual abuse disclosure. *Child Abuse & Neglect: An International Journal*, 28(11), 1213-122.

Alaggia, R., Collin-Vézina, D., and Lateef, R. (2019). Facilitators and barriers to Child Sexual Abuse (CSA) disclosures: A research update (2000–2016). *Trauma, Violence, & Abuse*, 20(2), 260–283.

Alexander, C. (2004). Imagining the Asian gang: Ethnicity, masculinity and youth after 'the riots.' *Critical Social Policy*, 24(4), 526–549.

Allnock, D. (2010). *Children and young people disclosing sexual abuse: An introduction to the research*. London: NSPCC

Allnock, D., and Miller, P. (2013). *No one noticed, no one heard: A study of disclosures of childhood abuse*. London: NSPCC.

Archer, L. (2001). 'Muslim brothers, black lads, traditional Asians': British Muslim young men's constructions of race, religion and masculinity. *Feminism and Psychology*, 11(1), 79–105.

Aziz, R. (2017). *Taking the strain: Second generation British Asian Muslim Males and arranged marriage in London*. PhD Thesis, City, University of London.

Balani, S. (2019). Anxious Asian men: 'Coming out' into neo-liberal masculinity. *Journal of Postcolonial Writing*, 55(3), 382–396

Balzani, M. (2010). Masculinities and violence against women in South Asian communities: Transnational perspectives. In R. K. Thiara and A. K Gill (Eds.) *Violence against women in South Asian communities: Issues for policy and practice*. Jessica Kingsley.

Bhanbhro S. (2021). Brothers who kill: Murders of sisters for the sake of family honour in Pakistan. In A. Buchanan, and A. Rotkirch (Eds.), *Brothers and sisters*. Palgrave Macmillan.

Begum, H. (2018). *An exploration of how British South Asian male survivors of childhood sexual abuse make sense of their experiences*. PhD thesis. Leicester: De Montfort University.

Begum, R., Khan, R., Brewer, G., and Hall, B. (2020). They will keep seeing young women murdered by men. Enough is enough-we have seen too many women lose their lives. Lessons for professionals working with victims of 'honour' abuse and violence. *Genealogy*, 4(3), 69.

Berrington, A. (2020). Expectations for family transitions in young adulthood among the UK second generation. *Journal of Ethnic and Migration Studies*, 46(5).

Biggeri, M. and Ciani, F. (2019). Emancipatory research as empowerment: an illustration from a research study of persons with disabilities in Palestine. In Clark, D.A., Biggeri, M., Frediani, A.A. (eds) *The capability approach, empowerment and participation: concepts, methods and applications*. London: Palgrave Macmillan.

Butler, I. (2002). Critical commentary: a code of ethics for social work and social care research. *British Journal of Social Work*, 32, 239–248.

Bux, W., Cartwright, D. J., and Collings, S. J. (2016). The experience of non-offending caregivers following the disclosure of child sexual abuse: Understanding the aftermath. *South African Journal of Psychology*, 46(1), 88–100.

Chambers, C. (2020). 'Burminggaon? Nottinggaon? Biradforrd?': British Asian Noir depictions of Bradford. *Forum for Modern Language Studies*, 56(3), 259–279.

Chiaramello, S., Cyr, M., McDuff, P., Laguerre, C.-E., Rodgers, R. F., Walburg, V., and Lignon, S. (2018). Effects of personality traits and characteristics of child sexual abuse on maternal reactions and support. *European Review of Applied Psychology*, 68(3), 99–106.

Collings, S.J., Griffiths, S., and Kumalo, M. (2005). Patterns of disclosure in child sexual abuse. *South African Journal of Psychology*, 35(2), 270–285.

Connell, R. W., and Messerschmidt. J. W. (2005). Hegemonic masculinity: Rethinking the concept. *Gender and Society*, 19(6), 829–859.

Corbett, A. (2016). Psychotherapy with male survivors of sexual abuse: The invisible men. London: Karnac.

Couture-Carron, A. (2020). Shame, family honor, and dating abuse: Lessons from an exploratory study of South Asian Muslims. *Violence Against Women*, 26(15–16), 2004–2023.

Cowburn, M., Gill, A.K., and Harrison, K. (2015). Speaking about sexual abuse in British South Asian communities: Offenders, victims and the challenges of shame and reintegration. *Journal of Sexual Aggression*, 21(1), 4–15.

Crane, S., and Broome, M. E. (2017). Understanding ethical issues of research participation from the perspective of participating children and adolescents: A systematic review. *Worldviews on evidence-based nursing*, 14(3), 200–209.

Crosson-Tower, C. (2014). *Confronting child and adolescent sexual abuse*. Sage.

Crowder, A. (2013). *Opening the door: A treatment model for therapy with male survivors of sexual abuse.* Routledge

Darko, N. (2021). *Engaging black and minority ethnic groups in health research: 'Hard to reach?' Demystifying the misconceptions.* Policy.

Depraetere, J., Vandeviver, C., Beken, T. V., and Keygnaert, I. (2020). Big boys don't cry: A critical interpretive synthesis of male sexual victimization. *Trauma, Violence, & Abuse*, 21(5), 991–1010.

Dey, B.L., Balmer, J., Pandit, A., Saren, M., and Binsardi, B. (2017). A quadripartite approach to analysing young British South Asian adults' dual cultural identity. *Journal of Marketing Management*, 33(9–10), 789–816.

Dodgson, J. E. (2019). Reflexivity in qualitative research. *Journal of Human Lactation*, 35(2), 220–222.

Dominelli, L. (2017). Social work challenges in the second decade of the 21st century: Against the bias. *Affilia*, 32(1), 105–107.

Draucker, C. B., Martsolf, D., Roller, C., Knapik, G., Ratchneewan, R., and Stidham, A. (2011). Healing from child sexual abuse: a theoretical model. *Journal of Child Sexual Abuse*, 20, 435–466.

Durham, A. (2003). Young men living through and with child sexual abuse: A practitioner research study. *The British Journal of Social Work*, 33(3), 309–323.

Easton, S. D., Saltzman, L. Y., and Willis, D. G. (2014). Would you tell under circumstances like that? Barriers to disclosure of child sexual for men. *Psychology of Men and Masculinity*, 15(4), 460-469.

Easton, S., and Parchment, T. M. (2021). "The whole wall fell apart, and I felt free for the first time": Men's perceptions of helpful responses during discussion of child sexual abuse. *Child abuse and Neglect*, 112.

Edwards, K.M., Probst, D.R., Tansill, E.C., and Gidycz, C.A. (2013). Women's reactions to interpersonal violence research: a longitudinal study. *Journal of Interpersonal Violence*, 28(2), 254–272.

Eisen, D. B., and Yamashita, L. (2019). Borrowing from femininity: The caring man, hybrid masculinities, and maintaining male dominance. *Men and Masculinities*, 22(5), 801–820.

Elkins, J., Crawford, K., and Briggs, H. E. (2017). Male survivors of sexual abuse: Becoming gender-sensitive and trauma-informed. *Advances in Social Work*, 18(1).

Eriksson, M. (2009). Girls and boys as victims: Social workers' approaches to children exposed to violence. *Child Abuse Review*, 18(6), 428–445.

Gagnier, C., and Collin-Vézina, D. (2016). The disclosure experiences of male child sexual abuse survivors. *Journal of Child Sexual Abuse*, 25(2), 221–321.

Gagnier, C., Collin-Vézina, D., and La Sablonnière-Griffin, M. D. (2017). The journey of obtaining services: The realities of male survivors of childhood sexual abuse. *Journal of Child and Adolescent Trauma*, 10, 129–137.

Gavey, N. (2005). *Just sex? The cultural scaffolding of rape*. Routledge.

Gilbert, P., Gilbert, J., and Sanghera, J. (2004). A focus group exploration of the impact of Izzat, shame, subordination and entrapment on mental health and service use in South Asian women living in derby. *Mental Health, Religion and Culture*, 7(2), 109–130.

Gill, A. K. (2008). 'Crimes of honour' and violence against women in the UK. *International Journal of Comparative and Applied Criminal Justice*, 32(2), 243–263.

Gill, A. K. (2021) 'Honour'-based violence. In *Wiley-Blackwell encyclopedia of sociology* (2nd ed.). Wiley-Blackwell.

Gill, A. K., and Harrison, K. (2017). Breaking down barriers: Recommendations for improving sexual abuse reporting rates in British South Asian communities. *The British Journal of Criminology*, 58(2), 273–290.

Gill, A. K., and Harrison, K. (2019). 'I am talking about it because I want to stop it': Child sexual abuse and sexual violence against women in British South Asian communities. *The British Journal of Criminology*, 59(3), 511–529

Gill, A. K., and Day, A. S. (2020). Moral panic in the media: Scapegoating South Asian men in cases of sexual exploitation and grooming. In Ramon, S., Lloyd, M., and Penhale, B. (Eds.), *Gendered domestic violence and abuse in popular culture*. Emerald: Bingley

Gill, A. K., and Walker, S. (2020). On honour, culture and violence against women in black and minority ethnic communities. In S. Walklate, K. Fitz-Gibbon, J. McCulloch, & J. Maher (Eds.), *Emerald handbook of criminology, feminism and social change*. Emerald.

Gill, S.S. (2020). 'I need to be there': British South Asian men's experiences of care and caring. *Community, Work & Family*, 23(3).

Gilligan, P., and Akhtar, S. (2005). Child sexual abuse among Asian communities: Developing materials to raise awareness in Bradford. *Practice*, 17 (4): 267-284.

Gilligan, P., and Akhtar, S. (2006). Cultural barriers to the disclosure of child sexual abuse: Listening to what women say. *British Journal of Social Work*, 36(8), 1361–1377.

Giwa, S. (2016). Surviving racist culture: Strategies of managing racism among gay men of colour—An interpretative phenomenological analysis. PhD Thesis, York University.

Goffnett, J., Liechty, J., and Kidder, E. (2020). Interventions to reduce shame: A systematic review. *Journal of Behavioral and Cognitive Therapy*, 30(2), 141–160.

Gupta, R. (Ed.). (2003). *From homebreakers to jailbreakers: Southall black sisters*. Zed Books.

Hardy, S. J., and Chakraborti, N. (2019). *Blood, threats and fears: The hidden world of hate crime victims*. Palgrave.

Harrison, K., and Gill, A. K. (2018). Breaking down barriers: recommendations for improving sexual abuse reporting rates in British South Asian communities. *British Journal of Criminology*, 58(2), 273–290.

Hesse, B. (2000). *Un/settled multiculturalisms*. Zed.

Hohendorff, J. V., Habigzang, L. F., and Koller, S. H. (2017). "A boy, being a victim, nobody really buys that, you know?": Dynamics of sexual violence against boys. *Child Abuse & Neglect*, 70, 53–64.

Hlavka, H. R. (2017). Speaking of stigma and the silence of shame: Young men and sexual victimization. *Men and Masculinities*, 20(4), 482–505.

Hunter, S. V. (2011). Disclosure of child sexual abuse as a life-long process: Implications for health professionals. *Australian and New Zealand Journal of Family Therapy*, 32, 159–172.

Izzidien, S. (2008). *"I can't tell people what is happening at home." Domestic abuse within South Asian communities: the specific needs of women, children and young people*. London: NSPCC.

Kaur C, Kaur A. (2020). Malaysian Sikh Youths' perception of diverse sexual identities. *Millennial Asia*. https://doi.org/10.1177/0976399620956289.

Jaffe, A. E., DiLillo, D., Hoffman, L., Haikalis, M., and Dykstra, R. E. (2015). Does it hurt to ask? A meta-analysis of participant reactions to trauma research. *Clinical Psychology Review*, 40, 40–56.

Jaspal, R. (2014). Arranged marriage, identity and psychological wellbeing among British Asian gay men. *Journal of GLBT Family Studies*, 10(5), 425–448.

Jaspal, R. (2019). Parental reactions to British South Asian young men who come out as gay. *Journal of GLBT Family Studies*.

Jaspal, R. (2020). Honour beliefs and identity among British South Asian gay men. In M. M. Idriss (Ed.), *Men, masculinities and honour-based abuse*. Routledge.

Javaid, A. (2017). The unknown victims: Hegemonic masculinity, masculinities, and male sexual victimisation. *Sociological Research Online*, 22(1), 28–47.

Kalra, V. S. (2009). Between emasculation and hypermasculinity: Theorizing British South Asian masculinities. *South Asian Popular Culture*, 7(2), 113–125.

Kia-Keating, M., Grossman, F., and Sorsoli, L. (2005). Containing and resisting masculinity: Narratives of renegotiation. *Psychology of Men and Masculinity*, 6(3), 169–185.

Kia-Keating, M., Sorsoli, L., and Grossman, F. K. (2010). Relational challenges and recovery processes in male survivors of childhood sexual abuse. *Journal of Interpersonal Violence*, 25, 666–683.

Kirkner, A., Relyea, M., and Ullman, S. E. (2019). Predicting the effects of sexual assault research participation: Reactions, perceived insight, and help-seeking. *Journal of Interpersonal Violence*, 34(17), 3592–3613.

Khubchandani, K. (2019). Queer South Asian diasporas. In *Oxford research encyclopedias: Literature*. Oxford University Press.

Kukreja, R. (2021). Recouping masculinity: Understanding the links between macho masculinity and self-exploitation among undocumented South Asian male migrants in Greece. *Geoforum*, 122, 164–173.

Kyler-Yano, J. Z., and Mankowski, E. S. (2020). What does it mean to be a real man? Asian American college men's masculinity ideology. *Psychology of Men & Masculinities*, 21(4), 643–654.

Legerski, J., and Bunnell, S. (2010). The risks, benefits, and ethics of trauma-focused research participation. *Ethics & Behavior*, 20, 429–442.

Lovett, J., Coy, M., and Kelly, L. (2018). *Deflection, denial and disbelief: Social and political discourses about child sexual abuse and their influence on institutional responses—A rapid evidence assessment*. London Metropolitan University.

MacGinley, M., Breckenridge, J., and Mowll, J. (2019). A scoping review of adult survivors' experiences of shame following sexual abuse in childhood. *Health and Social Care in the Community*, 27(5), 1135–1146.

Manay, N., and Collin-Vézina, D. (2021). Recipients of children's and adolescents' disclosures of childhood sexual abuse: A systematic review. *Child Abuse & Neglect*, 116(1).

Massey, C., and Widom, C. (2013). Reactions to research participation in victims of childhood sexual abuse. *Journal of Empirical Research on Human Research Ethics*, 8(4), 77–92.

McCarthy, A., Cyr, M., Fernet, M., and Hébert, M. (2019). Maternal emotional support following the disclosure of child sexual abuse: A qualitative study. *Journal of Child Sexual Abuse*, 28(3), 259–279.

McElvaney, R., Murray McDonnell, R., and Dunne, S. (2021). Siblings' perspectives of the impact of child sexual abuse disclosure on sibling and family relationships. *Family Process*.

McElvaney, R., and Nixon, E. (2020). Parents' experiences of their child's disclosure of child sexual abuse. *Family Process*, 59(4), 1773–1788.

McGregor, K. (2014). *Surviving and moving on: Self help for survivors of child sexual abuse*. Routledge.

McKeown, E., Nelson, S., Anderson, J., Low, N., and Elford, J. (2010). Disclosure, discrimination and desire: Experiences of Black and South Asian gay men in Britain. *Culture, Health and Sexuality*, 12(7), 843–856.

McTavish, J. R., Sverdlichenko, I., MacMillan, H. L., and Wekerle, C. (2019). Child sexual abuse, disclosure and PTSD: A systematic and critical review. *Child Abuse and Neglect*, 92, 196–208.

Mesquita, B. (2001). Emotions in collectivist and individualist contexts. *Journal of Personality and Social Psychology*, 80(1), 68–74.

Mitha, K., Ali, S., and Koc, Y. (2021). Challenges to identity integration amongst sexual minority British Muslim South Asian men. *Journal of Community and Applied Social Psychology*.

Morrison, S. E., Bruce, C., and Wilson, S. (2018). Children's disclosure of sexual abuse: A systematic review of qualitative research exploring barriers and facilitators. *Journal of Child Sexual Abuse*, 27(2), 176–194.

Mucina, M. K., and Jamal, A. (2021). Assimilation interrupted: Transforming discourses of culture and honour-based violence in Canada. *International Journal of Child, Youth and Family Studies*, 12(1), 1–12.

Noel, J.A. (2016). Promoting an emancipatory research paradigm in design education and practice. Design Research Society 50th Anniversary Conference, Brighton.

O'Leary, P., Easton, S. D., and Gould, N. (2017). The effect of child sexual abuse on men: Toward a male sensitive measure. *Journal of Interpersonal Violence*, 32(3), 423–445

O'Neill Gutierrez, C. and Chawla, S. (2017). *The child sexual exploitation of young south Asian women in Birmingham and Coventry. Exploring professional insight into young women's hidden journeys, silence and support.* The Children's Society.

Pabla, M. (2019). *Moral panics and the governance of South Asian gang involvement: The construction of a local 'cultural' problem.* PhD Thesis, University of Waterloo.

Pabla, M. (2020). The legacies of Bindy Johal: The contemporary folk devil or sympathetic hero. *Religions*, 11(5), 228.

Patel, P. (2008). Faith in the state? Asian women's struggles for human rights in the UK. *Feminist Legal Studies*, 16, 9–36.

Payne, J. S., Galvan, F. H., Williams, J. K., Prusinski, M., Zhang, M., Wyatt, G. E., and Myers, H. F. (2014). Impact of childhood sexual abuse on the emotions and behaviours of adult men from three ethnic groups in the USA. *Culture, Health and Sexuality*.

Peart, K. (2013). Visible identities in Yasmin and provoked. *South Asian Popular Culture*, 11(1), 31–46.

Petersson, C.C. and Plantin, L. (2019). Breaking with norms of masculinity: Men making sense of their experience of sexual assault. *Clinical Social Work Journal*, 47, 372–383.

Phillips, D., Davis, C., Ratcliffe, P. (2007). British Asian narratives of urban space. *Transactions of the Institute of British Geographers*, 32: 217–234.

Purkayastha, B. (2000). Liminal lives: South Asian youth and domestic violence. *Journal of Social Distress & the Homeless*, 9(3), 201–219.

Randall, D., Anderson, A., and Taylor, J. (2016). Protecting children in research: Safer ways to research with children who may be experiencing violence or abuse. *Journal of Child Health Care*, 20(3), 344–353.

Reavey, P., Majumdar, A., Ahmed, B. (2006). 'How can we help when she won't tell us what's wrong?' Professionals working with South Asian women who have experienced sexual abuse. *Journal of Community and Applied Social Psychology*, 16(3), 171–188.

Roberts S. (2020). Untold stories: Male child sexual abusers' accounts of telling and not telling about sexual abuse experienced in childhood. *Journal of Child Sex Abuse*, 29(8), 965–983.

Robertson, H.A., Chaudhary, Nagaraj, N., and Vyas, A.N. (2016). Family violence and child sexual abuse among South Asians in the US. *Journal of Immigrant and Minority Health*, 18, 921–927.

Roller, C., Martsolf, D. S., Draucker C. B., and Ross, R. (2009). The sexuality of childhood sexual abuse survivors. *International Journal of Sexual Health*, 21(1), 46–60.

Romo, J. (2013). Responsibilities of faith-based groups regarding child sexual abuse. *Family & Intimate Partner Violence Quarterly*, 6(1), 7–16.

Sahota, K. K. (2019). *Sharam Nahi Aundi? Navigating culture, religion, gender and sexuality in a colonized world.* Unpublished Master's dissertation, Arizona State University.

Sangar, M., and Howe, J. (2021). How discourses of sharam (shame) and mental health influence the help-seeking behaviours of British born girls of South Asian heritage. *Educational Psychology in Practice*.

Sawrikar, P., and Katz, I. (2017). The treatment needs of victims/survivors of Child Sexual Abuse (CSA) from ethnic minority communities: A literature review and suggestions for practice. *Children and Youth Services Review*, 79, 166–179.

Serin, H. (2018). Non-abusing mothers' support needs after child sexual abuse disclosure: A narrative review. *Child and Family Social Work*, 23(3), 539–548.

Sharma, A. (2020). The role of media in creating awareness on child sexual abuse among school students. *Journal of Education Culture and Society*, 11(2), 52–67.

Singh, S. (2019). What do we know the experiences and outcomes of anti-racist social work education? An empirical case study evidencing contested engagement and transformative learning. *Social Work Education*, 38(5), 631–653.

Sivagurunathan, M., Orchard, T., MacDermid, J. C., and Evans, M. (2019). Barriers and facilitators affecting self-disclosure among male survivors of child sexual abuse: The service providers' perspective. *Child Abuse & Neglect*, 88, 455–465.

Smith, J. A., Larkin, M., and Flowers, P. (2009). *Interpretative phenomenological analysis*: theory, method and research. London: Sage.

Sodhi, P.K. (2017). *Exploring immigrant and sexual minority mental health: Reconsidering multiculturalism*. Routledge.

Soni, S. (2013). *'Izzat' and the shaping of the lives of young Asians in Britain in the 21st century*. PhD Thesis, University of Birmingham, UK.

Stanko, E. A., and Hobdell, K. (1993). Assault on men: Masculinity and male victimization. *British Journal of Criminology*, 33(3), 400–415.

Stiller, A., and Hellmann, D. F. (2017). In the aftermath of disclosing child sexual abuse: Consequences, needs, and wishes. *Journal of Sexual Aggression*, 23(3), 251–265.

Szto, C. (2020). *Changing on the fly: Hockey through the voices of South Asian Canadians*. New Jersey: Rutgers University Press.

Spataro, J., Moss, S. A., and Wells, D. L. (2001). Child sexual abuse: A reality for both sexes. *Australian Psychologist*, 36, 177–183.

Spiegel, J. (2013). *Sexual abuse of males: The SAM model of theory and practice*. Routledge.

Swan, W. (2016) *Handbook of gay, lesbian, bisexual, and transgender administration and policy*. Marcel Dekker.

Tener, D., and Murphy, S. (2015). Adult disclosure of child sexual abuse: A literature review. *Trauma, Violence & Abuse*, 16(4), 391–400.

Tonsing, J., and Barn, R. (2017). Intimate partner violence in South Asian communities: Exploring the notion of 'shame' to promote understandings of migrant women's experiences. *International Social Work*, 60(3), 628–639.

Walklate, S. (2007). *Imagining the victim of crime*. Open University Press.

Walters, A. S., and Valenzuela, I. (2020) More than muscles, money, or machismo: Latino men and the stewardship of masculinity. *Sexuality & Culture*, 24, 967–1003.

Wamser-Nanny, R. (2017). Maternal support following childhood sexual abuse: Links to parent-reported children's outcomes. *Child Abuse and Neglect*, 67, 44–53.

Yancey, C. T., and Hansen, D. (2010). Relationship of personal, familial, and abuse specific factors with outcome following childhood sexual abuse. *Aggression and Violent Behaviour*, 15(6), 410–421.

4

Maternal Mimesis: The Impact of Intersectional Abuse on African-Caribbean British Maternal Responses to 'Tellings' of Child Sexual Abuse by Daughters

Joanne Wilson

Introduction

This chapter examines disclosure/'tellings'[1] (Summit 1983; Jones 2000) experiences between seven female African, African-Caribbean British[2] victim-survivors[3] of child sexual abuse (CSA) and their mothers. Taken from the findings of a doctoral thesis (Wilson 2017), the chapter proffers an explanation using the theory of intersectionality (Crenshaw 1991) to explain maternal responses, and the lack of any pursuit to justice from criminal justice, social welfare agencies after such 'tellings' by daughters. Mothers in the study (Op. cit.) were reported as using their own explicit/implicit disclosures of CSA, informed by the realities of intersectional racial, sexist, classist abuse and how these oppressions positioned them as overtly racialised women to inform daughters of how to cope with sexual and intersectional abuse(s) they would encounter in

J. Wilson (✉)
University of East London, London, UK
e-mail: joannerose.w@gmail.com

their everyday lives. Study participants explained how they were encouraged to mimic their mother's portrayal of the racialised stereotype of 'strong Black woman' (SBW) (Beauboeuf-Lafontant 2009). The concept of 'maternal mimesis' (Wilson 2017) draws heavily on postcolonial theories of alterity (difference, otherness) and mimesis (copying, becoming) (Taussig 1993; Bhabha 1984) and suggests that SBW was passed intergenerationally between mothers and daughters of African-Caribbean British descent as a coping strategy to live with both intersectional abuse and sexual abuse and further as a tool to protect Black male abusers and African-Caribbean British communities from further racial hostility by society. The chapter interweaves an analysis of the television series '*How to Get Away with Murder*' (HGAWM) with the accounts by study participants to illustrate how intersectional (race, class, gender and sexuality) abuse(s) both informs attitudes to help seeking and conflates with CSA experiences for women of African descent in Western societies. Where there has been a lack of research and representation of how women of African descent in the UK live with CSA, the television series although set in the U.S. reflected the participant accounts of how intersectional abuse(s) have historically and currently influence maternal responses to disclosures of CSA from daughters, especially where mothers had a similar history of CSA. The chapter attempts to demonstrate with the aid of HGAWM how this conflation of abuse(s) informs female subjectivity, agency, resilience and notions of 'resistance' to racism with the mimicry of SBW. Where mimicry of SBW has aided women of African descent in Western societies to live with the harsh realities of intersectional (Crenshaw 1991) and sexual abuse(s), the women expressed how its effectiveness over time waned as a coping mechanism to live with their CSA experiences. They cited psychological consequences and fractured family relationships, specifically the mother-daughter relationship as being negatively impacted well into adulthood. However, the chapter concludes with the potential of how maternal mimesis can be used to deconstruct through dialogues between mothers and daughters, how intersectional abuses informed agency and subjecthood for women of African descent, in Western climes during different temporal moments. As such, maternal mimesis attempts to curtail feelings of betrayal, shame and guilt for both daughters and mothers impacted by CSA.

(How to get away with Murder: S1 Ep. 13: "Mama's here now" 2015)
Scene 1 [Anna Mae confronts Mama in the kitchen about her CSA]

Mama: "Men were put on this planet to take things, you know. They take your money, they take your land, they take a woman, and they take any other thing they can put their grubby women".
Anna Mae: [chuckles].
Mama: "Did I say something funny?"
Anna Mae "Your definition of woman. I mean what have I ever cared for? What have I ever nurtured? What have I ever protected, cared for, or loved? What have you? Did you know? …Did you know what he did to me?" …So, you knew. Sam knew what happened to me the minute I stepped into his office. He said, "this thing that happened to me, what you ignored, is why I am the way I am"
Mama: "Your aunt Lynn was got out by her first- grade teacher. Reverend Daniels got me after choir practice. The first man I worked for; some of the men I dated…I told you men take things. They've been taking things since the beginning of time. Ain't no reason to talk about it and get all messy everywhere. Certainly, ain't no reason to go to a headshrinker for help. You ain't learned nothing".
Anna Mae: "No. I learned Anna Mae belongs in a hand me down box. Go home Mama… I don't need you".

Background

Whilst undertaking my doctoral thesis, I avoided watching any popular television which explored the themes of race, and especially sexual abuse and violence. I made the decision to postpone any viewing which might further immerse me or influence the analysis of my research data. On submission of my thesis (2017), I sat down to catch-up on the dramas I had previously refused to engage with. During series 1, episode 13 of 'How to get away with murder' (Rhimes 2015), I became overwhelmed and struck with awe of what was unfolding before me on the screen between the main characters Annalise Keating (Anna Mae) and her mother (Mama/Ophelia). The very lived experiences outlined by the African-Caribbean British study participants were emerging before my eyes. I had agonisingly laboured over their accounts to understand the often-negative responses by mothers to their daughter's experiences of CSA, and the study participants refused to approach sexual violence support agencies, preferring to draw on a supposed innate strength associated with Black womanhood to live with their histories of CSA. By contextualising both the participant's sense of hopelessness to address histories of abuse and their mothers' responses to disclosures of CSA, within a specifically British social and temporal context, I able to identify how the personal experiences of intersectional abuse described by the women informed their sense of agency and subjectivity. The concept of 'African-Caribbean British 'maternal mimesis" emerged out of their accounts. The term was later revised to maternal mimesis, due to its potential usefulness for understanding maternal responses to 'tellings' of CSA by daughters and mothers from ethnically diverse and minoritised communities which later emerged.

Having a television programme succinctly illustrate many of the issues raised by the doctoral participants was serendipitous, when it came to writing this chapter. Although the television series is set in the U.S. and the main character and her mother are of African American heritage, the impact of how intersectional abuses based upon race, gender and class inform agency and subjectivity within different temporal moments, for women of African descent in Western societies, reflects the often-negative effects of CSA on family relationships, a major theme which emerged throughout the interviews with the doctoral participants (Wilson 2017). As such, the TV series parallels some of the key findings from my research with African-Caribbean British victim-survivors of CSA. The early scenes between Annalise Keating (Anna Mae) and her mother (Ophelia Harkness) reflected the tensions described by the study participants (ibid.). However, the bedroom exchange between Anna Mae and her mother later in episode 13, where her mother speaks of how she was socially situated as a Black woman bringing up a family during an early time, in the Deep South enables Annalise/Anna Mae to finally understand her mother's lived experience, and her reluctance to hear her daughter's disclosure. Having finally listened to and understood how social inequalities and CSA informed her mother regarding seeking justice for her own and her daughter's history of CSA, and how these abuses impacted her mother's agency, the scene closes with mother and daughter embracing. It is this scene which further mirrors the potential of maternal mimesis as a concept, enabling understanding and reunification of maternal-daughter relationships impacted by CSA. The chapter seeks to extrapolate on these findings with reference to the TV show.

Maternal Mimesis

Maternal mimesis attempts to add a positive lens to discussions around the often-difficult mother/daughter relationships on disclosures of CSA. The concept offers an understanding of the impact of socio-cultural, socio-historic and socio-economic disadvantage on African-Caribbean British mothers. Locating mother's lived experiences within an intersectional (Crenshaw 1991) framework, maternal mimesis demonstrates the conflation of sexual and intersectional abuse(s) on maternal agency and responses to disclosures of CSA by daughters. The concept emerged from doctoral research (Wilson 2017), exploring African-Caribbean British female victim-survivors experiences of CSA. The women spoke of how mothers conveyed implicitly by ignoring daughters' 'tellings' of CSA and or explicitly, with mothers using self-disclosure to inform daughters of the futility of speaking of or seeking justice, support for either sexual abuse or systemic abuse(s) experienced by Black women in Western societies.

Mothers passed-down, intergenerationally a gendered stereotype of the strong Black woman (SBW) (Beauboeuf-Lafontant 2009) as a tool for daughters to mimic, and live with, the harsh realities of sexual and intersectional abuse they would encounter throughout their lives as Black women. Additionally, women spoke of an expectation by mothers, for daughters to remain silent, about their experiences of CSA. Remaining silent was also expected regarding the impact of racism, sexism and poverty and socio-economic disadvantage in their everyday lives. Silence was seen as both a form of resilience and resistance, to all forms of abuse and was an expectation of mothers; interestingly, expected more from daughters than Black male family members. Both the expectation to mimic and perform SBW, to defy all forms of social inequalities and sexual violence/abuse, portraying resilience and resistance is dramatically captured by the main characters in the hit U.S. TV series, '*How to Get Away with Murder*' (Rhimes 2015). Underpinning the drama is the sense of futility felt by those affected by intersectional abuse(s) of race, gender, sexuality, class and sexual abuse/violence, and how murder is often seen as the only option available to them, to both protect themselves and seek some manner of justice.

The relationship between the main characters Annalise Keating and her mother Ophelia illustrates both the maternal expectation of SBW and the tensions which arise from such a performance on her daughter's well-being. Interestingly, the character Annalise is childless. Yet she transfers SBW and resilience to her cohort of law students, clients and colleagues as a tool for them to live with a variety of adverse life experiences. Ironically, in her (Annalise) maternal capacity of protecting her colleagues, students and clients, it is Annalise who is ultimately demonised when things do not go as planned. As such, her experience mirrors to some extent Homi Bhabha's (1984) and Taussig's (1993) understanding of the subversive nature of mimicry, as it is revealed as a façade, by those who have replicated the stance of innate strength. What ensues is mockery of the usefulness of SBW by Annalise towards her mother and by Annalise's cohort towards herself.

The drama (Op. cit) is weaved throughout this chapter to assist in demonstrating the impetus of intergenerational transference of maternal mimesis in the mother-daughter relationship. Additionally, it is used to illustrate how dialogue between women, especially mothers and daughters with similar histories of CSA and intersectional abuse, may bridge gaps of misunderstanding, with respect to how socio-historical, socio-economic and socio-cultural social positions impact agency and justice for women of African descent, within different temporal moments in Western cultures. The following scenes between Annalise and her mother provide a useful visualisation of maternal mimesis at play, whilst further providing us with an example of how we may employ lived experience to better aid understanding and alleviate hurt after experiences of CSA.

Early on during the episode (both women in the kitchen) Anna Mae's responds to Mama's view on the attributes of women and men reveals old tensions which have not been sufficiently addressed and reconciled.

She analyses her mother's definition of woman as caring and protecting, asking her, '*what have you?*' (Cared for, protected) in relation to herself. She rebukes her mother with the words, '*this thing that happened to me, what you ignored, is why I am the way I am*'. Yet her mother's purposeful disclosure of her own and her sister's CSA history is used to both provide Anna Mae with a template of living with her CSA, and as a weapon to chastise her daughter for not being or embodying SBW. Mama cannot understand, why Anna Mae has allowed the CSA to make her weak, breaking down her SBW persona. She states, '*ain't no reason to talk about it and get all messy everywhere. Certainly, ain't no reason to go to a headshrinker for help. You ain't learned nothing*'. The employment of purposeful disclosures as a template of informing daughters of how to live with experiences of CSA, as in Mama's response to Anna Mae above, emerged in the doctoral participant accounts of victim-survivors. Purposeful disclosure by mothers will be discussed later in the chapter.

Underpinning each episode (How to get away with Murder) initially hidden, lurked the realities of how CSA negatively impacted victim-survivor characters and their families from diverse cultures. The two scenes outlined in this chapter are the most apt examples of maternal mimesis. Both speak of how agency to seek justice through the legal systems for experiences of CSA on both the abused and the mother/caregiver of that child is being informed by their social positioning. This is especially the case where intersectional (Crenshaw 1991) abuse(s) relating to one's class, race, gender, faith and sexuality is encountered and navigated on a daily occurrence. When these social considerations are acknowledged, we further begin to understand the title of the drama, making it more pertinent and insightful. Subsequently, we begin to understand why murder was portrayed as an option for many of the characters in the drama, when their back stories were eventually revealed as they experience some form of sexual abuse/violence. Sexuality, race, class and gender inequalities were also depicted throughout the drama as informing the choices of different characters, to approach conventional routes to justice.

Research (Chan et al. 2013) conducted into race and female homicide offenders in the U.S. found a link between homicides and women's experiences of sexual and domestic violence/abuse. African American female homicide offenders had higher rates of prosecution (8 out of 10) for homicide of male victims and partners, than their White female counterparts. Chan et al. (2013: 269) stress that these findings are noteworthy, due to the small percentage of African American women relative to White females, in the U.S. population. Yet Black females were disproportionately represented in the female sexual homicide population.

Similarly, a recent report (Centre for Women's Justice 2021) conducted in the UK found that Black, Asian and minoritised women's experiences of intersectional (race, culture, faith) abuse(s) informed their decisions regarding approaching sexual violence and criminal justice agencies to address domestic and sexual abuse experiences in their lives. Intersectional abuse, protection of faith and cultural communities combined with 'race loyalty' (White 2001) to African-Caribbean British communities often underpinned the reluctance of women to speak out about abuse they were experiencing within the home, externally. Protecting communities and particular groups (especially Black men) from further hostility or discrimination on the grounds of race, faith or culture from White society was reported in the women's accounts as superseding women's agency (Centre for Women's Justice 2021; Wilson 2017).

The drama further explored the long-term psychological and interpersonal damage to relationships with family members and friends caused by CSA. Yet the most compelling scenes are those between the mother and daughter characters, Anna Mae, and her mother Mama, as they grappled with each other's understanding of historic CSA in both their pasts. The intergenerational transfer of resilience of SBW as a coping strategy was depicted differently for Anna Mae and Mama. The difference suggests an acknowledgement of shifts in temporality, socio-cultural and socio-economic status in the lives of mother and daughter. Historically, the Mama character's lived experiences and life choices as a Black woman living in the Deep South would have differed greatly from Anna Mae's. Social mobility was shown to have enhanced Anna Mae's agency to speak of and seek support for her CSA, especially with her marriage to a White male (her psychiatrist). Additionally, her shift in social status via high educational attainment enables her to become an attorney and defend those clients with whom her own experiences resonate and whom she understands may have felt 'silenced' and excluded from conventional paths to justice for the inequalities and abuse(s) they lived with. At this point, we are unaware of the mimetic maternal role Anna Mae has unconsciously adopted, in portraying SBW attorney to protect her clients even when she is aware that they have committed murder.

The strategies adopted by each character living with a CSA history in the drama is subtly revealed, enabling the viewer to judge the usefulness of those coping strategies for each victim-survivor. The template Anna Mae inadvertently adopts, that of SBW from her mother, is revealed during an exchange between the two characters in the kitchen, as being wholly insufficient for Anna Mae to live with her own history of CSA. We are made aware of this with Anna Mae's subversive feelings towards her mother. Hence, the tensions between mother and daughter surface yet again. The inability of SBW to contain Anna Mae's pain is tangible.

Equally, we may question the usefulness of SBW for Mama. For Scene 1 demonstrates that a simple explanation of sexism and the sense of entitlement of men in her culture is futile to appease Anna Mae's anger. The inevitability of patriarchal privilege expressed by Mama of male entitlement '*Men were put on this planet to take things…they take any other thing they can put their grubby hands on*' contextualises experiences of gender inequality and loss in her life. The audience is made aware of her powerlessness as an African American woman and hence the lack of agency felt by Mama to address sexism and gender inequality and to 'keep' what she values in her life. Yet for Anna Mae, this distant and removed explanation by Mama is dismissed as simplistic for it does not contextualise or 'speak of' how intersectional inequalities have situated Mama's through her lived experience. However, in Western societies, Black patriarchal power tends to be obscured by narratives of racism against Black males within the public realm. Consequently, little investigation is made of patriarchal power and its impact in the everyday lives of women of African descent within Black communities in Western societies. This is especially the case in the UK with the paucity of knowledge exploring African-Caribbean British women's everyday lives, a grievance echoed by some of the study participants (Wilson 2017).

However, the concept of maternal mimesis can also act as a reunification tool, easing some of the tensions which occur between mother and daughter in the post-disclosure period, immediately or later in both women's lives. The following scene between Anna Mae (Annalise) and her mother Ophelia demonstrates how intergenerational dialogues between mothers and daughters, which recognise and employ lived experience, can help to contextualise parameters of agency, open to Black mothers, during different temporal moments. Outlining the socio-cultural, socio-political and socio-economic conditions of a woman's life creates better understandings and empathy of her social positioning, and hence even forgiveness. Dialogue which seeks to explain options available to disenfranchised groups and communities may serve to both promote critical-reflection and mutual understanding and soothe maternal/daughter tensions caused by histories of CSA and intersectional abuse, as outlined in the following scene.

Scene 2 [Bedroom-Mama combs anna Mae's hair]

> *Mama*: "I bought that house over on Peachtree when I was pregnant with you. I was so proud of that house. It wasn't much but it was mine. Built a porch-swing, tended a little garden that was just right out front… [Chuckling] I baked up a storm on that old stove. You know the one's that you had to light with a long match? …One winter, [sniffs] Uncle Clyde came by and said, "he needed a place to stay", just till he got on his feet, he said. Can't turn your back on family. Then one day I woke up in the middle of the night. I don't know what it was. I-I-I just woke up! I walked down the hall, to look in on you, and Clyde came out of your room, and I knew what he had done. He was a big man. Loved his liquor and his hooch. Smoked three packs of cigarettes a day…was always stinking up the house with cigarette smoke. All the time, he would just fall asleep on the couch, a cigarette hanging out his mouth… then one night, not too long after he fell asleep on the couch drunk as a skunk, that cigarette hanging out of his mouth…. I got you and your brothers and sisters out of bed, and we went over to Aunt Mabel's to sleep. And that house, that I loved so much burned to the ground and your Uncle Clyde burned right with it… Maybe you did something real, bad- I don't know and I don't care if you did. I know if you did, you had your reasons. Cause sometimes you got to do what you got to do…even if all you've got is a long match and a very

4 Maternal Mimesis: The Impact of Intersectional Abuse ...

flammable hooch" [Softly crying, Anna Mae reaches up and embraces her mother's arms. Her mother returns the embrace].

Later in the episode we glimpse how listening to the lived experiences of mothers can be transformative for daughters with their own experiences of CSA. It is whilst sitting between Mama's knees having her hair combed that Anna Mae finally understands and gains an understanding of her mother's life and hence her mother's unsupportive response to Anna Mae's 'telling' of CSA. It is in this harrowing yet tender moment where Mama outlines how she killed Uncle Clyde after she discovered that he was sexually abusing Anna Mae that some semblance of reconciliation occurs between mother and daughter. Mama's words, 'can't turn your back on family', further explains why Uncle Clyde was allowed to stay with the family. Protecting of the Black male from the racial inequalities emerged in the study (Wilson 2017) and has previously been used to explain the prioritisation of Black males needs over those of women of African descent in both the U.S. and the UK.[4]

Mama further explains her justification for murder and her own sense of isolation to address the CSA of her daughter by stating, '*maybe you did something real bad... I don't know and I don't care if you did. I know if you did you had your reasons. Cause sometimes you got to do what you got to do... even if all you've got is long match and a very flammable hooch*'. Her final words provide a glimpse into why she responded to Anna Mae's sexual abuse in the manner she did. For Mama, sometimes you can only work with what you have and suffer the consequences of your actions, for example provide a racialised template for your daughter to live with her experience of CSA.

The frustration expressed during the exchanges in scene 1, between Mama and Anna Mae, as each party strived to justify their positions and the yearning by Anna Mae for an appropriate supportive response on disclosing CSA, was present in my study participants' recollections. Women spoke of the numerous times they attempted to 'tell' and be heard. They spoke of the ongoing desire to raise questions relating to the acknowledgement of CSA by mothers. Adult abused daughters expressed anger towards mothers an emotion identified in previous research (Sanderson 1995). These feelings may explain the continuation of mistrust of mothers and women in general, alluded to by the victim-survivors in the study (Wilson 2017). Interestingly, this mistrust remained present throughout childhood into adulthood further impacting and straining mother/daughter and family relationships the participants outlined.

Victim-survivors spoke vividly of how their disclosures were dismissed; being physically beaten, how they were made to feel complicit in their abuse and blamed for daring to speak of, or for not 'coping' with their experiences of sexual abuse by what is believed to be an omnipotent mother. The women's accounts of disclosing revealed deep hurt, betrayal and shame, resulting from the maternal responses to their disclosures of CSA. According to Sanderson (1995), children frequently believe parents, especially mothers, to be omniscient and omnipotent, expecting mothers to be aware of the pain, hurt and anxieties. If mothers are unresponsive to these emotions the child feels that she has been abandoned and in later life feels betrayed (Sanderson 1995).

The Research

The doctoral research aimed to add the lived experiences of women of African, African-Caribbean British victim-survivors to existing knowledge on CSA. The disclosure experiences of seven African-Caribbean British victim-survivors (see Table 4.1) of CSA are discussed in this chapter. Also, where relevant the accounts of Black British feminists who were active in some manner on the issue of CSA from the 1970s to the present are added. These women were deemed 'Experts' as they articulated what social inequalities were considered priority for Black British/Black feminism from the 1970s onward. Additionally, three of the Experts disclosed their own experiences of CSA.

The victim-survivor accounts (Wilson 2017) are prioritised providing an explanation for the enduring embodiment of SBW amongst African-Caribbean victim-survivors of violence against women and girls (VAWG), especially CSA. However, the concept of 'maternal mimesis' (ibid.) was developed using the lived experiences of both the victim-survivors and Experts, to understand and articulate the impact of

Table 4.1 Participant details: three experts identifying as victim-survivors and the seven victim-survivor participants

Participant	Age	Education	Occupation	Relationship status	Self-identification	Dependants
Expert 1	60	Masters	Health Consultant	Married	African American/Black	0
Expert 2	52	Degree	Civil Servant	Single	Black/Jamaican	1
Expert 3	53	Degree	Managing Director	In relationship	Black African	0
Angel	39	NVQ4	Nursery Officer	Divorced/singles	Afro-Caribbean British	1
Bianca	51	No qualifications	Retail manager	Divorced/single	Black	3
Ciara	26	No qualifications	Unemployed	In relationship	Black Caribbean	3
Maria	48	A levels	Unemployed	Single	Black	4
Porsha	24	Access to Social Work	P/T Care Asst/Student	In relationship	Black Caribbean	1
Sar	38	Degree	Family support worker	Single	Dual heritage/Black	3
Sharon	41	Masters	Social Worker	Single	Black African	0

intersectional inequalities on mother and daughter agency in the wake of 'tellings' of CSA—furthermore, to understand the often-negative responses of parents, specifically mothers, to tellings of CSA by their daughters.

The research further assessed the impact of real and/or perceived personal recollections of intersectional (Crenshaw 1991), especially racist encounters on women's decisions to seek support for their experiences of CSA. Additionally, the participant accounts were analysed to explore whether parental, especially maternal, responses on first disclosure informed how daughters proceeded to live with their abuse experiences. In so doing, it aimed to understand if mothers were passing onto their daughters a coping strategy of resilience—a racialised strategy, specific to women of African descent to survive all manner of abuses, namely via the stereotype of SBW. The recollections of intersectional abuse are contextualised from an ecological (Bronfrenbrenner 1977; Hagan & Smail 1997) perspective enabling the socio-cultural, socio-political and socio-historical influences and conditions negatively impacting Black/African-Caribbean British women and girls historically and currently, to emerge.

Race/racism, racialisation and what White (2001) termed 'race loyalty' are employed to describe how the political concerns of Black women are tied to those of Black men in Western cultures. This supposed unification of 'Blackness' resulting in the 'de-gendering' of Black women, with embodiments of SBW, has served Black male patriarchy, enabling it to set women of African descent in the West within a separate sphere to archetypal womanhood. In this sphere, SBW cloaks womanhood, for women of African descent—replaced with historic racialised constructions of the emasculating 'Sapphire', sexually wanton (Hammond 1999; Spillers 1987) and deviant and hence silent as outlined by a study participant below.

> It is disrespectful to the family. They are scared of what friends and family are going to say. They say that you are lying because it can go either way; they believe you or they don't. Mainly with the black community, they will say you put that on yourself; it is your fault of the individual, other than the man…

(Bianca)

What is interesting about Bianca's reasoning to disclose her CSA experience within African-Caribbean British communities is her sense of knowing that these historic racialised negative stereotypes associated with Black womanhood continue to remain within the psyches of not only White members of society, but within psyches of people from African-Caribbean British backgrounds. Additionally, we see the protection of the Black male emerging, eclipsing the subjectivity and personal concerns of the Black females within these communities. Claims of Black-on Black rape or CSA problematises and compromises Black cultural solidarity globally suggests White (ibid.). White (2001) uses the African proverb, '*I am because we are*' to demonstrate the patriarchal privilege afforded the Black male in Western societies and the diminishment of gender for Black women.

When notions of racial/cultural solidarity are evoked for the purposes of race equality politics, there necessitates a silencing and suppression of personal experiences of historical abuse (White 2001). Personal concerns of African-Caribbean British women were reported as being relegated to a secondary position by the Experts in the study. The everyday intersectional abuses and exclusions had to take precedence in the lives of women of African descent in the UK as emerged in the accounts by the Experts below.

> You know we were looking at the racism in schools; why the children were not getting on; and it just snowballed. They (Black women) would come in and wanted to see what you were doing here; and 'Wha a gwaan'[5] and all this opened a can of worms.
>
> (Expert 2)

> We organised around a number of key issues, the SUS laws[6] which were laws which at the time young black boys were being stopped and searched a lot in Brixton. Black mothers, black sisters were saying we have got to do something about this. So, we did a lot of demonstrating outside Brixton Police station and elsewhere to say this practice has got to stop; you're targeting of black children basically. So that was one of the campaigns we waged. Another one was around sinbins[7] to get rid of the practice

of excluding black children, again black boys, from schools and sticking them in these, kind of no hope institutions where very little was expected of them. We campaigned around the Police [and] Criminal Evidence Bill. We campaigned against virginity testing at Heathrow Airport.

(Expert 1)

The Experts participants reported how during the 1980s and 1990s, African-Caribbean British mothers attended Black Feminist organisations like Brixton Black Women's Group (BBWG) in the first instance, to seek support and advice to address everyday intersectional inequalities, for example, housing, immigration, health issues and for advocacy to address what was deemed the over-zealous decisions by social services, educational institutions and racist policing and criminal justice systems and agencies. CSA emerged out of this context, as a secondary issue. The Expert recollections of what was considered 'personal' for African, African-Caribbean British women helped frame and contextualise both intersectional abuses experienced by women daily and helped to explain the sense of futility felt by mothers to seek support from existing sexual violence support agencies, criminal justice agencies and social service agencies for CSA experiences during that period. These factors influenced the conceptualisation of maternal mimesis. A discussion of how the lived experiences of the study participants underpinned the concept of maternal mimesis follows next. However, with the recent re-emergence of social movements such as Black Lives Matter, their very presence suggests that social inequalities continue to exist in the lives of communities of African descent in Western societies. Yet, one promising aspect of the current movement is that there appears to be a willingness by women of African descent to speak out more within public arenas regarding both intersectional abuse and sexual violence/abuse experiences occurring within the private realm.

Conceptualising the Research

With the paucity of research in the UK, exploring CSA and the lived experiences of how women associated with race, especially women from

African, African-Caribbean British backgrounds, the research (Wilson 2017) process was forced to engage with a multidisciplined framework. This included: critical race theory, psychology, history, Black/Black British feminist theory, anthropology and an auto-ethnographic epistemological lens as a reference guide. As the participants were the descents of migrants from former British colonies, postcolonial studies further aided the investigation into how race/racism and racialisation informed agency for CSA victim-survivors. With most of the research exploring the interconnections of race and sexual abuse from an African American context, a key task of the research aimed to elevate and add the voices of women with histories of CSA from African, African-Caribbean communities in the UK. In so doing, a specifically British perspective derived from women of African descent in the UK would be added to existing knowledges on CSA and the impact of such 'tellings' on mother-daughter relationships.

Crenshaw's theory of intersectionality (Crenshaw 1991) argues that women associated with colour[8] experience race, gender, class, poverty and sexual discrimination not independent of each other, but rather intersectionally producing multidimensional experiences of oppression and exclusion simultaneously. Crenshaw's theory of intersectionality was used in the doctoral research in conjunction with Bhabha (1994) and Taussig's (1993) postcolonial conceptualisations of alterity (difference, otherness) and mimesis (copying or becoming). This combined framework considers historical oppressions of race, gender, sexual and class, articulated from a British standpoint. In so doing, geographical location, migration, temporality and historical (slavery, colonialism) dimensions were incorporated to fully inform African, African-Caribbean British women's subjectivity, agency, identification and sense of belonging in the UK, and how these factors impact agency to seek support and speak of CSA.

Within postcolonial theories, the act of mimicry or 'becoming', copying and assimilating the other (alterity) is a means to harnessing the perceived power of one's coloniser, oppressor (mother) (Ashcroft et al. 2000). Taussig (1993), employed the theory of mimicry and alterity to explain his ethnographic work with the Cuna peoples of Panama who use replicas or 'magical figurines' of their colonisers to ward off evil spirits.

According to Taussig (1993) '*mimicry is a means by which one can be healed, cured or protected from evil spirits by portraying them*' (Taussig 1993: 13).

Therefore, the act of 'becoming' the other by embodying their qualities reduces alterity (difference, otherness) and fear of the other when it is embodied by the colonised oppressed. The participant accounts suggest how they suppressed their feelings and mimicked SBW as advised by their mothers—a necessary shift of mimicry (Bhabha 1984). Yet, this suppression of the self has been argued to be 'unintentionally subversive' (Bhabha 1984). For the very act of mimicking exposes and reveals the power of the other as façade. Mimicry of the other is never a true authentic copy (Bhabha 1984; Taussig 1993); it is by nature hybridised, comprised of the subjectivity of the copier. In this sense, it works to initially empower, yet ultimately inform the person mimicking, of the flaws and gaps (Bhabha 1984) in the supposed power of the other being replicated. For Bhabha (1984: 86), mimicry is ambivalent being resemblance, of mockery, and 'menace'.

Maternal mimesis was developed using the concepts of mimesis and alterity and intersectionality (Op. cit.) to explain the oftennegative parental, especially maternal, response, to 'telling's' (Alaggia 2004; Summit 1983) of child sexual abuse by daughters from AfricanCaribbean British backgrounds. The victim-survivors all expressed how they had continued to 'tell' throughout their childhoods into adulthood. The reaction by mothers was particularly harsh, often involving extensive physical abuse (beatings), to silence their daughters into submission. Interestingly, the participants expressed that on 'telling', mothers implicitly or explicitly outlined their own histories of sexual abuse. The support offered by mothers during this stage consisted of advising their daughters '*to be strong*'—that they were '*not the only ones*' who had experienced such abuses in their lives. Therefore, mothers appeared to use their own lived experiences of CSA as a tool to pass on to daughters to live with CSA experiences.

Mimetic performance emerged in the victim-survivors accounts during the study as women spoke of how they were advised to become SBW from their mothers, to live with everyday intersectional inequalities and CSA discussed below. Daughters were almost enticed by mothers to *harness* their (mother's) supposed power. This seemed most effective after a punitive response, supporting Taussig's (1993) theory of *becoming* the thing you feared to understand and dispel that fear. Yet, the continued tensions between mothers and daughters from childhood into adulthood support Bhabha and Taussig's (Opcit) acknowledgement of the subversive nature of mimetic performance. Where all seven victim-survivors initially described themselves as being SBW, at some point during the in-depth interviews, they all, similarly, declared the harsh difficulties they experienced being forced to perform strength, for other people in their lives. Women reported feeling vulnerable, alone, even suicidal at times. All ten victim-survivors, including the Experts (three) who disclosed during the interviews, outlined strained even broken relationships with families, especially mothers, whom many reported feeling contemptuous towards.

Intersectionality: A Precursor to Maternal Mimesis

One of the prerequisites to being a Black female identified by the participant accounts was the designation of strength (Beauboeuf-Lafontant 2009). If this characteristic is not present, then where do you belong? The following expert outlined the precariousness of displacement from the collective of Blackness for women of African descent in the UK below:

> No outside of black we will always hang on to that; being strong. I think at the moment all the while in the UK that black women face the kind of racism that we do, and all the while we are on the sharp end of all sorts of things... the cuts[9] are a really good example of that, we will always have that sense that we need to be stronger.
>
> (Expert 3)

That there is '...*no outside of black*' sums up how lived experiences of intersectional inequalities necessitate: '*we will always hang on to that*', the need for women of African descent in the UK to appear resilient in order to continue to function and survive. Both experts and victim-survivors described themselves as 'strong Black women'.

> My mother told me boil stones pretend that you are cooking soup.
>
> (Ciara)

Ciara words sum up the 'performance' of resilience associated with African-Caribbean British victim-survivors of CSA (Wilson 2017, 1993). Ciara's statement further illustrates how some African-Caribbean British mothers advise or coerce their daughters into hiding all manner of abuses, including CSA, by encouraging or demonstrating a racially specific way of being: 'strong and chaste'. The following section discusses the reality of living with constant intersectional inequalities and how this type of existence informs both mothers and young female victim-survivors of the need to reproduce an embodiment of 'strong Black woman' via the process of maternal mimesis.

Intersectional Experiences: Turning a Blind Eye

Ciara believed that her mother may have turned a blind eye to the sexual abuse because the abuser's financial assistance was needed. She stated:

> She said, she just didn't want to recognise it. Because when he came into our life, he owned his own business, he had money and we weren't poor anymore! So, I think if she got rid of him, we would be poor again. That's what I think, she hasn't said that that is my opinion because we had everything, we had a PlayStation, a big TV, you know we had big whole psyche hi-fi, we had chairs. Because before him it was carpet that didn't fit the floor; we all slept in the front room, but I did have my room before he came about actually, but we didn't have as much. So, I just think it might have been slightly living a comfortable life and she didn't want to give it up [Voice drops very low].
>
> (Ciara)

What Ciara outlines is how intersectional inequalities, specifically economic disadvantage and poverty, can create situations whereby sexual abuse can be 'ignored', almost sanctioned by the non-offending parent: '*She said she just didn't want to recognise it*'. Ciara's mother was a lone parent, and financial hardship may render a non-offending parent and household reliant on the income of the abuser.

Bianca stated that she had not discussed her CSA with her mother as a child because she feared that any disclosure may add to her mother's already turbulent life, as a single mother on a low income. She outlines her thoughts on this below:

> I must have been about eight or nine and the person lived in the house as a tenant… Because in those days everybody rented out rooms because they couldn't get houses. It was always a cousin, uncle or an aunty or somebody if one person had a house, they would rent a room out not to strangers to like an uncle or an aunt or a brother, so it was family not connected, but it was family.
>
> (Bianca)

Bianca notes here that her household depended on the financial contribution of this tenant and that to tell anyone may impact negatively on the economic status of her household. Therefore, in this instance, it is Bianca who could be seen as 'turning a blind eye' to the abuse she has experienced to safeguard the family finances and cultural considerations. Her hesitancy supports findings in previous research (Paine & Hansen 2002; Kazarian & Kazarian 1998) identifying cultural factors such as social isolation, immigration concerns, discrimination, racism (ibid. 2002, p. 275) and race solidarity (Wilson 2017: 147). In Bianca's account, intersections of gender, race and class are evident in the household composition. Additionally, recollections of the racism faced by Caribbean economic migrants in the UK, in Bianca's account, enable a glimpse of how historically racism disavowed agency for both Bianca and her mother.

Additionally, Angel expressed great empathy for her mother's refusal to acknowledge her abuse. She displayed an understanding of the consequence of coercive control (Stark 2007) on both her mother's agency in relation to her father and her mother's participation in her own sexual victimisation.

> I just thought that she didn't want me, that she didn't like me. Also, my Dad was very violent. My mum never gave me any cuddles; I think she resented me. I did hear an argument one time when she said, 'You promised you would stop hitting me if I had your child, and you didn't'. So, I realized that she really didn't want to have me, she was forced to ... I can definitely live without the sex thing. All the time I just picture my Mum all over me or her just lying there lifeless with my Dad.
>
> (Angel)

In the following account by Angel, she describes how her understanding of police racism influences her decision to remain silent about her CSA. Furthermore, she outlines the additional consideration for remaining silent; the protection of African-Caribbean British communities from any further hostility from criminal justice agencies like the police. Interestingly, her account further provides a glimpse of how historic racialised discourses regarding the supposed hypersexual nature of Black female sexuality (Hammond, 1999; Kempadoo 2004) as significantly influencing her entitlement to seek justice and support, and be seen as a victim of CSA by others.

> Because I know... because of the police that's why I wouldn't speak. That scares me especially with the black community, because they are racist (police) they are not going to believe you. Or they will say, she wanted that! So that is a scary thought... just being in that room being interviewed that is a scary thought. But also, as I said it is the friends, the family the community that's a hard thing to say.
>
> (Angel)

The participant accounts outline how intersectional experiences impacted the family life of African-Caribbean British families, especially mothers parenting alone as described in Bianca's account below:

> But it is interesting that when I told my mum [disclosure of CSA], my mum still stayed with my stepdad; and they actually split up after that, a

while after that because she'd had enough of his beatings. So, they didn't actually split up because of what he'd done to me, they split up because of what he'd done to her. I was angry with my mum for that; disappointed because she did believe me. They had words but I don't know what lies he told.

(Bianca)

Bianca's account of 'telling' her mother that her stepdad was sexually abusing her and mother's decision to remain in the relationship demonstrates how intersectional abuse, in this case domestic abuse, diminished her mother's agency to protect and support her daughter. The results of her mother 'turning a blind eye' created in Bianca feelings of complete betrayal and hatred, especially when her mother decides to stay with her abuser after Bianca has disclosed. Bianca outlined that she attempted to speak with her mother about the abuse later as an adult, to no avail.

Equally, Sar recalls how intersectional abuse experienced by her mother from her family for being a mother of two dual heritage girls, and from her domestically abusive father shaped her subjectivity and agency as a young girl.

Mum was still very protective of me and my sister but there was only so much she could do to protect us because she was being abused every day by her family for having black kids… battered about by my Dad… she must have spent about a year looking for a way to escape my Dad … because she actually met him… whilst escaping from her family who were not accepting of her size, because she is obese and of her … just the way the she is…(lesbian) she is not one for just being quiet and being hurt, physically, mentally by anybody…

He would be going on, and on about how she's a lesbian… and she's this and she's that. And he would go on and on about anyone. He hated Jamaicans, hated Nigerians, hated… he liked white people because he wanted to be accepted by the white people… I remember us going to his; and him…mimicking a white middle class voice; and going to a ballet when I was young … and being really like, I've gone to another part of the world; but enjoyed it as well. At the same time, it was weird. He would just go on, and on for about two hours cussing... so it was emotionally, physically draining ... [Inhales deeply] ... brainwashing...and traumatised.

(Sar)

She supports her mother's lack of support with the words, '*there was only so much she could do to protect us because she was being abused everyday...*' Sar's recollection of her mother's family's racism informs her sense of belonging. Although she is dual heritage, she self-identified as Black in the study. Interestingly, Sar further outlines how her Gambian father's '*hatred*' of *Jamaicans* and Nigerians, and his desire to be accepted by White middle-class society creates a feeling of ambivalence regarding her own sense of self, and where she belonged for her. She enjoys attending the ballet, '*being in another world*', yet simultaneously, '*it was weird*', listening to her father's angry rants about her mother's sexuality and internalised racism.

Staying close or belonging to a group, community was an additional theme which emerged during episode 13 of HGAWM (Rhimes 2015). One of the tensions in the mother-daughter relationship is Annalise's rejection of her birth name, Anna Mae. For Ophelia (Mama), Annalise's rejection of her birth name represents a rejection of her 'Blackness' and the Black community. In contrast, to Sar's father who wishes for his daughter to reject 'Blackness'; for Ophelia, her daughter's rejection of her birth name signifies a sense of displacement away from 'Blackness'. A position which Mama alludes will leave Annalise vulnerable as a Black female navigating a White world. Mama's anger at her daughters change of name demonstrates the illusionary 'power' of the collective of 'Blackness' as a safe-space for women of African descent in Western societies and the use of SBW as a template of existence. In contrast, Sar's account resonates with Homi Bhabha's version of mimesis and alterity and the *coloniser within the colonised*[10] on the part of her father. Compounding her understanding of her CSA experience is the fact that her radical feminist mother never acknowledged her CSA experience but fought the racism she and her sister experienced as young children and the homophobia from her mother's family and her father.

One of the most common responses of parents, especially mothers, was that the CSA was acknowledged and then ignored; 'this thing that happened to me that you ignored' (Rhimes 2015) an experience echoed by Anna Mae above. Being dismissive or 'turning a blind eye' to CSA has been linked, in the case of Caribbean communities, to cultural attitudes. Jones and Trotman Jemmot (2009) found that CSA was culturally bound and almost normalised as something which happened in their study conducted in the Eastern Caribbean. They reported an implicit social sanctioning, coupled with an atmosphere of secrecy, involving maternal complicity due to an overreliance on a male breadwinner ideology. Again, we see the privileging and protection of Black males with the disempowerment and abuse of young children. Yet, to understand the supposed impunity stance by mothers in the Caribbean, we must investigate how socio-economic, socio-cultural and socio-historic factors have situated subjectivity and impacted agency. It is too simplistic to assume that these mothers do not care for their children as we care for ours; just as Anna Mae believed her mother didn't care for her.

Multiple 'Tellings'

Much of the research into disclosures of CSA has focused upon the variables which may prevent victim-survivors telling purposefully: developmental maturity (Flathman 1997; Kelly et al. 1998; Bussey & Grimbeek 1995; Lamb 1999; Sas et al. 1993; Finkelhor 1984). Very little research has focussed upon how socio-cultural, socio-political, socio-historical and socio-economic factors influence disclosures by victim-survivors (Jones & Trotman Jemmot 2009) and maternal responses to those 'tellings'. The table below outlines the process of 'tellings' by the study participants. All seven women went through a process of disclosure which involved several stages of telling. Where previous research (Summit 1983) identified retracting of accusations by victim-survivors as common after first disclosures, none of the women in this study recanted. Rather, they like Anna Mae (Rhimes 2015) continued to 'tell' until they received an appropriate response or until their victimisation was validated and they felt some semblance of support.

As Table 4.2 demonstrates, two women told at all three stages of their lives: childhood, teenage years and in adulthood, and four told at two

Table 4.2 Process of telling

Name of participant	Disclosed under 10 years	Disclosed as teenager	Disclosed as an adult
Sar	✓	✓	✓
Bianca		✓	✓
Maria	✓		✓
Ciara		✓	✓
Porsha		✓	✓
Sharon	✓	✓	✓
Angel			✓

stages. Angel's abuse began before the age of 10, yet differs in that she was still being abused, disclosed this to her therapist when she was in her thirties, and then again to myself during the interview process. Interestingly, all the women reported disclosing again as adults. One explanation for this may be that the punitive treatment received by many could not occur during adulthood. The women outline these punitive maternal responses below.

Punitive Maternal Responses to 'Tellings' by Daughters

Participants further recalled being fearful of mothers because of their harsh responses, often involving severe physical abuse ('beatings') as a means of coercing daughters into silence.

> My mum has been very violent toward me, but that was the most violent I had ever seen my mum. She pulled chunks out of my hair, she was slapping me, she pushed me off the chair; in fact, she really beat me all over the front room but then like she'd calm down and leave the front room and go in the kitchen and she would be like, "yeah she thinks she is a big woman".
>
> (Ciara)

Ciara's recollection of physical abuse after her mother became aware that her boyfriend had sexually abused her daughter parallels the severity of physical abuse experienced by some young African-Caribbean British victim-survivors. Although Ciara was accustomed to being physically abused by her mother, the physical abuse she describes above suggests that during the post-disclosure period her mother's violence became more severe. The reference to '*she thinks she is a big woman*' implies that her mother held Ciara responsible in this situation for attracting the attention of her abuser. Thus, in her mother's eyes, she has become equal to mother, if she is 'engaging' in sexual activity. Even though her mother acknowledges her status as a minor with the words: '*she thinks*'. The fact that Ciara is only 13 years of age when her mother's boyfriend begins to make sexual advances towards her appears lost in her mother's statement as she transfers the responsibility of the abuse away from the abuser onto her daughter.

Similarly, Sharon's recollection of her mother rubbing chilli into her vagina when she was five years of age as a punishment for 'supposedly' playing inappropriately is another example whereby a girl is punished because it is felt that she is acting 'too womanly'. What Sharon describes in the two following accounts could be seen as informing a young victim-survivor that disclosing sexual abuse would carry severe consequences:

> ...So, I was playing; which is a common punishment back home; my mother used pepper, hot pepper on my vagina, as a punishment; and I wasn't supposed to cry. My mum physically beat me [long pause]. I remember she beat me so badly that there was some blood coming out of my head and she instructed me when I went back to tell my grandmother that I fell, and I complied [Begins to cry] ...
>
> (Sharon)

At age 13, Sharon had purposefully talked to her mother about the sexual abuse in front of her stepfather. Her recollections demonstrate the patriarchal respect that men are given within our cultures and the limited support for girls who are sexually abused.

> ...He just rushed me and started kicking me in the ribs, beating me. My mum was standing there by the heater telling me, while he's kicking me, "you respect him he is the man of the house". "Don't disrespect him in this house". The violence was getting quite severe, my mum then decided

to stop him and as my mum attempted to stop him, he physically lashed at my mum.

(Sharon)

When physical abuse occurs after disclosures or discoveries of CSA, it may lead girls to think that the abuse occurred because of the unruliness of their body, read by the racially inscribed abused child as confirmation of the inadequacy of the Black sexually violated body. Acts of corporal punishment may remove responsibility of the sexual abuse away from the abuser by transferring it firmly onto the corporeality of the young girl. Therefore, physical abuse may initiate and intersect with dissociative coping strategies, producing a loathing of the physical for the victim-survivor, and fuel the desire to '*become*' (Bhabha 1984; Taussig 1993) the mother who is seen as all powerful.

Physical punishment combined with the failure of caretakers to address CSA not only informs victim-survivors of the uselessness of disclosing further but may convey and deter others within the family from speaking out. Maria's account below reflects the precarious position faced by family members to inform parents that a sibling may be being sexually abused.

> He must have forgotten his schoolbook and he came back to the house and saw… but he has never mentioned anything to me. If he had of said to mum, "mum oh, mummy I think such and such is happening" or whatever, my mum would have beat him.
>
> (Maria)

The use of physical abuse within African-Caribbean British communities has traditionally created a state whereby all parties aware of the CSA face the dilemma of whether to tell. Yet, it must be stressed that the use of physical abuse as a means of 'correcting' a child is not exclusive to African-Caribbean British or West African cultures. However, the circumstances that the women describe suggest physical abuse within African-Caribbean British communities were used to punish any sexual acts by children, chosen or coerced. The physical abuse outlined by the women in this study after they dared to 'tell' indicates that this practice may be employed to reinforce hierarchies of control based on age and gender (Reynolds 2005). Furthermore, disclosing CSA as outlined in Bianca's earlier account does not guarantee that the abuse will end. The choices for victim-survivors narrow once they understand the impunity given to abusers and the possible dismay of their experiences by parents who seek to ensure silence with the use of physical abuse. Awareness of physical abuse occurring within African-Caribbean British communities against young children, by such agencies as social services, may have checked to some extent this punitive style of parenting. Pheonix and Husain (2007) suggest that temporal and cultural exchanges must be considered in any examination of parenting and ethnicity (2007: 24). However, the parental/maternal response of 'turning a blind eye' to 'tellings' of CSA as discussed below may continue unchecked as they leave no physical scars.

Parental/Maternal Responses

Six women expressed a range of emotion from deep sorrow to anger towards their mothers as adults; one had never felt the need to discuss her experience because her mother played a part in her abuse as a child and as an adult. Angel expressed great empathy for her mother's refusal to acknowledge her abuse. She displayed an understanding of the consequence of coercive control (Stark 2007) on both her mother's agency in relation to her father and her mother's participation in her own sexual victimization (Table 4.3).

Maternal Tellings and Disclosures: Implicit/Explicit

Three of the participants expressed how their mothers had explicitly offered their own histories of CSA and intersectional abuse, as a template for daughters to replicate and live with their own experiences of sexual and racial abuse. Two strongly believed that their mothers had implicitly

Table 4.3 Response of parents to disclosures of CSA

Name of participant	Parent believed and was supportive	Parent believed but was unsupportive	Parent did not believe	Response to daughter's disclosure by parent(s)	External support taken to support daughter
Sar		✓		After disclosure mother focused on abuser not daughter. Has not spoken of sexual abuse since	
Bianca		✓		Mother has not spoken of sexual abuse to date	
Maria		✓		Father beat brother (abuser). Mother discovered abuse but has not spoken of it since. Called Maria a liar	
Ciara		✓		Mother supported abuser. Beat daughter badly	

4 Maternal Mimesis: The Impact of Intersectional Abuse ...

Name of participant	Parent believed and was supportive	Parent believed but was unsupportive	Parent did not believe	Response to daughter's disclosure by parent(s)	External support taken to support daughter
Porsha	✓			Initially supported by family. Abuse characteristic (anal rape) prevents parents from speaking of abuse since disclosure by police	✓
Angel		✓		Sexual abuse ongoing into present	
Sharon		✓		Mother and abuser beat her. Shamed publicly to family and friends	

Table 4.4 Explicit, implicit disclosures by mothers

Name of participant	Mother named own abuse	Mother implicitly suggested	No disclosure by mother
Sar			✓
Bianca			✓
Maria		✓	
Ciara	✓		
Porsha	✓		
Angel		✓	
Sharon	✓		

disclosed their own experiences of CSA, whilst Sar and Bianca's mothers had neither implicitly/explicitly disclosed personal experiences of CSA (see Table 4.4).

Ciara illustrates the role her mother's explicit revelation played.

> My mum actually said that she was sexually abused as a child; so, I don't understand. I mean my mum raised me to [shouts] if anyone touches you, make sure that you tell me. I mean der, der, der! She was really quite vigilant with us, so I don't understand why she just put it to the back of her mind?
>
> (Ciara)

Ciara's confusion is linked to her mother's refusal to acknowledge or address what has happened to her, considering earlier cautions: she is perplexed and frustrated.

Porsha infers that her mother's disclosure was a means of explaining her felt inadequacies as a parent.

> *I*: Can I just ask what type of abuse your mother experienced?
> *P*: Domestic violence and CSA.
> *I*: Did she tell you this?
> *P*: Yeah...
> *I*: In what context did she disclose her CSA to you?

> Well, I was aware of the domestic abuse that was going on around me. I found out at quite an early age when I was about 10 or 11 about what happened to my mum, and I suppose my mum had insecurities about

how she mothered. I think I was a bit young to hear it but I didn't get the full extent until later... I kind of took on the role of not parenting but you know being strong for my brothers and sisters; not really showing any weakness for their sake or my situation.

(Porsha)

Porsha's awareness of how her mother's disclosure had situated her, not just as a child, but later with her own experience of CSA was truly insightful. Her self-awareness '*I didn't get the full extent until later on*', and '*not really showing any weakness for their sake or my situation*' suggests that on reflection she has become aware of the impact of the legacy of her mother's disclosure on both her own life and those of her siblings.

Because I was kind of raised and taught to handle situations... being an overcomer you know just getting on with stuff like you know the plate that you are served I suppose. So just, just fighting the battle regardless.
(Porsha)

Fighting on regardless and being an 'overcomer' are attributes which have traditionally been associated with being Black and especially female which is articulated by the 'strong Black woman' stereotype (Beauboeuf-Lafontant 2009).

Sharon's account of her mother's implicit purposeful disclosure provides a glimpse of how African-Caribbean British negative maternal responses inform their daughters through purposefully, implicitly revealing of their own experiences of CSA. Maternal mimesis is conveyed and adopted through certain behaviours and standpoints on how to live with sexual abuse and provides daughters with a type of template of resistance to cope with experiences of CSA.

My mum has been angry at me and she said why don't I just let this go? I am acting as if I am the only child who has been abused; the way she coped with it was by ignoring it. Because when she said that to me she also said why don't I just let it go? You know why do I need to push it? I'm not the only child that has been abused and that was all she said to me she never said more than that to me.

(Sharon)

The harsh lived experiences of intersectional inequalities appear to inform mothers and eventually daughters to the possibility that nothing will come of speaking of the abuse especially to family and friends within the community. The women accounts suggest that mothers who have themselves experienced CSA often inform their daughters of how to 'live with' sexual abuse.

The rationale for African-Caribbean British mothers to disclose their own histories of CSA purposefully implicitly could be seen as they attempt to inform their daughters of the perils of disclosing within African-Caribbean British communities. Maternal mimesis may not be a coping strategy exclusive to African-Caribbean British communities as it has been depicted in the U.S. drama 'How to get away with Murder' (Rhimes 2015) and outlined in the accounts of women with West African heritage. However, the subjugated knowledge held by African-Caribbean British mothers regarding the negative consequences to their daughters if they disclose within our communities may be impetus enough for the reproduction of a mimetic performance of resilience of strong Black woman by African-Caribbean British women from one generation to the next.

Conclusion

Due to the small number of participants, and the lack of previous research conducted on CSA and especially disclosure experiences of women from African-Caribbean British backgrounds, more research is required in the future to expand our understanding of how intersectional inequalities and racialisation inform subjectivity and agency for both non-abusing parents and victim-survivors from African-Caribbean British communities.

However, the accounts of the participants in the study enable us not only to name the barriers which continue to inhibit African-Caribbean British women's choices regarding histories of sexual abuse but to also gain a fuller understanding of how these are experienced within everyday lives. Culture and racialisation/racism impact on both how victim-survivors make sense of CSA and opportunities for recognition and seeking support. Their decisions are not only understood and shaped through gender (Finkelhor 1984; Kelly et al. 1998; Sas et al. 1993; Lamb 1999) but additionally through a lens of culture, racialisation and political Blackness and continued intersectional abuse, which unfortunately continues with each new generation. Where previous research has highlighted the distinction between 'disclosure' and 'telling' (Jones 2000; Summit 1983), this study found that the women told their caregivers, with disclosure to an external agency rarely the aim or even an option if the abuse was intra-familial. Women continued to 'tell' until they received what they felt was an appropriate response especially if the maternal response was negative.

Where the abuser was a mother's partner, boyfriend or son, the maternal response tended to be negative followed in most cases by physical abuse by mothers who located responsibility on the abused girl. In the two cases where the abuse was reported to an external agency, it served the interests of parents rather than the child and created a further set of contradictions. Although all the women remained in contact with their families, for all but one it was the mother-daughter relationship which was strained. The women's accounts were analysed through a concept of racialised gendered mimesis, passed on intra-generationally between mother and daughter: this functioned as a coping strategy and mode of resistance which enabled them to live with the adversities of life such as CSA histories, poverty and racism until adulthood. The process of maternal mimesis: the transference of a coping strategy is imparted verbally/non-verbally through silences ('turning a blind-eye'), avoidance of or eclipsing of the child's own experience of sexual victimisation through disclosures of the mother's own. With the limited options available to African-Caribbean British victim-survivors, maternal mimesis underscores the lack of 'space to speak' for experiences of CSA for African-Caribbean British female victim-survivors.

However, maternal mimesis does not attempt to further castigate non-offending mothers. Rather, it suggests that mothers were aware of the futility of complaining or 'speaking out' about the intersectional injustices they experienced on the grounds of race, gender, class and sexuality in their own lives and those of their children. The concept is used to explain the accounts of the study participants and to describe what seemed to be a sense the futility felt by both African-Caribbean British mothers and their daughters after a disclosure of CSA. The women in the study described how intersectional lived experiences, especially experiences of racism (externally) and racialisation (within African-Caribbean British communities, home), eroded any sense of entitlement to seek justice via traditional routes. The inevitable gifting of racialised embodiments of SBW as a coping strategy for intra-generational victim-survivors of CSA may yet be rebuked if we enable and encourage mothers to speak of their own experiences in a more socially contextualised manner. If daughters acknowledge the impact of intersectional histories of abuse upon mothers' responses and decisions such as that which occurred in the exchange between Anna Mae and Mama, we may be able to create a bridge of understanding of the 'other', expelling both notions of becoming the 'other' in order to harness their power and curtail feelings of betrayal, shame and hurt from being carried into adulthood by another generation of victim-survivors.

Notes

1. Tellings/telling is used to describe the numerous unofficial ways victim-survivors informed parents, friends of their experiences. Disclosure is used in the study to convey official reporting to criminal justice agencies.
2. The term African-Caribbean refers to peoples whose origins and heritage consists of both these ethnicities, who make up the largest and most recognisable Caribbean migrant community in the U.K. (Goulbourne 2002). The added British component reflects the present stage of our diasporic journey, recognising our present geographical location and hopefully, our sense of citizenship and belonging. The women in the original research study often self-identified as 'Black'; their words were not changed. Equally, African may also prefix African-Caribbean British to include and acknowledge those of West African and dual heritage who identified as Caribbean during the time being explored. As such, African, African-Caribbean British will be used throughout in conjunction with the ethnic racial category Black https://www.ethnicity-facts-figures.service.gov.uk/style-guide/ethnic-groups.

3. The term victim-survivor was used in the original study when participants expressed how they had moved from being sexually victimised during their early childhoods, to living with, and surviving histories of sexual abuse. The position of victim was claimed for the first time for five of the participants during the interviews. The study participants expressed on reflection, how their race, racialisation, informed how their identification as 'survivor'. The term 'victim' was initially viewed as running counter to representations of Black femininity and womanhood, associated with strength and resilience strong Black woman (SBW) hence initial identification with 'survivor'. On reflection, participants felt that that 'victim-survivor' represented the transitory nature of women's experiences and understandings of child sexual abuse in their lives.
4. See Wilson, J. (2017) Doctoral thesis for more in-depth discussion of protecting the African-Caribbean British male and communities (pp. 120–130).
5. Jamaican patois for 'What's happening'; 'How are you?' Used as a greeting.
6. SUS Laws were the predecessor to what is now termed 'Stop and Search'. Derived from the 1824 Vagrancy Act of England and Wales, the law permitted police to stop and search and potentially arrest anyone whom they felt was in violation of vagrancy laws. By the 1970s–1980s, the law was used by police officers to predominantly stop and search members from Black and ethnic minority communities, especially men from those communities.
7. The expulsion of Black British children from mainstream schools and placed in 'no hope' pupil referral units (Sin Bins).
8. It is customary for the term 'people or women of colour' to be used to describe those who are not White. The chapter acknowledges that White is a colour used for racial identity, although it occupies a normative, position. As such, the term 'associated with colour' is used as a means of including Whiteness within the process of racialisation.
9. Austerity cuts by Conservative Government from 2010 onward.
10. My emphasis with use of italics.

References

Alaggia, R. (2004). Many ways of telling: Expanding conceptualizations of child sexual abuse disclosure. *Child Abuse & Neglect*, 28, 1213–1227.

Angel. (2012, October 2). Sour Milk: African Caribbean British survivors experiences of childhood sexual abuse (J. Wilson, Interviewer).

Ashcroft, B., Griffiths, G., and Tiffin, H. (2000). *Post-colonial studies: The key concepts*. Routledge.

Beauboeuf-Lafontant, T. (2009). *Behind the mask of the strong black woman: Voice and the embodiment of a costly performance*. Temple University Press.

Bhabha, H. (1984). Of mimicry and man: The ambivalence of colonial discourse. *Discipleships: A Special Issue on Psychoanalysis, Spring*, 28, 125–133.

Bhabha, H. (1994). *The location of culture*, Oxon and New York, Routledge.

Bianca. (2012, April 4th). Sour Milk: African Caribbean British survivors experiences of childhood sexual abuse (J. Wilson, Interviewer).

Bronfrenbrenner, U. (1977). Toward an experimental ecology of human development. *American Psychologist*, 32, 513–531.

Bussey, K., & Grimbeek, E. J. (1995). Disclosure processes: Issues for child sexual abuse victims. In K. Rotenberg (ed.), *Disclosure processes in children and adolescents* (pp. 166–203). Cambridge University Press.

Centre for Women's Justice. (2021). *The decriminalisation of rape: Why the justice system is failing rape survivors and what needs to change*. Report by the Centre for Women's Justice, End Violence Against Women Coalition, Imkaan, and Rape Crisis England and Wales in response to England and Wale's Government's 'End to End' Review of the Criminal Justice Systems Response to Rape. https://www.centreforwomensjustice.org.uk/s/Decriminalisation-of-Rape-Report-CWJ-EVAW-IMKAAN-RCEWNOV-2020.pdf

Chan, H., Frei, A., and Myers, C. W. (2013). Female sexual homicide offenders: An analysis of offender racial profiles in offending process. *Forensic Science International*, 265–272.

Ciara. (2012, June 18th). Sour Milk: African Caribbean British survivors experiences of childhood sexual abuse (J. Wilson, Interviewer).

Crenshaw, K. (1991). Mapping the margins: Intersectionality, politics, and the violence against women of colour. *Stanford Law Review*.

Finkelhor, D. (1984). *Child sexual abuse: New theory and research*. New York: Free Press.

Flathman, M. (1997). Trauma and delayed memory: A review of the "repressed memories" literature. *Clinical and Research Review*, 1–23.
Golbourne, H. (2002). *The caribbean transnational experience, pluto press & arawak publications*, London and Kingston, JA.
Hagan, T., and Smail, D. (1997). Power-mapping—I background and basic methodology. *Journal of Community & Applied Social Psychology*, 7, 257–267.
Hammond, E. (1999). Toward a genealogy of black female sexuality: The problematic of silence. In J. Price, & M. Shildrick (Eds.), *Feminist theory and the body: A reader* (pp. 93–103). Edinburgh University Press.
Jones, A., and Trotman Jemmot, E. (2009). *Child sexual abuse in the Eastern Caribbean: The report of a study carried out across the Eastern Caribbean during the period October 2008 to June 2009*. Huddersfield University: UNICEF/Government of the Eastern Caribbean Programme of Cooperation/Department for International Development.
Jones, D. (2000). Editorial: Disclosure of child sexual abuse. *Child Abuse & Neglect*, 267–271.
Kazarian, S., and Kazarian, L. Z. (1998). Cultural aspects of family violence. In S. Kazarian, & D. R. Evans (Eds.), *Cultural clinical psychology: Theory, research and practice* (pp. 316–347). Oxford University Press.
Kelly, L., Burton, S., and Regan, L. (1998). *Legacies of abuse: "It's more complicated than that". A qualitative study of meaning and impacts of sexual abuse in childhood*. CWASU/ESRC Project .
Kempadoo, K. (2004). *Sexing the caribbean: Gender, race and sexual labor*, New York and Oxon, Routledge.
Lamb, S. (1999). *New versions of victims: Feminist struggles with the concept*. New York University Press.
Paine, M., and Hansen, D. (2002). Factors influencing children to self-disclose sexual abuse. *Clinical Psychology Review*, 22, 271–295.
Pheonix, A., and Husain, F. (2007). *Parenting and ethnicity*. Joseph Rowntree Foundation.
Porsha. (2012, October 4th). Sour Milk: African Caribbean British survivors experiences of childhood sexual abuse (J. Wilson, Interviewer).
Reynolds, T. (2005). *Caribbean mothers: Identity and experience in the UK*. The Tufnell Press.
Rhimes, S. (2015, February 19). How to get away with murder: S1 Ep. 13: Mama's here now. *Shondaland TV/ABC*.
Sanderson, C. (1995). *Counselling adult survivors of child sexual abuse*. Jessica Kingsley Publishers.

Sas, L., Hatch, A., Malla, S., Dick, T., and Hurley, P. (1993). *Three years after the verdict: A longitudinal study of the social and psychological adjustment of child witnesses referred to the child witness project.* Washington, DC: U.S. Department of Justice: Office of Justice Programs.

Spillers, H. (1987). Mama's baby, papa's maybe: An American grammar book. *Diacritics*, 17(2), 64–81.

Stark, E. (2007). *Coercive control: How men entrap women in personal life*, Oxford and New York, Oxford University Press.

Summit, R. (1983). The sexual abuse accommodation syndrome. *Child Abuse & Neglect*, 7, 177–193.

Taussig, M. (1993). *Mimesis and alterity: A particular history of the senses.* Routledge.

White, A. (2001). I am because we are: Combined race and gender political consciousness among African American women and men anti-rape activists. *Women's Studies International Forum*, 24(1), 11–24.

Wilson, J. (2017). 'Spaces to speak' of sour milk: Exploring African-Caribbean women's activism and agency on child sexual abuse from the 1980's to the present. *Doctoral Thesis*.

Wilson, M. (1993). *Crossing the boundary: Black women survive incest.* Virago Press.

5

'Preserving What for Whom?' Female Victim/Survivor Perspectives on the Silence Behind Child Sexual Abuse in Britain's South Asian Communities

Vanisha Jassal

Introduction

Child sexual abuse (CSA) often has lifelong implications for victims/survivors, resulting in serious psychological and physical problems (Crisma et al. 2004; Office of the Children's Commissioner 2014; McElvaney 2016; Nelson 2016; MacIntosh and Ménard 2021; Manay et al. 2022). Many victims/survivors do not disclose, either as children or as adults, due to feelings of shame, guilt, fear and confusion (Martin et al. 2014; Dubowitz 2017; Kelly and Karsna 2018). Consequently, disclosures and reporting of CSA in Britain is discussed as being far lower than official statistics suggest (Children's Commissioner for England 2015; McNeish and Scott 2018). Reporting of CSA has been documented as being particularly low from Britain's South Asian communities, with

---

V. Jassal (✉)
School of Social Policy, Sociology and Social Research (SSPSSR),
University of Kent, Kent, UK
e-mail: v.jassal@kent.ac.uk

official and academic research centring around cultural barriers, predominantly *shame* and *honour*, which are likely to be hindering disclosures and reporting (Cowburn et al. 2015; Gilligan and Akhtar 2006; Gohir 2013; House of Commons Home Affairs Committee Report 2013; Martin et al. 2014; Office of the Children's Commissioner 2014, 2015; Fox 2016; Gill and Harrison 2019; IICSA 2020). Although existing research indicates the need to improve knowledge about the experiences of CSA amongst South Asian victims/survivors, the preliminary literature review undertaken by this study discovered that attempts to address this have been notably minimal.

This chapter shares initial findings from a study, the primary aim of which was to research in greater depth, the lived experiences of British female South Asian CSA victims/survivors and barriers to disclosing and reporting. The research sample comprised 15 women who were willing and brave enough to share their stories. Pseudonyms and other non-identifying features for the women have been employed in this chapter. The study recruited female victims/survivors due to the majority of CSA cases being perpetrated by males against females (Office of the Children's Commissioner 2014; Dubowitz 2017; Gauthier-Duchesne et al. 2021). The South Asian category in the study refers to Bangladeshi, Indian and Pakistani communities and this was deemed to be the most suitable form of homogenising the data sample for a number of reasons. Firstly, official government statistics record incidences of CSA for the three communities as a single group under the category of South Asian (Department of Education 2016, 2021) (also including Chinese and any other communities of South Asian background). Secondly, the three communities form the largest South Asian grouping in the UK with just under three million people recorded in 2020 (ONS 2020). Thirdly, the three communities have a common history due to being a part of pre-colonial India, sharing similar religious, social and cultural norms.

There has been a noticeable absence of minoritised ethnic women from Western CSA research, both as researchers and as research participants, yet experiences of CSA as shared by victims/survivors remain critical to developing practice and policy (Office of the Children's Commissioner 2014; Fox 2016), indicating that the absence of voices from any particular ethnic community requires due consideration. Attempts to address this have been made by several scholars, including Bernard (2001) and Davies (2019), exploring CSA amongst Black girls, and Gilligan and Akhtar (2006), Begum (2018) and Gill and Harrison (2019), exploring CSA in South Asian communities. Such research has highlighted the need for an intersectional approach to CSA research where in addition to gender (be it abuse against females or males), race, ethnicity and culture are also duly explored. Intersectionality was therefore chosen as the most appropriate theoretical framework for this study, a particular point of interest being whether the ethnicity of a South Asian woman, in addition to her gender, was increasing her vulnerability to CSA and impacting her experience of abuse. As intersectional approaches have begun to be used to examine ethnic and gender disproportionalities more generally in child safeguarding practice (Webb et al. 2020), this chapter further highlights the benefit of adopting this theoretical framework in seeking to understand experiences of abuse amongst minoritised ethnic communities.

A second aim of the study was to respond to a body of research which illustrates that although the UK child protection system is built upon a long-established culture of child welfare and consists of rigorous legal and policy frameworks (Children's Act 1989, 2004; Equality Act 2010; HM Government 2018; BASW 2021), practice and services for children and families from minoritised ethnic communities have also been described as inadequate and ineffective (Qureshi et al. 2000; Barn 2007; Chand 2008; Bernard and Harris 2016, 2019; Kirton 2018; Laird and Tedam 2019). A pivotal study highlighting the issue of CSA within British South Asian communities was the Gilligan and Akhtar (2006) study which suggested that CSA is under-reported in South Asian communities. The study recommended the need for professionals and support services to more carefully consider the culture of South Asian communities when responding to CSA, highlighting that framing the abuse solely within a Western paradigm was limiting and hindering accessible and effective outreach work. More recent research continues to argue the need for culturally sensitive approaches to CSA (Gill and Harrison 2019; IICSA 2020; Jassal 2020; Ali et al. 2021).

Legal and professional responsibilities in terms of CSA include identifying risks, helping children to disclose and report and providing effective support services (Children's Commissioner 2015). As shame and honour, or cultural barriers of any type, have been identified as an impediment to safeguarding children from South Asian communities (Gohir 2013; Office of the Children's Commissioner 2015; Fox 2016), this study argues that a more rigorous investigation of such barriers is warranted. Without a good enough understanding of these barriers, professionals will remain insufficiently informed and ill-equipped to safeguard effected children. This chapter, therefore, also includes implications for child protection practice and policy.

Researching British South Asian Female Victims/Survivors of CSA

Approval for the research was granted by the Research Ethics Committee at the University of Kent. Participants were recruited through purposive sampling, via third sector organisations and the author's social media channels which she had created for her research. While recruiting for a sample of victims/survivors of CSA was always expected to be a challenging aspect of the field work, it was found to be particularly slow-paced. Hesitancy of women volunteering for the research was coupled with difficulties resulting from the Covid-19 pandemic; the research method requiring face-to-face meetings with the women. Nevertheless, from August 2018 to September 2021, a sample size of 15 women participated in the research, with some conversations having to be transferred online due to continuing restrictions enforced by the pandemic. The ethnic breakdown of the 15 women was as follows: 2 Bangladeshi, 9 Indian and 4 Pakistani. The ages of participants ranged between 21 and 61, with the majority being in the 21–31 and 32–41 age bands.

The method of research was a guided conversation with each of the women, a method which reflects *'an interest in other individuals' stories because they are of worth'* (Seidman 2013, p. 9). This sense of worthiness lay at the heart of the study because of the significant absence of South Asian women's experiences of CSA. This style of interviewing was also appropriate due to the sensitivity of the topic, creating an environment which allowed the participant to feel more at ease and facilitating a conversation rather than a sense of being interviewed. It provided the women the time, space and freedom to share their experiences. At this point, I wish to thank the 15 women who participated in this study for their courage, time and enthusiasm for the research. They have made an important contribution in highlighting the need to more effectively safeguard children at risk of CSA across South Asian communities living in Britain today.

The women's accounts were analysed through the framework of *narrative analysis,* which focuses primarily on human experiences as told solely by those who have experienced them (Riessman 2008; Josselson and Hammack 2021). Its central premise is *listening* to individuals *telling* their own stories, with a focus on how they themselves are making sense of what they have experienced. How and why this sense-making is taking shape in the form it is, and in that particular period of their lives, is what is of value to narrative researchers (Hinchman and Hinchman 2001; Etherington 2000, 2011). Each guided conversation was recorded and transcribed by the author and due to the ethical framework guiding the research, no third party was involved in the transcribing nor in the analysis stage. Although this placed a considerable onus on the author as the sole researcher of what was considerably emotive content, it created an important intimacy between the author and the data, allowing her complete immersion in it from the outset. In addition, it contributed to a trusting rapport with the women which was a critical objective for the author and for the research itself, leading to the participants sharing their stories quite openly and unreservedly. Although defining researcher positionality as an 'insider' or 'outsider' can appear to simplify what is a complex and nuanced dyadic interaction between a researcher and who she is researching (Hayfield and Huxley 2015), it is helpful to use these concepts in terms of defining both the value added and the limitations of a research project. The author was an 'outsider' in that she is not a victim/survivor of CSA, although her credentials as a child protection academic is likely to have addressed this to some extent. Being a female of South Asian origin, she was an 'insider' in that she shared certain cultural experiences with the women, including being a descendant of first-generation immigrants from the Indian Sub-Continent. Cultural norms and values around family life, reputation and concerns around shame and honour, were not unfamiliar to the author and this appeared to be a key reason as to why many of the women responded to her research advert which had included the author's gender and ethnicity.

Due to the nature of CSA being a highly sensitive topic of research, this 'insider' role brought considerable advantages to the process and is likely to be a fundamental reason for the women sharing their experiences in the depth that they did. Some of the women stated that a shared culture influenced their decision to participate. They felt that the author understood the challenges they faced simply because she had raised shame and honour as relevant factors in CSA cases, and they felt relieved that they did not have to explain these to her. They were comfortable with the author and keen to share whatever they felt would help develop child protection practice for South Asian victims/survivors:

> Finally, somebody's actually doing some research into it because it's something that needs to be done.
> (Laila, aged between 21 and 31, Bangladeshi)

> Being a survivor, I want to come into this line of work and help other survivors. Come to the other side…I've been absolutely down in the dumps and now I want to come into this field and help other survivors…I want to kind of wake our community up. Open your eyes and realise this is going on.
> (Zara, aged between 32 and 41, Pakistani)

Key Findings

Shame and Honour in the Context of Family and Community Life

A specific cultural barrier in the context of South Asian CSA disclosure and reporting is *shame* and *honour* or *sharam* and *izzat* as they are known amongst the communities. Although separate constructs with multiple meanings when applied to universal settings, in the context of this study, *shame* and *honour* refer primarily to cultural norms around social behaviour. Norms which must not be broken and if they are, can result in serious consequences for the individual (Gill 2013). This expectant behaviour includes avoiding incidences deemed to be shameful (sharam) and thereby harmful to the honour (izzat) of a family or community. These constructs have been reported to be a factor in the low rates of disclosure and reporting of sexual, domestic and honour-based abuse and violence perpetrated by males against females across South Asian communities (Gill 2004; Gilligan and Akhtar 2006; Thiara and Gill 2010; Gohir 2013; Gill and Brah 2014; Cowburn et al. 2015; Aplin 2017; Harrison and Gill 2017; Idriss 2017; Mansoor 2017). This study sought to extend this body of knowledge by exploring these constructs in the context of South Asian victim/survivor experiences of CSA in Britain.

Shame is a complex and universal emotion and discussed by Scheff and Mateo (2016) as still being a largely taboo and invisible emotion in modern societies. It is widely documented that CSA victims/survivors across the spectrum of ethnicity, culture and gender experience intense shame from the abuse, creating a barrier to disclosure (Crisma et al. 2004; Lemaigre et al. 2017; McElvaney et al. 2021). However, the context of shame in this study sought to explore shame beyond this very internal and individual nature of shame. Although this remained important to the research, and indeed to the sensitivities around the researcher-participant dyad, the study sought to primarily explore how shame in South Asian communities tends to transcend the individual and locate itself into a broader arena (Gill et al. 2018).

Family and community relations are important in providing an individual's social and psychological foundation and continued sense of security (Bronfenbrenner and Morris 2006). In some communities, these relations can take on greater intensity due to a lesser focus on the *individual* and more on the *collective* (Hofstede et al. 2010). Research illustrates that individuals who are part of collective communities perceive CSA through a lens where reactions of the wider community may take prominence over the experience of the individual victim/survivor. This has been reported to be the case in Chinese, Arab and other communities defined as collective (Futa et al. 2001; Haboush and Alyan 2013; Sawrikar and Katz 2017). South Asian communities can also demonstrate this, often influenced by *shame* and *honour* or *sharam* and *izzat* (Gill 2004; Gohir 2013; Gill and Brah 2014) and this study sought to explore this specifically in the context of CSA. Examining what these constructs meant to the 15 female victims/survivors was therefore a key aim of the research project:

> I think shame could actually be the biggest thing that's stopping anyone complaining or going to the relevant authorities, and I think it's also fear from the backlash, from the community... (not wanting) dishonour or any of that, you know, because if you do this, if you did that, nobody will want to marry you, you know.
> (Priya, aged between 51 and 61, Indian)

> Sharam (shame) to me means keeping yourself private. The way you act outside, the news will go back to your parents. You've always got to keep sharam in mind. You've got to make sure nobody knows too much of your business.
> (Laila, 21–31, Bangladeshi)

These excerpts indicate that the community to which the women belong is considered to be a significant aspect of the women's existence, in terms of influencing and impacting their life. Many of the women confirmed that a fear of their family's or community's perception of their abuse was an overriding factor in their decision not to disclose. Such fears were also reported by Gilligan and Akhtar (2006) in their CSA research with South

Asian communities in Bradford. For some, this concern continues even in present times, as recounted below by one research participant:

> That's why I stay quiet now, as well, because I know there's going to be a big fight and relationships are going to break and everything. And I don't want to be the reason for that. I wish it was different though. We shouldn't have to be like that, you know, if someone's done wrong, one person's done wrong, that person should get punished, not everybody else.
>
> (Zara, aged between 32 and 41, Pakistani)

Acknowledging the injustice she feels in not disclosing, Zara continues to feel that this is the right decision for her because it avoids the severe ramifications she believes will unfold for her should the abuse be known amongst extended family members. Such preservation of family relations and protecting one's family from shame and dishonour were common themes in the women's narratives. The literature review for the study had already indicated that this was likely to be the case but it was the *meaning* the women were giving to these constructs within the loci of CSA which was the point of interest for this study: what did shame and honour mean to them at the time of the abuse and now as adult survivors? This line of inquiry led to detailed descriptions and granular insights into how shame and honour affected their experience of CSA and through this data, the study seeks to provide a more fulsome knowledge base of the influence and impact of these constructs for South Asian victim/survivors of CSA. Drawing upon this extended source of knowledge, practitioners and policymakers are likely to be better informed about the *extent* and *depth* to which these constructs are embedded into the women's consciousness and therefore, the extent to which they are likely to influence their experience of CSA.

Shame/*sharam* and Gender Inequality

Women spoke about how notions of shame/*sharam* had always been a part of their life, since childhood. Parents were reported as being overly concerned about their physical appearance as female children, such as what clothing they were wearing and *how* they were wearing it. There tended to be a preoccupation with their behaviour in everyday activities and how this could be labelled as shameful: what they said; how they said it; what they did; and what they did not do:

> [Sharam] is engrained into us since birth.
> (Laila, aged between 21 and 31, Bangladeshi)

> As soon as I... started puberty and grew breasts I had to always wrap a shawl around my chest area. Simple things like... when I would do my laundry... and then take it out, my mum would make us... put things like our bras and our underwear on the washing line and then she'd put like a sheet over it.
> (Sonam, aged between 21 and 31, Bangladeshi)

Such behavioural expectations had created a consciousness which rested upon the fragility of what was deemed right and wrong and what could or could not be spoken about. A shift in the 'wrong' direction could destabilise family life and lead to disapproval. Although expectations and norms associated with parenting are integrated across communities and countries (Nomaguchi and Milkie 2020), this study identified narratives around what *people* would think about certain behaviours and what impressions these behaviours would create about the family. Women described childhoods as being heavily weighted towards not only what parents thought about their behaviour, but also extended family members and even the local community. This mattered to their parents and was a critical factor in parents wanting to have an unproblematic family life. The women shared how CSA was a significant threat to this sought out and desired stable, family life.

Shame was also discussed in the context of gender differences, with women sharing narratives of how it was girls and women who were raised to be alert and aware of shame and its implications, rather than boys and men:

> The blame is always going to be on the woman... so sometimes it's best not to say anything as the blame will always be on you.
> (Laila, aged between 21 and 31, Bangladeshi)

Hopefully our generation is going to change and let girls know that you don't have to hold all of this on your shoulders. Its girls and boys, not just girls who hold the shame. And then if something goes wrong, it's the girls who get punished for it as well. When the man does wrong, the girl gets punished, when the girl does wrong, the girl gets punished. So, the man gets away scot-free every single time. And it's not fair.
(Zara, aged between 32 and 41, Pakistani)

The burden of honour/*izzat*

Although connected with shame or sharam, the women's narratives relating to honour or *izzat* were more serious and affirmative in tone and language:

Honour isn't just about you, it's about your entire family. The family name... family's really important in the Asian community... it's never just about you... It's always about what are people going to say... it's about how people see you.
(Laila, aged between 21 and 31, Bangladeshi)

While the constructs of shame and honour are not only experienced by South Asian females—as discussed by Begum (2018) in the context of South Asian male CSA and Mansoor (2017) in relation to the Muslim South Asian community as a whole—they have been reported to predominantly govern and impact the lives of females. Again, narratives relating to honour were often interwoven with narratives about gender differences:

Izzat (honour) is something the girl has to protect. The girl is the family's izzat. But if somebody came and... raped me... that would be the family's izzat gone. Not just my izzat. So, it's my job to protect this izzat. And if somebody takes it away from me, it's my fault, and I will have to pay for it. So, it's always on the woman. We have to hold it and it's such a heavy thing to hold for all our life... and then we have to pass it onto our daughter, right? You know, it's just... it's not fair. Where does the man come into it?

(Zara, aged between 32 and 41, Pakistani)

Zara's account explicitly conveys honour as being a construct wholly embodied by the female rather than the male, manifesting itself within her. Honour as a construct relevant to violence against women has been increasingly discussed and integrated into UK policy following a series of honour-based killings of females from minoritised communities (Siddiqui 2018). Begum et al. (2020) discuss how defining and managing female behaviour through the lens of honour/*izzat* remains a contemporary threat to females in minoritised communities. Zara also expressed her fears concerning honour killings indicating that the subject of CSA can be perceived by some members of South Asian communities, as compromising honour, which has inevitable implications for disclosing and reporting:

> I knew that it's [CSA] not something that's spoken about. I was scared to say something because of what might happen and I'd heard stories about honour killings and being sent to your country to get married and you know, all those things. They really put me off [from disclosing].
> (Zara, aged between 32 and 41, Pakistani)

Although discussed substantively in relation to male perpetrated abuse and violence against South Asian women (Thiara and Gill 2010; Gill and Brah 2014), an exploration of the construct of honour in the context of CSA in Britain's South Asian communities had not been undertaken in a substantial way—hence the evolution of this study.

Preserving What for Whom?

A consequence of how the women felt about shame and honour in their lives and their subsequent silence about the abuse was that many of them were living in a vacuum of secrecy and isolation. However, they themselves felt little if any affiliation with the constructs, expressing disdain, disappointment and disgust at how debilitating the constructs can be for South Asian women experiencing abuse:

I think it [shame] is a very destructive notion, and I think it's a very silencing tool and it can manifest in such a way that creates masses of mental health issues and deprives a community of its wellbeing.

(Yasmin, aged between 32 and 41, Pakistani)

The excerpt below provides an example of the human cost of preserving shame and honour:

You know, he's (perpetrator) followed me all my life. Every time I move houses, he moves houses, to a couple of streets away from me. Even now he lives a couple of streets away from me. And that's one thing, I know, he's promised me. No matter where I go in the world, he's going to follow me. And I've learned to deal with that.

(Zara, aged between 32 and 41, Pakistani)

As the women had a genuine disconnect with the constructs and shared the damaging effect of them on their lives, the author was curious as to why the constructs still appeared to resonate in their lives—for some more than others. *What were they continuing to preserve and for whom?* The author wishes to emphasise that she does not judge the women who have not disclosed or reported their abuse. Through getting to know them, before, during and after the research, she has immense respect and admiration for them and understands through their narratives, why they remain silent and preserve family harmony. Rather, the author wants to direct the question of *preserving what for whom*, to future efforts and enquiries into CSA amongst South Asian communities, believing that further exploring this preservation of honour is fundamental to unlocking change and reaching a position whereby victims/survivors of CSA do not feel that they need to *preserve anything for anyone.*

The answer to this question provides a critical point of learning for child protection practice and policy and highlights the need to persist in efforts to discover more about cultural barriers to disclosure. The result will be a wider knowledge base from which practitioners and policy-makers can work: providing more insights into why disclosure may not take place; explaining why referrals to statutory services are lower than expected; and guiding professionals and services to improve their engagement with South Asian children and families so that their access to and experience of relevant services is improved.

Women's Lived Experiences of Shame and Honour

This study has provided important and unique insights into how British South Asian victims/survivors of CSA made sense of what they had experienced. Through the narrative approach of 'storying' (Clark et al. 2021), their very personal experiences have been given a voice and many have shared how this has been a therapeutic process in their journey of recovery, but also enabled them to reflect on their experiences in a different way. Reassuringly for the author, some feeling less guilty and having less self-blame than before. Several of the women spoke about how this had been the first time that they had really thought about the constructs of shame and honour in such depth and the influence that the constructs had had upon their experience of CSA. This illustrates the value of narrative research in exploring the human lived experience (Andrews et al. 2013):

> It's definitely made me think about things with a different perspective, because obviously it's weird… I mean sharam (shame) definitely and izzat (honour)… plays a huge part in my life. It's constantly there. It's like that shadow that will never leave you kind of thing, but I've never really broken it down the way I've done today, so I found it quite helpful.
> (Sonam, aged between 21 and 31, Bangladeshi)

Female CSA victims/survivors from South Asian communities appear to not only internalise their individual feelings of shame, but also find themselves having to digest wider implications of this shame—considering the consequences for extended family and community members. Although disclosures of CSA by children remain rare (Alaggia 2004; Solberg et al. 2021), it appears noteworthy that from a sample of 15, only one of the women disclosed her abuse to her non-abusing caregiver as a child. There was a shared sense amongst the women that they did not feel that a disclosure would lead to a supportive response from families due to concerns about shame and honour. There was also a consensus that a disclosure would jeopardise family honour and threaten the stability of family life.

Responses from non-abusing family members to CSA disclosures can vary (Crisma et al. 2004; Tener et al. 2018), and therefore a lack of support from families is not singly a point of significance. However, its relevance is heightened in terms of *why* they felt that support would be lacking, which was centred around concerns about shame and honour. This again indicates that by being both a female and South Asian presents an added layer of complexity for victims/survivors and reaffirms the relevance of an intersectional perspective to expose what is possibly a dual vulnerability.

Another concerning factor within the nexus of shame, honour and being female is the advantage that these factors provide to South Asian male perpetrators of CSA. Aware of the entrenched efforts to preserve family honour through female behaviour, they feel assured that the victim/survivor will not disclose the abuse:

> He (perpetrator) had a very good grasp of that (shame and honour) and he used that as a weapon against me. Yeah, yeah, it definitely protected him… because he knew that this stuff (CSA) wasn't discussed in our communities. He knew what it meant to be a girl being raised in a Punjabi family, he knew.
> (Parminder, aged between 32 and 41, Indian)

> If it does come out, the parents just push it under the carpet and kind of not let anyone find out… people can look at them (the girls) in a bad way. The perpetrator always gets away.
> (Laila, aged between 21 and 31, Bangladeshi)

Perpetrators can therefore be emboldened by the constructs of shame and honour. This can facilitate abuse and allow it to continue. Examining the narratives around this was beyond the scope of this chapter but is continuing to be explored by the author due to having significant implications for child protection practice and keeping children safe. Furthermore, although additional research would be required to explore the influence of shame and honour across generations, many of the women shared narratives suggesting that the constructs remain prevalent in British South Asian family life today. Such areas of concern underline the need to continue exploring the lived experiences of South Asian victims/survivors of CSA with the intent to better guide and design child protection practice and policy.

Statutory Safeguarding Responsibilities

The protection of children at risk in Britain is governed by national and international law (Children's Acts 1989, 2004; United Nations n.d.) and policy guidance such as *Working Together to Safeguard Children* (HM Government 2018) and *Keeping Children Safe in Education* (Department for Education 2022) which guide child protection practice in England (Scotland and Wales having their own equivalents). These legal and policy frameworks have been established around principles seeking to safeguard all vulnerable children, regardless of race and ethnicity.

Although legal frameworks can never ensure the safety and protection of all children, several high-profile child deaths involving children from minoritised communities (Chand 2008; Bhatti-Sinclair and Price, 2016; Bernard and Harris 2019) and discussions concerning perennial inequalities in safeguarding practice, centred around race and ethnicity (Webb et al. 2002; Harrison and Turner 2011; Bernard and Harris 2016, 2019; Bywaters et al. 2017; Laird and Tedam 2019), does call into question how effective child protection practice and policy is in meeting the needs of minoritised children.

The argument for improved cultural competency amongst practitioners; the over-representation of Black children in the child protection and care system (Welbourne 2002; Barn 2007; Owen and Statham 2009; Tilbury and Thoburn 2009; Webb et al. 2020); and the under-representation of children from South Asian communities (Ahmed 2005; Tilbury and Thoburn 2009; Webb et al. 2020) are topics that have been documented for many years.

In similar discussions, the inaccessibility and ineffectiveness of preventative and support services have also been critiqued (Qureshi et al. 2000; Ahmed 2005), often highlighting the need for practitioners and services to be more sensitive to the needs of minoritised children and families (Bernard 2001; Welbourne 2002; Tilbury and Thoburn 2009; Chand 2008; Laird and Tedam 2019). Inadequacies in provision include limited access to interpreting services and the need for greater consideration of language barriers (Qureshi et al. 2000; Chand 2005; Gilligan and Akhtar 2006; Bernard and Harris 2019). Service users have been reported as feeling 'demeaned and degraded' (Ahmed 2005, p. 93) or misunderstood and misinterprete d (Featherstone and Fraser 2012). With regards to CSA services specifically, whilst exploring the uptake of CSA services amongst the South Asian communities in Bradford, Gilligan and Akhtar (2006) found that many women were unaware that such services even existed. Allnock et al. (2012) found that CSA services appeared to be less available/accessible to minoritised ethnic children, and the Office of the Children's Commissioner (2015) reported that children from minoritised ethnic communities are known to receive a poorer quality of service than their peers. In recent times, the UK Independent Inquiry into Child Sexual Abuse (IICSA) researched barriers to accessing services and identified a number of themes, including shame and honour, which must be addressed to ensure more effective and equitable service provision for minoritised children experiencing CSA (IICSA 2021). In short, the needs of minoritised ethnic children remains a point of concern for child protection practice and policy in Britain. This chapter argues that efforts to address such inequities must be addressed with increased fervour and urgency.

A key means of addressing shortfalls in practice is to effectively research the lived experiences of victims/survivors of CSA. If we are not sufficiently informed enough of all children's experiences of child sexual abuse, we are limited in how we can identify risk and provide relevant support. This study makes a contribution to this extension of knowledge, illustrating that responding to CSA requires greater consideration of a victim/survivor's race, ethnicity and culture (in addition to gender). This provides a fuller insight into her experience of abuse, and provides important knowledge for those tasked with protecting children.

Employing such an intersectional framework to their analysis of child protection decision-making in England, Germany and the Netherlands, Middel et al. (2020) also explore the need to understand the lives of children at risk in the context of multiple familial factors. They discuss how a more holistic approach provides a more effective framework for safeguarding vulnerable children.

Conclusions

This chapter has shared initial findings from a research study which is exploring the lived experiences of British South Asian female victims/survivors of CSA. Early data is substantiating existing research concerning the significance of shame and honour on South Asian women's experiences of male-perpetrated abuse. It extends this learning to encompass CSA and discusses how these constructs can be just as pervasive and oppressive in incidences of CSA as they have been in other forms of male-perpetrated abuse of South Asian women. Through probing further into the constructs, this study enables practice and policy to move beyond what has been quite a fixed child protection practice and policy narrative of *cultural barriers*. Through the narratives of the women, *what* they are preserving and for *whom* becomes clear. The *what*—shame and honour—envelops a complex set of feelings and expectations and potentially lifelong implications. The perceived risk of thrusting family members—the *whom*—into situations of shame and dishonour appears too great, inhibiting disclosures and reporting.

By applying an intersectional lens, the study exposes what can be deemed to be a *dual vulnerability* for South Asian women; by being female and vulnerable to male-perpetrated sexual abuse, and by being South Asian and impacted by constructs of shame and honour. This study encourages those responsible for safeguarding children to become more cognisant of this amplified position of vulnerability.

The challenge of recruiting South Asian victims/survivors has also been highlighted by this study, emphasising a need to persist in engaging research participants from South Asian communities, and to think more attentively and creatively about how such recruitment can take shape. Only through hearing more from this group of women can their experiences be more fully documented. For instance, as the current study progresses, additional narratives are emerging which relate to experiences beyond shame and honour. It is therefore important to understand that although shame and honour are significant constructs in the experiences of South Asian women, they are not the only factors which ought to be considered and pigeon-holing experiences within this framework must be avoided.

Those working in the field of CSA remain concerned and inquisitive about the lower-than-expected rates of CSA disclosures and reporting, and this must also remain an active line of enquiry when supporting children from South Asian communities. This chapter calls for a greater onus to be placed upon practitioners, services and policy-makers, to better understand the extent to which shame and honour is embedded within South Asian communities and to more rigorously investigate cultural barriers. Table 5.1 outlines key messages and implications for policy, practice and research. Only through a process of continuous exploration, examination and review of this issue will necessary adaptations to child protection practice and policy be made and children facing such barriers be more effectively protected from risk.

Table 5.1 Key messages and implications for policy, practice and research

Referral rates for CSA amongst Britain's South Asian communities are reported as being lower than expected due to cultural barriers	• Practitioners are recommended to remain professionally curious about low referral rates from South Asian communities, and through studying peer reviewed research/government reports in which experiences of victims/survivors from South Asian communities are shared, are encouraged to strengthen their understanding of this • Practitioners are advised to remain invested in effective culturally competent practice, enabling them to acquire and develop relevant practice skills • Children's services—from universal, to child in need, to child protection—are advised to strengthen systems through which ethnicity data of children and families is collated. Consistency in data collection across services is critical for developing knowledge about the needs of minoritised communities • This data should be reviewed regularly and compared to local ethnicity data. This will help identify ethnic disproportionalities which may indicate that the needs of a particular community are not being effectively met • Should disproportionalities exist, actions within services should be taken to address this
Without a more concerted effort to address CSA in South Asian communities, children and young people are likely to remain at risk	• Practitioners and organisations are mandated to safeguard all children and should be able to demonstrate that they are undertaking this responsibility to the best of their ability • Intersectional perspectives, encompassing racial, ethnic and cultural factors and related barriers, facilitate the development of more effective practice when investigating CSA. Assessment models and interventions across child protection services are encouraged to develop and integrate intersectional approaches

A proactive and innovative approach is required to address cultural barriers such as shame and honour

- Policy, practice and research must move beyond foundational and peripheral discussions about cultural barriers, and about shame and honour, and develop concrete plans of action
- Pre- and post-qualifying programmes should include teaching and learning about lived experiences of child abuse (including CSA) across all minoritised ethnic communities in Britain
- Agencies are encouraged to embed into their organisations the issue of increased vulnerabilities to abuse amongst some groups of children (because of ethnicity, disability, sexual orientation) and develop means of designing action and services to address this
- This can be through simple and resourceful means such as watching relevant training videos, reading and discussing specific case studies each week at team meetings, engaging in more interactive training mediums and inviting expert speakers or organisations to raise awareness about the issues (see Jassal 2020).
- There is a steady increase in research into CSA experiences of minoritised children which should be made accessible to practitioners and child protection agencies

Research into CSA amongst Britain's minoritised communities is critical in strengthening child protection practice and policy and helping keep children safe

References

Ahmed, S. (2005). What is the evidence of early intervention, preventative services for Black and Minority Ethnic group children and their families? *Practice*, *17*(2), 89–102. https://doi.org/10.1080/09503150500148107.

Alaggia, R. (2004). Many ways of telling: Expanding conceptualizations of child sexual abuse disclosure. *Child Abuse & Neglect*, *28*, 1213–1227.

Ali, N., Butt, J. and Phillips, M. (2021). *Improving responses to the sexual abuse of Black, Asian and minority ethnic children*. CSA Centre. Available via https://www.csacentre.org.uk/documents/improving-responses-csa-of-black-asian-minority-ethnic-children/. Accessed 14 July 2021.

Allnock, D., Radford, L., Bunting, L., Price, A., Morgan-Klein, N., Ellis, J. and Stafford, A. (2012). In demand: Therapeutic services for children and young people who have experienced sexual abuse. *Child Abuse Review*, *21*, 318–334.

Andrews, M., Squire, C. and Tamboukou, M. (2013). *Doing narrative research*. London: Sage.

Aplin, R. (2017). Exploring the role of mothers in 'honour' based abuse perpetration and the impact on the policing response. *Women's Studies International Forum*, *60*, 1–10.

Barn, R. (2007). 'Race', ethnicity and child welfare: a fine balancing act. *British Journal of Social Work*, *37*, 1425–1434. https://doi.org/10.1093/bjsw/bcm145.

BASW (2021). *The BASW Code of Ethics for Social Work*. Available via https://www.basw.co.uk/about-basw/code-ethics. Accessed 21 October 2021.

Begum, H. (2018). *An exploration of how British South Asian male survivors of childhood sexual abuse make sense of their experiences*. PhD thesis. De Montfort University. Available via https://dora.dmu.ac.uk/handle/2086/18315. Accessed 13 December 22.

Begum R., Khan R., Brewer G., and Hall, B. (2020). "They will keep seeing young women murdered by men. Enough is enough-we have seen too many women lose their lives". Lessons for professionals working with victims of 'honour' abuse and violence. *Genealogy*, *4*(3), 69. https://doi.org/10.3390/genealogy4030069

Bernard, C. (2001). *Constructing lived experiences: Representations of Black mothers in child sexual abuse discourses*. Abingdon: Routledge.

Bernard, C. and Harris, P. (2016). *Safeguarding Black children: Good practice in child protection*. London: Jessica Kingsley Publishers.

Bernard, C., and Harris, P. (2019). Serious case reviews: The lived experience of Black children. *Child & Family Social Work*, *24*(2), 256–263. https://doi.org/10.1111/cfs.12610.

Bhatti-Sinclair, K., and Price, D. (2016). Evaluation: Serious case reviews and anti-racist practice. In C. Williams and M. J. Graham (Eds.), *Social work in a diverse society: Transformative practice with Black and minority ethnic individuals and communities* (pp. 217–228). Bristol: Policy Press.

Bronfenbrenner, U. and Morris, P. A. (2006). *The bioecological model of human development. Handbook of child psychology: Theoretical models of human development*, 793–828.

Bywaters, P., Kwhali, J., Brady, G., Sparks, T. Bos, E. (2017). Out of sight, out of mind: ethnic inequalities in child protection and out of-home care intervention rates. *British Journal of Social Work*, *47*, 1884–1902.

Chand, A. (2005). Do you speak English? Language barriers in child protection social work with Minority Ethnic families. *British Journal of Social Work*, *10*, 169–178.

Chand, A. (2008). Every Child Matters? A critical review of child welfare reforms in the context of minority ethnic children and families. *Child Abuse Review*, *17*(1), 6–22.

Children's Act 1989. https://www.legislation.gov.uk/ukpga/1989/41/contents. Accessed 3 August 2021.

Children's Act 2004. https://www.legislation.gov.uk/ukpga/2004/31/contents. Accessed 3 August 2021.

Clark, T., Foster, L., Sloan, L., and Bryman, A. (2021). *Bryman's Social Research Methods* (Eds). Oxford University Press.

Cowburn, M., Gill, A. K. and Harrison, K. (2015). Speaking about sexual abuse in British South Asian communities: offenders, victims and the challenges of shame and reintegration. *Journal of Sexual Aggression: An International, Inter-Disciplinary Forum for Research, Theory and Practice*, *21*(1), 4–15. https://doi.org/10.1080/13552600.2014.929188.

Crisma, M., Bascellia, E., Paci, D. and Romito, P. (2004). Adolescents who experienced sexual abuse: fears, needs and impediments to disclosure. *Child Abuse & Neglect*, *28*, 1035–1048. https://doi.org/10.1016/j.chiabu.2004.03.015

Davies, J. (2019). 'Where are the Black girls in our CSA services, studies and statistics?'. https://www.communitycare.co.uk/2019/11/20/where-are-the-black-girls-in-our-services-studies-and-statistics-on-csa/. Accessed 6 January 2022.

Department for Education (2016–21). *Statistics: Children in Need and Child protection.* https://www.gov.uk/government/statistics/characteristics-of-children-in-need-2014-to-2015;2016-to-2017;2018-to-2019. Accessed 22 April 2021.

Department for Education (2022). *Keeping Children Safe in Education.* Available via https://assets.publishing.service.gov.uk/government/uploads/system/uploads/attachment_data/file/1101454/Keeping_children_safe_in_education_2022.pdf. Accessed 1 February 2022.

Dubowitz, H. (2017). Child sexual abuse and exploitation—A global glimpse. *Child Abuse & Neglect, 66,* 2–8.

Equality Act (2010). Available via https://www.legislation.gov.uk/ukpga/2010/15/contents. Accessed 4 January 2002.

Etherington, K. (2000). *Narrative approaches to working with adult male survivors of child sexual abuse. The clients', the counsellor's and the researcher's story.* London: Jessica Kingsley Publishers.

Etherington, K. (2011). Narrative Case Study Research: On endings and six session reviews. *Counselling and Psychotherapy Research, 11*(1): 11–22.

Featherstone B., Fraser, C. (2012). 'I'm just a mother. I'm nothing special, they're all professionals': Parental advocacy as an aid to parental engagement. *Child & Family Social Work, 17*(2), 244–253.

Fox, C. (2016). 'It's not on the radar'. The hidden diversity of children and young people at risk of sexual exploitation in England. Barnardos. Available via https://www.basw.co.uk/system/files/resources/it_s_not_on_the_radar_report_0.pdf. Accessed 14 January 2022.

Futa, K. T., Hsu E. and Hansen, D. J. (2001). Child sexual abuse in Asian American families: An examination of cultural factors that influence prevalence, identification, and treatment. *Clinical Psychology: Science and Practice, 8*(2), 189–209.

Gauthier-Duchesne, A., Hébert M. and Blais, M. (2021). Child sexual abuse, self-esteem, and delinquent behaviours during adolescence: The moderating role of gender. *Journal of Interpersonal Violence.* https://doi.org/10.1177/08862605211001466

Gill, A. K. (2004). Voicing the silent fear: South Asian women's experiences of domestic violence. *The Howard Journal, 43*(5), 465–483.

Gill, A. K. (2013). Feminist Reflections on Researching So-called 'Honour' Killings. *Feminist Legal Studies, 21,* 241–261. https://doi.org/10.1007/s10691-013-9249-6

Gill, A. K. and Brah, A. (2014). Interrogating cultural narratives about 'honour'—Based violence. *European Journal of Women's Studies, 21*(1), 72–86.

Gill, A.K., Cox, P., and Weir, R. (2018). Shaping Priority Services for UK victims of honour-based violence/abuse, forced marriage, and female genital mutilation. *The Howard Journal of Crime and Justice, 57*(4), 576–595. https://doi.org/10.1111/hojo.12287.

Gill, A.K. and Harrison, K. (2019). 'I am talking about it because I want to stop it': Child sexual abuse and sexual violence against women in British South Asian Communities. *The British Journal of Criminology, 59*(3), 511–529. https://doi.org/10.1093/bjc/azy059.

Gilligan, P. and Akhtar, S. (2006). Cultural barriers to the disclosure of child sexual abuse in Asian communities: Listening to what women say. *British Journal of Social Work, 36*, 1361–1377.

Gohir, S. (2013). *Unheard voices: the sexual exploitation of Asian girls and young women.* Muslim Women's Network UK. Available via https://www.mwnuk.co.uk/go_files/resources/UnheardVoices.pdf. Accessed 9 January 2022.

Haboush, K.L. and Alyan, H. (2013). Who can you tell? Features of Arab Culture that influence conceptualization and treatment of childhood sexual abuse. *Journal of Child Sexual Abuse, 22*(5), 499–518.

Harrison, G. and Turner, R. (2011). Being a 'culturally competent' social worker. Making sense of a murky concept in practice. *British Journal of Social Work, 41*, 333–350.

Harrison, K. and Gill, A. K. (2017). Breaking down barriers: recommendations for improving sexual abuse reporting rates in British South Asian Communities. *The British Journal of Criminology, 58*(2), 273–290.

Hayfield, N. and Huxley, C. (2015). Insider and outsider perspectives: Reflections on researcher identities in research with lesbian and bisexual women. *Qualitative Research in Psychology, 12*(2). https://doi.org/10.1080/14780887.2014.918224.

Hinchman, L. P. and Hinchman, S. K. (2001). *Memory, identity, community. The idea of narrative in the human sciences.* Albany: State University of New York Press.

HM Government. (2018). *Working together to safeguard children. A guide to inter-agency working to safeguard and promote the welfare of children.* Available via https://assets.publishing.service.gov.uk/government/uploads/system/uploads/attachment_data/file/942454/Working_together_to_safeguard_children_inter_agency_guidance.pdf. Accessed 8 February 2022.

Hofstede, G., Hofstede, G. J. and Minkov, M. (2010). *Cultures and organizations: Software of the mind—Intercultural cooperation and its importance for survival.* London: McGraw-Hill.

House of Commons Home Affairs Committee. (2013). *Child sexual exploitation and the response to localised grooming.* Available via https://publications.parliament.uk/pa/cm201314/cmselect/cmhaff/68/68i.pdf. Accessed 9 October 2021.

Idriss, M. M. (2017). Not domestic violence or cultural tradition: Is honour-based violence distinct from domestic violence? *Journal of Social Welfare and Family Law, 39*(1), 3–21.

IICSA. (2020). *"People don't talk about it": Child sexual abuse in ethnic minority communities.* Available at https://www.iicsa.org.uk/document/%E2%80%9Cpeople-dont-talk-about-it%E2%80%9D-child-sexual-abuse-ethnic-minority-communities. Accessed 14 December 22.

IICSA. (2021). *Engagement with support services for ethnic minority communities.* Available at https://www.iicsa.org.uk/key-documents/26008/view/engagement-report-ethnic-minority-communities-29-april-2021.pdf. Accessed 13 January 22.

Jassal, V. (2020). *Sexual abuse of South Asian children: What social workers need to know.* Available via https://www.communitycare.co.uk/2020/08/20/sexual-abuse-south-asian-children-social-workers-need-know/. Accessed 5 January 2022.

Josselson, R. and Hammack, P.L. (2021). *Essentials of Narrative Analysis.* American Psychological Association.

Kelly, L. and Karsna, K. (2018). *Measuring the scale and changing nature of child sexual abuse and child sexual exploitation: scoping report.* Barkingside: Centre of Expertise on Child Sexual Abuse. Available via https://www.csacentre.org.uk/documents/scale-and-nature-scoping-report-2018/. Accessed 13 January 2022.

Kirton, D. (2018). Neoliberalism, 'race' and child welfare. *Critical and Radical Social Work, 6*(3), 311–327.

Laird, S. and Tedam, P. (2019). *Cultural diversity in child protection: Cultural competence in practice.* London: Red Globe Press.

Lemaigre, C., Taylor, E. P. and Gittoes, C. (2017). Barriers and facilitators to disclosing sexual abuse in childhood and adolescence: A systematic review. *Child Abuse & Neglect, 70*, 39–52.

MacIntosh, H. B. and Ménard, A. D. (2021). Where are we now? A consolidation of the research on long-term impact of child sexual abuse. *Journal*

of *Child Sexual Abuse*, *30*(3), 253–257. https://doi.org/10.1080/10538712.
2021.1914261.
Manay, N., Collin-Vézina, D., Alaggia, R., and McElvaney, R. (2022). It's complicated because we're only sixteen: A framework for understanding child sexual abuse disclosures to peers. *Journal of Interpersonal Violence*, *37*(3–4). https://journals.sagepub.com/doi/10.1177/0886260520933052
Mansoor, N. (2017). *Exploring honour and shame for South Asian British Muslim men and women*. PhD thesis. University of Manchester. Available via https://www.proquest.com/openview/5d819b4811471b5a2c0353c7 4ea22eff/1?pq-origsite=gscholar&cbl=51922&diss=y. Accessed 5 November 22.
Martin, L., Brady, G., Kwhali, J., Brown, S. J., Crowe, S. and Matouskova, G. (2014). *Social workers' knowledge and confidence when working with cases of child sexual abuse. What are the issues and challenges?* NSPCC. Available via https://www.basw.co.uk/system/files/resources/basw_113949-6_0.pdf. Accessed 15 December 2021.
McElvaney, R. (2016). *Helping children to tell about sexual abuse. Guidance for helpers*. London: Jessica Kingsley Publishers.
McElvaney, R. Lateef, R., Collin-Vézina, D., Alaggia, R. and Simpson, M. (2021). Bringing shame out of the shadows: Identifying shame in child sexual abuse disclosure processes and implications for psychotherapy. *Journal of Interpersonal Violence*, 1–23. https://doi.org/10.1177/088626052 11037435.
McNeish, D. and Scott, S. (2018). *Key messages from research on intra-familial child sexual abuse*. Centre of Expertise on Child Sexual Abuse. Available via https://www.csacentre.org.uk/resources/key-messages/intra-familial-csa/. Accessed 9 October 2021.
Middel, F., López, M. L., Fluke, J., and Grietens, H. (2020). The effects of migrant background and parent gender on child protection decision-making: An intersectional analysis. *Child Abuse & Neglect*, 104. https://doi.org/10.1016/j.chiabu.2020.104479.
Nelson, S. (2016). *Tackling child sexual abuse: Radical approaches to prevention, protection and Support*. Bristol: Policy Press.
Nomaguchi, K. and Milkie, M. A. (2020). Parenting and well-being: a decade in review. *Journal of Marriage and Family*, *82*(1), 198–223.
Office of the Children's Commissioner. (2014). *"It's a lonely journey": a rapid evidence assessment on intrafamilial child sexual abuse*. Available via https://www.childrenscommissioner.gov.uk/wp-content/uploads/2017/07/Its-a-lonely-journey-REA-on-Intrafamilial-child-sexual-abuse.pdf. Accessed 10 September 2021.

Office of the Children's Commissioner. (2015). *Protecting children from harm: a critical assessment of child sexual abuse in the family network in England and priorities for action.* Available via https://dera.ioe.ac.uk/25409/3/Protecting%20children%20from%20harm%20-%20executive%20summary_0.pdf. Accessed 16 October 2021.

ONS (2020). *Population of England and Wales.* Available via https://www.ethnicity-facts-figures.service.gov.uk/uk-population-by-ethnicity/national-and-regional-populations/population-of-england-and-wales/latest#by-ethnicity Accessed 8 Sept 2021.

Owen, C. and Statham, J. (2009). *Disproportionality in child welfare: the prevalence of Black and minority ethnic children within the 'Looked After' and 'Children in Need' populations and on Child Protection Registers in England.* Research Report DCSF-RR12. Available via https://bit.ly/34pmINt. Accessed 23 November 2021.

Qureshi, T., Berridge, D. and Wenman, H. (2000). *Where to turn? Family support for South Asian communities: A case study.* National Children's Bureau. Available via https://www.jrf.org.uk/report/where-turn-family-support-south-asian-communities. Accessed 23 January 2022.

Riessman, C. K. (2008). *Narrative methods for the human sciences.* Albany: SUNY Press.

Sawrikar, P. and Katz, I. (2017). Barriers to disclosing child sexual abuse (CSA) in ethnic minority communities: A review of the literature and implications for practice in Australia. *Children and Youth Services Review, 83,* 302–315.

Scheff, T. J. and Mateo, S. (2016). The S-Word is Taboo: Shame is Invisible in Modern Societies. *Journal of General Practice, 4*(1). https://doi.org/10.4172/2329-9126.1000217.

Seidman, I. (2013). Interviewing as qualitative research: a guide for researchers. In D. Silverman (Ed.), *Interpreting qualitative data.* London: Sage.

Siddiqui, H. (2018). Counting the cost: BME women and gender-based violence in the UK. *Progressive Review, 24*(4), 361–368. https://doi.org/10.1111/newe.12076

Solberg, E., Tvedt, H., Jorunn, E. and Stige, S. H. (2021). What do survivors of child sexual abuse believe will facilitate early disclosure of sexual abuse? *Frontiers in Psychiatry,* 12. https://doi.org/10.3389/fpsyt.2021.639341

Tener, D., Lusky, E., Tarshish, N. and Turjeman, S. (2018). Parental attitudes following disclosure of sibling sexual abuse: a child advocacy centre intervention study. *American Journal of Orthopsychiatry,* 88, 661–669. https://doi.org/10.1037/ort0000311.

Thiara, R. and Gill, A.K. (2010). Understanding violence against South Asian women: What it means for practice. In Thiara, R. and Gill, A. K. (Eds.), *Violence Against Women in South Asian Communities: Issues for Policy and Practice* (pp. 29–54). London: Jessica Kingsley.

Tilbury, C. and Thoburn, J. (2009). Using racial disproportionality and disparity indicators to measure child welfare outcomes. *Children and Youth Services Review, 31*(10), 1101–1106.

United Nations (n.d.). *Convention on the Rights of the Child.* Available via https://www.ohchr.org/EN/ProfessionalInterest/Pages/CRC.aspx. Accessed 2 February 2022.

Webb, E., Maddocks, A. and Bongilli, J. (2002). Effectively protecting Black and minority ethnic children from harm: Overcoming barriers to the child protection process. *Child Abuse Review, 11*, 394–410.

Webb, C., Bywaters, P., Scourfield, J., Davidson, G. and Bunting, L. (2020). Cuts both ways: Ethnicity, poverty, and the social gradient in child welfare interventions. *Children and Youth Services Review*, 117. https://doi.org/10.1016/j.childyouth.2020.

Welbourne, P. (2002). Culture, children's rights and child protection. *Child Abuse Review*, 11, 345–358.

6

Survivors Speak Up: Improving Police Responses to Sexual Abuse Cases in Black and Racially Minoritised Communities

Aisha K. Gill and Yasmin Khan

Introduction

This chapter first outlines the super-complaint filed by the Halo Project—the charitable arm of the Tees Valley Inclusion Project—regarding police handling of sexual abuse cases in which both the victim and perpetrator were from Black and racially minoritised communities. Next, it provides some background information on the Halo Project and the work it does with both sexual abuse survivors/victims and Cleveland Police. The chapter cites current figures for reported sexual abuse

---

A. K. Gill (✉)
Faculty of Social Sciences and Law, School of Policy Studies, University of Bristol, Bristol, UK
e-mail: ak.gill@bristol.ac.uk

Y. Khan
Middlesbrough, UK
e-mail: yk@haloproject.org.uk

© The Author(s), under exclusive license to Springer Nature Switzerland AG 2022
A. K. Gill and H. Begum (eds.), *Child Sexual Abuse in Black and Minoritised Communities*, https://doi.org/10.1007/978-3-031-06337-4_6

cases in England and Wales and presents some of the reasons why abuse victims often fail to report their experiences. It then details the Halo Project's key findings on police responses to victims/survivors who do report, the effects these responses have on survivors/victims of sexual abuse and the damage they cause at both personal and structural/social levels. Drawing on two case studies of familial abuse, the chapter examines each failing and weakness in police practice. It concludes by offering concrete suggestions for how to address these failings, such as offering appropriate police officer training and monitoring translators and interpreters. It also stresses the importance of establishing a national Black and racially minoritised sexual violence reference group that can influence national police guidance and training and scrutinise the responses to these cases.

Background: The Halo Project

The Halo Project, which was founded in 2011, is a national charity that supports victims/survivors of honour-based violence, forced marriages and female genital mutilation. It aims to protect victims/survivors from indefensible human rights abuses that can, in extreme cases, take the form of abduction, serial rape and murder. It also seeks to educate the community about these forms of abuse. By working closely with Cleveland Police, the Halo Project creates and maintains links with relevant agencies and organisations in order to provide emergency and non-emergency services to victims/survivors. From April 2018 to March 2021, the Halo Project dealt with 152 forced marriage cases, 53 female genital mutilation cases (49 international and four UK-based) and 450 honour-based violence/abuse cases. It should be noted that these are only the recorded cases; it is likely that many more were never reported.

In August 2020, the Halo Project filed a super-complaint to Her Majesty's Inspectorate of Constabulary and Fire & Rescue Services regarding systemic failings in police handling of sexual abuse cases in England and Wales—specifically, in cases where the victim and perpetrator were both from Black and racially minoritised communities. However, although the College of Policing (CoP) and the Independent

Office for Police Conduct assessed the super-complaint as eligible for investigation, they have not yet provided any timelines indicating when the investigation will be completed. The Halo super-complaint details nine key failures in police responses to reports of sexual abuse within Black and racially minoritised communities. The charity claims that individually and cumulatively, these failures demonstrate the ineffectiveness of police investigations of sexual abuse cases in these communities and materially dent community confidence in the police's commitment to properly investigating these serious allegations. The super-complaint highlights barriers created by the police that hamper sexual abuse investigations in these communities. These include, but are not limited to, the following:

- an 'overuse of voluntary suspect interviews', where alleged perpetrators can attend police interviews at their own convenience
- the 'failure to consider honour-based abuse' when complainants face family reprisals in response to the abuse.
- a 'disproportionate focus on community impact'.

In particular, the Halo Project identified police failure to consider honour-based violence a key impediment to justice for Black and racially minoritised victims.

Sexual Abuse Prevalence and Reporting

The Crime Survey for England and Wales (CSEW) for the year ending March 2020 estimates that 773,000 adults aged 16 to 74 years were victims of sexual assault (including attempted assault). There were almost four times as many female victims (618,000) as male victims (155,000) (ONS, 2021a, 2021b). Although the volume of sexual offences recorded by the police has almost tripled in recent years, the latest figures for the year ending March 2020 show a decrease of 0.7% to 162,936 offences compared with the previous year's figures. While changes in police recording practices and victims' willingness to report are likely to result in annual variations in the number of offences recorded by the police, that figure nevertheless remains well below the number of victims estimated by the Office for National Statistics (ONS) survey (2021a, 2021b). Latest estimates from the CSEW show that fewer than one in six (16%) female victims and fewer than one in five (19%) male victims aged 16 to 59 years who had been sexually assaulted by rape or penetration since the age of 16 years had reported their abuse to the police (ONS, 2021a, 2021b).

The reasons why people fail to report sexual abuse are varied and complex. According to Lorenz, Dewald and Venema (2021), most sexual assault victims make the conscious decision to *not* report to the police. Concerns about police response appear to feature prominently in victims' decision-making processes and include lack of trust in criminal justice agencies, concern about not being taken seriously and fear of being revictimised by the police's handling of the case (Stern 2010). As Gill and Harrison (2017) state, while these barriers transcend individual characteristics, they are nonetheless compounded by the multiple aspects that form an individual's identity, such as gender, age and ethnicity.

Police Responses to Black and Racially Minoritised Sexual Abuse Victims

In the UK, the relationship between the police and Black and racially minoritised communities has a chequered history, and institutional racism is often cited as a fundamental reason for this. Research consistently shows that those from 'Asia, Africa and the Islands of the sea' are less satisfied with their experiences of the police than their White counterparts (Bowling et al. 2008: 611). Some of the many reasons for this dissatisfaction can be attributed to the way the police handled the racially motivated murder of Black teenager Stephen Lawrence in 1993 and the ongoing overuse of stop-and-search powers against Black and racially minoritised communities. Distrust of the police is exacerbated by the disproportionate number of Black deaths in police custody: Black people account for just 3% of the population, yet they comprise 8% of deaths in custody. In addition, Black people are 18 times more likely to be stopped under Section 60, according to an analysis of the official figures by the Liberal Democrats (Dodd, 2020; Harrison and Gill, 2017a, b).

This pattern of distrust and ineffective policing is also apparent in the context of domestic violence. For example, Belur's research (2008) raised concerns around the policing of such incidents in Asian communities, arguing that institutionally racist practices compounded the ability of police forces to appropriately respond to Asian victims of domestic violence. Consequently, many South Asian women opt to use informal support services or report directly to domestic abuse services (Imkaan, 2008, 2020), thus bypassing the need for police contact. At present, limited research has been conducted on police responses to reports of sexual abuse when both the victim/survivor and the perpetrator are members of Black and racially minoritised communities; consequently, little is known about the social wider impacts these responses might have (Gutierrez and Chawla, 2017).

Key Findings Regarding Police Response Failures

In preparing its super-complaint, the Halo Project found that police responses to reports of sexual abuse within Black and racially minoritised communities fall far short of acceptable standards. It contends that such inadequate responses have a detrimental impact on these communities by deterring Black and racially minoritised sexual abuse victims/survivors from reporting to the police, a situation that compounds the already low levels of reporting among these victims. These inadequate responses create a sense of injustice and a lack of safety among community members; furthermore, Black and racially minoritised perpetrators feel able to continue carrying out their abuse without fear of prosecution.

In the process of producing the super-complaint, the Halo Project had the opportunity to work with victims/survivors of historical familial sexual abuse. These individuals shared their stories of abuse in many meetings, interviews and informal conversations, and the experiences they recounted clearly demonstrate the extent to which they were failed by the criminal justice system, particularly the police. The Halo Project's research identified these key failures in police responses to reports of sexual abuse within Black and racially minoritised communities, and these failures are summarised below.

Using voluntary suspect interviews

The CoP's Authorised Professional Practice (APP) guidance includes information about how police officers should deal with child sexual abuse (CSA) investigations. It states that 'the timing, coordination and extent of any arrests, potential victim or witness approaches, research enquiries (including with multi-agency partners) and evidential searches could, if not properly considered, have a detrimental effect on evidence gathering and, subsequently, on any prosecution (e.g. by alerting suspects)' (CoP, 2018). Despite this guidance, the use of voluntary suspect interviews has risen significantly in recent years and is proven to have a negative impact on victims. In particular, voluntary interviews take away the police's power to use bail and impose conditions, leaving victims/survivors who have reported their abuse vulnerable to potential violence and intimidation from their perpetrators and others. Furthermore, voluntary suspect interviews may detrimentally harm the investigation by inadvertently giving suspects the time they need to collude with others and destroy key evidence, such as that stored on phones or laptops.

Not Considering Honour-Based Abuse a Safeguarding Concern After Reporting

The CoP (2017) defines honour-based abuse as follows:

> an incident or crime involving violence, threats of violence, intimidation, coercion or abuse (including psychological, physical, sexual, financial or emotional abuse) which has or may have been committed to protect or defend the honour of an individual, family and/ or community for alleged or perceived breaches of the family and/or community's code of behaviour.

Many sexual abuse victims/survivors from Black and racially minoritised communities may be vulnerable to honour-based abuse from their family and wider community after they report sexual abuse, as their reporting may be seen as bringing dishonour and shame to their family and/or community—especially when the perpetrators belong to that same family and/or community. The Halo Project's research identified a theme whereby the police a) failed to identify particular behaviours as honour-based abuse and thus failed to understand the level of risk present and b) failed to act and adequately safeguard victims following reports of abuse.

Not Keeping Victims/survivors Informed After Reporting

According to the Victims' Code, victims of crime are entitled to be kept updated about their case and the police investigation. In particular, they have statutory rights to the following:

- a written acknowledgement of the crime reported (a letter, email, text or handwritten document) that includes the basic details of the offence
- a clear explanation of what to expect from the criminal justice system
- information about how often they will receive updates on the status of the case following discussions with the police
- an explanation, within five working days of reporting, of a police decision not to investigate a crime.

Gill, Cox and Weir's (2018) research suggests that the police were not meeting their statutory obligation, as per the Victims' Code (2015/2020), to keep victims/survivors informed during the investigation process. Many of the victims/survivors in this study reported constantly having to chase the police for updates, which caused significant distress and a sense that their case was not being taken seriously. They also experienced a lack of empathy from the police that compounded their distress. Similarly, victims/survivors were not given adequate information during the prosecution process. In particular, the police and Crown Prosecution Service (CPS) did not discuss special measures with victims/survivors, make them aware of their entitlements or provide relevant trial updates, such as letting them know why/when a trial was adjourned.

Disproportionately Focusing on Community Impact

In her report into the investigation of child sexual exploitation (CSE) in Rotherham, former Victims' Commissioner Louise Casey addresses in depth what she calls 'the race factor'. The report interviews conducted by key partners, including voluntary sector workers and police officers, make clear how significantly race has shaped the police and council's responses to reports of CSE. According to one voluntary sector worker:

> The issue [of CSE perpetrators] was predominately Asian men and they were scared that this would cause a problem. We would tell them that in the forums and they were uncomfortable. Stats on ethnicity were taken out of presentations. There was resistance to focusing on who the perpetrators were. (Casey 2015: 32)

A former key partner echoed this belief:

> The number one priority was to preserve and enhance the [Pakistani heritage] community—which wasn't an unworthy goal, but it wasn't right at the time. It was difficult to stand up in a meeting and say that the perpetrators were from the Pakistani heritage community and were using the taxi system—even though everyone knew it. (Casey 2015: 35)

Senior and lower-ranking police officers and frontline voluntary sector workers seemed to share this view:

> They wanted to use any other word than 'Asian males'. They were terrified about [the effect on] community cohesion. I got this sense from overhearing conversations between [senior members] and [senior officers] ... they were terrified of the BNP [British National Party]. (Casey 2015: 35)

Casey aptly sums up the impact of this attitude on both the Pakistani community and the victims/survivors:

> Rotherham's suppression of these uncomfortable issues and its fear of being branded racist has done a disservice to the Pakistani heritage community as well as the wider community. It has prevented discussion and effective action to tackle the problem. This has allowed perpetrators to remain at large, has let victims down, and perversely, has allowed the far right to try and exploit the situation. These may have been unintended consequences, but the impact remains the same and reaches into the present day. (Casey 2015: 36)

The super-complaint indicates that this kind of disproportionate focus on community impact overlooks the specific experiences of victims/survivors in favour of homogenising diverse communities and can thus seriously compromise sexual abuse investigations.

Failures at Trial

Those interviewed for the super-complaint believed that the heritage of their perpetrators played a significant role in how police handled their case. They felt that the police seemed disproportionately focused on how their investigation of a complaint involving members from a particular ethnic community may have affected community cohesion rather than on addressing the victim/survivor's wellbeing and safety. Furthermore, all the victims/survivors interviewed believed that their own racial background, coupled with the police's lack of cultural awareness and 'political correctness', negatively influenced the treatment they received.

However, the Victims' Code states that victims of crime are entitled to enhanced support throughout the criminal justice process if they are:

- victims of the most serious crime (this includes a sexual offence)
- persistently targeted victims
- vulnerable or intimidated victims (Ministry of Justice 2015).

It also states that victims of crime who are vulnerable or intimidated witnesses are entitled to have special measures made available to them so that they can give their best evidence in court. These measures include:

- screens/curtains in the courtroom (and, in some cases, the public gallery) so the witness does not have to see the defendant
- a live video link that allows a witness to give evidence away from the courtroom (i.e. from a separate room within the court or via a dedicated live link site outside the court building)
- the ability to give evidence in private (the public gallery can be cleared in cases involving a sexual offence or human trafficking, or where the court is satisfied that someone other than the accused may seek to intimidate the witness)
- removal of wigs and gowns by judges, defence and prosecution advocates
- the ability to give video-recorded statements—these allow a witness to use a pre-recorded video statement as their main prosecution evidence (Ministry of Justice 2015).

Case Study 1: 'Shoiab', British Pakistani Male [Police Area A]

Between the ages of five and nine years old, Shoiab was sexually abused by his three maternal cousins. The abuse first began after Shoiab moved to Pakistan with his mother and siblings for around 18 months between 1969 and 1970. The cousin who perpetrated the abuse during this period was around 13 years old. When Shoiab returned to England, he began to be sexually abused by two of his other cousins, who were the older brothers of the initial perpetrator in Pakistan. This abuse occurred regularly and continued for many years in a variety of different locations, including a slaughter house, a flat above the shop where Shoiab and his cousins worked, and in Shoiab's own home; it often occurred while Shoiab's mother and sisters were in the next room, although they had no idea the abuse was taking place. Shoiab stated that the abuse was often premeditated: his cousins would take him out and buy him gifts before abusing him. Shoiab revealed that the first time his own father brought him a gift—a watch—years after the abuse had ended, Shoiab's initial reaction was crippling fear that this meant his father would violate him. The abuse stopped when the eldest and most prolific abuser married Shoiab's older sister and told Shoiab that he had 'no further use for him anymore'.

Shoiab struggled in silence for years before making his first disclosure to his partner in 2003. He then made further disclosures to his sons and a family friend in 2007/8. In early 2010, Shoiab disclosed to a doctor at a medical centre. Weekly consultations with the doctor resulted in Shoiab revealing the details of his abuse in much more depth than in his previous disclosures. Once the doctor realised that the perpetrators were UK residents and were still in contact with children from Shoiab's family, she began urging Shoiab to inform the police.

Shoiab then made the decision to contact an officer who was also a friend—PC Welsh—to informally discuss what had happened to him. Shoiab was subsequently put in touch by PC Welsh with DC Marilyn, who encouraged him to make a formal statement attesting to the abuse so that the case could be brought forward. On multiple occasions, the police told Shoiab that his case would be a landmark one, as it is very uncommon for a male to report sexual abuse to the police and even more uncommon for an Asian male to do so. Shoiab wanted personal justice, but he also wanted to help the wider community, and he hoped that his decision to formally disclose would encourage other victims/survivors to follow suit. Shoiab stated in various meetings with the Halo Project that his own experiences of abuse were not isolated incidents but that no one in his community spoke up about sexual abuse, and he hoped his case could help lift this veil of secrecy. In July of that year, Shoiab spent more than five harrowing and traumatic hours giving his formal statement, articulating his abuse in as much excruciating detail as he was able to.

Key Failure 1: Using Voluntary Suspect Interviews

After Shoiab gave his statement, police assured him that the suspects would be questioned promptly. The next day, child protection took away the children who lived with the suspects. However, it then took more than three months for the police to bring those suspects in for questioning; when this finally did occur, it was via an appointment the suspects made themselves. During that three-month period, the suspects were able to collaborate, rehearse their stories and contact lawyers, and an uncle of the youngest suspect was able to travel to Pakistan and return to England with falsified documents stating that he had been younger than 13 at the time of the alleged abuse.

Clearly, the APP guidance about how to handle CSA cases was not followed in this instance. In addition, because the suspects were interviewed voluntarily, the police's power to impose bail conditions was lost. As a result, Shoiab's abusers were able to approach him in the lead-up to the trial. As this case illustrates, the use of voluntary interviews not only potentially reduces the strength of the investigation and chances of a successful prosecution but also puts the victim/survivor at risk and so undermines or negates the intent of the Victims' Code.

Key Failure 2: Ineffective Use Police Resources and Under-Resourcing

DC Marilyn, who took Shoiab's formal statement alongside DC Heath, was removed from the case without any explanation to work 'elsewhere' when the investigation began. DC Heath was thus the only detective assigned to the case. Shoiab explained that his meetings with her were frequently cut short due to her personal commitments. He described one incident in which DC Heath said the police could not contact the farmer, Mr Brooks, who owned the slaughterhouse where Shoiab had been abused because they did not have an available police car to travel to Mr Brooks's farm in Area D. According to Shoiab, during an internal review meeting after the trial, Second in Command of Police Area A along with PC Adams and PC McCormack confirmed that the investigation was under-resourced by as many as three to four detectives, again demonstrating that Shoiab's case was clearly not handled in line with the official guidance.

Key Failure 3: Not Keeping Victims/survivors Informed After Reporting

Shoiab made clear that the police officers he encountered during the investigation and after the trial did not conduct themselves with professionalism or empathy. For example, he described one incident in which he pressed an officer to answer questions about the investigation—question Shoiab had asked repeatedly to no avail—only to be told that he needed 'mental help'. In addition, during the internal review meeting, Shoiab was told that the police had made some mistakes but that Shoiab now needed to 'get on with his life'.

Key Failure 4: Not Considering Honour-Based Abuse a Safeguarding Concern After Reporting

The notions of culture, izzat (honour) and shame represent some of the most substantial reasons why Asian victims/survivors are less likely to report sexual abuse than their White counterparts. Many members of the Asian community feel that reporting sexual abuse will bring shame to themselves and their families and that the abuse is better kept a dirty secret. This reluctance is often compounded by family and wider community pressure not to report. Fear of the consequences of going against this pressure, which can range from ostracism to honour-based abuse and forced marriage, also plays a part in the decision not to report.

In their study *Policing the Culture of Silence*, Harrison and Gill (2017a, b) found that aspects of community policing still suffer from institutional racism. They quote an officer describing the distinction he made between the seriousness of reporting consequences in Asian and White British communities:

> People tend to fall out over matters within the white British community, or what you might call it, but don't tend to take any retribution, in my experience. Whereas I tend to find there is a very real-life threat of retribution within the South Asian community. (Harrison and Gill, 2017a, b: 8)

Shoiab experienced—and continues to experience—abuse, intimidation and harassment from the Asian community as a result of disclosing to the police. During the investigation, he was directly approached on numerous occasions by community elders who stated he must drop the charges and 'forgive' the accused. Some even asked him, 'But did you enjoy [the abuse] at the time?' He recalled a relative of the accused travelling from South of England to pressure Shoiab into retracting his allegations. Shoiab was even approached by the perpetrators themselves, who attempted to force him to drop the case. He explained that he was 'subject to emotional blackmail and threats' and, when these did not work, was 'offered a blank cheque' to drop the charges. Shoiab reported each of these incidences to the police, and yet they did nothing tangible to prevent further abuse or mitigate the abuse already committed. He stated that DC Heath 'resolutely refused to take any action when informed' and failed to keep the promises she made to ensure the safety of Shoiab and his family. Shoiab ultimately felt that he had no option but to move away from the area where he and his abusers lived.

Fundamentally, the police failed to understand the link between this abuse and community honour. They did not identify Shoiab's treatment at the hands of his community as honour-based abuse, consider the risk of honour-based abuse in the first place nor act upon Shoiab's reports of further abuse/intimidation. From the outset, the police should have given serious consideration to any culturally specific safeguarding concerns in this case, particularly given that Shoiab was a Pakistani male who had reported three other members of the Asian community to the police for sexually abusing him over many years and that he was subject to threats and harassment from the wider community after reporting. The police also failed to consider the potential of community collusion. One member ['Riaz'] of an independent advisory group in Police Area A was a relative of both Shoiab and the perpetrators. Shoiab explained that during the investigation process, Riaz contacted Shoiab's friends to make threats against him and spread false information about him. Shoiab reported this to DC Heath, who said there was nothing she could do. Shoiab also believed that Riaz held information that only the police should have known and shared it with a witness for the prosecution.

Failure 5: Disproportionately Focusing on Community Impact

The 'Rotherham effect' was starkly apparent in Shoiab's situation (Halo 2020: 20). He believed that the Pakistani heritage of his perpetrators strongly influenced how the police dealt with the case. The officers involved seemed concerned about how their investigation of a complaint involving Pakistani suspects would affect community cohesion and, more importantly, how it would influence their institutional relationship with the Pakistani community. From Shoiab's perspective, the police prioritised these concerns over his safety. For example, after spending five harrowing hours giving his statement, the first thing DCs Marilyn and Heath asked Shoiab was if he could 'foresee any hindrance from the community in picking up the accused?' and whether he thought the community might react violently to police involvement. Shoiab was understandably upset by these questions at this stage, given that, according to Shoiab, 'DC Heath had [already] made it clear that the accused had not been picked up due to concerns over community impact'. Shoiab also felt that the police had failed to act on the harassment and intimidation he received from the Pakistani community after reporting because they did not want to harm their relationship with that community, a particularly large and entrenched one in that area of the UK.

Failures at Trial

At their subsequent trial, none of the three perpetrators was found guilty of sexual abuse. Shoiab must live with the fact that they can now continue their lives freely despite the destruction they have caused in his. This outcome is partly the result of the significant failures that occurred during the trial. While these failings are not solely attributable to the insufficient police response, they are nonetheless part of a pattern of failures associated with trials involving Black and racially minoritised sexual abuse victims/survivors. In this case, Shoiab and his family harboured particular concerns over the quality and neutrality of the interpreter present at the trial. The interpreter made comments to a security guard that the 'case is all about money', and when this was reported to the clerk, no action was taken. Furthermore, the interpreter was observed answering questions himself, reading aloud answers from a diary in court instead of purely interpreting the words spoken by the defendants and having lengthy discussions with the defendants during trial proceedings rather than purely interpreting their words.

Shoiab and his family also felt that the judge allowed inappropriate comments to be made during the trial proceedings. For example, he recalled the defence barrister asking him if he made his abuse allegations because he was angry that the Asian community did not accept the fact that he had a 'White woman [partner] and kids. Shoiab found this exceedingly offensive and racist, yet the judge said nothing. In addition, during her summing up of the case, the judge informed the jury that the defendants had no previous convictions; for Shoiab, she delivered this information in a manner that inferred he did have previous convictions or that the defendants' lack of previous convictions was relevant. Shoiab and his family believed that the judge seemed to have more empathy for the defendants than for them. Shoiab also felt let down by the prosecution barrister, who was given the case no more than two weeks before trial because the original barrister was unable to attend. As a result, he did not seem 'up to speed and missed opportunities to probe witnesses further'. For example, Mr Brooks, the slaughterhouse owner, appeared as a defence witness. Under questioning, Mr Brooks seemed more concerned with demonstrating that he had adhered to all of the relevant farming laws, and the prosecution barrister failed to steer him towards more germane ground.

Case Study 2: 'Zak' (British Pakistani Male), 'Saima' (British Pakistani Female) and Their Brother 'Haris' (British Pakistani Male), [Police Area B]

Siblings Zak, Saima and Haris were victims/survivors of familial CSA. 'Haris' is a pseudonym, as he did not wish to be directly named in the super-complaint but was happy for his experiences to be included in this case study. The assessment of the police response presented below is therefore based on all three victims/survivors' experiences and feelings. As children, Zak and Haris were subject to abuse perpetrated by both their maternal uncle and their mother's cousin. Saima was abused by her uncle when she was nine years old, 11 years old and 19 years old. Zak was 10 years old when the abuse began and 13 when it ended. Haris was six years old when the abuse began and 10 when it ended. Zak kept his abuse a secret until 2002, when he disclosed his experiences to friends. Like Shoiab, he then disclosed to a medical professional, telling his GP in October 2016. Then, in March 2017, Zak told his family, and in April 2017, he disclosed to the police. Saima made her first disclosure to her aunt in Pakistan when she was 11 years old, but her aunt did nothing with this information. In 2010, she disclosed the abuse to a therapist. In 2016, she disclosed the abuse to her mother and Haris. She went to the police in July 2017. Haris made his first disclosure to Saima and his mother in 2016, at the same time Saima told them about her abuse; in July 2017, he also went to the police.

Failure 1: Not Considering Honour-Based Abuse a Safeguarding Concern After Reporting

Following their disclosure of sexual abuse to the police, Zak, Saima and Haris were ostracised from their wider family and community and subjected to honour-based abuse. The police failed to clearly identify this treatment as honour-based abuse and thus failed to understand the level of risk it presented; they also neglected to act on reports of the abuse. These failures left all three victims/survivors feeling unsafe and vulnerable.

Zak explained that one of the abusers was their mother's younger brother, which meant that:

> The family were against us throughout and still are. We were very intimidated, scared and frightened on many occasions by the family and mostly by [one of the perpetrator's older brothers], who is a committee member of the mosque in South West England.

Zak stated that he and his siblings tried to make the police understand that they were experiencing honour-based abuse because by reporting their CSA, they were perceived by the community as having compromised their family's honour:

> We tried on several occasions to explain and make the police understand the consequences of the [mother's] older brother's influence and intimidation tactics, but it was always disregarded and never taken seriously. He is still using these tactics and yet the police are sitting on their hands. I just hope that nothing has to happen for them to realise how it affects us daily.

Saima described one occasion when her ex-husband called to pressure her into retracting her statement, telling her that he was glad she had been raped. According to Zak:

> She rang me, distressed and crying, to explain what had happened. I called him [the ex-brother-in-law] but knowing that there was an active case going on, I was very careful in what I said yet firm in telling him not to contact us.

He then described the shocking response he received from Police Area B:

> I informed Police Area B of the situation and to this date nothing has been done about it. I was instead called by Police Area B and told not to speak to my ex-brother-in-law or they would arrest me. After an hour

of explaining the situation, he [officer from Police Area B] still would not listen or investigate the situation of witness intimidation.

The siblings also received death threats on Facebook from family members of the perpetrators. Yet still, 'Police never took the death threats seriously and every time we contacted them, we were not helped at all'. The siblings detailed one incident in which a police officer said 'What do you want us to do?' in response to an abuse report. Sam explained:

> We told our case officer who said if we start going in for 'tit for tat' the courts will not look into the case, but more into these particular incidents and this could affect our case. We then had more threats, but it just seemed pointless telling the police.

At no point did the police classify the treatment to which Zak, Saima and Haris were subjected as honour-based abuse, which demonstrates their failure to understand the level of risk the siblings faced from their family and community. Furthermore, the police never acted upon reports of the abuse to ensure the siblings' safety. Saima continued receiving abuse from her ex-husband as a result of her disclosure to the police. She recalled him telling her, in October 2018, that if he ever saw her outside, he would kill her. Saima did not report this threat to the police because she did not believe, based on their past inaction, that they would respond to it appropriately.

Haris also faced continued threats. In April 2021, when he uploaded a photo of his child to Facebook, someone posted an image beneath it that showed a person covered in blood and a threat written in Urdu. Haris, like Saima, did not report this incident to the police because he did not trust that they would take it seriously or act upon it. By this stage, Haris felt unable to see his friends and family in South West England because he did not feel safe there: 'I regret reporting my abuse to the police, totally and utterly.' The siblings concluded, 'we are still suffering abuse from the community and we don't know who to turn to as we now realise the police will not help'.

Failure 2: Not Keeping Victims/survivors Informed After Reporting

Despite the rights to which they are entitled under the Victims' Code, Zak, Saima and Haris revealed that they were constantly having to chase the police for updates, spending hours on the phone and having to speak to numerous different officers to obtain information about the case and their reports of honour-based abuse:

> We had spoken to several police officers and were given numerous crime numbers when we reported incidences of abuse and intimidation and yet to this day, the police have failed to provide us with any updates about what they are doing.

Zak reported receiving death threats on Facebook from a perpetrator's family member to the police. He was understandably very concerned about these threats and about the safety of his children. Despite Zak's very real worries about this apparent death threat, the police failed to keep him updated with their response to it and he had to keep contacting them to find out what developments, if any, had occurred. Eventually, Zak was told that the individual sending the threats was in Pakistan and thus constituted no immediate risk. Zak stated that if the police had communicated this fact to him straight away, rather than waiting for him to chase them for answers, he would not have had to endure so much anxiety.

For Saima, too, it was virtually impossible to receive updates from the police, as they never contacted her. She said this treatment of her case made the whole process even more distressing, and it was a significant reason why she would not recommend that a friend report a crime to the police. Saima wished that she had never involved the police in the first place.

Failures at Trial

Ultimately, both perpetrators were successfully prosecuted. The siblings' uncle was sentenced to 10 years in prison and their mother's cousin was sentenced to six years. However, during the prosecution process, the police and the CPS gave Zak, Saima and Haris little to no information. Most particularly, they were not made aware of the special measures that could be used in court, nor were they kept fully informed of developments in the court case (for example, when/why the trial was being adjourned or why the jurors were dismissed). In an already stressful and difficult situation, these failings made them feel even more unsupported and anxious about the trial. Given that all three siblings were sexual abuse victims/survivors and had experienced intimidation as a result of reporting their abuse to the police, they should have automatically received enhanced support throughout the criminal justice process as per the Victims' Code. That they did not indicates a serious shortcoming in police safeguarding procedure in this case.

It is the responsibility of the police and the CPS to consult with victims/survivors about what special measures are available and what measures they may wish to have applied. Despite this obligation, Zak, Saima and Haris were not informed of their special measures entitlements. The police had told the siblings during the investigation stage that if they became witnesses, the public gallery would be closed when they gave evidence—yet just two weeks before the court case began, the usher informed the siblings that such closure never happened and the public gallery would have to remain open. Receiving this information at this late juncture understandably caused significant distress, particularly to Saima, who came very close to not proceeding with the trial due to her anxiety about who would be in the public gallery watching her give evidence. Indeed, those present in the gallery during the trial included the very same relatives of the perpetrators and members of the community who had subjected Zak, Saima and Haris to honour-based abuse. Throughout the court case, these individuals were seated right behind the siblings.

Zak, Saima and Haris were left so uninformed about any developments or changes during the prosecution process that Sam felt he was being treated 'like someone who had no involvement in the case'. He continued:

The trial was adjourned every month and it took six months before sentencing was passed. Going back and forth with no explanation as to what was going on was mentally and physically exhausting, not to mention the difficulty in continuously trying to resource multiple trips to court.

On one occasion we went to court and the guard at the door had to tell us we were not on today and it was only after ringing the police and witness care that we were told it was cancelled.

The siblings also felt that they were not given any practical information by the police during the prosecution process. According to Zak:

I was not made aware of times or places to arrive in court and nearly got arrested for going in with the jurors.
    Three days into our uncle's trial we were told that the jurors had been dismissed and that they cannot tell us anymore and we need to go home. The next day I get a call from the head of CID [Criminal Investigation Department] saying my uncle has pleaded guilty to a lesser charge. He told me my brother and sister have agreed to this lesser charge and they are now just waiting on me. He told me I had 30 minutes to make the decision. I called my brother and sister, who tell me that they agreed because the police officer had told them I had already agreed. I called the head of CID back, who explained that we might lose the case if we do not agree to the lesser charge. He could not explain any legalities, such as whether my uncle could appeal. He just wanted me to accept the lesser charge. After an hour of hell, we accepted the lesser charge as we were told by the police the CPS were going to accept it either way so we had no choice. Nothing was actually explained to us. With no legal explanation or advice how could we be forced to make a decision of such magnitude in 30 minutes?

Zak, Saima and Haris felt that the officer in this situation behaved unprofessionally by lying to all three parties about who had already agreed to a lesser charge in an attempt to pressure them into agreeing with this charge as soon as possible.

The Effects of Systemic Police Failures on Victims/Survivors of Sexual Abuse

As the striking similarities in the cases above demonstrate, systemic failures in police handling of sexual abuse cases, particularly those that involve victims/survivors from Black and racially minoritised communities, can have serious consequences for those who report their abuse. Impact statements from the victims/survivors in these case studies powerfully capture the devastating and long-term ramifications of these systemic failures—and of the police's failure to own their mistakes.

For Zak, the police response he received compounded his mental health difficulties:

> Hurt, scarred, scared to move forward in my life. I think about ending my life every day and then to endure this with services who are supposed to help us. The police forces are not performing to what they should be doing.

Zak said he was made to feel like a criminal:

> As a victim I have felt through the investigation and trials like I was the criminal. No information, no correct communication, no support. Please, please, please can someone answer me this, why was I treated this way?

Shoiab felt that disclosing his abuse left him in an even worse position than he was in before:

> Going to the police and the following investigation and trial traumatised me so heavily that I found myself in a worse situation than ever. The failings of the police and CPS resulted in the abusers being acquitted and my feeling of total injustice was overwhelming.
>
> Following the trial I have had many meetings with the police at medium and higher levels and the outcome is similar to the response of the Asian community. Comments like 'although we (the police) have made mistakes, you need to get on with your life'. 'Steve Gregory' [a police officer involved in Shoiab's case] made the comment that most shocked

me in front of seven or eight family members and friends that I needed 'mental help'. I have been monitored on a regular basis by two successive GPs for nine years now and this is set to continue indefinitely. I have been declared unfit for work by my GP due to depression and emotional problems. This shows no sign of changing soon.

'Giles', a close friend of Shoiab, also provided a statement explaining the impact of the police response to Shoiab's case:

Shoiab was clearly now in a worse emotional position than ever and we would regularly meet up just to chat over things. I became involved in meetings with Shoiab called by the police as due to pressure they finally admitted that they had made mistakes. I'm sure the police now find the content and narrative of these meetings particularly embarrassing. The whole upshot was that it seemed to be an exercise in making Shoiab feel better by praising him in an attempt to keep the lid on the whole thing.

Evidence of Systemic Failures in Cases Involving Victims/Survivors From Black and Racially Minoritised Communities and Their Implications

The Halo Project's research and super-complaint are not the only evidence that police failures run far deeper than the failings highlighted in the above two cases. For example, research conducted by the Muslim Women's Network UK reveals that during the prosecution process, abuse victims/survivors lacked information from the police and CPS about trial updates and special measures that could/ought to be put in place (Gohir, 2019). Gohir (2019) also identifies police failure to identify particular behaviour as honour-based abuse and to adequately safeguard victims/survivors. A super-complaint made by the Centre for Women's Justice in 2020 discusses the use of voluntary suspect interviews from the perspective of how they might affect the safety of victims/survivors who have reported their abuse: when a suspect is interviewed voluntarily, the police have no power to impose bail conditions (Ofer, 2019). As Shoiab's case demonstrates, if the suspects had not been voluntarily interviewed, bail conditions would have been imposed and these might have deterred them from indirectly and directly contacting Shoiab to intimidate and harass him into dropping his charges.

Victim Support's 2011 *Left in the Dark* report focused on whether police keep victims/survivors informed about their case to an acceptable standard (Victim Support, 2011). More than 10 years ago, this report addressed why this high level of communication is imperative and noted the detrimental impact of keeping victims/survivors in the dark. Such lack of information can lead to victims becoming revictimised and fearing for their safety. Poor communication can have as significant an effect on victims/survivors' confidence in the police as their perpetrators being brought to justice. The experiences of Zak, Saima and Haris also strongly support that finding. Devastatingly, the police's lack of communication with the siblings led Saima and her brother to wish they had never reported the abuse to begin with. Failing to communicate with victims/survivors after they report these kinds of crimes may affect victims/survivors' perceptions of case management and contribute to their feeling uncertain and isolated, which can worsen the distress caused by the crime itself and harm the public interest in terms of procedural justice. Nonetheless, similar to the Halo Project's findings, *Left in the Dark* revealed that victims/survivors' needs and desires to be kept informed have long gone unmet, and this situation does not appear to be changing.

Inadequate police responses to reports of sexual abuse from Black and racially minoritised victims/survivors have far-reaching impacts: when victims/survivors lack confidence in the criminal justice system, they do not report their abuse nor receive the support and justice they deserve (EVAW 2021; Victims Commissioner 2021). Most crucially, a belief that their cases have been poorly managed can lead individuals who have reported abuse to deter other victims/survivors in those communities from disclosing, consequently allowing perpetrators to continue their abuse, confident in the knowledge that they will not be held culpable.

Remedying Systemic Failures

In addition to echoing some of the findings in the reports mentioned above, Harrison and Gill (2017a, b) attribute such failures to a lack of adequate police training. They conclude that as long as culturally specific training falls short of acceptable standards, victims/survivors are and will continue to be left vulnerable. While many of the police officers interviewed by Harrison and Gill (2017a, b) acknowledged that shame and dishonour play a large role in South Asian culture, they also revealed that there are little to no sound training processes in place that can help police officers understand South Asian culture and honour-based abuse. Harrison and Gill's (2017a, b) research concluded that out of the four UK police forces studied, only one had an acceptable level of cultural awareness training. They also found that

> individual police officers are not passive agents awaiting the next policy edit on how to police diverse communities and do not act in completely risk-averse ways around Black and racially minoritised communities. Rather, they noted innovativeness and creativity at work in terms of how officers are engaging with this particular ethnic group and how the police can be a force for good in challenging victimisation and vulnerability and, in turn, driving through change. (Harrison and Gill 2017a, b: 15)

Ultimately, if such strengths are to be built upon and disseminated to all police forces, stronger training is required.

Conclusion

Deciding to come forward as a victim of sexual abuse, regardless of gender or race, is an incredibly difficult and brave step to take. However, victims/survivors from Black and racially minoritised communities who decide to report sexual abuse perpetrated by members of their own community often face different, specific and even more complex barriers than those confronting their White counterparts. All victims/survivors who put their trust in the criminal justice system deserve to be treated with respect and to feel confident about how the police will handle their case. However, the Halo Project's super-complaint, along with other studies, suggest that the police often fail to adequately respond to reports of sexual abuse from Black and racially minoritised communities. The case studies explored in this chapter reveal deep systemic failings on the part of the police that are adversely affecting both individual Black and minoritised victims/survivors and the communities of which they are a part. The terrible experiences of victims/survivors such as Shoiab, Zak, Saima and Haris inevitably and understandably damage their faith in the criminal justice system and deter future reporting; these experiences also compound the victimisation that is already more pronounced for Black and racially minoritised individuals due to the intersecting inequalities they face.

While this chapter has highlighted the experiences of victims/survivors served by both Police Area A and Police Area B, the wider studies included here represent a national problem. They not only provide evidence that systemic failures exist across a number of police forces but also that systemic change is urgently needed if victims/survivors of sexual abuse from Black and racially minoritised communities—and, indeed, from any communities—are to receive the response they deserve from the police when they report their abuse. In order to support and encourage discourses related to sexual abuse and police reform, responses to these crimes need to include a national police training program to ensure that all officers possess detailed knowledge of the other cultures that exist in Britain today. This program should not simply take the form of diversity training—stand-alone diversity training that is divorced from community contexts is not going to fix the problem because it carries the risk of simply affirming people's existing biases. Rather, cultural awareness training that can enable police forces to develop a deeper understanding of the cultural contexts in which Black and racially minoritised community victims/survivors live is essential if the police are to properly investigate honour-based abuse, forced marriage and female genital mutilation and to understand how these link to sexual abuse.

Furthermore, change clearly needs to be implemented in a number of specific areas in order to address the failures explored in this chapter. First, police officers and the criminal justice system itself need to take seriously their statutory obligation, as stated in the Victims' Code, to keep victims/survivors informed and updated during the investigation and prosecution process. There must also be greater accountability when lack of compliance is identified on the part of the police and other actors across the criminal justice system. When it comes to interacting with victims/survivors, police officers need to consider the language they use and ensure they are communicating appropriately and with empathy. Police officers must also seriously consider whether the use of voluntary suspect interviews is appropriate in all sexual abuse cases, particularly in terms of victim/survivor safety and the strength of the investigation. In addition, as it is imperative that interpreters are neutral and professional during both the investigation and prosecution processes, efforts should be made to ensure that interpreters have sufficient cultural understanding and knowledge in CSA cases involving Black and racially minoritised victims. When concerns are expressed about the competence of an interpreter, they must be taken seriously and acted upon if deemed necessary. Finally, a national Black and racially minoritised sexual violence reference group should be established. This group must comprise not only experts and sexual abuse survivors who have lived experience of the current system's failings but must also be able to influence national police guidance and training and to scrutinise cases. It is hoped that the Halo Project's super-complaint will bring us at least one step closer to achieving those ends and producing better outcomes for victims/survivors of sexual abuse nationally.

Note

1. Source: *So-Called Honour-Based Abuse and Forced Marriage: Guidance on Identifying and Flagging cases.* https://www.cps.gov.uk/legal-guidance/so-called-honour-based-abuse-and-forced-marriage-guidance-identifying-and-flagging.

References

Belur, J. (2008). Is policing domestic violence institutionally racist? A case study of south Asian Women. *Policing and Society, 18*(4), 426–444.

Bowling, B., Parmar, A., and Phillips, C. (2008). Policing minority ethnic communities. In T. Newburn (Ed.), *Handbook of Policing* (2nd ed., pp. 611–641). Routledge.

Casey, L. (2015). *Reflections on child sexual exploitation*. https://assets.publishing.service.gov.uk/government/uploads/system/uploads/attachment_data/file/418394/Louise_Casey_report_into_CSE_template_format__4_.pdf. Accessed 10 September 2021.

Centre for Women's Justice. (2020). *Super-complaint by Centre for Women's Justice: Failure to address police perpetrated domestic abuse*. https://assets.publishing.service.gov.uk/government/uploads/system/uploads/attachment_data/file/913084/Police_perpetrated_domestic_abuse.pdf. Accessed 15 September 2021.

College of Policing. (2017). *Forced marriage and honour-based abuse*. https://www.app.college.police.uk/app-content/major-investigation-and-public-protection/forced-marriage-and-honour-based-violence/?highlight=honour%20based%20abuse?s=honour+based+abuse. Accessed 3 September 2021.

College of Policing. (2018). *Managing complex child abuse investigations*. https://www.app.college.police.uk/app-content/major-investigation-and-public-protection/child-abuse/complex-investigations/. Accessed 2 September 2021.

Dodd, V. (2020). Black people nine times more likely to face stop and search than white people. *The Guardian*. https://www.theguardian.com/uk-news/2020/oct/27/black-people-nine-times-more-likely-to-face-stop-and-search-than-white-people. Accessed 7 September 2021.

End Violence Against Women. (2021). *Victims' Commissioner's survey finds victims' confidence in the justice system is worryingly low*. https://www.endviolenceagainstwomen.org.uk/victims-confidence-justice-system-low/. Accessed 15 September 2021.

Gill, A. K., Cox, P., and Weir, R. (2018). Shaping priority services for UK victims of honour-based violence/abuse, forced marriage and female genital mutilation. *Howard Journal of Criminal Justice, 57*(4).

Gohir, S. (2019). *Muslim Women's Experiences of the Criminal Justice System*. https://www.mwnuk.co.uk/go_files/resources/Muslim_Women_and_Criminal_Justice_FINAL.pdf. Accessed 7 September 2021.

Gutierrez, C., and Chawla, S. (2017). *The child sexual exploitation of young South Asian Women in Birmingham and Coventry. Exploring professional insight into young women's hidden journeys, silence and support*. The Children's Society.

Halo Project. (2020). *Invisible survivors: The long wait for justice. Police response to BAME victims of sexual abuse*. https://assets.publishing.service.gov.uk/government/uploads/system/uploads/attachment_data/file/963007/Invisible_survivors___The_long_wait_for_justice.pdf. Accessed 6 September 2021.

Harrison, K. and Gill, A.K. (2017a). Breaking down barriers: Recommendations for improving sexual abuse reporting rates in British South Asian communities. *British Journal of Criminology, 58*(2), 273–290.

Harrison, K., and Gill, A. K. (2017b). Policing the culture of silence: strategies to increase the reporting of sexual abuse in British South Asian communities. *Policing and Society, 29*(3), 302–317.

Imkaan. (2008). *No recourse—No duty to care? Experiences of BAMER women and children affected by domestic violence and insecure immigration status in the UK*. https://static1.squarespace.com/static/5f7d9f4addc689717e6ea200/t/61e6a77f9b3bf9708d007261/1642506112688/2008+_+Imkaan+_+No+Recourse+-+No+Duty+to+Care.pdf. Accessed 12 September 2021.

Imkaan. (2020). *The impact of the dual pandemics: Violence against women & girls and COVID-19 on black and minoritised women & girls*. https://rapecrisis.org.uk/get-informed/reports/reports-archive/the-impact-of-the-two-pandemics-vawg-and-covid-19-on-black-and-minoritised-women-and-girls/. Accessed 15 September 2021.

Lorenz, K., Dewald, S., and Venema, R. (2021). "I was worried I wouldn't be believed": Sexual assault victims' perceptions of the police in the decision to not report. *Violence and Victims, 36*(3), 455–476.

Ministry of Justice. (2015). *Code of practice for victims of crime*. https://www.cps.gov.uk/sites/default/files/documents/legal_guidance/OD_000049.pdf. Accessed 9 September 2021.

Ministry of Justice. (2020). *Code of practice for victims of crime*. https://assets.publishing.service.gov.uk/government/uploads/system/uploads/attachment_data/file/936239/victims-code-2020.pdf. Accessed 9 September 2021.

Ofer, N. (2019). Too many rape and abuse victims are being let down by the police. *The Guardian*. https://www.theguardian.com/commentisfree/2019/mar/21/rape-abuse-victims-let-down-police-women. Accessed 14 September 2021.

Office for National Statistics. (2021a). *Sexual offences in England and Wales overview: year ending March 2020*. https://www.ons.gov.uk/peoplepopulatio nandcommunity/crimeandjustice/bulletins/sexualoffencesinenglandandwale soverview/march2020. Accessed 2 September 2021.

Office for National Statistics. (2021b). *Nature of sexual assault by rape or penetration, England and Wales: year ending March 2020*. https://www.ons. gov.uk/peoplepopulationandcommunity/crimeandjustice/articles/natureofs exualassaultbyrapeorpenetrationenglandandwales/yearendingmarch2020. Accessed 2 September 2021.

Stern, V. (2010). *The Stern Review. A report by Baroness Vivien Stern CBE of an independent review into how rape complaints are handled by public authorities in England and Wales*. https://evaw-global-database.unwomen.org/-/media/ files/un%20women/vaw/full%20text/europe/stern%20review%202010/ stern%20review%20-%202010.pdf?vs=655. Accessed 4 September 2021.

Victims' Commissioner. (2021). *Victims' experience: Annual survey*. https:// s3-eu-west-2.amazonaws.com/victcomm2-prod-storage-119w3o4kq2z48/ uploads/2021/09/VC-2021-survey-of-victims.pdf. Accessed 14 September 2021.

Victim Support. (2011). *Left in the dark: Why victims of crime need to be kept informed*. https://www.victimsupport.org.uk/wp-content/uploads/docume nts/files/Left%20in%20the%20dark%20-%20why%20victims%20of% 20crime%20need%20to%20be%20kept%20informed.pdf. Accessed 15 September 2021.

7

Institutional Responses to Child Sexual Abuse in Ethnic Minority Communities

Rachel Hurcombe, Theresa Redmond, Holly Rodger, and Sophia King

They forgot about the person that was being hurt.
(Female focus group participant)

Introduction

Child sexual abuse affects all communities but less is known about how child sexual abuse affects ethnic minority communities in England and Wales. There is a general consensus that victims and survivors from ethnic minority communities often face additional barriers to disclosing

---

R. Hurcombe (✉) · H. Rodger · S. King
Independent Inquiry Into Child Sexual Abuse, London, UK
e-mail: rachel.hurcombe@norfolk.police.uk

T. Redmond
Policing Institute for the Eastern Region (PIER), Anglia Ruskin University, Cambridge, UK
e-mail: theresa.redmond@aru.ac.uk

child sexual abuse, and research has shown that people from Caribbean, African and Asian backgrounds in the UK may find it especially difficult to report child sexual abuse and get the right kind of support (for example, see Gill and Harrison 2018; Warrington et al. 2017; Bernard and Harris 2016; Cowburn et al. 2015; Gohir 2013). This chapter seeks to explore how people from ethnic minority communities experience and perceive institutional responses to child sexual abuse, and the support needs of victims and survivors from these communities.

This chapter is predominantly based on a research study carried out by the Independent Inquiry into Child Sexual Abuse ('the Inquiry') in collaboration with the Race Equality Foundation, a national UK charity that aims to tackle racial inequality in order to improve the lives of Black, Asian and ethnic minority communities. Set up as a statutory inquiry in March 2015, the Inquiry was tasked with considering the extent to which state and non-state institutions in England and Wales have failed to protect children from sexual abuse and exploitation and to consider the steps which it is necessary for these institutions to take to help ensure that children are better protected from sexual abuse in the future, and to publish a report with recommendations. The research findings of the study entitled *'People don't talk about it': Child sexual abuse in ethnic minority communities* was published by the Inquiry in June 2020 ('the research report'). The research findings arising from the study do not constitute formal recommendations by the Inquiry's Chair and Panel and are separate from evidence obtained in investigations and hearings.

The aims of the research, discussed in detail in the report, were to explore:

1. how different ethnic minority communities perceive and experience barriers to disclosing and reporting child sexual abuse;
2. their experiences of, and interactions with, institutions in relation to child sexual abuse; and
3. the support needs of victims and survivors from ethnic minority communities

The first phase of the study entailed a literature review, focusing on research from England and Wales published between 2009 and 2019.

The second phase comprised 11 focus groups, carried out with 82 people across England and Wales between September 2019 and January 2020. Participants came from a range of ethnic minority communities, particularly from Caribbean, African and South Asian[1] ethnicities. Three focus groups were with victims and survivors of child sexual abuse. The remaining eight were with members of the public who had no known experiences of abuse, recruited by the Race Equality Foundation through organisations that work with people from ethnic minority communities. Sixty-eight participants identified as female, 13 as male and one participant identified as both female and transgender. As male voices tend to be underrepresented in research in this field, a male-only focus group was carried out to ensure their inclusion. The age of participants ranged from 19 to 74 years old, with over three quarters of participants aged between 30 and 59 years old.[2]

This small-scale, qualitative research provides contemporary insight from people in these communities and amplifies their voices and experiences. However, the research findings are based on a small sample and cannot be generalised to all ethnic minority communities. This chapter also references a number of more recent studies regarding child sexual abuse and ethnic minority communities, which do not appear in the research report. They are referenced in this chapter to provide updated information about research carried out in this area and to provide examples of how interactions with institutions might be improved. This chapter also offers further reflections on the findings from the research study. The views expressed here are those of the authors alone.

Definitions

There is no universal definition of child sexual abuse. The research report and this chapter use the term 'child sexual abuse' to refer to behaviours that involve forcing or enticing a child or young person to take part in sexual activities. The activities may involve physical contact, and non-contact activities such as involving children in looking at, or in the production of, sexual images, watching sexual activities, encouraging children to behave in sexually inappropriate ways or grooming a child in preparation for abuse including via the internet. Child sexual abuse includes child sexual exploitation. Although demographic data on perpetrators of child sexual abuse is lacking, data has shown that abuse can be perpetrated by adults or peers, and perpetrators often tend to be male, although sexual abuse can also be perpetrated by females (Kelly and Karsna 2018).

Terminology associated with ethnicity can be problematic and often exclusionary, in part due to a lack of consensus regarding what constitutes an ethnic group and because membership of an ethnic group is 'self-defined and subjectively meaningful to the person concerned' (Office for National Statistics 2019). For this chapter, we have used participants' own words when describing their ethnic backgrounds and we use the phrase 'ethnic minority communities' as an umbrella term.

However, we recognise the limitations of the term 'ethnic minority communities', as well as the limitations of specific ethnic group categories that are often used (e.g. the Office for National Statistics' categories of 'Black', 'Black Caribbean', 'Asian' and 'Indian'). These refer to a number of different aspects of identity, including nationality or country/continent of heritage (e.g. 'Asian') and physical attributes (e.g. 'Black'), as well as tacit associations with immigration status, nationality and religion. Discussions of ethnicity can also fail to recognise and take into account the other overlapping identities held by the individuals within different communities, such as age, class, gender and disability (Thoburn 2016). The use of such terms and problems with combining, and sometimes conflating, different aspects of identity while ignoring others can make it difficult to see and understand the factors behind different perceptions and experiences within and between groups. As such, we recognise the different identities within and between ethnic minority communities, and our usage of the phrase is not intended to present these diverse groups as homogeneous. Bearing in mind these caveats, research that explores the relationship between ethnicity and child sexual abuse is still a valuable endeavour and is important for identifying and addressing child sexual abuse in all communities. We use the term culture to describe the ways of life, customs, habits and beliefs of a particular group of people. Cultural competency within an institution includes factors such as having an ethnically diverse workforce, trained interpreters, regular staff training, multicultural framework and mandatory data collection (Sawrikar 2020).

We use the term 'institution' to refer to a range of organisations that is a group of people who work together in an organised way for a particular shared purpose, and settings where such organisations are based, for example a government department, the police, children's social care services, hospitals, prisons, schools or religion-based settings. Statutory institutions are institutions set up by law to carry out public activities, for example the police and children's social care services. Voluntary sector organisations are non-governmental and non-profit organisations that undertake activities for social benefit, including charities. Formal support refers to support services that are provided by professionals in statutory and voluntary sector organisations. Informal support refers to support provided by peers, family and the wider community.

Literature Review Findings

The literature review highlighted how ethnic minority victims and survivors can face additional barriers to disclosing and reporting child sexual abuse, with these barriers often linked to ethnic background and gender. This can sometimes be a consequence of institutional racism or conversely, the desire among professionals to appear culturally sensitive can mean that they may not intervene and respond appropriately in cases of suspected sexual abuse.

Research has revealed some institutions' resistance to acknowledging that ethnic minority children can be victims of sexual abuse (Ali et al. 2020). Among Asian victims, this has been attributed to a lack of awareness among professionals of the risk of exploitation, particularly in relation to boys, due to masculinity and stigma, and also due to professionals being better at identifying inappropriate relationships between men and girls than men and boys. Resistance has also been attributed to a failure to believe the victims' accounts, a lack of coordinated services (Gohir 2013) and to the media portrayal of the 'Asian perpetrator/white victim' dynamic of child sexual exploitation (The Children's Society 2018). In some organisations, appropriate responses can be thwarted by institutional racism, which can stem from harmful personal beliefs, assumptions and narratives about ethnic minorities, and unconscious bias resulting from a less diverse workforce (Cowburn et al. 2015; Thiara et al. 2015; Fontes and Plummer 2010; Gilligan and Akhtar 2005). However, there is also research evidence that some organisations are managing to identify victims from ethnic minorities, in particular ethnic minority, faith, and statutory and voluntary sector youth justice agencies (Berelowitz et al. 2012).

The desire to be culturally sensitive can mean that professionals may fail to investigate instances of child sexual abuse through fear of disrupting community cohesion and perceived potential resistance by communities (Gohir 2013). Fears of allegations of racism can also affect responses and result in a different level of service being provided to ethnic minority communities (O'Neill Gutierrez and Chawla 2017). Much of the literature suggests that there is a disproportionately low take-up of statutory, formal support services from ethnic minority victims and survivors. This can stem from a lack of awareness of services and how to access them (Sawrikar and Katz 2017b; Cowburn et al. 2015; Rehal and Maguire 2014; Gilligan and Akhtar 2005). There can also be a mistrust of services, which may stem from previous negative interactions in their native country or experiencing racist attitudes from some professionals (O'Neill Gutierrez and Chawla 2017; CEOP 2011; Gilligan and Akhtar 2005) and concerns around the potential consequences of engaging with services (Sawrikar and Katz 2017a, b; CEOP 2011; Fontes and Plummer 2010; Gilligan and Akhtar 2005).

Some studies suggest that specialist, local services that are directed towards the specific priorities and needs of ethnic minority communities are more accessible and there is a perception that an ethnically or culturally similar professional could aid disclosure (Harrison and Gill 2017; O'Neill Gutierrez and Chawla 2017; Rehal and Maguire 2014). However, for some, this could act as a barrier as there may be a fear that if the professional is from their own community they would not maintain confidentiality, or would prioritise protecting the community reputation over the needs of the victim and survivor (Gilligan and Akhtar 2005, 2006; Webb et al. 2002).

Informal support, from families and communities, is often utilised more than formal support services in ethnic minority communities. However, some victims and survivors may receive negative responses from families (Rehal and Maguire 2014) and informal support systems may also prevent victims and survivors from accessing further help through fear of bringing shame upon the family (O'Neill Gutierrez and Chawla 2017). Overall, the literature highlights how victims and survivors from ethnic minority communities are less likely to report sexual abuse and are often less likely to be recognised as victims by statutory services. The literature also reveals how victims and survivors may have less positive interactions with institutions due to experiences of racism and poor responses from professionals. These themes were explored in depth during the second stage of the research study, which comprised focus groups with people from ethnic minority communities. The following sections discuss the findings from these focus groups, in particular drawing on the experiences of victims and survivors.

Participants' Perceptions and Experiences of Institutions in Relation to Child Sexual Abuse—Focus Group Findings

Discussions regarding institutions and child sexual abuse generally revealed negative perceptions and experiences, particularly in relation to statutory services like the police and children's social care services. Although it was occasionally not clear whether participants were referring to statutory institutions or voluntary organisations, most of the discussions around institutions focused on statutory services.

Knowledge of Institutions Responsible for Identifying and Responding to Child Sexual Abuse

Participants identified a number of institutions as having a responsibility to respond to child sexual abuse, including the police, children's social care services, schools, health services, religious institutions and voluntary sector organisations. There was an acknowledgement among participants that schools can be a good place for a child to disclose abuse because they often have appropriate staff, such as counsellors or learning mentors, which can give children a place to speak without telling their family.

> If you're a child in school, you might not tell your parents or your family, but you could tell your teacher ... because in schools they've got counsellors and all that.
>
> (Female focus group participant)

The safeguarding role of children's social care services was also recognised by participants, particularly victims and survivors who often had direct experiences of them, and a few participants recognised the support that they can offer. There was also an acknowledgement of the importance of religion and faith in some communities, with a shared view that people should be able to disclose sexual abuse to religious institutions and receive support from them.

Factors That Influence Willingness to Engage with Institutions

Although many participants recognised the role of statutory institutions in responding to cases of child sexual abuse, there was a lack of consensus among participants regarding their willingness to engage with institutions. Some participants said that they would notify authorities, but often highlighted that other members of their community would not. Other participants expressed a reluctance to report to statutory institutions, saying they would prefer to deal with child sexual abuse within their own community or to report to voluntary sector organisations. There was a perception among some participants that institutional responses would '*make the situation worse*'. Some of the reluctance to engage with institutions reflected concerns about the ability of institutions to deal with cases of child sexual abuse and handle information confidentially. Other concerns were more explicitly related to how these services may interact with people from ethnic minorities; specifically, how misconceptions and stereotypes about ethnicity and culture on the part of professionals may mean that they fail to identify or acknowledge child sexual abuse, and may also fail to respond appropriately and offer the support and help that all children are entitled to.

Competency in Dealing with Child Sexual Abuse Cases

> I think the police knew that they'd made a mistake. They had me straight back in there … But they do make mistakes. The CPS made a mistake.
> (Female focus group participant)

Some participants, particularly victims and survivors, talked about having little confidence in the system, perceiving institutions to be insufficiently resourced and '*not set up properly*', with '*holes, gaps everywhere*'. In particular, several victims and survivors described negative experiences with police and the criminal justice system. Participants talked about the police's general approach as being off-putting, of not acting '*quick enough*' or being '*not really that interested*'. One victim and survivor talked very angrily about the '*serious, serious, serious negligence*' in the way the police had handled her case.

A number of participants expressed doubts about whether the police were best placed to deal with allegations of child sexual abuse. Some participants argued that the needs of the victim should come first and this may not include reporting to police:

> Why would you call the police, knowing that someone has done something wrong, but then having a victim you want to care for? You wouldn't necessarily call the police for that ... if your focus is on the victim.
>
> (Male focus group participant)

One participant discussed how it is '*a bit of a myth that Black people don't call the police*' but what is relevant are the circumstances in which they will call the police. There was a perception that the police are better able to respond to more general crimes, such as burglary, than child sexual abuse. Some participants recognised the challenges police face and queried whether they have sufficient resources to put into issues like child sexual abuse. There was also a perception that they lack the sensitivity needed, with one participant highlighting that police '*are just not trained in the art of dealing with people psychologically*'.

Experiences with the criminal justice system were also described by victims and survivors of child sexual abuse as difficult and talking about these experiences left some participants angry and tearful. Most of the participants who had been through the court system described their experiences negatively, for example as '*another abuse*' and '*an absolute trauma*'. Some participants believed that the professionals had made mistakes in their cases. In some instances, victims and survivors had to wait years for their case to get to court and they were not always kept properly informed throughout the process.

Information Sharing and Confidentiality

A common theme in the focus groups related to concerns about how institutions would share information about disclosures of child sexual abuse, and with whom. There was a strong concern that information shared with institutions may then be passed on to other institutions without the person's consent or knowledge and may get back to other members of the community or family.

> So they'll [the school] involve the social services and then obviously they will call in the parents, so now that child is already put in a position like, 'Oh, my God, my parents know I've done this'.

(Female focus group participant)

Some participants expressed how they would not want others in their community to know if they reported child sexual abuse to an institution. This was related to not wanting others to know about the sexual abuse and also to the shame associated with informing authorities. In particular, some South Asian participants described how it was not regarded as a good thing to '*name and shame*' by reporting sexual abuse and that this leads to '*a lot of covering up*', for example by adults removing a child from harm but not notifying authorities of sexual abuse and not seeking support for the victim. Participants said that some people from their communities may not be aware of confidentiality and the laws that protect the anonymity of the victim and survivor. It was suggested that if people were more aware of the processes they might be more willing to come forward.

Failing to Identify Child Sexual Abuse

> If the social worker's white and we're from an ethnic minority I think the social worker's scared of being accused of being racist, so they just stay clear.
>
> (Female focus group participant)

Victims and survivors gave numerous examples of institutions failing to identify signs of child sexual abuse and described the considerable impact this had had on their lives. In some cases, these failures were a consequence of professionals failing to recognise that participants were victims and instead viewing them as children displaying behavioural problems. In particular, several participants described how schools failed to pick up on changes in behaviour that should have been warning signs that something was wrong. As adults, participants recognised that these behaviours were a cry for help, but the adults around the child at the time did not tend to explore the reasons behind the behaviour and the opportunity to identify the sexual abuse or provide the child with emotional support was missed:

> I find school like very – an emotive topic because they were people that were seeing me every day; they were seeing my behaviour and they were punishing me and not investigating. I find that really – I find that really hard to forgive.
>
> (Male focus group participant)

In some cases, these failures were a consequence of victims being overlooked by professionals as a result of stereotyping. One participant felt that his '*bad*' behaviour was interpreted by professionals as '*typical*' for a Black child and he believed that a White child would have been responded to more effectively:

> I did a lot of bad things; I was playing up, and I think it should have been picked up on that something's wrong … But I think if a child of colour or Black kid or Asian kid maybe plays up and, you know, does things and gets violent or whatever, it's sometimes seen as typical. It's not investigated … Where I feel if it's a White kid that maybe does something wrong it's: 'Oh, something's got to be wrong; let's look into it. Let's find out why he's behaving this way'.
>
> (Male focus group participant)

Stereotyping according to gender and family background was also noted by participants. One participant felt that professionals just saw him as '*a difficult Black boy*', which resulted in a failure to identify him as '*a vulnerable person … who was actually crying out for help*'. Another participant described how she was behaving erratically at school, but was taken to one side by a teacher and told that she should be '*grateful*' for the family she had as she was one of the few children in a two parent household. Similar concerns about being stereotyped were expressed more broadly by participants in the focus groups and were cited as reasons for not disclosing child sexual abuse to institutions. One participant stated that social services frame ethnic minorities as '*actually quite dysfunctional*' and several participants revealed a perception that involving children's social services could lead to a child being removed from the family and taken into care, sometimes due to cultural misunderstandings.

But unfortunately sometimes it's reported and the child is removed from the home, put into foster care and all sorts of other things.
(Female focus group participant)

Similarly, another participant described how '*the police frame us [ethnic minorities] as actually being quite criminal*'. Participants described the police as '*the enemy*' who may be contacted for help but would actually be scrutinising people from ethnic minorities or low income backgrounds. Another participant shared this view:

The police can be against us. You could call the police because you are suffering from domestic abuse and the police can come in and say, 'Yes, but are you legally here?'. They may be more interested in [that].
(Female focus group participant)

Failing to Respond to Disclosures of Child Sexual Abuse

You don't need somebody to understand all the laws. You don't need somebody to understand all the cultures, all the diversities, you just need somebody to just be a human being and just give you the information and not make comments.
(Female focus group participant)

In some cases, victims and survivors described how professionals failed to respond appropriately to disclosures of sexual abuse because of what appeared to be a lack of cultural competence. This can arise in part from a lack of cultural diversity within institutions and was cited as a reason by some participants for not wishing to engage further with statutory services. A lack of diversity can exacerbate a sense of difference for people from ethnic minorities, even when the services are helpful:

I was going to say that all these people are helpful, but the thing that I found really difficult was being able to relate with somebody, because unfortunately all these people … they all have one thing in common:

they're White, and they just don't appreciate – like whether the – it's not intentional or whatever, but, you know, they just don't appreciate that culture – cultural barrier and like gap.

(Female focus group participant)

Several participants also talked about professionals' fears of '*stepping on cultural sensitivities*' and of '*the community accusing them of being racist*', resulting in failures to respond appropriately to allegations of child sexual abuse. One victim and survivor described how this left her unprotected:

I just wish social services just barged in and took me into care, and took me and my siblings into care ... but they were so intent on not coming across racist or coming across culturally insensitive, that they forgot about the person that was being hurt here.

(Female focus group participant)

For other participants, racist stereotyping and misunderstandings were the reasons for poor responses. Participants suggested that professionals sometimes had a different idea of what is 'normal' for ethnic minority children and families compared to White children and families. At the stereotypes at play varied between ethnic groups and were also based on other characteristics such as gender, age and class. For example, participants mentioned long-held problematic historical narratives that sexualise Black people or that suggest that intra-familial sexual relations are common and acceptable in Asian ethnic groups.

Among many participants, a fear of being stereotyped or 'othered' by professionals created a feeling of mistrust. Participants discussed discrimination and the tendency for anything that happens in an ethnic minority community to be seen as representative of that entire community or ethnic group. By disclosing or even discussing child sexual abuse in ethnic minority communities, there was a perceived risk that "*they'll think we're all like that*".

To them it's like I think there's an external view of our people which is: 'Oh, you lot do that anyway, don't you? You marry each other.'

(Female focus group participant)

Some victims and survivors explicitly linked the poor response they received from professionals to the fact that they were from an ethnic minority and the professional was White. These experiences related to both physical and sexual abuse. Two participants discussed revealing they had been physically abused to a teacher at school, but nothing was done in response. In one of these cases the victim and survivor was told that it was a '"*culture clash*"'. Another victim and survivor shared her experience of disclosing sexual abuse as a child to a social worker and revealed how the sexual abuse was denied, with the abusive behaviour instead attributed to her culture:

> The social worker was White, okay, and she said to me, 'This is not sexual abuse. This is your culture'. Even today, I'm so traumatised by this.
> (Female focus group participant)

She then described how she has, over the years, sought reassurance and validation from other professionals in different institutions that '"*This is sexual abuse. This is not Asian culture or Indian culture. This is sexual abuse.*"' In this case, the failure to acknowledge the sexual abuse became a traumatic experience in itself. Conversely, one participant spoke about how she would prefer not to see a professional from the same ethnicity as herself. This was due to a concern of being judged by that person—fearing that consideration of ethnicity and culture may take precedence over her needs as a victim and survivor. This view was echoed by another participant who described how she was told by her Bengali GP to consider the impact of disclosing sexual abuse on her family:

> When I told her [GP], she told me, she's Bengali, so she was like, 'In your community … you'll have to weigh up the pros and cons of telling the family, how the family will take it, and whether or not you should report it to the police.'
> (Female focus group participant)

However, not all experiences were negative and a few participants did experience positive responses from institutions in relation to child sexual abuse. What helped make these experiences positive, which was lacking in so many other accounts, was the acknowledgement of the sexual abuse—naming what had happened—and the support that was offered throughout the process. One participant approached the police to talk about the sexual abuse of another child, but found that they helped her to recognise and name her own sexual abuse:

> 'I was just going to say, because mine's quite the opposite, as in it was the police that really supported me to say the word ... to deal with it, 'You've been abused' ... they have been very, very supportive, the police, the court, straightaway knew what it was, called it what it was.'
>
> (Female focus group participant)

Support Services for Victims and Survivors of Child Sexual Abuse—Focus Group Findings

Many participants recognised that victims and survivors of child sexual abuse may require professional help and support, possibly over an extended period of time. However, victims and survivors often spoke about not receiving adequate support for sexual abuse as a child and in general described how services offering support were just not available. Sometimes this lack of support was related to gender or class. In one focus group, male participants talked about how institutions are not able or willing to hear the views of young, aggressive males and suggested that there are more opportunities for females to access help from institutions. Another participant explained how she was unable to access support at the university she attended as they were used to admitting '*White, very very middle class, private school educated kids*' and they did not know how to support her. This participant felt unable to continue with her medical degree as a result, which she described as one of her biggest regrets.

Where victims and survivors had accessed services, although some experiences were positive, many participants spoke about poor experiences that were related to a lack of understanding on the part of professionals about child sexual abuse or about ethnicity and culture. Overall, there were conflicting views regarding whether support should be formal or informal and whether institutions are able to provide trauma-informed, culturally appropriate care.

Professionals' Understanding of Child Sexual Abuse

> Because nobody ever – unless they've gone through it, they will never really understand.
> (Female focus group participant)

Some victims and survivors attributed negative experiences with support services to the fact that the professionals involved did not seem to understand how they may have been affected or how to treat them. One participant discussed being made to take anti-depressant medication prescribed by a psychiatrist that she felt was not a suitable treatment for a child under 18. Another participant described how his therapist assumed that as a consequence of experiencing child sexual abuse he would possibly commit a sexual or violent offence, highlighting the prejudice that victims and survivors can face:

> The psychologist had this thought that I would turn out to be a rapist or a murderer myself out of some sort of revenge, and I was so disgusted I stopped going.
> (Male focus group participant)

Such accounts demonstrate how responses were not trauma-informed. Some participants felt that they needed to share their experience with someone who had had a similar experience in order to be understood, though others disagreed. One participant felt that '*sometimes you don't want people around you that have walked [in] your shoes*', and said that she would prefer to access the kind of support that would give her the tools and resources required to move on. Another participant, who had volunteered with Childline, pointed out that other volunteers were able to offer support to callers without having had the same experience.

Professionals' Understanding of Culturally Appropriate Support

> It meant so much to me ... that my paediatrician was Hindu and, later on, that my psychiatrist was Muslim, because they understood what it's like being a woman in the Asian community. I didn't need to explain.
>
> (Female focus group participant)

The fears around stereotyping and a lack of cultural competence discussed in relation to statutory services were also expressed with regards to support services. Participants were concerned that racist views, whether implicit or explicit, might affect the support that someone from an ethnic minority community would receive. Participants also described how services can be less accessible for people from ethnic minority communities due to the gap in understanding and the fear of being misunderstood:

> And a lot of the organisations that are out there that can offer the support do not look like yourselves, so therefore you may be reluctant to go to them, because they will not be culturally aware of what's going on for you, or they may not be able to comprehend, or even – they may not be able to recognise what's going on for you, just because there are so many differences.
>
> (Focus group participant)

In many of the focus groups, participants reflected on the benefits of receiving support from someone with a similar ethnic or cultural background. Some victims and survivors described how important it had been not to have to explain how their culture had influenced the experience and the impacts of sexual abuse. Knowledge of culture and ethnicity often intersected with other factors, such as gender or personal experiences of sexual abuse, as helping to foster understanding around the particular struggles individuals may face:

> She understood not only as a Black woman being abused, sexually abused. She ticked all my boxes. Everything I said she got me. And I realised how

important, how much I needed that. Someone that I could look at, I recognised, but understood me.

(Female focus group participant)

Other benefits of being supported by someone from the same ethnicity or culture related to them being more likely to understand the language and not be judgemental. However, several participants highlighted that what matters the most is someone's understanding of the issues and emphasised that this does not have to mean that a professional is from the same ethnicity. Some victims and survivors spoke about positive experiences with professionals from White ethnicities and in one focus group, some male participants expressed scepticism of the view that simply because an individual looked like them they would therefore be able to provide more effective support. One participant felt that a professional's behaviours and understanding will be shaped by the training and induction process within institutions, which can be reflective of the institutional practices within which they work, rather than their background or heritage:

But there's a real dilemma there that I have with that, which is about the assumption that because somebody's skin tone looks like mine he's going to be able to understand my worldview. So, for somebody to go into any of the general professions, they are trained to not be themselves.

(Male focus group participant)

Informal Support for Victims and Survivors of Child Sexual Abuse

Many participants spoke about the value of peer support in helping them to process the experience of child sexual abuse. The importance of this may be heightened by people's negative experiences with institutions, and may also reflect the significance of collectivist values to some ethnic minority communities (Sawrikar and Katz 2017b). As some victims and survivors can be ostracised from their families and communities as a consequence of talking about child sexual abuse, this kind of support can play a crucial role for victims and survivors.

Without the opportunity to talk about child sexual abuse with other victims and survivors, some participants described feeling isolated. For some victims and survivors, participating in the focus group was the first time that they had met with people with similar experiences. After one group, some victims and survivors stayed behind to chat and exchanged contact details in order to keep in touch.

> This is also the first time I've come together with a group of people who've had that experience, and it's very moving for me and very supportive and cathartic and everything, just to be in the room with the people who've been through experiences of abuse.
> (Female focus group participant)

Participants also described how meeting with others with similar experiences could help build strength among victims and survivors. This was seen as part of a process of starting to open up a wider conversation within communities about child sexual abuse and gradually break down the wall of silence:

> The more we talk about it the more strong we get and then the more we might collectively have a voice to say, 'It happens and it's happening in our community and, do you know what, we need to talk'. But we need to build that strength like it needs to start from somewhere. So, we need somewhere where we can get together and get healing.
> (Female focus group participant)

Due to a lack of culturally aware support services, some participants had started their own support groups for ethnic minority communities. One participant described how she would be setting up a support service because in her view White members of staff do not have enough in-depth understanding of the traditions and lifestyles of other cultures. Another participant had set up a peer support organisation for people from ethnic minority communities, with an emphasis on sharing what works:

I set up an organisation myself, and we get people from different BME communities. Peer empowerment is so important. We're able to come together once a month, and able to empower and encourage each other.

(Female focus group participant)

Reflections

Child sexual abuse is an issue that affects all communities, ethnicities and cultures. There are many experiences in relation to child sexual abuse that are common across communities, including difficulties in talking about child sexual abuse and poor responses to disclosure. However, experiences are not universal and this research has highlighted some experiences that are specific to ethnic minority communities. These include experiences of institutional racism and discrimination, and professionals' concerns about appearing culturally sensitive, that can impede the identification and disclosure of, and responses to, child sexual abuse. However, addressing these issues is complex; there was a lack of consensus among participants regarding the need for specialist support services and participants expressed sometimes contrasting views on the type of support they would like to receive. These research findings highlight the need to ensure that services can respond to a diverse range of needs and are responsive to the individual.

In participants' accounts, some professionals appeared to demonstrate bias in relation to children from ethnic minority communities. In comparison to children from majority ethnicities, some professionals appeared to have a different threshold for judging whether behaviours described by victims and survivors from ethnic minority communities were sexually abusive. Professionals also appeared to demonstrate a different threshold for judging behaviours among ethnic minority children, particularly boys, to be troubling or disruptive. These kinds of biases can lead to differences in the reported prevalence of child sexual abuse and to differences in interventions and treatment; research in the US for example has demonstrated racial bias in the substantiation of child sexual abuse cases, with children of Native North American or

Latinx ethnicity having a reduced likelihood of substantiation[3] (Fix and Nair 2020).

The accounts of victims and survivors from ethnic minority communities point to their struggles in dealing with the trauma of the sexual abuse alongside the trauma of interacting with institutions that, through bias, may have heightened their vulnerability to sexual abuse, failed to identify it and failed to provide an appropriate, supportive response. Racist stereotyping and assumptions about culture led some victims and survivors to question their own experiences and even created confusion about their own culture. As accounts highlighted, where responses fail to acknowledge a person's experience or they devalue the person, the response itself can become a trauma.

Participants' accounts revealed how fear of discrimination and racist stereotyping can prevent people from ethnic minority communities reporting cases of child sexual abuse. This can sometimes mean that sexual abuse is dealt with within the community or may not be dealt with at all, leaving the victim and other children at risk of further abuse. Victims and survivors may not be able to access formal support and may not receive suitable support from within the family or community, further compounding the impacts of child sexual abuse (Rodger et al. 2020). It can also mean that children from ethnic minority communities are underrepresented in prevalence statistics and service data, making it challenging for practitioners and policymakers to appreciate the scale of the issue and plan effective, culturally appropriate responses.

There were a number of occasions where participants spoke positively about changes that are occurring, both within communities and institutions. For example, some participants said their communities now have a better understanding of child sexual abuse and its impacts and are more open to talking about it. Participants described younger generations as being better informed due to media and education and said that they would sometimes pass this understanding on to older generations; some participants who were parents described learning from their children about how to respond appropriately to abuse. Some participants also felt that institutions, particularly schools, are in a better position to respond to child sexual abuse and one participant felt that the criminal justice system is becoming more supportive of victims than it used to be. However, many of the research findings from this study echo findings from previous research and highlight how change is not happening quickly enough to ensure that all children are protected from child sexual abuse.

What many participants in this research wanted was for professionals to see and acknowledge their experience for what it was, without it being distorted by assumptions about victims and survivors, their ethnicity or any other demographic characteristics. In particular, naming the experience can be important for victims and survivors and can be particularly powerful for children from communities where experiences of sexual abuse may be shrouded in silence and shame, and the words or language needed to communicate what has happened might not be available.

Improving Interactions with Institutions

This study did not speak directly with professionals but it has highlighted that many victims and survivors felt that professionals had fallen short in terms of providing support that is both trauma-informed and culturally aware. Professionals face the challenge of needing to avoid cultural blindness—assuming that victims and survivors of child sexual abuse are a homogeneous group who face universal issues—while also avoiding cultural incompetence, whereby behaviours that are abusive fail to be recognised or responded to appropriately. Participants also highlighted how racism and stereotyping continue to impede prevention, identification and responses to child sexual abuse among ethnic minority communities. Participants' accounts suggest that there are a number of factors that could improve interactions with institutions for people from ethnic minority communities, including institutional measures such as training and diversity, and community-based measures such as peer support and community engagement.

Appropriate Training for Professionals Coming into Contact with Victims and Survivors

Participants highlighted how professionals need appropriate training, both to improve understanding of ethnicity and culture, and to improve understanding around child sexual abuse. Such training was regarded as important for all professionals, regardless of background or personal experience. Participants also highlighted how peer supporters need to be trained in order to know how to support victims and survivors effectively.

In terms of the specific areas in which professionals may benefit from training, Sawrikar (2020) suggests that service providers should be educated about the following:

- Child sexual abuse (prevalence, perpetrators and myths).
- Cultural knowledge (awareness of the importance/relevance of supportive responses, racism and family reputation).
- Cultural competency (ethnically diverse workforce, trained interpreters, regular staff training, multicultural framework and mandatory data collection).
- Pros and cons of medicalising mental illness due to child sexual abuse over the use of a sociological framework.
- The importance of encouraging additional self-help, family and group therapy.

Participants' experiences of racial, gender and class bias highlight how any interventions designed by service providers need to be culturally aware and intersectional. In one study, service professionals suggested using an intersectional approach to design a framework/tool for professionals working with Black, Asian and ethnic minority communities, which would focus on both prevention of child sexual abuse in those communities and one-to-one work with children and young people affected by child sexual abuse. They considered that this framework/tool should be informed by the experiences—in terms of disclosure, the legal and court system, and therapeutic services—of victims and survivors from Black, Asian and minority ethnic communities (Ali et al. 2020).

Access to Support Services that Meet People's Preferences

In terms of support, there was no consensus among participants regarding the need for specialist support services targeted at victims and survivors from ethnic minority communities, highlighting the need for diversity and choice within services. Some participants pointed to the limitations of "*all-White organisations*" in being able to understand the traditions and lifestyles of ethnic minority communities and argued for support services targeted at these groups. Other participants felt they would prefer not to see a professional from their own ethnicity. Choice about the gender of professionals was also mentioned by some participants. In one group, participants argued for the need to have gender-specific support, such as women's centres, which were seen as bringing women together and strengthening them. Participants also pointed to the need for safe havens for men who have experienced abuse and suggested that men may prefer to talk to another male about abuse.

Some victims and survivors said that they would prefer to be supported by someone who has experience of child sexual abuse. They felt that other victims and survivors can provide the most empathic support and that professionals who have experienced sexual trauma are more likely to understand the impacts of child sexual abuse. Other researchers have highlighted how some professionals who work with this cohort will be victims and survivors, and providing adequate support and training for these practitioners is essential. Sanchez et al. (2019) discuss how a trauma-informed approach recognises that those providing support are often victims and survivors but point out that there can often be little space for professionals to be open about their experiences due to a fear of stigmatisation from colleagues. They argue that trauma-informed organisations will create opportunities for healing among staff and celebrate the strength that they bring.

Other participants, however, felt that as child sexual abuse is an issue that affects all communities, there are no specific support needs for particular communities. In talking about what participants wanted from professionals responding to child sexual abuse, being '*human*', non-judgemental and seeing the whole person were emphasised by participants, reflecting a person-centred approach that takes into account a person's ethnicity and culture, without reducing their experience to cultural factors.

Peer Support and Informal Ways of Sharing Experiences

Participants spoke about the value of peer support in enabling victims and survivors to talk to other people with similar experiences and from similar backgrounds. Forums were therefore suggested as one way to help people move forward. One such example comes from Siblinghood Survivor Listening Circles, a project run with survivors of child sexual abuse, which was held with culturally specific organisations in the US from 2016–2017. Using a focus group format, the groups explored themes on healing, trust and safety, and justice and accountability. The authors suggest that practitioners, rape crisis centres and culturally specific organisations should be exploring these concepts to support survivors who are healing individually, without family and community support, and also consider their role in healing communities (Sanchez et al. 2019).

Initiatives That Engage the Community

Many participants spoke about the need to open up the conversation around child sexual abuse and engage members of their communities in these discussions. Other research has suggested that services can play a role in raising awareness of child sexual abuse within communities (Ali et al. 2020). One participant for this research gave an example of a school that ran a parent support programme which addressed issues of abuse and provided childcare for the parents so they were able to attend, illustrating a proactive approach to safeguarding.

Sanchez et al. (2019) argue that central to the approach of many trauma-informed, community-based organisations is the embeddedness of communities and the creation of approaches alongside and led by community members and survivors themselves. Such approaches can also help to raise the visibility of services; research has shown that support services are insufficiently visible and accessible, particularly to people who do not speak English fluently (Ali et al. 2020). However, researchers emphasise the need to recognise how family, community and peers can be an important source of support in some cases but may also be a source of trauma (Sanchez at el. 2019). One way of navigating this complexity, advocated by participants in this research, is through approaches that empower children and young people, and victims and survivors. Placing the voice of the victim and survivor at the centre of any response or treatment can help professionals to determine where community involvement may be beneficial and where it may not.

Conclusion

This chapter was based on a study with people from different ethnic minority communities that explored their perceptions and experiences of the barriers to disclosing and reporting child sexual abuse, their experiences and interactions with institutions, and the support needs of victims and survivors of child sexual abuse from these communities. The focus of this chapter has been participants' interactions with institutions and experiences of support services. The research findings revealed how, while some victims and survivors reported positive experiences with institutions and support services, many reported negative experiences that can create barriers to disclosing child sexual abuse. These negative experiences include a lack of cultural competence in institutions and experiences of racism and stereotyping. Participants also raised concerns about confidentiality and the competence of institutions to manage cases of child sexual abuse. These negative perceptions and experiences of institutions are one reason why victims and survivors from ethnic minority communities may be less likely to disclose sexual abuse. The tendency of some professionals to stereotype also helps to elucidate why victims from ethnic minority communities may be less likely to be recognised as victims by institutions and may not receive the support they are entitled to. However, the varying needs and experiences of victims and survivors and the lack of consensus on some issues, such as specialist support services and sharing characteristics with professionals, highlight how victims and survivors would benefit from flexible and multifaceted responses from institutions.

Some positive messages did emerge from this research. Some participants acknowledged the important role that institutions like schools and children's social care services play in responding to child sexual abuse, and there was some indication that younger generations of people from ethnic minority communities are more willing to approach authorities. More work remains to be done however, and participants discussed how improved training for professionals, increased diversity within institutions, and better engagement between institutions and communities would improve relationships and outcomes for victims and survivors of child sexual abuse from ethnic minority communities.

> **Summary—Participants' Suggestions for Change**
>
> Participants' accounts highlighted how many victims and survivors experienced cultural incompetence and racism or discrimination from institutions in relation to child sexual abuse. Some victims and survivors also felt that professionals lacked knowledge and understanding in relation to the impacts of child sexual abuse. Many victims and survivors cited peer support from those with similar backgrounds as important for their recovery and talked about the need to open up the conversation around child sexual abuse more widely. To improve institutional responses in the future, participants suggested the following.
>
> 1. Appropriate training for professionals coming into contact with victims and survivors:
>   - Training on ethnicity and culture, and child sexual abuse, with culturally aware interventions.
> 2. Access to support services that meet people's preferences:
>   - Diversity within services and choice in relation to seeing professionals with similar or different characteristics.
> 3. Peer support and informal ways of sharing experiences:
>   - Forums and other groups that provide a safe space for victims and survivors to discuss their experiences with others who have had similar experiences.

4. Initiatives that engage the community:
   - Institutions working closely with the community to improve responses to child sexual abuse.

   Further research in this field could explore victims and survivors' experiences with different service models and approaches. Research could also explore the characteristics of peer support that aid recovery.

Notes

1. We use the term 'South Asian' to refer to the Indian subcontinent. In our sample, participants from South Asian ethnic groups included individuals with Bangladeshi, Indian and Pakistani ethnicities.
2. It should be noted that as all victims and survivors in this study were adults, their experiences of child sexual abuse were non-recent.
3. Meaning a case was founded or determined to have occurred by state law.

References

Ali, N., Butt, J., and Phillips, M. (2020). *Improving responses to the sexual abuse of Black, Asian and minority ethnic children*. Centre of Expertise on Child Sexual Abuse. https://www.csacentre.org.uk/documents/improving-responses-csa-of-black-asian-minority-ethnic-children/

Berelowitz, S., Firmin, C., Edwards, G., and Gulyurtlu, S. (2012). *"I thought I was the only one. The only one in the world." The Office of the Children's Commissioner's Inquiry into Child Sexual Exploitation in Gangs and Groups Interim report*. Office of the Children's Commissioner. https://www.childrenscommissioner.gov.uk/wp-content/uploads/2017/07/I-thought-I-was-the-only-one-in-the-world.pdf

Bernard, C., and Harris, P. (2016). Introduction. In C. Bernard, and P. Harris, (Eds.), *Safeguarding Black children: Good practice in child protection* (pp. 11–37). Jessica Kingsley.

Child Exploitation and Online Protection (CEOP). (2011). *Out of mind, out of sight: Breaking down the barriers to understanding child sexual exploitation.* CEOP. https://www.basw.co.uk/system/files/resources/basw_101409-2_0.pdf

Cowburn, M., Gill, A., and Harrison, K. (2015). Speaking about sexual abuse in British South Asian communities: Offenders, victims and the challenges of shame and reintegration. *Journal of Sexual Aggression, 21*(1), 4–15. https://doi.org/10.1080/13552600.2014.929188

Fix, R. L., and Nair, R. (2020). Racial/ethnic and gender disparities in substantiation of child physical and sexual abuse: Influences of caregiver and child characteristics. *Children and Youth Services Review, 116*, 1–9. https://doi.org/10.1016/j.childyouth.2020.105186

Fontes, L., and Plummer, C. (2010). Cultural issues in disclosures of child sexual abuse. *Journal of Child Sexual Abuse, 19*(5), 491–518. https://doi.org/10.1080/10538712.2010.512520

Gill, A., and Harrison, K. (2018). 'I am talking about it because I want to stop it': Child sexual abuse and sexual violence against women in British South Asian communities. *British Journal of Criminology, 59*(3), 511–529. https://doi.org/10.1093/bjc/azy059

Gilligan, P., and Akhtar, S. (2005). Child sexual abuse among Asian communities: Developing materials to raise awareness in Bradford. *Practice, 17*(4), 267–284. https://doi.org/10.1080/09503150500426735

Gilligan, P. and Akhtar, S. (2006). Cultural barriers to the disclosure of child sexual abuse in Asian communities: Listening to what women say. *British Journal of Social Work, 36*(8), 1361–1377. https://doi.org/10.1093/bjsw/bch309

Gohir, S. (2013). Unheard voices: *The sexual exploitation of Asian girls and young women.* Birmingham, Muslim Women's Network. https://www.mwnuk.co.uk/go_files/resources/UnheardVoices.pdf

Harrison, K., and Gill, A. (2017). Policing the culture of silence: Strategies to increase the reporting of sexual abuse in British South Asian communities. *Policing and Society, 29*(3), 302–317. https://doi.org/10.1080/10439463.2017.1405958

Kelly, L., and Karsna, K. (2018). *Measuring the scale and changing nature of child sexual abuse and child sexual exploitation: Scoping report (updated).* Centre of Expertise on Child Sexual Abuse. https://www.csacentre.org.uk/documents/scale-and-nature-scoping-report-2018/

Office for National Statistics (ONS). (2019). *Ethnic group, national identity and religion. Measuring equality: A guide for the collection and classification of ethnic group, national identity and religion data in the UK*. ONS. https://www.ons.gov.uk/methodology/classificationsandstanda rds/measuringequality/ethnicgroupnationalidentityandreligion

O'Neill Gutierrez, C., and Chawla, S. (2017). *The child sexual exploitation of young South Asian women in Birmingham and Coventry. Exploring professional insight into young women's hidden journeys, silence, and support*. Children's Society.

Rehal, M., and Maguire, S. (2014). *The price of honour: Exploring the issues of sexual violence within South Asian communities in Coventry*. Coventry Rape and Sexual Abuse Centre.

Rodger, H., Hurcombe, R., Redmond, T., and George, R. (2020). *"People don't talk about it": Child sexual abuse in ethnic minority communities*. Independent Inquiry into Child Sexual Abuse. https://www.iicsa.org.uk/publications/res earch/child-sexual-abuse-ethnic-minority-communities

Sanchez, D., Benbow, L. M., Hernández-Martínez, M., and Serrata, J. V. (2019). Invisible bruises: Theoretical and practical considerations for Black/Afro-Latina survivors of childhood sexual abuse. *Women & Therapy, 42*(3–4), 406–429. https://doi.org/10.1080/02703149.2019.1622903

Sawrikar, P. (2020). A conceptual framework for the prevention and treatment of child sexual abuse (CSA) in ethnic minority communities. In I. Bryce, and W. Petherick (Eds.), *Child sexual abuse: Forensic issues in evidence, impact, and management* (pp. 625–641). Elsevier Academic Press. https://doi.org/10.1016/B978-0-12-819434-8.00028-3

Sawrikar, P., and Katz, I. (2017a). Barriers to disclosing child sexual abuse (CSA) in ethnic minority communities: A review of the literature and implications for practice in Australia. *Children and Youth Services Review, 83*, 302–315. https://doi.org/10.1016/j.childyouth.2017.11.011

Sawrikar, P., and Katz, I. (2017b). The treatment needs of victims/survivors of child sexual abuse (CSA) from ethnic minority communities: A literature review and suggestions for practice. *Children and Youth Services Review, 79*, 166–179. https://doi.org/10.1016/j.childyouth.2017.06.021

The Children's Society. (2018). *Supporting black and minority ethnic children and young people experiencing child sexual exploitation. Guidance for professionals*. The Children's Society. https://www.csepoliceandprevention.org.uk/sites/default/files/cse_guidance_bame.pdf

Thiara, R. K., Roy, S., & Ng, P. (2015). *Between the lines. Service responses to Black and minority ethnic (BME) women and girls experiencing sexual violence*. Imkaan and University of Warwick. https://www.imkaan.org.uk/research

Thoburn, J. (2016). Foreword. In C. Bernard, and P. Harris (Eds.), *Safeguarding Black children: Good practice in child protection* (pp. 11–37). Jessica Kingsley.

Warrington, C., Beckett, H., Ackerley, E., Walker, M., and Allnock, D. (2017). *Making noise: Children's voices for positive change after sexual abuse. Children's experiences of help-seeking and support after sexual abuse in the family environment*. Office of the Children's Commissioner. https://www.beds.ac.uk/media/86813/makingnoise-20042017.pdf

Webb, E., Maddocks, A., and Bongilli, J. (2002). Effectively protecting black and minority ethnic children from harm: Overcoming barriers to the child protection process. *Child Abuse Review, 11*, 394–410. https://doi.org/10.1002/car.760

Open Access This chapter is licensed under the terms of the Creative Commons Attribution 4.0 International License (http://creativecommons.org/licenses/by/4.0/), which permits use, sharing, adaptation, distribution and reproduction in any medium or format, as long as you give appropriate credit to the original author(s) and the source, provide a link to the Creative Commons license and indicate if changes were made.

The images or other third party material in this chapter are included in the chapter's Creative Commons license, unless indicated otherwise in a credit line to the material. If material is not included in the chapter's Creative Commons license and your intended use is not permitted by statutory regulation or exceeds the permitted use, you will need to obtain permission directly from the copyright holder.

8

Addressing Harmful Sexual Behaviours Among Children and Young People: Definitional and Regulatory Tensions

Elizabeth Agnew and Anne-Marie McAlinden

Introduction

With the advent of digital technology, sexually abusive or exploitative behaviours among children and young people have become a greater concern. 'Peer-on-peer abuse' can occur in a wide variety of settings including within organisational or group contexts and within families or close inter-personal relationships (Firmin and Curtis 2015). Most recently, however, it is arguably non-contact or digital forms of sexual violence involving 'new media' (interactive digital forms of communication via the internet or mobile technologies) which have provoked the most concern (see e.g. Shariff 2015; McAlinden 2018). This chapter

---

E. Agnew (✉) · A.-M. McAlinden
Queen's University Belfast, Belfast, Northern Ireland, UK
e-mail: e.agnew@qub.ac.uk

A.-M. McAlinden
e-mail: a.mcalinden@qub.ac.uk

considers some of the key definitional and regulatory tensions which such behaviours present.

The digital world has changed the socio-cultural landscape around sexual norms and behaviours and increased opportunities for 'risky' sexual behaviours among adults as well as children (McAlinden 2018). This is evidenced, for example, in a wide range of relatively new criminal offences such as 'grooming' (McAlinden 2012), 'sextortion' (Wolak et al. 2018), 'revenge pornography' (Hall and Hearn 2017), 'upskirting' (Thompson 2020) and 'cyberflashing' (McGlynn et al. 2021), as part of the official recognition of 'image-based sexual abuse' (McGlynn and Rackley 2017). In relation to children and young people specifically, these new forms of behaviour have manifested as instances of non-consensual sharing of sexually explicit images as 'sexting' (Mori et al. 2020), as well as a number of high-profile cases of the filming and distribution of videos or photographs of rape or sexual assault.[1]

As research has explored further, the significance of technology and its role in sexual violence is not only that it has increased the potential and opportunities for peer forms of sexual abuse and exploitation to occur, but it has also blurred the demarcation between 'normal' and 'harmful' sexual behaviours. These difficulties are also reflected in professional and legal discourses which often struggle to discern motivations as 'harmful' or otherwise or even to differentiate between 'victims' or 'perpetrators' of harmful sexual behaviour. Moreover, these variables also impact how children and young people view sexual behaviours wherein the cultural normalisation of 'risky' or 'harmful' sexual behaviour impacts their perceptions of 'coercion' and 'consent' and, consequently, their potential status as victims.

Indeed, within social and legal discourses, there are a number of key variables which collectively impact how harmful sexual behaviours among children and young people are conceptualised and ultimately responded to. First, 'gender' is a dominant factor within both cultural and professional discourses where masculinity is often equated with offending behaviour and femininity with victimhood (McAlinden 2018:

---

[1] See for example, the 2012 sexual assault case in Steubenville, Ohio, USA, where the 16-year-old victim only learned of the sexual assault committed against her by her peers while she was unconscious due to photographs and videos of the assault being posted on social media.

175–177). However, in reality, the motivations for harmful sexual behaviour are usually more complex and young females can also be the 'perpetrators' as well as the 'victims' of sexting (Agnew 2021a). Further, the nuances and complexities of 'gender' and sexual identity are only beginning to be articulated within the literature on peer forms of sexual abuse and need to be understood more broadly beyond male/female heteronormative terms and also include LGBTQ+ identities (see e.g. Van Ouytsel et al. 2021).

Second, within public discourses, there may be a fundamental cultural reticence to even acknowledge the existence of peer forms of sexual abuse, as children are usually seen as the 'ideal' victims of child sexual abuse, rather than as 'perpetrators' (McAlinden 2014). However, in reality, as Firmin and Curtis (2015) explain, a child or young person may be victimised at the hands of another but simultaneously abuse or exert power over someone else. This may be particularly problematic in relation to abuse within organisational or groups settings such as within residential care homes, schools or gangs. In practice, the 'victim-offender overlap' (Jennings et al. 2012), or 'the victim-offender continuum' (McAlinden 2014), means that within complex forms of peer abuse where abusive behaviours have become normalised, the identification of the 'victim' or 'perpetrator' is not always easy or clear cut.

Third, there are inherent problems within legal frameworks in terms of how 'children' and 'young people' are defined across a wide variety of social and legal contexts within the UK. Within England, Wales and Northern Ireland, for example, one of the most noteworthy examples is the potential tension between the age of criminal responsibility (10); the age of consent for sexual activity (16); and the threshold for criminal liability concerning 'indecent images' of children (18). These anomalies can create regulatory tensions in terms of how harmful sexual behaviour among peers is responded to. Indeed, as a whole, the law and legal frameworks, made by adults and focused on adult-child forms of sexual abuse, are somewhat out of date in relation to capturing peer forms of abuse. In particular, prevailing cultural 'pre-existing conceptualisations of abuse' (Firmin 2013: 38) are centred around 'an offender who is often imagined to be a predatory, middle-aged white man' (Hasinoff 2015: 149) or on younger children as victims within intra-familial contexts. As a result, the law has often utilised legislation to criminalise children which was originally designed to protect them such as the use of 'indecent images' or 'child pornography' legislation as a response to adolescent 'sexting' (McAlinden 2018: Ch. 7).

This chapter draws on some of the themes which emerged from three broader empirical studies conducted by the authors respectively in Northern Ireland (McAlinden 2018; Agnew 2021a, b). The first two comprised Agnew's doctoral and post-doctoral research on young people, 'sexting' and 'consent.' This primary research initially comprised focus groups and interviews with 15 young people aged 13–17, and 28 professional interviews across a range of sectors (e.g. education, criminal justice, children's charities and safeguarding organisations) (March 2015–May 2016). This was supplemented by a small amount of additional fieldwork on the specific issue of 'consent' during an ESRC post-doctoral fellowship including interviews with 10 professionals and 61 attitudinal self-completion surveys with young people aged 14–18 (January 2020–May 2021). The third was a research project and resulting monograph on peer-based sexual exploitation and abuse by children and young people by McAlinden, funded by NOTA, encompassing both online and offline forms of abuse. The empirical research conducted for this study entailed 32 in-depth semi-structured interviews with a wide range of professionals who work with children or young people displaying or impacted by harmful sexual behaviour across the criminal justice, legal, health, education, charity and victim support sectors (February–November 2016).

This chapter intersects with a number of broader themes which run throughout this collection. First, and in the main, it considers some of the key difficulties presented by cultural and social contexts in terms of how peer forms of child sexual abuse are conceptualised culturally as well as their knock-on effects for regulatory and legal discourses. Second, it unpacks some of the key debates and challenges for contemporary discourses on harmful sexual behaviour by children and young people chiefly in terms of investigating and managing peer abuse in terms, for example, of separating out consensual and non-consensual behaviour, avoiding over-criminalisation and recognising the complexities of 'harm.'

Third, and to a lesser extent, while highlighting the complexities of gender within peer forms of sexual abuse, it also underscores the need for further research in this area along intersectional dimensions including race, class, disability and sexual identity.

The structure of the chapter is as follows: the chapter begins by outlining what is known about the nature and extent of harmful sexual behaviour among children and young people including core definitions and typologies. The main part of the chapter examines key issues and debates in this area in terms of social and cultural influences, the role of gender and the resulting blurring of the boundaries around 'harmful' behaviour, along with the consequent effects for legal and policy frameworks in investigating and managing peer forms of abuse. The concluding section will draw out current and future challenges as well as practical and preventive strategies in terms of education initiatives.

Nature and Extent

To begin, it is useful to provide some definitional context in terms of the nature and extent of harmful sexual behaviour. As noted above, there are a range of anomalies within the law in relation to how children, childhood and the capacity to consent are interpreted and defined (McAlinden 2018). Within this broader context, assessment and intervention frameworks commonly distinguish between children under 12 and those aged 12–18 which can become determining factors for whether a child displaying harmful sexual behaviour enters the child protection or criminal justice system (Ashurst 2016). For the purposes of our respective research projects, we adopted the collective term 'children and young people' to include those under the age of 18.

The term 'harmful sexual behaviour' ('HSB') is now widely accepted within academic and professional discourses when referring to children and young people in preference to 'offender' orientated terms which have a tendency to label and stigmatise. One much cited definition is that suggested by Palmer (1997: 11): 'Young people (under 18) who engage in any form of sexual activity with another individual, that they have powers over by virtue of age, emotional maturity, gender, physical strength, intellect and where the victim in this relationship has suffered a betrayal of trust.' This interpretation conveys the imbalance of power between the abuser and the abused—derived in a range of circumstances—which sits at the core of peer forms of abuse. While our analysis below is predominantly focused on digital forms of HSB, the term includes a wide range of behaviours including contact forms of abuse (e.g. touching, masturbation and penetration) and non-contact forms (e.g. grooming, voyeurism, and sexting or digital recording and distribution of sexual acts) (Ashurst 2016).

The term 'peer-on-peer' abuse is another umbrella term which captures a broad range of abusive or exploitative behaviours. Caroline Firmin and others (Firmin 2013; Firmin and Curtis 2015) classify these into four principal categories encompassing both contact and non-contact forms of child sexual abuse or exploitation: (1) *abuse*, including sexual abuse, and control within intimate relationships (such as within families or peer-based settings); (2) sexual abuse or exploitation within the context of exploitative *relationships or contexts* (such as within the context of gangs or groups); (3) sexual behaviour outside of the normative *parameters of development* (see e.g. Hackett 2010); (4) and serious violent *offences* (such as rape or assault) [emphasis added]. Examples of these are discussed further below. Moreover, such behaviours may also oscillate between these categories and thus often exist on a continuum.

Stemming from these broad definitions, a number of typologies of HSB have emerged with the overall aim of distinguishing between 'normal'/development sexual behaviours towards more 'risky'/problematic behaviours and ultimately towards 'harmful' sexual behaviour (McAlinden 2018: Ch. 6). O'Callaghan and Print (1994: 146), for example, have utilised 'normal', 'problematic' and 'abusive' sexual behaviours, while Ashurst (2016: 3) prefers 'experimental', 'exploitative' and 'abusive' behaviours. Hackett's (2010) much cited continuum is broader and more nuanced encompassing 'normal', 'inappropriate', 'problematic', 'abusive' and 'violent' behaviours. The essence of these typologies is that risk-taking behaviour and sexual experimentation is a normal or healthy part of adolescence and so not all peer-based sexual behaviours are necessarily problematic or even exploitative or harmful. As discussed further, making this important distinction between experimental and exploitive behaviour involves going beyond the extrinsic behaviour itself to consider not only the internal motivation of the alleged 'perpetrator' but also a range of contextual factors such as coercion and power or age differentials between the parties (McAlinden 2018).

Within the broader context of debates on the incidence and prevalence of child sexual abuse as a whole, considered elsewhere within this volume, there is a related body of work on the extent of HSB among children and young people. While figures vary across studies, it is generally thought that up to two-thirds of contact child sexual abuse is committed by those under 18 (Radford et al. 2011) with peer forms of abuse within schools emerging as an area of particular concern. For example, the Girlguiding Girls' Attitudes Survey 2017 found 64% of girls aged 13–21 had experienced sexual violence or sexual harassment at school or college in the past year.[2] Similarly, in 2018, Childline reported a 29% increase in the number of children seeking help for incidents of peer-on-peer abuse where many were unclear about the meaning of consent.[3] While adolescent males account for the majority of those who display HSB, adolescent females and children under 12 account for a growing number of such cases (Hackett et al. 2013).

The prevalence and range of non-contact or digital forms of HSB among peers globally are also issues of growing concern (Shariff 2015). For example, a 2020 meta-analysis of 50 published prevalence studies on sexting among 'emerging adults'—defined in this study as the developmental period between 18 and 29 years of age—found that sending, receiving and reciprocal texting was around 40% (ranging from 38.3 to 47.7%) with 'non-consensual forwarding' or 'third party dissemination'

---

[2] See https://www.girlguiding.org.uk/girls-making-change/girls-attitudes-survey/?301=yes. Accessed 28 January 2022.
[3] See S. Weale, (2018, 18 September) Rise in young people seeking help over peer-on-peer abuse in UK. The Guardian. https://www.theguardian.com/society/2018/sep/18/childline-rise-young-people-seeking-help-peer-on-peer-abuse-uk Accessed 15 October 2021.

of sexual images accounting for 15% (Mori et al. 2020). However, there is an acknowledged underestimate to official figures on peer abuse which would not include, for example, unknown cases which have not come through the criminal justice or child protection systems (Ashurst and McAlinden 2015) nor indeed the significant underreporting by males and minority groups (Juyal et al. 2017). In addition, and as discussed further, while girls are victimised at a disproportionately higher rate than boys, more recent studies show that the underlying motivations of both boys and girls are considerably more complex than traditional gendered stereotypes might suggest (see e.g. Lee and Crofts 2015; Agnew 2021a; Bianchi et al. 2021).

Motivations and Influences

Having recognised the nature and extent of HSB among children and young people and definitional issues more specifically, the next section will unpack and examine the key motivations and influences associated with peer-based HSB. In so doing, a nuanced understanding of the complexity of peer-based HSB will be provided. In particular, how social and cultural landscapes are shaping a paradigm shift which is influencing how children and young people conceptualise and understand sex, sexuality and healthy sexual relationships.

HSB does not develop in a void but must be understood alongside the evolving social and cultural environments within which it manifests and operates (Rich 2011). Indeed, a range of socio-cultural pressures have been recognised as significant and determining factors in understanding peer-based sexual abuse and the normalisation of 'risky' and 'harmful' sexual behaviours (McAlinden 2018). One of the authors of this chapter has made reference to five fundamental contexts within which HSB among children and young people can be located, including: (i) 'new media' and digital communication; (ii) a 'culture of sex' alongside the 'cultural sexualisation' of children; (iii) changes in dating practices; (iv) emergence of 'gang' and 'party' culture; and (v) unlimited access to pornography (McAlinden 2018: Ch. 4; see also Agnew and McAlinden 2021: 111–113). The analysis will explore each of these in turn.

First, 'new media' is recognised as an 'alternative social space' and has created new and varied opportunities for children and young people to connect online with peers and engage in a range of online activities including social networking and gaming (McAlinden 2018: 93; see also Livingstone et al. 2018). Such technological advancements have provided young people with a valuable tool to forge and maintain relationships and friendships (including long distance relations), learn new skills and enhance their knowledge base (Livingstone et al. 2018). In spite of a number of notable benefits, there are a range of broader online risks children and young people are exposed to, primarily grounded in their unlimited and often unrestricted access to the internet. Most children have access to media outlets in their homes, bedrooms and even on their person (e.g. SMART phones, laptops, iPads, games consoles, televisions), thus increasing their daily media consumption substantially and in turn, their exposure to online risks (Kirsch 2010). Not surprisingly, a 'history of concerns'[4] surrounding various forms of child abuse has now translated online (see McAlinden 2018). Within this specific context, contemporary concerns include exposure to a wide range of pernicious sexual content, online sexual abuse/harassment, grooming and cyberbullying, to name a few (Buckingham and Bragg 2005; McAlinden 2012; Ringrose et al. 2012). Research has further established a causal link between young people's exposure to prejudicial sexual content/language both on and offline and the development of 'harmful' sexual attitudes/norms (see Brown and Strasburger 2007; Ringrose et al. 2012).

Second and interrelated to 'new media', a 'culture of sex' alongside the 'premature sexualisation' and 'commercialisation' of children have prompted social, political and legal debates on what is considered to be 'healthy' and 'harmful' peer-based sexual behaviours (see Ashurst and McAlinden 2015). Living within 'a risk-averse culture', that is a society which primarily views young people's exposure to any sexual content as 'risky' and 'harmful' (Tsaliki 2015: 500; see also Agnew, 2021a), it is not surprising to learn that an extensive body of literature exists which documents growing societal fears surrounding certain aspects of celebrity

---

[4] Traditionally, a 'history of concerns' associated with child sexual abuse included intra-familial abuse, institutional abuse and grooming, for example (see McAlinden 2012).

and pop culture and the potential detrimental and harmful impact it can have on young people (Tsaliki 2015: 500). Identifiable risks include, the proliferation of toxic masculinity, infantilisation of women, the normalisation of stereotypical gender roles and unrealistic expectations within relationships (see e.g. McAlinden 2018; Agnew 2021b; Henry et al. 2021). One of the most prominent concerns associated with a culture of sex is the popular imaging of young people, in particular adolescents, as 'sexually charged' and 'sexually obsessed', which has culminated in the premature sexualisation and sexual socialization of children and young people (Kirsch 2010: 175, 176). The sexual messaging surrounding youth sexual identity significantly influences young people's attitudes, beliefs and values associated with sex and sexuality, their bodies' potential and worth, how they represent themselves both on and offline and how they understand and conceptualise healthy relationships (see Scraton 1997; Kirsch 2010: Ch. 9).

Third, with the introduction of SMART technology, material changes in modern dating practices have been documented. Indeed, a shift in dating norms has been noted with more young people communicating and negotiating intimate and personal relationships via the use of social networking sites, online dating platforms and apps (see e.g. Ringrose et al. 2012; Shariff 2015). Within the literature, 'traditional' dating (within an offline context) is often described as more serious whereas online relationships have been referred to as 'transient' and 'disposable' (Hobbs et al. 2017: 274). This transformation from off to online dating is evident not only in the use of language—including the use of emoji's, emoticons and abbreviations to illustrate how an individual is feeling such as '143' (I love you) and 'ASL' (Age/Sex/Location)—but also in how young people behave (McAlinden 2018: 99, 100). Indeed, a greater number of sexual risks have been associated with the use of online dating platforms. As an illustration, a relationship has been noted between users of dating apps among university students and emerging sexual risks including engagement in unprotected sex (see Choi et al. 2016).

Fourth, is the emergence of both 'gang' and 'party' culture. The scale and nature of gang-associated sexual violence and exploitation can include pressure and manipulation to engage in sexual activities for material gain, protection or 'perceived' status (Beckett et al. 2013; see also

Melrose 2013). Young people can also be groomed to recruit peers to gain 'favour' with the perpetrators often referred to as exchanging 'sex for popularity' (Melrose 2013: 162). The 'party house' scenario has also been noted by scholars as a place where sexually exploitative and abusive behaviours can exist (Beckett 2011). This often involves young people, primarily young girls, who are invited to 'parties' where they will be provided with alcohol and drugs and then encouraged to engage in sexual activities with older adults (Beckett 2011). Of course, 'party' culture goes beyond the 'gang' context and 'house parties' are now very much part of how many young people socialise and interact with their peers (see Melrose 2013). Within the peer-to-peer 'party' context, however, young people can be pressured to engage in sexual behaviours earlier than they might feel ready to due to peer pressure (see McAlinden 2018: 108–112). Further, due to the complex relationship traits at play within both 'gang' and 'party' cultures, young people involved may not see themselves as a 'victim' (Melrose 2013) or as satisfying 'ideal' victim status (Christie 1986: 18), thus rendering themselves as 'underserving' of help (McAlinden 2014: 190). This inevitably presents numerous problems for professionals and practitioners tasked with identifying, managing and investigating harmful and abusive sexual behaviours, discussed further below.

Fifth and finally is the accessibility and availability of pornography online. A relationship between exposure to violent and overtly sexual pornography (unwanted and deliberate) among young people and their engagement in HSB and other sexualised behaviours has been documented (see Bleakley et al. 2011; McAlinden 2018; Stanley et al. 2018). Associated concerns include: (i) how young people perceive 'risk' and 'danger'; (ii) young people's attitudes and values associated with sexual relationships including the development of 'risky' sexual scripts; (iii) the fostering of highly gendered sexual stereotypes; and (iv) the blurring of boundaries between 'consent' and 'coercion' (see Gagnon and Simon 1987; Horvath et al. 2013; Ashurst and McAlinden 2015). As an illustration, a relationship between regular viewing of pornography, unrealistic attitudes about sex and 'healthy' relationships and young people's engagement in sending sexual imagery ('sexting') within coercive and manipulative contexts has been noted (see Stanley et al. 2018).

In addition, the range of socio-cultural influences young people are exposed to, including access to pornographic content, is perpetuating a range of gendered myths and stereotypes which in turn are influencing how young people understand gender roles, sexual norms, 'healthy' and 'unhealthy' relations as well as how they perceive 'value' and 'risk' within relationships (McAlinden 2018; Stanley et al. 2018; Setty 2020). The myth that girl's or women's bodies are the property of boy's/men, for example, can lead to a range of harmful presumptions surrounding sexual agency and choice (see Ringrose et al. 2012). In addition, stereotypical narratives associated with genetics and evolution have been noted to significantly impact young people's perceptions of sexual norms. That is, girls are seen as being inherently submissive while boys are seen as sexually aggressive and dominant (see Buckingham and Bragg 2005; Ringrose and Renold 2012). Overall, however, a significant relationship has been established between problematic assumptions associated with gender identity and roles on the one hand and engagement and exposure to HSB on the other (Stanley et al. 2018; McAlinden 2018; Agnew 2021a).

The gendered culture surrounding some forms of HSB exposes the broader tensions associated with gender socialisation and the public scrutiny of female bodies (Fredrickson and Roberts 1997; Ringrose and Renold 2012; Agnew 2021a). Sexual harassment, for example, is predominantly directed at females and is deeply connected to misogyny as well as patriarchal and sexist attitudes and beliefs (see Henry et al. 2021). Relatedly, the cultural acceptance of gendered myths and stereotypes often results in a dangerous shift in how HSB cases are conceptualised and more widely understood. For instance, cases involving a young female who does not fit 'ideal' victim status can result in a victim blame narrative (see McAlinden 2014). That is, there is often a shift in dialogue from what did the perpetrator do or say to what did the victim (young person) do or say? This often arises when a young female, for example, challenges traditional gender roles and is subsequently blamed for her victimisation simply because she showed signs of a positive sexuality (see e.g. Penney 2016). Indeed, the range of socio-cultural influences and pressures young people are exposed to both on and offline is both persistent and prevalent. Consequently, identifying sexual behaviours as within or outside the boundaries of 'normal' sexual development becomes problematic.

In highlighting the complexities of gender within peer-based forms of sexual abuse, it also raises questions surrounding the intersectional dimensions of harm including race, class, disability and sexual identity. Further, when it comes to harmful behaviours including harassment and HSB (in particular image-based sexual abuse), research demonstrates an intersectional impact for girls and women from racial and ethnic minority groups as well as adverse relational impacts by LGBT+ respondents (Henry et al. 2021: Ch 3). Henry et al. (2021: 50) note a further potential relationship between image-based sexual abuse and exposure to hate crime while Juyal et al. (2017) note significant underreporting of abuse by males and minority groups. Prevailing and problematic gendered and intersectional norms and harms therefore impact how harmful sexual behaviours are conceptualised, reported and ultimately responded to by professionals within law, policy, child protection and welfare.

Investigating and Managing HSB: Key Tensions

Due to the complexity of harms and range of variables at play when young people engage in or are exposed to peer-based forms of HSB, investigating and managing HSB among children and young people inevitably presents a number of challenges. Here, we identify two principal areas of concern: (i) understanding issues of consent and the key 'motivations' of young people when differentiating between 'explorative' and 'exploitative' sexual behaviours; (ii) fears associated with the 'over-criminalisation' of young people who participate in certain forms of HSB.

First, as noted earlier in this chapter, legal responses to HSB have tended to apply laws made by adults to protect children from adult-child forms of sexual abuse to criminalise children. At the level of practice, however, a key area of concern among professionals and practitioners is the proper identification and labelling of the sexual behaviour(s) as 'harmful' (see e.g. Hackett 2010; Firmin 2013). In this respect, inextricably linked to distinguishing between 'explorative', 'exploitative' or 'harmful' sexual behaviour(s) are issues of consent. As such, both academics and practitioners have noted 'free and informed' consent as being a significant factor in determining whether the sexual behaviour is explorative or exploitative in nature (see Albury and Crawford 2012). Yet, consent remains a 'vague concept' and abstract accounts of consent often fail to consider the complex power dynamics at play, including gendered power relations (Dowds 2020: 3; see also Dowds 2021; Serisier 2021). The online world also presents unique challenges when negotiating and identifying consent (or lack thereof) more broadly within relationships. For example, image-based sexual abuse may be used as a 'tool' to maintain coercive relationships and/or to continue to perpetrate sexual violence and harms (see Henry et al. 2021: Ch. 6). It is therefore not surprising to learn that young people are struggling to understand key consensual concepts, particularly in online contexts, including the notion that consent is *ongoing* and can be *withdrawn* at any time (Agnew 2021b). Consequently, the misinformed narrative surrounding issues of consent can result in young people presuming consent has been given 'freely' when in fact the young person is in a coercive relationship or situation.

There are a number of contexts in which consent can be presumed to be given but it is actually, what has been termed, 'abused consent' which can exist within both coercive and normalised settings (Pearce 2013: Ch 4). In relation to 'coerced' consent, as noted above, a young person might be introduced to drink and drugs within 'party' and 'hook-up' culture in exchange for sex and/or participation in other sexual activities (Melrose 2013). The young person may feel they are in control and have a choice, when in fact they have been provided with narcotics to lower their inhibitions and are in an exploitative setting (Pearce 2013; see also McAlinden 2018). Such environments are coercive and therefore 'free' and 'informed' consent does not and cannot exist. In addition, the notion of 'normalised' consent explores the complex dynamics of intimate relationships among young people within contemporary culture. Several scholars have noted how the overt sexualisation of young people, for example within pop culture, has normalised certain sexual behaviours or sexual norms including sexting and sexual bullying (Pearce 2013: 61; see also Kirsch 2010). Consequently, sexually coercive and violent behaviours (including bullying behaviours) become normalised within relationships and young people may fail to recognise and/or challenge them as 'unhealthy' and 'harmful' (Pearce 2013: 62; see also Agnew 2021a). This can lead to underreporting of HSB among children and young people, as referenced earlier in this chapter. Indeed, two common reasons for underreporting among young people include: (i) they do not see themselves as being in a harmful or coercive relationship and therefore do not self-identify as a 'victim' and/or (ii) young people who *do* recognise the sexual behaviour(s) as harmful may not come forward through fear they will be blamed for somehow being 'implicit' in the sexual behaviour(s) (Pearce 2013; Ashurst and McAlinden 2015).

Second, another issue of concern is growing fears associated with HSB and the 'over-criminalisation' of young people. To fully understand the substance of such debates, it is useful here to provide some context in terms of the developing body of literature which illustrates how a significant amount of fear surrounding children, young people and their participation in a range of sexual behaviours, is based on traditional, and often misplaced, perceptions and ideologies of 'childhood' and 'youth sexuality' (see e.g. Scraton 1997). For example, the 'true essence' of childhood is believed to be a time of innocence and an 'asexual and peaceful existence' (Kitzinger 1988: 78, 79). Yet, such misplaced assumptions can lead to dangerous and problematic outcomes including labelling typically 'healthy' sexual behaviour as 'deviant' and 'harmful' and/or categorising young people as 'offenders' without proper attention being afforded to the context and settings of the behaviour(s). For example, within social and sometimes professional discourses, children who are not 'passive' participants in the commission of harmful sexual behaviours can be partially or fully blamed for the harm caused to them—thus also making the defendant less blameworthy (see McAlinden 2014).

Further, adolescence is understood to involve a 'dramatic' developmental shift, including physical, sexual, psychological and social developmental changes (World Health Organisation 2021). In addition, it has been noted that adolescents have a predisposition to engage in 'risk-taking' behaviour which has been described as the 'hallmarks of typical adolescent behaviour' (Kelley et al. 2004: 27). In spite of this, sometimes children and young people who engage in *any* form of 'risk-taking' behaviour, including some sexual behaviours, are automatically labelled 'deviant' within social discourses and their behaviour as 'harmful' and in need of legal regulation (see e.g. Powell 2010). It becomes apparent, therefore, that how these key terms (childhood, adolescence and youth sexuality) are conceptualised and understood is significant and informs the administration of justice and shapes current laws and policies on HSB (see e.g. Gillespie 2013; McAlinden 2018; Agnew 2021a).

The precarious cultural narrative associated with childhood and youth sexuality has also translated to online forms of peer-based HSB. As new platforms for peer interaction emerge, particularly within the online dating landscape, in tandem with the vastness and the 'unknown' dimensions of the online world, public anxieties surrounding online youth sexual behaviours heighten (see Henry and Powell 2014). Further, as technology continues to grow and advance, exposure to harmful behaviours, including HSB, has become more prevalent. The law has therefore had to adapt and reform in an attempt to regulate certain sexual behaviours. By way of example, a new criminal offence of 'upskirting' has recently been introduced in England and Wales under s67A Sexual Offences Act 2003. The practice has seen victims as young as seven up to 70 years (Oppenheim 2019) with the sexually exploitative behaviour mostly being targeted at females (see e.g. Thompson 2020). Yet, while the sexual harms that can manifest online are vast, not all online sexual behaviours are coercive and in need of regulation.

As noted previously, some forms of sexual behaviour(s) among young people have 'outstripped the law' (Richards and Calvert 2009: 3) and are categorised as 'harmful' before due consideration of the circumstances surrounding the behaviour. A good example would be the sharing of naked or semi-naked images by persons under 18 years (known colloquially as 'sexting'). This sexual behaviour is a criminal offence under s1 Protection of Children Act 1978 (as amended by s45 Sexual Offences Act 2003).[5] Yet, literature illustrates that peer-based sexting should

---

[5] s 45 of the Sexual Offences Act 2003 amended the definition of 'child' from those aged under 16 years to those aged under 18 years.

be understood as a continuum of behaviour and therefore a form of sexual conduct which cannot easily be placed into distinct categories (McAlinden 2018). Indeed, the diverse contexts in which sexting can manifest include as a flirting tool (part of the courting process), to establish and form a relationship and/or as a form of sexual expression/identity (Phippen 2012; Albury and Crawford 2012).

In spite of this, sexting among young people can and does enter more coercive and manipulative contexts. The boundaries between consensual and coercive sexting behaviours therefore often become blurred as relationships break down (both intimate and friendship based) and what was once consensual potentially becomes exploitative and ultimately harmful (Ringrose et al. 2012; Agnew 2021b). Further, as noted above, the context in which certain sexual behaviours occur, including sexting, is influenced by what McAlinden (2018: 122) has termed, a 'culture of confusion'. This backdrop shapes how young people understand issues of consent and healthy sexual norms. With this in mind, the laws (as they are currently written), fail to account for the complexity of peer-based sexual behaviour (see Albury and Crawford 2012). Moreover, using criminal law to regulate and manage the nuances of sexual behaviour young people are engaging in is failing to understand the systemic social and cultural dimensions attached to the sexual behaviour.

What becomes clear is that young people are engaging in and/or are exposed to a wide range of sexual behaviours both on and offline. This, alongside the diverse range of harmful outcomes young people may be subject to, can make identifying the most relevant support and intervention difficult. In terms of settings, young people's participation and exposure to HSB can start online and subsequently be accompanied by contact (offline) sexual harms (Hackett and Smith 2018). In addition, young people can be victimised while also participating in recruiting their peers for abuse, referred to earlier as the 'victim-offender continuum' (McAlinden 2014). This makes identifying a 'victim' and 'offender' in certain cases a much more complex process than one might think. Studies are further illustrating that participation with and exposure to HSB is happening at a younger age and thus managing 'appropriate' interventions for those more junior age ranges can become extremely challenging (see Hackett et al. 2013). Indeed, short- and/or long-term potential effects include family conflict, alcohol/drug use, eating disorders, poor mental health and low self-esteem (see Barbaree and Marshall 2008: 8; Ringrose et al. 2012: 40–52). In addition, the often 'siloed' working practices of key agencies alongside the limited resources and guidance available to staff creates problems when it comes to prioritisation of cases and responding to HSB (Hackett et al. 2016: 26). All of the above makes managing and identifying HSB as well as initiating appropriate interventions an extremely complex process.

Conclusion: Prevention and Education

This chapter has explored some of the key tensions associated with defining, conceptualising and responding to HSB among children and young people. We have argued that to have a nuanced understanding of peer-based sexual behaviours, including HSB, one must dismantle and discern the broader social and cultural landscape within which the behaviours are manifesting and operating (see also McAlinden 2018; Setty 2020; Henry et al. 2021). Not all sexual behaviours among young people are 'harmful', yet popular and prevailing discourses on childhood and youth sexuality create a misinformed narrative that *all* sexual behaviours among young people must be regulated, often resulting in over-criminalisation. It is recognised that there may be a place for the law to intervene in peer-based HSB which involves manipulation and coercion, including some forms of sexting behaviours.

Yet, of paramount, but sometimes neglected importance, is the consideration of the often-complex settings, motivations and influences within which peer-based sexual behaviours may manifest and operate. To overlook these important dimensions is potentially counter-productive and often creates unnecessary adverse outcomes for young people. Indeed, antiquated legal responses fail to account for the diverse and complex range of behaviours young people present with and the critical issue of consent within varying behavioural contexts. In addressing the core definitional and regulatory tensions, it is clear that peer-based HSB alongside key concepts including consent has competing interpretations which impact not only on the delivery of support but also on identifying 'victims' and 'offenders' as well as managing what interventions are considered to be most appropriate for young people. Better efforts should therefore be directed towards ensuring key service providers receive appropriate resources (including information sharing across relevant agencies) and the necessary education and tools to properly manage and identify HSB among young people (see also Hackett et al. 2016; McAlinden 2018).

In sum, the authors strongly believe that best practice for addressing the above concerns is primarily based in broader educative responses. Educating young people, parents/guardians, professionals and practitioners on (i) the ever-changing social and cultural landscape within which children and young people are operating; (ii) the complex dynamics at play when young people negotiate relationships, including intimate relationships, both on and offline; (iii) addressing misplaced presumptions associated with issues of consent and how broader social and cultural influences impact on how consent is understood and conceptualised; and (iv) the prevailing and misplaced traditional perceptions of children and young people as 'innocent' and 'asexual'. Against this backdrop, long-established myths and stereotypes associated with children and young people, including the notion that a young person who engages in any form of sexual behaviour is 'deviant' and/or 'harmful', will be challenged. In addition, comprehensive education programmes should also provide children and young people with the necessary tools and knowledge to better recognise and identify 'harmful' and 'abusive' sexual behaviours for themselves. This would also assist in reporting, investigating and managing HSB so that the most appropriate support and interventions are initiated as early as possible.

References

Agnew, E. (2021a). Sexting among young people: Towards a gender sensitive approach. *The International Journal of Children's Rights, 29*(1), 3–30.

Agnew, E. (2021b). Sexting, consent and young people: Regulatory challenges. queen's policy engagement, February, Policy Paper 9.

Agnew, E., and McAlinden, A. M. (2021). Harmful sexual behaviour among children and young people online: Cultural and regulatory challenges. In R. Killean, E. Dowds, and A. M. McAlinden (Eds.), *Sexual violence on trial: Local and comparative perspectives* (pp. 109–121). Routledge.

Albury, K., and Crawford, K. (2012). Sexting, consent and young people's ethics: Beyond Megan's story. *Continuum: Journal of Media and Cultural Studies, 26*(3), 463–473.

Ashurst, L. (2016). Children and young people with harmful sexual behaviour. Policy Paper prepared for NOTA (copy supplied to the author).

Ashurst, L., and McAlinden, A. (2015). Young people, peer-to-peer grooming and sexual offending: Understanding and responding to harmful sexual behaviour within a social media society. *Probation Journal, 62*(4), 374–388.

Barbaree, H. E., and Marshall, W. L. (2008). *The juvenile sex offender*, 2nd edition. The Guilford Press.

Beckett, H. (2011). *Not a world away: The sexual exploitation of children and young people in Northern Ireland*. Barnardo's Northern Ireland.

Beckett, H., with Brodie, I., Factor, F., Melrose, M., Pearce, P. J., and Warrington, C. (2013). 'It's wrong – but you get used to it': A qualitative study of gang-associated sexual violence Towards, and exploitation of, young people in England. Report commissioned by the Office of the Children's Commissioner's Inquiry into Child Sexual Exploitation in Gangs and Groups'. University of Bedfordshire.

Bianchi, D., Morelli, M., Nappa, M. R., Baiocco, R., and Chirumbolo, A. (2021). A bad romance: Sexting motivations and teen dating violence. *Journal of Interpersonal Violence, 36*(13–14), 6029–6049.

Bleakley, A., Hennessey, M., Fishbein, M., and Jordan, A. (2011). Using the integrative model to explain how exposure to sexual media content influences adolescent sexual behaviour. *Health Education and Behaviour, 38*(5), 530–540.

Brown, J. D., and Strasburger, V. C. (2007). From Calvin Klein to Paris Hilton and myspace: Adolescents, sex, and the media. *Adolescent Medicine: State of the Art Reviews, 18*(3), 484–507.

Buckingham, D., and Bragg, S. (2005). Opting in to (and out of) childhood: Young people, sex and the media. In J. Qvortrup (Ed.), *Studies in modern childhood* (pp. 59–77). Palgrave Macmillan.

Choi, E., Wong, J., Lo, H., Wong, W., Choi, J., and Fong, D. (2016). The association between smartphone dating applications and college students'

casual sex encounters and condom use'. *Sexual and Reproductive Healthcare, 9*, 38–41.
Christie, N. (1986). The Ideal victim. In E. A. Fattah (Ed.), *From crime policy to victim policy* (pp. 17–30). Palgrave Macmillan.
Dowds, E. (2020). Sexual consent in Northern Ireland: The social and legal dimensions. Queen's policy engagement, May, Policy Paper 6.
Dowds, E. (2021). Rethinking affirmative approaches to consent: A step in the right direction. In R. Killean, E. Dowds, and A. M. McAlinden (Eds.), *Sexual violence on trial: Local and comparative perspectives* (pp. 162–173). Routledge.
Firmin, C. (2013). Something old or something new: Do pre-existing conceptualisations of abuse enable a sufficient response to abuse in young people's relationships and peer groups. In M. Melrose, and J. Pearce (Eds.), *Critical perspectives on child sexual exploitation and related trafficking*. Palgrave Macmillan.
Firmin, C., and Curtis, G. (2015). *Practitioner briefing# 1: What is peer-on-peer abuse?* MsUnderstood Partnership.
Fredrickson, B. L., and Roberts, T. (1997). Objectification theory: Toward understanding women's lived experiences and mental health risks. *Psychology of Women Quarterly, 21*(2), 173–206.
Gagnon, J. H., and Simon, W. (1987). The sexual scripting of oral genital contacts. *Archives of Sexual Behaviour, 16*(1), 1–25.
Gillespie, A. (2013). Adolescents, sexting and human rights. *Human Rights Law Review, 13*(4), 623–643.
Hackett, S. (2010). Children and young people with harmful sexual behaviours. In C. Barter, and D. Berridge (Eds.), *Children behaving badly? Peer violence between children and young people* (pp. 121–135). Blackwell Wiley.
Hackett, S., Holmes, D., and Branigan, P. (2016). *Harmful sexual behaviour framework: An evidence-informed operational framework for children and young people displaying harmful sexual behaviours*. Project report. National Society for the Prevention of Cruelty to Children. NSPPC.
Hackett, S., Phillips, J., Masson, H., and Balfe, M. (2013). Individual, family and abuse characteristics of 700 British child and adolescent sexual abusers. *Child Abuse Review, 22*(4), 232–245.
Hackett, S., and Smith, S. (2018). *Young people who engage in child sexual exploitation behaviours: An exploration study*. Durham University; Centre of expertise on child sexual abuse.

Hall, M., and Hearn, J. (2017). *Revenge pornography: Gender, sexuality and motivations*. Routledge.

Hasinoff, A. A. (2015). *Sexting panic: Rethinking criminalization, privacy, and consent*. University of Illinois Press.

Henry, N., McGlynn, C., Flynn, A., Johnson, K., Powell, A., and Scott, A. (2021). *Image-based sexual abuse: A study on the causes and consequences of non-consensual nude or sexual imagery*. Routledge Critical Studies in Crime, Diversity and Criminal Justice.

Henry, N., and Powell, A. (2014). Beyond the 'sext': Technology-facilitated sexual violence and harassment against adult women. *Australian and New Zealand Journal of Criminology, 48*(1), 104–118.

Hobbs, M., Owen, S., and Gerber, L. (2017). Liquid love? Dating apps, sex, relationships and the digital transformation of intimacy. *Journal of Sociology, 53*(2), 271–284.

Horvath, M. A., Alys, L., Massey, K., Pina, A., Scully, M., and Adler, J. R. (2013). *Basically... porn is everywhere: A rapid evidence assessment on the effects that access and exposure to pornography has on children and young people*. London, Office for the Children's Commissioner.

Jennings, W. G., Piquero, A. R., and Reingle, J. M. (2012). On the overlap between victimization and offending: A review of the literature. *Aggression and Violent Behavior, 17*(1), 16–26.

Juyal, D., Yadav, D., Sethuraman, G., Kumar, A., Shende, T., Gupta, S., and Dhawan, B. (2017). Sexual abuse in males: An underreported issue. *Indian Journal of Sexually Transmitted Diseases and AIDS, 38*(2), 187–188.

Kelley, A., Schochet, T., and Landry, C. (2004). Risk-taking and novelty seeking in adolescence. *Annals New York Academy of Sciences, 1021*(1), 27–32.

Kirsch, S. (2010). *Media and youth: A developmental perspective*. Wiley-Blackwell.

Kitzinger, J. (1988). Defending innocence: Ideologies of childhood. *Feminist Review, 28*, 77–87.

Lee, M., and Crofts, T. (2015). Gender, pressure, coercion and pleasure: Untangling motivations for sexting between young people. *British Journal of Criminology, 55*(3), 454–473.

Livingstone, S., Mascheroni, G., and Staksrud, E. (2018). European research on children's internet use. *New Media & Society, 20*(3), 1103–1122.

McAlinden, A. M. (2012). *'Grooming' and the sexual abuse of children: Institutional, internet, and familial dimensions*. Oxford University Press.

McAlinden, A. M. (2014). Deconstructing victim and offender identities in discourses on child sexual abuse: Hierarchies, blame and the good/evil dialectic. *British Journal of Criminology, 54*(2), 180–198.
McAlinden, A. M. (2018). *Children as 'risk': Sexual exploitation and abuse by children and young people.* Cambridge University Press.
McGlynn, C., Johnson, K., Rackley, E., et al. (2021). It's torture for the soul: The harms of image-based sexual abuse. *Social & Legal Studies.* https://doi.org/10.1177/0964663920947791
McGlynn, C., and Rackley, E. (2017). Image-based sexual abuse. *Oxford Journal of Legal Studies, 37*(3), 534–561.
Melrose, M. (2013). Twenty-first century party people: Young people and sexual exploitation in the new millenium. *Child Abuse Review, 22*, 155–168.
Mori, C., Cooke, J. E., Temple, J. R., Anh, L., Lu, Y., Anderson, N., Rash, C., and Madigan, S. (2020). The prevalence of sexting behaviors among emerging adults: A meta-analysis. *Archives of Sexual Behavior, 49*(4), 1103–1119.
O'Callaghan, D., and Print, B. (1994). Adolescent sexual abusers: Research, assessment, and treatment. In T. Morrison, M. Erooga, and R. Beckett (Eds.), *Sexual offenders against children: Practice, management, and policy.* Routledge.
Oppenheim, N. (2019, April 12). Victims aged seven to 70 subject to upskirting last year, police figures show. *Independent.*
Palmer, T. (1997). Young people who sexually abuse. In M. Calder, S. Goulding, H. Hanks, K. Rose, J. Skinner, and J. Wynne (Eds.), *Juveniles and children who sexually abuse. A guide to risk assessment.* Russell House Publishing.
Pearce, J. (2013). A social model of abused consent. In M. Melrose, and J. Pearce (Eds.), *Critical perspectives on child sexual exploitation and related trafficking.* Palgrave Macmillan.
Penney, R. (2016). The rhetoric of the mistake in adult narratives of youth sexuality: The case of Amanda Todd. *Feminist Media Studies, 16*(4), 710–725.
Phippen, A. (2012). *Sexting: An exploration of practices, attitudes and influences.* UK Safer Internet Centre, NSPCC.
Powell, A. (2010). *Sex, power and consent: Youth culture and the unwritten rules.* Cambridge University Press.
Radford, L., Corral, S., Bradley, C., Fisher, H., Bassett, C., Howat, N., and Collishaw, S. (2011). *Child abuse and neglect in the UK today.* NSPCC.

Rich, P. (2011). *Understanding, assessing and rehabilitating juvenile sexual offenders*, 2nd ed. Wiley.

Richards, R. D., and Calvert, C. (2009). When sex and cellphones collide: Inside the prosecution of a teen sexting case. *Hastings Communication and Entertainment Law Journal, 32*(1), 1–40.

Ringrose, J., Gill, R., Livingstone, S., and Harvey, L. (2012). *A qualitative study of children, young people and 'sexting': A report prepared for the NSPCC*. IOE London, LSE, Kings College London and NSPCC.

Ringrose, J., and Renold, E. (2012). Teen girls, working-class feminity and resistance: Retheorising fantasy and desire in educational contexts of heterosexual violence. *International Journal of Inclusive Education, 16*(4), 461–477.

Scraton, P. (1997). Whose 'childhood'? what 'crisis'? In P. Scraton (Ed.), *'Childhood' in 'crisis'?* UCL Press.

Serisier, T. (2021). From date rape jeopardy to (not) drinking tea: Consent humour, ridicule and cultural change. *Australian Feminist Law Journal, 46*(2), 189–204.

Setty, E. (2020). *Risk and harm in youth sexting culture: Young people's perspectives*. Routledge.

Shariff, S. (2015). *Sexting and cyberbullying defining the line for digitally empowered kids.* Cambridge: Cambridge University Press.

Stanley, N., Barter, C., Wood, M., Aghtaie, N., Larkins, C., Lanau, A., and Overlien, C. (2018). Pornography, sexual coercion and abuse and sexting in young people's intimate relationships: A European study. *Journal of Interpersonal Violence, 33*(19), 2919–2944.

Thompson, C. (2020). Skirting around the issue: Misdirection and linguistic avoidance in parliamentary discourses on upskirting. *Violence Against Women, 26*(11), 1403–1422.

Tsaliki, L. (2015). Popular culture and moral panics about 'children at risk': Revisiting the sexualisation of young girl's debate. *Sex Education, 15*(5), 500–514.

Van Ouytsel, J., Walrave, M., De Marez, L., Vanhaelewyn, B., and Ponnet, K. (2021). Sexting, pressured sexting and image-based sexual abuse among a weighted-sample of heterosexual and LGB-youth. *Computers in Human Behavior.* https://doi.org/10.1016/j.chb.2020.106630

Wolak, J., Finkelhor, D., Walsh, W., and Treitman, L. (2018). Sextortion of minors: Characteristics and dynamics. *Journal of Adolescent Health, 62*(1), 72–79.

World Health Organisation. (2021). *Adolescent health.* https://www.who.int/southeastasia/health-topics/adolescent-health. Accessed 14 October 2021.

9

He Didn't Want Any of That: Considerations in the Study and Theorization of Black Boys' Sexual Victimization in the United States

Tommy J. Curry

Introduction

Child sexual abuse is an under-researched area of public health scholarship and family conflict studies. Research acknowledging the sexual abuse of Black boys is practically non-existent. Over the last decade, the National Intimate Partner and Sexual Violence Survey conducted by the Center for Disease Prevention and Control (CDC) has shown that Black males over the age of eighteen suffer some of the highest rates of sexual coercion and made to penetrate violence over a 12-month period. Despite this data, boyhood studies scholars, gender theorists, and public health researchers remain indifferent to these findings and consider the evidence showing Black men (6.5%) in the United States experiencing contact sexual violence (which includes rape, being made to penetrate, sexual coercion, and unwanted sexual contact) as often as

T. J. Curry (✉)
University of Edinburgh, Edinburgh, Scotland, UK
e-mail: t.j.curry@ed.ac.uk

© The Author(s), under exclusive license to Springer Nature Switzerland AG 2022
A. K. Gill and H. Begum (eds.), *Child Sexual Abuse in Black and Minoritised Communities*, https://doi.org/10.1007/978-3-031-06337-4_9

Black women (5.8%) in a given year, or have rates of sexual victimization higher than White women (3.6%) to be incredulous (Smith et al. 2017: 18, 21, 28). Much of the current theoretical and sociological research on race and racism in the United States ignores the sexual victimization of Black males. Even when scholars invoke intersectionality as a framework for understanding Black boys and sexual violence, there is little understanding of this group or the causal or correlative determinants that produce the Black male vulnerability to sexual violence (Curry 2018a, b, 2021a, b). The inability to recognize Black boys as victims of sexual victimization and coercion impedes our ability to conceptualize sexual victimization and violence against Black males, or their vulnerability to various forms of sexual violence, as enduring throughout their lives. Whereas our narration of sexual violence against women generally anticipates a particular vulnerability the female body has to rape and sexual violence throughout girlhood and womanhood, this explanatory schema is absent in how researchers and theorists conceptualize male sexual victimization, particularly Black male sexual vulnerability from boyhood to manhood.

The scant research on the sexual abuse of Black children reaches back to the 1980s, however, the focus of these few studies mentioning Black children's sexual victimization focuses primarily on the sexual abuse of young Black girls by a male perpetrator and rarely acknowledged the sexual assault or rape of young Black boys (Ashbury 1993; Hampton and Oliver 2006; Hampton 1987). Contemporary studies into sexual abuse and early sexual debut, which often occurs as statutory rape, systematically ignore Black males' experiences of rape and sexual assault to hold fast to the idea that Black males are primarily perpetrators of sexual violence, not victims to it be they adults or children (Curry 2017a, b; Curry and Utley 2018). The early sexual debut of Black boys is referred to as "any adolescent boy engaging in sexual intercourse before he is 15 years old" (Lohman and Billings 2008, p. 724). Statutory rape is often understood as an adult, or older peer in some cases, having sex with someone under the age of consent (Goodwin 2013). Age of consent laws have historically sought to protect young people from sexual exploitation by adults (Sutherland 2003), however, the race and sex of the victim often determine whether courts see any violation at all. Statutory rape laws are highly prejudicial and have primarily focused on convicting men and boys for sexually violating women and girls (Sutherland 2003), consequently, boys sexually coerced by older women or girls are not recognized by courts to be victims of any sexual violation at all (Burrow et al. 2020). When Black boys are coerced into having sex with older girls or women, they are believed to have wanted these sexual events to occur and consequently are thought to be unaffected by these coercive sexual debuts.

These interpretative gaps are as much an expression of our cultural biases as they are the manifestation of the habits academic disciplines have in narrowly construing sexual violence. Unfortunately, many of our academic assumptions about gender, sexuality, and Black masculinity are rooted in racist and classist assertions that have very little evidence to support them. Many of our current gender theories concerning Black masculinity rely on outdated subcultural analyses concerning Black men and boys drawn from outdated criminological theories claiming that poor young Black males have compensatory masculinity that is uniquely predatory (Curry 2021a, b). Compensatory masculinity theory asserts that Black males use violence—specifically rape, intimate partner abuse, and homicide—to define their masculinity, because they are denied access to mainstream education and employment. Historically, feminist analyses of Black masculinity have asserted that young poor Black men are violent, and particularly hypersexual and sexually aggressive (Brownmiller 1975; Cooper 2006; White 2008; Garfield 2010). Throughout bell hooks' work *We Real Cool: Black Men and Masculinity* (2004), for instance, she insists that violence against women be it physical or sexual is foundational to Black male identity. Without evidence or ethnographic accounts, she asserts that young Black boys have been so seduced by the myth of Black male hypersexuality that they will seek out sexual conquests, even if it means raping innocent women, without reflection or hesitation and regardless of consequence (hooks 1990, p. 63). Drawing inspiration from subculture of violence theories arguing that Black masculinity was uniquely violent and rape prone—operating on different and deficient values (Wolfgang and Feracutti 1967; Amir 1971)—the analyses of hooks relies on popularly accepted stereotypes concerning Black males and offers no evidentiary support or ethnographies for her claims about Black male hypersexuality (Pitt and Sanders 2010). Unfortunately, these claims have dictated the interpretation of Black boys' sexual vulnerability for the last several decades.

Black boys are aware of the negative racial and sexual myths associated with Black manhood that are imposed upon them as young children (Hust et al. 2008). Recent research has suggested that some pubertal Black boys begin manifesting depressive symptoms given their anxiety toward approaching Black manhood (Carter et al. 2020). These negative ideations affect Black boys' realizations of themselves as sexual beings. More recent research (Curry and Utley 2020) has sought to humanize Black boys and explain their choices regarding sexual debut as a complex personal decision. Interviews with Black men about their first sexual experiences have shown that Black boys are reflective and emotional beings who not only show trepidation over their sexual debut but prefer their first time to be with close friends whom they trust. Contrary to the literature framing Black males as hypersexual and predatory, Black boys are often aware of the sexual scripts imposed on Black men and chose close intimate friendships to experiment and comfort their anxieties regarding sex. Academic discussions fail to approach the study of Black boys' sexuality as a serious inquiry into experiences individuals from this group have when negotiating structural racism and sexual victimization (Curry 2017a, b) and often interpret young Black males in line with pathological assertions and unsubstantiated presumptions about Black males as a group. The exploration of Black boys' sexual victimization must keep in mind that these individuals are experiencing trauma and sexual violence in a world that often denies such violence is possible.

While the ethnographies and research into Black male sexual vulnerability are slowly increasing, Claudia Bernard's (2019) recent statement that "we lack knowledge of Black boys who are affected by sexual exploitation and the needs and issues of vulnerable and at-risk Black boys are little understood" is accurate and must be remedied (p. 195). Investigations concerning the sexual victimization of Black boys through child sexual abuse or rape require the researcher to confront various stereotypical assumptions and ideological assertions about Black males. Social scientific research into Black male sexual victimization, even as children, is still thought to be controversial within the academy. This controversy is not as much about the victimization of young Black boys as it is about the perpetrators of violence against them. Our exploratory study (Curry and Utley 2018) revealed that many Black men recount their earliest experiences with sex as coercive adult violations. Many of these violations were at the hands of women who were family friends, caretakers, or older peers. While our initial research did capture several cases of older men abusing young Black boys, most of the testimonies described female perpetrators.

This chapter aims to explore some of the conceptual and interpretive obstacles in our understanding of Black male vulnerability to sexual assault and child sexual abuse. The recent intervention around Black male sexual vulnerability in Black male studies (Curry 2017a, b, 2021a; Kitossa 2021) has introduced a nascent conversation concerning the role that statutory rape, early sexual debut, and made to penetrate violence have over the life course of Black boys in the United States and abroad. While the dearth of scholarly research on the sexual violence that Black boys suffer tends to give the impression that rape and sexual coercion almost solely affect girls, this chapter aims to convince the reader that Black boys' sexual victimization requires not only public health interventions but more rigorous theoretical engagements within academia.

Defining Child Sexual Abuse

The CDC defines child sexual abuse as "the involvement of a child (person less than 18 years old) in sexual activity that violates the laws or social taboos of society and that he/she: does not fully comprehend, does not consent to or is unable to give informed consent to, or is not developmentally prepared for and cannot give consent to" (CDC 2022). Research by practitioners, clinicians, and public health scholars have stressed that child sexual abuse can be from peers, adolescents, and older children, as well as adults or caretakers (Shaw, Lewis, Loeb, Rosado, and Rodriguez 2000), and asked for more numerous categories of child sexual abuse that account for a range of age differences between victim and perpetrator. These differences in interpretive approaches dictate how researchers interpret what is taken to be child sex abuse and more importantly what they believe constitutes violence toward young children. These debates have serious consequences for what is reported as the prevalence and incidence of child sexual abuse and rape in various communities.

> Accurate measurement of the prevalence of childhood CSA is made difficult by several methodological issues. Definitions of CSA typically vary across studies, such as in terms of the age used to define childhood, whether an age difference is specified, or if peer abuse is included, as well as the types of acts considered as sexual abuse (e.g., both contact and noncontact). (Murray et al. 2014: 323)

The variability of definition not only makes epidemiological analyses of child sexual abuse difficult or inaccurate but complicates the ability of researchers, especially theorists, to formulate strict criteria for the violation of consent or coercion among children and adolescents (Leeb et al. 2008; Mathews and Collin-Vezina 2019). If one believes that sexual abuse or coercive practices among peers constitute a more symmetrical power relationship than that of a child and an adolescent, the researcher creates a rationalization that may overlook the vulnerability the child and adolescent have to larger sexualized or traumatic environments. How researchers and theorists conceptualize the *asymmetrical power relation* and how that relationship is established between children and peers, or children/adolescents and adults, determines the seriousness of the violation. Throughout the literature on child sexual abuse, epidemiological concerns are translated into moral claims and public health agendas based primarily on what one perceives as constituting a sexual violation, statutory rape, or sexual violence and child compliance (Hines and Finkelhor 2007; Lanning 2005). How one defines the act of violence, deeming it child rape or molestation, for instance, affects one's sense of urgency and the measure of violence imposed on a child or group. At a practical level, "varying and inconsistent definitions and stereotypical and inaccurate perceptions can influence how cases are investigated, prosecuted, and decided" (Lanning 2017, p. 317).

Alongside inaccurate definitions is the problem of compliance or the willing child or teenager under the age of consent that freely chooses to engage in sexual intercourse with an older peer or adult. Statutory rape laws tend to assert that it is primarily young girls that need protection from older boys and adult men, so the willingness of the young girl is irrelevant to how the state asserts its need to protect her from a male perpetrator (Goodwin 2013), however, this is not the case for Black boys. The presumption of compliance or the sexually willing, sexually curious, and sexually insatiable Black boy is an enduring myth throughout sexual violence scholarship (Curry and Utley 2018). Some of the first descriptions of Black boy sexual victimization were found in the scholarship of Kardiner and Ovesey, two white sociologists studying the sexual behaviors of lower-class Black males to show that the segregated Black boy is more sexually active than his white counterparts. In Kardiner's and Ovesey's (1951) *The Mark of Oppression: Explorations in the Personality of the American Negro*, the authors describe the early age of Black boys' first sexual experience as an indication of the Black race's premature sexual development compared to whites'. Kardiner and Ovesey (1951) argue that, unlike their white middle-class counterparts who learn about sex from their mothers and fathers, Black boys "learn about sex in the streets, masturbation generally begins early six to eight. On the whole, masturbation does not play much of a role in the growing lower-class boy. This is due to the early opportunities for relations with women. First, intercourse at seven or nine is not uncommon, and very frequent in early adolescence usually with girls much older" (Kardiner and Ovesey 1951: 68). The sexual activity of Black boys has historically been framed as a particular race-sex trait among Black males. There was no worry of Black boys suffering trauma from their early sexual debut with female peers or statutory rape by adult women because Black boys were prone to sexual excess and embraced a view of masculinity that sought out sexual conquest. This mid-twentieth-century idea of Black male sexual development is only beginning to be challenged in scholarly research, and only being interpreted as evidence of Black male sexual abuse and statutory rape over the last several years (Curry 2017a, b; Curry and Utley 2018, 2020). Black male studies scholars have begun to interrogate intersectional feminism's reliance on white criminology and second-wave feminist assumptions about Black men and boys that pathologize Black masculinity as hypermasculine and violent. By tracing the sources of prominent theories concerning Black masculinity, Black male studies scholars have not only shown how intersectional feminist theories concerning Black males are inaccurate (Oluwayomi 2020) but depict dangerous racist tropes as cutting-edge gender theory (Curry 2021a, b). These theories often insist upon the invulnerability of Black men and boys to sexual violence, unless this abuse occurs at the hands of other men (Curry 2019).

Child abuse is not an exceptional form of violence inflicted upon children living under repressive social conditions. It is part of an ecology of violence and trauma that exists within the home and throughout the community which is often the product of marginalizing structures within a society. As Murray et al. (2014) explain: "Childhood sexual abuse often occurs alongside other forms of abuse or neglect, and in family environments in which there may be low family support and/or high stress, such as high poverty, low parental education, absent or single parenting, parental substance abuse, domestic violence, or low caregiver warmth" (p. 324). Male victims of child abuse tend toward the sexual coercion of future sex partners, increased risk-taking behavior, post-traumatic stress syndrome, substance abuse, affective numbing, and sexual promiscuity (Hernandez, Lodico and DiClemente 1993; Lohman and Billings 2008). Male victims of child sexual abuse also suffer from depressive symptoms and multiple mental health issues well into adulthood (Shaw et al. 2000; Homma et al. 2012).

Black boys are particularly susceptible to negative health consequences caused by child sexual abuse because of racism and the lack of positive support structures enabling Black male victims to deal with the trauma (Gray and Rarick 2018). Similarly, Wyatt (1990) found that structural racism amplifies the negative consequences of child sexual abuse physiologically and psychologically for young, racialized children. Hernandez, Lodico, and DiClemente's research (1993) found that:

> Black children are at higher risk of abuse than white children, particularly black males. Children from single-parent households and of lower

socioeconomic status are more common targets, as are children with physical, neurological, or emotional problems; black males are overrepresented in all those situations...Although age of onset of abuse is similar across genders, girls are generally abused up to an older age, as boys begin to fend off abusers sooner. Actual or attempted intercourse is more common with boys, as is extrafamilial abuse. (Hernandez et al. 1993: 594)

The higher risk Black boys have to attempted and completed sexual abuse is contrary to the cultural assumptions that researchers and the at-large public have about child sexual abuse. These assumptions, or more accurately biases, not only limit research but the ability of this information to change the intellectual and social culture around child sexual abuse.

Prevalence of Sexual Violence Against Black Boys in the United States

The lack of national data makes it extremely difficult to authoritatively show repetitive patterns of Black boys' sexual victimization. Prevalence data concerning made to penetrate violence and sexual violence against Black boys is largely unavailable within national datasets in the United States. The CDC understands made to penetrate violence as a form of sexual violence similar to rape. According to the CDC, made to penetrate violence occurs if "the victim was made to, or there was an attempt to make them, sexually penetrate someone without consent as a result of physical force or when the victim is unable to consent due to being too drunk, high, or drugged, (e.g., incapacitation, lack of consciousness, or lack of awareness) from their voluntary or involuntary use of alcohol or drugs" (Smith et al. 2017, p. 17). The Child Maltreatment Surveys produced by the Children's Bureau under the U.S. Department of Health and Human Services does not report rates of child sexual abuse by race and sex in the yearly publications, nor does the CDC's National Intimate Partner and Sexual Violence Survey (NISVS) racially disaggregate their age of first made to penetrate victimization data (Smith et al. 2017: 170). The CDC NISVS dataset does show that roughly twenty-five percent of made to penetrate victimization of males in the

United States occurs before the age of eighteen (Ibid). The lifetime prevalence of contact sexual violence for Black males in the United States is roughly twenty percent which translates into about 2.5 million Black male victims (Smith et al. 2017, p. 21) according to the most recent NISVS data. Contact sexual violence includes various kinds of violence including rape/made to penetrate violence, unwanted sexual contact, and sexual coercion.

The little research that does exist about sexual violence against Black boys consists of some periodical sources trying to convince America that Black boys under the age of eighteen are children (NPR 2009; New York Public Radio 2021) and bring more public attention to the fact that the sexual abuse of Black men by other men and women does happen in the United States (Woodyatt 2022) as well as a few peer-reviewed sources which will be discussed below. A recent study tracking the sexual debut of U.S. adolescents has noted an especially early age of first sexual experience for Black males which would fall within the ages of pre-consent or statutory rape. Cavazos-Rehg, Krauss, Schootman, Bucholz, Peipert, Sander-Thompson, Cotttler, and Bierut (2009) used the National Youth Risk Behavior Survey (YRBS) from 1999 to 2007 to analyze trends in the sexual debut of racial and ethnic groups analyzed by sex and was not able to ascertain consent or coercion throughout their study. Using a Kaplan-Meir analysis, the authors showed that Black boys had the earliest sexual debut of all groups, or were the least likely to survive to the age of twelve without sexual debut compared to whites, Asians, Hispanics, and their female counter (p. 161). Kaplan Meir estimates for surviving until one's 17th birthday without sexual debut for Black boys at the age of twelve was 0.85 (95% CI: 0.83–0.86), by the age of thirteen was 0.72 (95% CI:0.700–0.74), by the age of fourteen was 0.58 (95% CI: 0.55–0.60), by the age of fifteen was 0.42 (95% CI: 0.40–0.45), by the age of sixteen was 0.28 (95% CI: 0.25–0.31), and by the age of seventeen was 0.18 (95% CI: 0.16–0.20). These survival estimates were lower than all groups of boys and girls across the selected age groups (see Table 9.1).

Cavazos-Rehg et al. (2009) considered that the higher rates of sexual debut among Black boys did not seem compatible with the ages of sexual debut among Black girls. At the age of twelve, roughly 96% of Black girls survive without sexual debut while only 85% of Black boys do. By the

Table 9.1 Kaplan Meier (KM) estimates for surviving free of sexual debut through 17th birthday, according to race and gender

Time point (age)	Caucasian		African American		Hispanic*		Asian	
	KM estimate	95% CI	KM estimate	95% CI	KM estimate	95% CI	KM estimate	95% CI
Males								
12.0	0.97	0.96–0.97	0.85	0.83–0.86	0.94	0.93–0.95	0.97	0.95–0.98
13.0	0.94	0.93–0.95	0.72	0.70–0.74	0.88	0.87–0.89	0.95	0.93–0.97
14.0	0.89	0.88–089	0.58	0.55–0.60	0.77	0 76–0.79	0.93	0.90–0.94
15.0	0.79	0.78–0.81	0.42	0.40–0.45	0.64	062–0.66	0.87	0.84–0.90
16.0	0.65	0.64–0.67	0.28	0.25–0.31	0.47	0.45–0.49	0.80	0.75-0.84
17.0	0.47	0.45–0.49	0.18	0.16–0.20	0.31	0.29–0.33	0.67	0.61–0.73
Female*								
12.0	0.98	0.98–0.99	0.97	0.96–0.98	0.98	0.98–0.98	0.98	0.97–0.99
13 0	0.97	0.96–0.97	0.92	0.90–0.93	0.96	0.95–0.96	0.98	0.96–0.99
14.0	0.93	0.92–0.93	0.83	0.81–0.85	0.90	0.89–0.91	0.96	0.94–0.97
15.0	0.82	0.80–0.83	0.66	0.63–0.68	0.78	0.76–0.79	0.91	0.88–0.93
16.0	0.63	0.61–0.65	0.45	0.43–0.48	0.59	0.57–0.61	0.85	0.81–0.88
17.0	0.42	0.40–0.45	0.26	0.23–029	0.41	0.39–0.43	0.72	0.64–0.78

*Includes multiracial Hispanic

age of fourteen, roughly 83% of Black girls have not had sex while only 58% of Black boys report they have not. While 26% of Black girls tend to delay their sexual debut at the age of seventeen, only 18% of Black boys managed the same. Cavazos-Rehg et al. (2009) explain, "From the data, we are unable to identify the sexual partners of these adolescents. Black girls tend to have a later sexual debut than their male counterparts. However, because far fewer female adolescents have had a sexual debut at a very early age, we can speculate that these young African-American males were exaggerating reports of sexual debut or are having their first sexual intercourse with older females" (p. 161). It is important to note that the selected ages of Cavazos-Rehg et al. (2009) are under the age of consent which is 18 in most states in the United States. The early sexual debuts of these Black boys would likely constitute statutory rape or some form of sexual coercion if their sexual partners are indeed older women or girls who may be slightly older peers.

In a more recent study by French, Tilghman, and Malebranche (2015) analyzing sexual coercion among high school and college male students in the United States, the authors found that Black men from their cohort of 284 males reported the highest rates of sexual manipulation (43%) and statutory rape (67%) compared to white, Asian, Latino, and multiracial male (p. 47). In a subsequent study, French, Teti, Suh, and Serafin (2019) found that racialized men sexually abused by women of color were more likely not only to engage in risky sexual behaviors but "more likely to endorse stereotypes of hypersexuality about women in their racial group" (p.8). Being sexually victimized by Black women from a racial or ethnic minority enables racialized boys to more easily believe that these women are aggressive, untrustworthy, promiscuous, or dangerous as a way to make sense of the sexual violence they suffered. French et al. (2019) show that racialized males internalize the harm that women of their groups enact against them. The negative racialized ideations of the society, specifically the various myths of racial inferiority, are assimilated by the young racialized male as a way to explain the harm non-white inflict on them. It is important to understand how previous sexual abuse conditions intra-racial conflicts among young men and women. Often current works analyzing Black masculinity insist that Black boys hold negative stereotypes about Black women because of sexism or patriarchy (hooks 2004). None of that work considers that some Black boys hold negative views of Black women because of the sexual abuse and coercion they experience throughout their lives from female caretakers and peers.

Our Curry and Utley (2018) study suggested that the lack of a nationally representative sample to obtain prevalence data provided the opportunity to utilize qualitative interviews with Black men discussing their early sexual experiences to better contextualize the harms of such experiences throughout their lives. Our study selected five narratives from "a larger collection of 60-min semi-structured phone interviews with 27 black men over the age of 18 who were asked to define a sexual experience, describe their early sexual experiences, and discuss how those sexual experiences impacted them as adults" (Curry and Utley 2018: 215). These Black men were from various parts of the United States and held various occupations. They answered a call for interviews on Black men's early sexual experiences which was advertised on multiple social media platforms and academic discussion forums. Like the larger quantitative studies, the sample showed both early peer exploration (Curry and Utley 2020) and adult sexual abuse of minors. In the stories describing the sexual abuse of minors, the perpetrators were predominately identified as older women or caretakers. Our testimonies showed that Black males had various experiences of sexual violation and abuse as children. Even when they felt or knew something was wrong at the ages of three, or nine, they were never taught to think of themselves as victims of sexual violence. There was simply no cultural script that Black boys had access to that allowed them to understand older women and girls making them perform cunnilingus against their will or making them penetrate their vaginas as an act of rape or sexual violence. In some cases, Black boys were abused by older boys or white teenagers. While the male perpetrators were more easily identified as wrong, the Black boys did not see the violence as an act of rape. In several of those interviews, the Black male did not disclose the events of their abuse that happened before the age of ten in some cases until there were well within their thirties. The suppression of the trauma associated with these sexual violations had a profound effect on how the subjects of our study perceived sex as adults and their ability and willingness to trust women in relationships.

Risk Factors and Challenges

Black boys are placed in multiple negating social contexts in the United States (Curry 2017a, b; Kitossa 2021). The relative isolation of Black males through downward economic mobility, mass incarceration, police homicide, and domestic abuse compared to other race-sex groups conditions their societal vulnerability to the will of other more powerful and recognizable groups (Curry 2018a; Smith et al. 2020). The negative stigmas associated with Black boys make their recognition as victims of abuse and sexual violence difficult for Americans regardless of racial or ethnic background (Curry and Utley 2018; Curry 2017a, b). Across all the available studies, the evidence showed that Black boys are sexually vulnerable to men and women as well as older boys and girls. From the perspective of the Black boy victims, it cannot be overlooked that there was an inability of Black boys to recognize themselves as victims of rape and child sexual abuse until much later in life. While the disclosure of child sexual abuse among men often occurs later in life for various reasons (Alaggia and Millington 2008), the reticence of Black boys must be contextualized within ongoing and daily negations of Black male life and the over-representation of Black males in death. While the disbelief of males as sexual victims is common throughout American society as well as the very institutions created to treat and reassure victims of sexual violence (Hlavka 2016), the violence inflicted upon the Black male child stems from a degradation—an imposed devolution of his kind—which insists as a Black male he is nothing more than the pathologies other assert about him. He is thought to be the cause of his suffering. His existence dooms him to suffer within the disbelief that he is injured by the acts of violence others commit against him. This creates an immense problem for the public health scholar and social worker who would attempt to develop interventions to remedy this problem.

Child sexual abuse literature rarely engages how racism and systemic oppression affect the child victim. Lisa Fontes (1995) was one of the first child sexual abuse researchers to introduce the idea of studying child sexual abuse within an eco-systemic approach that recognized the interplay between "individual, familial, cultural, and societal factors" (p. 1). "Although researchers sometimes consider race and culture as demographic labels, culture as a complex web of behaviors, values, and attitudes has hardly been discussed in relation to sexual abuse," writes Fontes (1995: 2). Fontes maintained that previous research primarily understood race and ethnic markers as demographic labels of targeted populations, not an indicator of cultural meaning or societal location. Consequently, previous research failed to understand how different cultural meanings and definitions of abuse were operating under systems of oppression that did not trust the police or social workers to remedy the abusive conditions. The deleterious effect of maleness on the life chances of Black boys requires researchers to think more carefully about how Black men and boys make sense of a world that primarily depicts them as violent deviants and denies their ability to be victimized by violence other than death.

Early explorations of Black and Latino populations' perception of child sexual abuse from men and women did not consider the possibility that boys were regularly victimized or that Black boys could be victimized by women (Fontes et al. 2011). Racial scripts in the Black community regularly depict the sexual victimization of Black boys as rare, a white problem that does not affect Black children, especially Black male children (McGuffey 2008). Abney and Priest (1995) similarly observed that:

> significant segments of the African American community have traditionally taken a twofold thematic variation of "see no evil, hear no evil." On one hand, sexually abusing children is something other ethnic groups do. On the other hand, if, in fact, African Americans do engage in incestuous acts or other sexually abusive behavior with children, it is not to be talked about because it is thought that acknowledging sexual child abuse will be used in some damnable way to further exclude African Americans from the American mainstream. (Abney and Priest 1995: 11)

This culture of silence and unbelievability is especially disadvantageous to collect data, stories, and design meaningful interventions into the sexual victimization of Black boys. The distrust of police, social workers, and academic researchers who have all historically harmed the Black community makes remedying and understanding the dynamics of Black male victims of child sexual abuse a formidable task.

Understanding the Overdetermination of Black Males as Predators and Incapable of Sexual Victimization

The history of American racism has not only involved the demonization of Blackness as inferior to whiteness but also created sexual narratives legitimated by "science" that established Black males as sexual predators. In the 1800s, ethnologists asserted that Black males were primitive beasts who were less evolved than white men. This perception that Black males were incapable of developing proper manhood and patriarchal virtues such as chivalry, sexual restraint, and paternalism meant that Black men were to remain devolved and trapped by their insatiable sexual appetites (Curry 2017a, b; Stein 2015). This was an evolutionary pattern of sexual development that was codified in the very being of Black males. In the 1890s, ethnologists termed the sexual insatiability of Black males furor sexualis. George Frank Lydston, a noted nineteenth-century physician explained that there was not "any difference from a physical standpoint between the sexual furor of the negro and that which prevails among the lower animals...the furor sexualis in the negro resembles similar sexual attacks in the bull and elephant, and the running amuck of the Malay race" (McGuire and Lydston 1893, p. 17). Such theories were not uncommon at the dawn of the twentieth century. William Lee Howard, a well-regarded sexologist, once wrote that:

> With the advent of puberty the Negro shows his genesic instincts to be the controlling factor of his life. These take hold of his religion, control his thoughts, and govern his actions. I the increase of rape on white women we see the explosion of a long train of antecedent preparation. The attacks on defenseless white women are evidences of racial instincts that are about as amenable to ethical culture as is the inherent odor of the race. When education will reduce the large size of the Negro's penis... then will it also be able to prevent the African's birthright to sexual madness and excess. (1903: 424)

The description of Black male sexuality as a racial and primitive instinct is thought to be a fact of racial differentiation scientifically proven by nineteenth-century ethnologists. Early twentieth-century social scientists merely extended these assumptions through ethnographic studies of Black populations across the world. For example, the British psychologist Havelock Ellis argued in *The Psychology of Sex Volume III* (1913) that primitive peoples have breeding seasons like most animals. However, the peculiar sexual development among Negroes gave Black men a novel sexual power to delay ejaculation. According to Ellis (1913), Black males had slower ejaculation because "of his blunter nervous system which takes three times as long to reach emission as the white man" (p. 271). This made him a better lover for the white woman, but also a sensual being designed primarily for sexual excess and incapable of sexual restraint.

The sociological account of poor Black American culture insisted upon the predator nature of the Black male adolescent. As a creature driven almost solely by external stimuli and immediate gratification, poor Black boys in urban environments (i.e., ghettos) were thought to pursue sexual conquests over young girls due to compensatory masculinity (Williams and Holmes 1981). Sociologists and ethnographers believed that the satyrical disposition of the young Black men and boys indicated a primordial bio-cultural tendency in less developed racialized males. Subculture of violence scholars insisted that the strong cultural and racial inclination of Black males to use sexual aggression and violence to display masculine prowess was an expression of an antecedent and repetitive trait that could be observed in the sexual activity of Black boys as early as the age of seven in some cases (Hannerz 1969; Rainwater 1970; Curtis 1975). Ira Reiss's (1964) study on the sexual permissiveness of the Negro compared to whites insisted that the racial difference, or more accurately the racial distance, between Blacks and whites, explained why Blacks engaged in premarital sex more easily than whites. Reiss suggested that Blacks were culturally disposed to premarital sexual permissiveness, while whites were a much more adaptable population whose morals could be corrected through church attendance and social environment. Blacks, especially Black men, were simply a more morally debased racial group. Unsurprisingly, he concluded his study with a lesson on Black male sexuality. Reiss (1964) wrote "white women's permissiveness is affected by all the variables investigated [race, church attendance, romantic love, and frequency of falling in love]; that of Negro men is affected by none of them" (Reiss 1964: 698). Black Americans were thought to not only be more culturally inferior to whites, but sexually permissive than whites because of their primitive and undeveloped moral virtues as a race. Black men were of worry because their lack of moral conscience and sexual insatiability posed a danger to white racial reproduction and white women's safety, but also the rampant impregnating of Black girls and women in slums (Rainwater 1966a, b, 1966a).

Robert Staples (1972) explained that this racist imagery of "Black people as a sexually animated group that is immune to any restraints on its sexual conduct…has inculcated in the public mind a host of myths concerning the sexual behavior of Afro-Americans" (p. 183). Recognizing that much of white sociology's analysis of Black promiscuity was geared toward proving the unamenable sexual behavior of the Black male, Staples (1972) insisted once age was controlled for, larger samples of Blacks were taken Black men (as well as women) were not vastly different from whites. Robert Staples argued that racial differences in sexual activity between whites and Black were not due to some innate racial traits or cultural deficit, but the simple fact that white men and women substituted heavy petting, masturbation, and fellatio for sexual intercourse (Robert, 1972: 185). Staples understood that the attack on lower-class Black men and boys' sexuality was not simply about the class biases of white social scientists, but rather part of a racist program that made the sexual behavior of lower-class Blacks the presumed norm for all Black people in the United States regardless of class background or educational attainment. Recent research has sought to complicate the long-standing view that the earlier sexual debut of Black Americans is simply cultural differences. Biello et al. (2013) does support previous research showing that there is a verifiable Black-white disparity in the age of sexual debut, however, their results suggest that "residential racial segregation may help to explain this disparity" (p. 28). The authors concluded "In hyper-segregated areas, black participants were at increased odds of adolescent first sexual intercourse compared with white people. This racial disparity did not exist in non-hyper-segregated areas" (Biello et al. 2013: 31).

These sexual myths came to define the twentieth-century accounts of Black male sexual development. While one may find the renderings of sexologists such as William Lee Howard a testament to the ignorance of white racist pseudo-science, these theories impacted sociologists, psychologists, criminologists, and feminists well into the 1970s and 1980s when gender theorists were beginning to formulate the systematic accounts of rape and masculinity. Unfortunately, feminist theories offered by Susan Brownmiller's *Against Her Will: Men, Women, and Rape* (1975), and Joyce Williams' and Karen Holmes' *The Second Assault: Rape and Public Attitudes* (1981) would come to define the boundaries of sexual victimization and male sexual predation for the next several decades. Throughout these texts, Black males are depicted as culturally maladjusted predators incapable of civility and defined by sexual pathology and aggression. By depicting Black males, poor young Black boys as sexual predators who used rape and sexual violence to reclaim the manhood lost from racist oppression, these theories bolstered the criminological and carceral logics of the racist American state (Bumiller 2008) to incarcerate and murder young Black men and boys to protect women and girls. This formulation of gender, which placed Black males outside the realm of victimization, became canonized theory and a foundational assumption of intersectional theory (Curry 2021a, b).

Black males are primarily depicted in Black feminist theory as hypersexual threats to women in intimate relationships. Speaking about the aggression of Black working-class men who spend their time on the streets, Patricia Hill Collins (2004) argues: "When joined to understandings of booty as sexuality, especially raw, uncivilized sexuality, women's sexuality becomes the actual spoils of war. In this context, sexual prowess grows in importance as a marker of Black masculinity. For far too many Black men, all that seems to be left to them is access to the booty, and they can become depressed or dangerous if that access is denied. In this scenario, Black women become reduced to sexual spoils of war, with Black men defining masculinity in terms of their prowess in conquering the booty" (p. 151). In *We Real Cool*, bell hooks (2004) similarly warns that intimacy with Black men is a perilous endeavor "Since so many black males, especially young black males, feel that they are living on borrowed time, just waiting to be locked down (imprisoned) or taken out (murdered), they may as well embrace their fate—kill and be killed" (p. 57). Like the subcultural criminologists before her (Amir 1971; Curtis 1975, 1976), hooks (2004) asserted with no evidence whatsoever that challenges the masculinity of Black men—interrupting the idea they have of themselves from movies as "fearless, insensitive egocentric and invulnerable"—causes them to respond with "anger and sexual predation to maintain their dominator stance" (p. 57). According to these aforementioned theories, Black men and boys are perpetrators of sexual violence against women, not victims of sexual violence by women. This meant that the testimonies and early sexual experiences of Black males documenting statutory rape, sexual coercion, or highly sexual childhood encounters at the hands of a female perpetrator were thought to be the consequences of the young Black boys' agency and desire for sexual intercourse.

It is not simply that the nineteenth and twentieth centuries created racist and biased pseudo-scientific scholarship depicting Black males negatively, what is of central concern, is how these pseudo-scientific claims concerning Black males are culturally inculcated and conceptually solidified in how academics and the public think about the properties thought to be natural and essential to the bodies claimed under the general idea of "Black maleness." If Black maleness is thought to be violent or exhibiting sexual excess, then all those bodies that fit that definition are almost intuitively (analytically) asserted to have these properties. Previous research on race and gender theory has referred to this as the failure of the concept, or the inability of our abstractions and general categories of thought to accurately depict groups as they exist in the real world (Curry 2021b). The historical and contemporary demonization of Black males in media, gender theory, and American society (Curry 2017a, b) creates a crisis of thought whereby the very category/abstraction/concept we have of Black maleness is inextricably tied to the pathological excesses believed to be incidental to other bodies or race-sex groups.

What constitutes a sexual violation, an act of sexual violence, or rape against young Black boys has remained a conceptual and sociological problem for over a century among historians, sociologists, and public health scholars in the United States. Only recently have historians begun to unearth the narratives and archival documents showing that the rape of Black men and boys during slavery and Jim Crow were a normal and regular occurrence in the United States (Foster 2019, 2011; Curry 2017a, b, 2018a, b). Being the kind of body that was assumed to be completely sensual and consequently irrational makes Black males incapable of being seen as victims of sexual violence. The Black brute was invulnerable to sexual violence because rape and pedophilia emanated from his primitive satyriasis (Curry 2017a).

The sexuality of Black males continues to be theorized as hypermasculine and hypersexual, as well as aggressive, immoral, and dangerous (Pass, Benoit and Dunlop 2014). The enduring myths of Black male hypersexuality and promiscuity are not fixed stereotypes or idle ideas about a group. These caricatures of Black boys are dynamic and integral to the interpretive schema of researchers (Pitt and Sanders 2010). Gail Wyatt (1990) once recalled her experience at a symposium on adolescence where a well-known researcher said, "you have to go to the second grade to find adequate samples of Black male virgins to include in research" (Wyatt 1990: 339). As a researcher of Black male sexual vulnerability, it is not uncommon to hear scholars make similar remarks despite being thirty years after Wyatt's account. As a philosopher, integrating public health perspective or epidemiological findings to theorize the sexual victimization of Black boys is often met with hostility and distrust of data that contradicts the anecdotal experiences of theorists. At a national philosophy conference where I suggested that young Black boys experience rape as young children and suggested the need to track Black male sexual vulnerability into manhood, a female professor said, "You cannot rape Black boys, they always want sex." These are not simply statements of racial ignorance but indicate the presence of a cultural-disciplinary schema that codifies (or more accurately ontologizes) the invulnerability of the Black male to sexual violence by pathologizing the Black male body (Okello 2022).

The ethnological characterizations of Black men and boys that are routinely dismissed as racist sciences from a long-gone era nonetheless influence our twenty-first-century notions of Black male bodies and sexuality. Like the sexologists of the early twentieth century, contemporary gender theorists, public health scholars presume the Black male body cannot be harmed by sexual violence in ways that produce negative psychological symptomologies and harm Black boys' socio-cultural development. Working from the assumption that Black boys are anti-social and deviant, and exhibit these deficits throughout their journey toward manhood, researchers often cannot conceptualize what aspect of Black males' personality is harmed by abuse. Whereas other race-sex groups are thought to suffer physical injury and psychological harms that increase the likelihood that they (as a victim of sexual violence) will engage in anti-social behavior, riskier sexual practices, and more interpersonal conflicts with friends, peers, and intimate partners, Black males are assumed to engage in these behaviors without suffering injury or experiencing a traumatic event. Said differently, non-Black male groups are thought to be more civil and socially adjusted than Black men and boys, so the etiology of anti-social behavior and promiscuity for these groups would have to be due to an external event that changes their psychological and behavioral norms. For Black males, anti-sociality and hypersexuality are thought to be endemic traits and ultimately unaffected by early sexual debut, sexual violation, or rape/made to penetrate violence.

Conclusion

The small amount of published research on Black boys and sexual assault makes evidence-based analyses of child sexual assault exploratory at best, however, the increasing interest and recognition of Black male sexual victimization make further research necessary to any efforts attempting to decrease sexual violence within Black communities in the United States. Despite the evidence, academia remains resistant to the study of Black boys as victims of child sexual abuse and sexual violence. Theories that should be evaluated for their explanatory power given the sociological, epidemiological, and historical evidence available to researchers are politicized and moralized as sacred and beyond contestation. Accepting that Black boys and young Black males are victims of sexual violence at rates comparable to their female counterparts upset the asymmetrical accounts of gendered violence found throughout various disciplines. While liberal academics are more willing to accept that Black men and boys could be victimized by other men (Curry 2019), there is outright hostility to theorizing the consequences of female perpetration of sexual violence against Black boys. The data and stories of Black male survivors show that Black boys are suffering and hurting. Regardless of the resistance to or outright hatred of this research, public health scholars and ethicists have a responsibility to lessen the harm experienced by vulnerable groups.

Public health scholars would better serve Black boys victimized by child sexual abuse if Black males were educated about their risk to sexual abuse and sexual violence more generally (Curry and Utley 2018). Black males currently have no publicly available materials educating them about sexual violence and child sexual abuse. Among many Black Americans, the sexual victimization of Black boys is thought to be a minor problem that occurs at the hands of men, not women or older girls. The risks and associated consequences of child sexual abuse and statutory rape need to be provided to young Black boys as early as six to nine years old in some cases. Parents also need to be educated about the characteristics of perpetrators who given the available evidence tend to be female caretakers or older female peers. This pattern of female perpetration also holds over many Black men's adult life since roughly 80% of made to penetrate violence against men are committed by women (Smith et al., 2017, p. 32). The deleterious mental health effects of child sexual abuse are compounded by the widespread aversion and fear white Americans have of Black men. Black boys are rarely believed to be victims of sexual violence. The myths of hypersexuality and sexual predation are still part of the American cultural schema. Consequently, Black boys will be depicted as compliant at best, or at worse the sexual aggressor. This means that public health officials and counselors need to specifically engage and unlearn the misandric stereotypes associated with Black males to effectively treat them (Smith et al. 2020).

Black boys need protection from sexual assaults by women and girls as well as other men and boys. To acknowledge these forms of sexual vulnerability requires massive resocialization programs involving schools, universities, social workers, doctors, and scholars working on sexual violence and child sexual abuse. This is not only about recognizing the vulnerability of Black boys but accepting that their victimization fundamentally challenges our cultural schema which not only maintains that Black boys are not victims of sexual abuse, but that Black women and girls are not perpetrators of sexual violence either. For academics, grant awarding agencies and universities must insist on inclusive research practices that not only include male victims of sexual violence and rape but address the racial variation in prevalence throughout men's lives. Despite Black boys having the earliest sexual debut of all racial groups in the United States, and Black men (over the age of 18) having the highest rates of sexual victimization over a twelve-month period, Black males remain absent from ongoing research and recent publications engaging sexual violence. The silence surrounding the statutory rape and sexual abuse of Black boys must end if scholars and public health practitioners aim to truly help all victims of child sexual abuse.

References

Abney, V., and Priest, R. (1995). African American and sexual child abuse. In L. Fontes (Ed.), *Sexual abuse in nine North American cultures* (pp. 11-30). Thousand Oaks: Sage.
Alaggia, R., and Millington, G. (2008). Male child sexual abuse: A phenomenology of betrayal. *Clinical Social Work Journal, 36*, 265–275.
Amir. M. (1971). *Patterns of forcible rape.* Chicago: University of Chicago Press.
Ashbury, J. (1993). Violence in Families of Color in the United States. In R. Hampton, T. Gullotta, G. Adams, and R. Weissberg (Eds.), *Family violence: prevention and treatment* (pp. 159–178). London: Sage.
Bernard, C. (2019). Using an intersectional lens to examine the child sexual exploitation of black adolescents. In J. Pearce (Ed.), *Child sexual exploitation: Why theory matters* (pp. 193–208). Bristol: Policy Press.
Biello, K. B., Ickovics, J., Niccolai, L., Lin, H., and Kershaw, T. (2013). Racial differences in age at first sexual intercourse: Residential segregation and black-white disparity among U.S. adolescents. *Public Health Reports, 128*, 23–32.
Brownmiller, S. (1975). Against Our Will: Men, Women, and Rape. New York: Fawcett Columbine.

Burrow, J., Isom-Scott, D., and Mikell, T. (2020). No man's land: the denial of victimisation in male statutory rape cases. *Journal of Sexual Aggression*, 26(3), 316–333.

Carter, R., Seaton, E., and Blazek, J. (2000). Comparing associations between puberty, ethnic–racial identity, self-concept, and depressive symptoms among African American and Caribbean black boys. *Child Development*, 91(6), 2019–2041.

Cavazos-Rehg, P., Krauss, M., Spitznagel, E., Schootman, M., Bucholz, K., Peipert, J., Sanders-Thompson, V., and Bierut, L. (2009). Age of sexual debut among U.S. adolescents. *Contraception, 80*, 158–162.

Collins, P.H. (2004). *Black Sexual Politics: African Americans, Gender and the New Racism*. New York: Routledge.

Cooper, F. R. (2006). Against Bipolar Black Masculinity: Intersectionality, Assimilation, Identity Performance, and Hierarchy. *U.C. Davis Law Review*, 39(3), 853–904.

Curry, T. J. (2017a). *The man-not: Race, class, genre and the dilemmas of Black Manhood*. Philadelphia: Temple University Press.

Curry, T. J. (2017b). This nigger's broken: Hyper-masculinity, the buck, and the role of physical disability in white anxiety toward the black male body. *Journal of Social Philosophy, 48*(3), 321–343.

Curry, T. J. (2018a). He's a Rapist, Even when He's Not: Richard Wright's Man of All Work as an Analysis of the Rape of Willie McGee. In J. Gordon, and C. Zirakzadeh (Eds.), *The Politics of Richard Wright: Perspectives on Resistance* (pp. 132–152). Lexington: University of Kentucky Press.

Curry, T. (2018b). Killing boogeymen: phallicism and the misandric mischaracterizations of black males in theory. *Res Philosophica*, 95(2), 235–272.

Curry, T. (2019). Expendables for whom: terry crews and the erasure of black male victims of sexual assault and rape. *Women Studies in Communication*, 42(3), 287–307.

Curry, T. (2021a). Decolonizing the Intersection: Black Male Studies as a Critique of Intersectionality's Indebtedness to Subculture of Violence Theory. In R. Beshara (Ed.), *Critical Psychology Praxis: Psychosocial Non-Alignment to Modernity/Coloniality* (pp. 132–154). New York: Routledge.

Curry, T. (2021b). Must there be an empirical basis for the theorization of racialized subjects in race-gender theory. *Proceedings of the Aristotelian Society, 121*(1), 21–44.

Curry, T., and Utley, E. (2018). She touched me: five snapshots of adult sexual. *Kennedy Institute of Ethics Journal, 28*(2), 205–241.

Curry, T., and Utley, E. (2020). She's just a friend (with benefits): Examining the significance of Black American Boys' partner choice for initial sexual intercourse. In M. Hopson, & M. Petin (Eds.), *Reimagining Black Masculinities and public space: Essays on race, gender and social activism* (pp. 33–52). Lanham: Lexington Books.

Curtis, L. (1975). *Violence, race, and culture.* Lexington, MA: Lexington Books.

Finkelhor, D. (1987). The trauma of child sexual abuse: two models. *Journal of Interpersonal Violence, 2*(4), 348–366.

Finkelhor, D., and Browne, A. (1985). The traumatic impact of child sexual abuse: a conceptualization. *American Journal of Orthopsychiatry, 55*(4), 530-541.

Fix, R., and Nair, R. (2020). Racial/ethnic and gender disparities in substantiation of child physical and sexual abuse: influences of caregiver and child characteristics. *Children and Youth Services Review, 116*, 1–9.

Fontes, L. A. (Ed.). (1995). *Sexual Abuse in Nine North American Cultures: Treatment and Prevention.* Thousand Oaks: SAGE Publications.

Fontes, L., Cruz, M., and Tabachnick, J. (2011). Views of child sexual abuse in two cultural communities: an exploratory study among african americans and latinos. *Child Maltreatment, 6*(2), 103–117.

Foster, T. (2011). The sexual abuse of black men under american slavery. *Journal of the History of Sexuality, 20*(3), 445–464.

Foster, T. (2019). *Rethinking rufus: Sexual violations of enslaved men.* Athens: University of Georgia Press.

French, B., Tilghman, J., and Malebranche, D. (2015). Sexual coercion context and psychosocial correlates among diverse males. *Psychology of Men and Masculinity, 16*(1), 42-53.

French, B., Teti, M., Suh, H., and Serafin, M. (2019). A path analysis of racially diverse men's sexual victimization, risk-taking, and attitudes. *Psychology of Men and Masculinities, 20*(1), 1–11.

Garfield, G. (2010). *Through Our Eyes: African American Men's Experiences of Race, Gender, and Violence.* New Brunswick: Rutgers University Press.

Goodwin, M. (2013). Law's limit: regulating statutory rape law. *Wisconsin Law Review, 2*, 481–540.

Gray, S., and Rarick, S. (2018). Exploring gender and racial/ethnic difference in the effects of child sexual abuse. *Journal of Child Sexual Abuse, 27*(5), 570–587.

Hannerz, U. (1969). *Soulside: Inquiries into Ghetto culture and community.* Chicago: University of Chicago Press.

Hampton, R. L. (Ed.). (1987). *Violence in the Black Family: Correlates and Consequences.* Hoboken: Prentice-Hall.

Hampton, R. L., & Oliver, W. (2006). Violence in the Black Family: What We Know, Where Do We Go? In R. L. Hampton, & T. Gullotta (Eds.), *Interpersonal Violence in the African-American Community: Evidence-Based Prevention and Treatment Practices* (pp. 1–15). New York: Springer.

Hernandez, J., Lodico, M., and DiClemente, R. (1993). The effects of child abuse and race on risk-taking in male adolescents. *Journal of the National Medical Association, 85*(8), 593–597.

Hines, D., and Finkelhor, D. (2007). Statutory sex crime relationships between juveniles and adults: a review of social scientific research. *Aggression and Violent Behavior, 12*, 300–314.

Hlavka, H. (2016). Speaking of stigma and the silence of shame: Young men and sexual victimization. *Men and Masculinities, 20*(4), 482–505.

Homma, Y., Wang, N., Saewyc, E., and Kishor, N. (2012). The relationship between sexual abuse and risky sexual behavior among adolescent boys: a meta-analysis. *Journal of Adolescent Health, 51*, 18–24.

hooks, b. (1990). *Yearning: Race, gender and cultural politics.* Boston: South End Press.

hooks, b. (2004). *We real cool: Black men and masculinity.* New York: Routledge.

Howard, W.L. (1903). The negro as a distinct ethnic factor in civilization. *Medicine* 9, 423–426.

Hust, S., Brown, J., and L'Engle, K. (2008). Boys will be boys and girls better be prepared: an analysis of the rare sexual health messages in young adolescents' media. *Mass Communication and Society, 11*(1), 3-23.

Kardiner, A., and Ovesey, L. (2014). *The mark of oppression: Explorations in the personality of the American Negro.* Mansfield Center: Martino Publishing.

Kim, H., and Drake, B. (2018). Child maltreatment risk as a function of poverty and race/ethnicity in the USA. *International Journal of Epidemiology, 47*(3), 780–787.

Kitossa, T. (2021). *Appealing because he is appalling: Black masculinities, colonialism, and erotic racism.* Edmonton: University of Alberta Press.

Lanning, K. (2005). Compliant child victims: Confronting and uncomfortable reality. In E. Quayle and M. Taylor (Eds.), *Viewing child pornography on the Internet: Understanding the offence, Managing the offender, Helping the victims* (pp. 49–60). Regis: Russel House Publishing.

Lanning, K. (2017). Sexual victimization of children: Rape or molestation. In R. Hazelwood and A. Burgess (Eds.), *Practical aspects of rape investigation: A multidisciplinary approach* (5th ed., pp. 305–318). Boca Raton: CRC Press.

Lanning, K., and Dietz, P. (2014). Acquaintance molestation and youth serving organizations. *Journal of Interpersonal Violence, 29*(15), 2815-2838.

Leeb, R., Paulozzi, L., Melanson, C., Simon, T., and Arias, I. (2008). *Child maltreatment surveillance: Uniform definitions for public health and recommended data elements.* Atlanta: Centers for Disease Control and Prevention: National Center for Injury Prevention and Control.

Lohman, B., and Billings, A. (2008). Protective and risk factors associated with adolescent boys' early sexual debut and risky sexual behaviors. *Journal of Youth and Adolescence, 37*, 723–735.

Mathews, B., and Collin-Vezina, D. (2019). Child sexual abuse: toward a conceptual model and definition. *Trauma, Violence, and Abuse, 20*(2), 131–148.

McGuffey, C. (2008). "Saving masculinity": Gender reaffirmation, sexuality, race, and parental responses to male child sexual abuse. *Social Problems, 55*(2), 216–237.

McGuire, H., & Lydston, G. F. (1893). *Sexual Crimes among the Southern Negroes.* Louisville: Renz and Henry

Murray, L., Nguyen, A., and Cohen, J. (2014). Child sexual abuse. *Child and Adolescent Psychiatric Clinics of North America, 23*(2), 321–337.

New York Public Radio. (2021, February 24). *The overlooked and Pervasive sexual abuse of boys and young men.* New York. Retrieved from https://www.wnycstudios.org/podcasts/takeaway/segments/overlooked-and-pervasive-sexual-abuse-boys-and-young-men

NPR. (2009, July 13). Sexual Abuse is Often Taboo for Black Boys. *NPR.* Retrieved from https://www.npr.org/templates/story/story.php?storyId=106538016&t=1643974387370

Okello, W. (2022). "We've never seen this": Reckoning with the impossibility of black [males'] vulnerability to sexual violence. *International Journal of Qualitative Studies in Education, Online First*, 1–13.

Oluwayomi, A. (2020). The man-not and the inapplicability of intersectionality to the dilemmas of black manhood. *Journal of Men's Studies, 28*(2), 183-205.

Pitt, R.N. and Sanders, G. (2010). Revisiting hypermasculinity: shorthand for marginalized masculinities? In W.S. Harris and R. T. Ferguson (Eds.), *What's up with the brothers: Essays and studies on African-American Masculinities* (pp. 33–51). Harrimon: Men's Studies Press.

Rainwater, L. (1966a). The negro lower class family. *Daedalus, 95*(1), 172–216.

Rainwater, L. (1966b). Some aspects of lower-class sexual behavior. *Journal of Social Issues, 22*, 96–108.

Rainwater, L. (1970). *Behind Ghetto Walls: Black families in a Federal Slum.* Chicago: Aldine Publishing Company.

Reiss, I. (1964). Premarital sexual permissiveness among negroes and whites. *American Sociological Review, 29*, 688–698.

Shaw, J., Lewis, J., Loeb, A., Rosado, J., and Rodriguez, R. (2000). Child on child sexual abuse: psychological perspectives. *Child Abuse & Neglect, 24*(12), 1591–1600.

Smith, S., Chen, J., Basile, K., Gilbert, L., Merrick, M., Patel, N., Welling, M., and Jain, A. (2017). *The national intimate partner and sexual violence survey (NISVS): 2010–2012 State Report.* Atlanta: National Center for Injury Prevention and Control, Centers for Disease Control and Prevention.

Smith, W., David, R., and Stanton, G. (2020). Racial Battle Fatigue: The long-term effects of racial microaggressions on African American Boys and Men. In R. Majors, K. Carberry and T. Ransaw (Eds.), *The international handbook of Black Community mental health* (pp. 83–92). Bingley: Emerald Publishing.

Staples, R. (1972). Research on black sexuality: its implication for family life, sex education, and public policy. *The Family Coordinator, 21*(2), 183-188.

Sutherland, K. (2003). From jailbird to jailbait: age of consent law and the construction of teenage sexualities. *William and Mary Journal of Race, Gender, and Social Justice, 9*(3), 313–349.

White, A. (2008). *Ain't I a Feminist?: African American Men Speak Out on Fatherhood, Friendship, Forgiveness, and Freedom.* New York: SUNY Press.

Williams, J., and Holmes, K. (1981). *The Second Assault: Rape and Public Attitudes.* Santa Barbara: Praeger.

Woodyatt, A. (2022, February 2). More than 1,000 students were sexually abused at this university. An ex-NFL player wants their stories to be heard. *CNN.com.* Retrieved from https://edition.cnn.com/2022/01/29/sport/university-of-michigan-robert-anderson-victims-intl-spt/index.html

Wyatt, G. (1990). Sexual abuse of ethnic minority children: Identifying dimensions of victimization. *Professional Psychology: Research and Practice, 21*(5), 338–343.

10

Child Sexual Abuse in Latinx Populations in the United States: An Examination of Cultural Influences

Maureen C. Kenny, Claire Helpingstine, and Maheshi Pathirana

Introduction

Few studies examine childhood sexual abuse (CSA) in Latinx[1] populations, and even fewer study the intersections of Latinx identity and trauma. In this chapter, we will summarize the current literature on CSA in Latinx populations. Attention will be paid to risk factors and cultural norms surrounding this form of victimization. In the United States (US), the Latinx community is the second largest and includes individuals from numerous countries with their own ethnic identities, languages, and cultural values. While the authors recognize the diversity among Latinx in the US, the goal of the chapter is to present the existing literature in an attempt to give attention to the potentially unique influences and intersections of Latinx cultural identity as related to the trauma of CSA. Intersectionality is important to consider when

---

M. C. Kenny (✉) · C. Helpingstine · M. Pathirana
Florida International University, St, Miami, FL, USA
e-mail: kennym@fiu.edu

discussing CSA among Latinx as it frames sexual abuse within a larger system of inequity and injustice. Intersectionality refers to the role of overlapping and vulnerable individual level factors (e.g., gender, race, economic status, and immigration status) which relate to an individual's power within larger systems in which they are embedded (Crenshaw 1991). Within this framework, these identities may shape how CSA is discussed, viewed, and influence norms around abuse disclosure within Latinx families and communities. Most of the existing literature on CSA is dated and presents contradictions in the occurrence of, and characteristics related to CSA in Latinx groups. This chapter will examine these inconsistencies in the research and the role of culture on incidence, disclosure, and family, victim and perpetrator characteristics among US-based Latinx populations. A critique of the current weaknesses in the literature, including incongruities and recommendations for future research are also presented.

Prevalence of Childhood Sexual Abuse in the United States

In 2019 in the US, there was a reported 62,961 new victims of CSA (US Department of Health and Human Services 2021). It is estimated that one in seven girls and one in 25 boys will be victims of CSA prior to turning 18 (Townsend and Rheingold 2013). CSA affects youth of all ages across all ethnic, racial, and cultural groups (US Department of Health and Human Services 2021). The majority of the perpetrators of these crimes are known to children in the form of family members or acquaintances (Finkelhor and Shattuck 2012). Effects of CSA include psychological issues (e.g., depression, anxiety), sexual risk-taking (e.g., multiple sexual partners), and increased substance use (see a 30-year longitudinal study by Fergusson, et al. 2013). The economic costs of CSA—specifically, the projected average lifetime cost for female victims of nonfatal CSA—is a staggering $282,734 per victim and $74,691 for male victims (Letourneau et al. 2018). The cost for males is projected lower as there was insufficient information on productivity losses to be included in the analysis. These expenses include childhood health care costs, adulthood medical costs, productivity losses, child welfare costs, violence/crime costs (including costs associated with assault, robbery, burglary, and theft), special education costs, and suicide death costs (Letourneau et al. 2018). All of these facts combined, make CSA a major public health issue in the US.

Latinx Population in US

Latinx includes individuals from various birth countries in North, Central, and South America. Latinx, similar to Latino/a, "is a pan-ethnic label typically used to describe individuals in the US who are descendants of, or direct immigrants coming from, Latin America" (Santos 2017: 8). The term Latinx is applied to those who come from Spanish-speaking countries; however, beyond sharing a common language, these individuals represent diverse religions, racial groups, and traditions (Kenny and Wurtele 2013). Although it is important to recognize the substantial diversity among Latinx, it has been argued that many different Latinx cultures (e.g., Mexican, Cuban, Honduran, Chilean) have underlying similarities, often related to the effects of imperialism and imposed colonization: for example, the introduction of Catholicism (Lefkowitz et al. 2000).

There is a tremendous Latinx population in the US that has experienced exponential growth in the last decade. The 2020 US Census included 62 million Latinx of which 33% were foreign-born (Krogstad and Noe-Bustamante 2021). Despite a slight decrease in the growth rate over the last few years (Noe-Bustamante et al. 2020), the Latinx population is the second largest population in the US. Latinx children currently comprise 26% of all children in the US and are projected to remain the largest ethnic minority group among children in the US (Child Trends 2018). Nationwide, the 2020 US Census identified 19% of the US population to be represented by Latinx, yet many of the mental and physical health needs of Latinos are largely unexplored (Arreola et al. 2005). All cultures have norms that increase the risk of CSA while also having values that protect children (Fontes 1995) and those from Latinx communities are no exception. Given the prevalence of Latinx cultures in the US, there is a need to examine CSA in these populations, how the experience of living as Latinx in the US may contribute to family climates where CSA occurs, may hinder disclosure and the ability of individuals from these communities to access help after CSA.

One difficulty with research that has been conducted with Latinx groups is that many studies simply refer to participants as Latino/a or Hispanic, without specifically describing their origins. Fontes (1995) identified the hazards of "ethnic lumping" referring to when researchers collapse many diverse individuals into broad, overly general categories. As Leenarts et al. (2013) conclude after their review of child maltreatment and ethnic minority groups, there are insufficient numbers of participants from different ethnic minority groups in recent studies of trauma symptoms among victims of CSA. This may contribute to the "ethnic lumping" that occurs in research. In this chapter, where possible, we will use descriptions provided in studies about their Latinx participants to more specifically describe their national roots.

Prevalence of CSA in Latinx Populations

Despite their population growth, there is little investigation of CSA among Latinx populations in the US. Much of the early research into CSA neglected to examine race and ethnicity, often failing to mention or parse out these demographic characteristics. The available research on CSA that examined race and ethnicity was conducted in the 1980s and 1990s, and the authors have chosen not to include these studies currently due to their age (see Kenny and McEachern 2000). This chapter will only include studies that have been conducted in the last 20 years in order to represent the current state of research on this topic.

The lack of available consistent research findings on CSA in Latinx makes estimates of prevalence in this population difficult, however, the available data indicate that Latinx youth experience higher rates of CSA than White youth. The US Department of Health and Human Services, *Child Maltreatment* report does not provide ethnicity of victims within the categories of abuse; it simply provides race across all types of maltreatment (i.e., White (43.5%), Hispanic (23.5%), African American (20.9%)) (US Department of Health and Human Services 2021). The National Survey of Children's Exposure to Violence (NatSCEV) (Gewirtz-Meydan and Finkelhor 2020) on children and adolescents found the highest rates of CSA in Black youth (5.7%), and then Hispanic (4.1%), followed by White non-Hispanic (3.1%). Analysing the 2018 National Child Abuse and Neglect Data System, Luken et al. (2021) found that based on population ratios, Latinx-identified children were over-represented for CSA in nine US states as compared to CSA overrepresentation for Black children as found in 30 states (Lukenet al. 2021). However, the authors' findings point to underreporting among Latinx as underrepresentation for all types of child abuse in about half of the US states. The National Incidence Study 4 reported CSA incidence rates of Latinx children (1.8 per 1000) were a bit higher than those of White non-Latinx children (1.4 per 1000), but the differences were not statistically significant (Sedlak et al. 2010).

Adult Retrospective Studies

Many studies on CSA in Latinx communities have employed a retrospective research design, asking women to recall experiences of CSA. In fact, this is often the most common type of research methodology for CSA studies, regardless if culture is being examined (Murray et al. 2014). Bowman, and colleagues (2009) found that 46.8% of a sample of community dwelling Latinx reported a history of CSA. Two recent studies (one using the Latinx data from the National Latino and Asian American Study (NLAAS)) found rates of 15–18% of Latinx women in their studies reported CSA (McCabe et al. 2018; Ai and Lee 2018). Similarly, 12.2% of participants from the Sexual Abuse Among Latinas Study (Cuevas and Sabina 2010), a national study of lifetime sexual violence among a sample of mostly Mexican American women, reported experiencing at least one incident of CSA. In a sample of predominantly Mexican and Mexican American women, Ulibarri, et al. (2009) found that 35% of the women reported some form of sexual abuse experience in childhood or adolescence. In sum, the ranges from these retrospective studies are 12.2 to 46.8%, representing a wide variability, although consistent with lifetime prevalence rates found in studies where ethnicity is not considered (Finkelhor et al. 2014).

College Students

Given the presence of researchers in academia and the availability of undergraduates as research participants, there are some studies with this population which show quite high, but consistent, rates of CSA. In a study with primarily Mexican American female college students, Ernst and colleagues (2009) found that 1 in 3 reported being a victim of sexual abuse prior to age 18. This is very similar to the results by Cordero (2020) with a sample of 95 male Latinx undergraduate students of Mexican descent who found over one-third had experienced CSA in their lifetime. In a college sample, Ullman and Filipas (2005) found some ethnic differences in prevalence of any CSA, with more Black survivors (40.3%) reporting a CSA experience than Hispanic survivors (33.3%). Finally, in another sample of Mexican American college students, Clemmons et al. (2003) found 38% reported CSA.

Youth/Young Adults

The Reteniendo y Entendiendo Diversidad para Salud (Project RED, Grest et al. 2021) data found that 15.8% of Latinx youth reported sexual abuse. This data set is a longitudinal study of youth in the US in selected schools where 70% or more of student enrolment was Latinx. Another study using the National Longitudinal Study of Adolescent to Adult Health (Brown et al. 2021) found that 5% of the sample (aged 10–19 years old) reported CSA and there were no significant differences between Latinx and non-Latinx.

Men

Much of the research on CSA and Latinx men has predominantly focused on men who have sex with men (MSM) and HIV risk. Thus, the majority of the literature is limited to prevalence rates and sexual risk-taking behaviours among this population. Only a handful of studies within the past decade have sought to explore the long-term related health outcomes among Latino MSM who have experienced CSA in general (Arreola et al. 2009; Levine et al. 2018; Mattera et al. 2018; Sauceda et al. 2016). Previous research has suggested that Latinx MSM are more likely to have experienced CSA (Mimiaga et al. 2009; Welles et al. 2009). Arreola et al. (2005) found that almost twice as many Latinx MSM have experienced CSA (prior to age 13) as non-Latinx MSM. When examining Latinx MSM specifically, other studies have reported higher rates. For example, in a study conducted with HIV positive MSM, Welles et al. (2009) found that 58% of Latinx MSM had experienced CSA. Further, in a sample of Latinx men (predominantly Mexican (35%) and Puerto Rican (17%)), Arreola et al. (2005) found that 22% of Latinx MSM reported experiencing at least one instance of CSA before the age of 13 as compared to their non-Latino counterparts (12%). Variations in prevalence rates of CSA among this population may be due in part to the ways in which participants conceptualize CSA. For example, some studies have shown that Latinx MSM may not view age-discordant sexual experiences as abuse (Camacho et al. 2021; Carballo-Diéguez et al. 2012; Bruce et al. 2012). Negative perceptions of LGBTQ+, cultural bias, and discrimination towards members of this community within the Latinx context has been noted in previous research. From a religious standpoint, the Catholic Church has actively supported the inequitable and unjust treatment of the LGBTQ+ community by refusing to recognize LGBTQ+ people and partnerships. These homophobic environments and attitudes can contribute to Latinx MSM emotional or psychological distress. Latinx men and boys in particular may not be able to disclose CSA due to fear of the repercussions of being viewed as gay (Camacho et al. 2021). While CSA disclosure is critical for intervention, homophobic environments may also contribute to feelings of shame or other emotionally distressing experiences in addition to the CSA. Arreola et al.

(2009) found that after the CSA had ended, Latinx MSM still experienced homophobia in childhood and adulthood, leading them to engage in maladaptive coping behaviours.

CSA in general has been linked to distress intolerance, or the inability to withstand periods of emotional discomfort leading to impulsive and avoidant coping strategies. MSM from 17 countries in Latin America (mostly Mexico (34%), Brazil (15%), Columbia (13%), and Venezuela (10%)) who participated in Wang et al. (2017) study, reported higher levels of distress intolerance as compared to those who had not experienced CSA. This increased level of distress intolerance was associated with increased odds of participating in negative health behaviours such as substance and alcohol abuse. The links between CSA and substance abuse have been well-documented in the literature, and the same is true for Latinx MSM with a history of CSA as well (Lee et al. 2020; Levine et al. 2018). In particular, men who have experienced CSA are more likely to engage in heavy drinking in general, but Latinx MSM are more likely to report binge drinking and heavy drinking (Levine et al. 2018) which have been shown to place MSM at greater risk of sexual risk-taking (e.g., anal intercourse without condoms) (Lee et al. 2020; Levine et al. 2018).

Latinx MSM with a history of CSA are known to face heightened risk of negative mental health outcomes (Sauceda et al. 2016). Findings from Levine et al. (2018) suggest that among a sample of Latinx MSM (28% Central American, 28% South American, 17% Puerto Rican), those that experienced CSA were 3.5 times more likely to be clinically depressed, particularly if they only spoke Spanish. This is in line with findings from Mattera et al. (2018) who reported higher odds of clinical depression among bisexual Latinx men who had experienced CSA, and Sauceda et al. (2016) who reported the same among a sample of Latinx MSM. Relatedly, in a study comparing Latinx MSM and Black non-Hispanic MSM, Downing et al. (2020) found significantly greater PTSD symptoms in Latinx MSM. In a study conducted on Latinx MSM in three large metropolitan areas in the US (Los Angeles, Miami, and New York), Arreola et al. (2009) reported higher rates of depression, anxiety, and suicidality among their sample.

Characteristics of Abuse

Severity

While there is some general consensus on the definition of CSA, given the range of actions and behaviours involved, severity of the abuse varies. CSA can include both contact and non-contact forms of abuse. The later may involve forcing the child to witness sexual acts or taking photos of the child for pornographic purposes. When considering severity, factors such as the frequency, duration, nature of the acts, relationship of the perpetrator, force, and number of perpetrators are considered (Fortier et al. 2009). Some studies will use indicators of severity such as forced intercourse as well as the length of time the abuse occurred (Clemmons et al. 2003). The results on severity of CSA experienced by Latinx victims is inconsistent. Niu, et al. (2021) found that 14.5% of their Black Hispanic sample and 41.8% of their non-Black Hispanic sample of young women (ages between 13 and 23 years) reported severe sexual abuse. In a sample of Latinx (self-identified as Mexican American, Hispanic, or Latina), Bowman et al. (2009) found a greater proportion of participants (22.6%) reported extreme severity for sexual abuse compared to the other forms of maltreatment. Contrary to these findings, in a sample of low-income African-American and Latinx adults, Myers, et al. (2015) found that both men and women reported severe histories of CSA involving penetration, with Latinx women reporting the lowest levels of CSA severity. Ullman and Filipas (2005) found that severity of CSA also differed by ethnicity with higher percentages of Black and Latinx college student survivors reporting minor abuse (e.g., 29.2% and 23.5% reported exposure or fondling, respectively) compared to Asian or White survivors. Further, 19% of Black survivors more often reported attempted or completed penetration compared to 9.9% of Latinx survivors. Examining Latinx and African-American girls who had experienced CSA, Shaw et al. (2001) found that the African-American girls in this sample were more likely to experience CSA involving penetration compared to the Latinx girls.

Perpetrators

CSA in Latinx communities seems to fit broader patterns of CSA with regard to perpetrators. Specifically, as is true of most cases of CSA, family members and individuals known to the child (in the form of family friends, boyfriends, or acquaintances) pose the biggest risk for offending (Finkelhor and Shattuck 2012). Ullman and Filipas (2005) found that most perpetrators reported by their college student sample were family members or relatives of Latinx victims (63%). In their Mexican–American sample, Ulibarri et al. (2009) found that most of the perpetrators were family members (31%), a boyfriend (27%), a friend or acquaintance (25%), and the lowest percent were strangers (14%). Moreover, of the women who experienced rape before age 13, the perpetrators were friends and boyfriends. Among their predominantly Mexican–American sample in Cuevas and Sabina's (2010) study, perpetrators were most commonly relatives (42.6%) and non-familial individuals (38.1%) known to the family. Similarly, Clemmons et al. (2003) found that extended family members and acquaintances were most often identified as perpetrators among Mexican–American college students recollecting CSA. In a qualitative study conducted with Mexican–American women, Marrs Futchsel (2013) found that perpetrators comprised of family members (brothers, aunts, cousins), boys, and a Catholic priest. Shaw et al. (2001) found Latinx girls were more likely to report abuse perpetrated by their fathers or stepfathers (45%) than other non-related adult males (34%). Graham et al. (2016) analysed secondary data from the 2012 National Child Abuse and Neglect Data System Child File to determine if Latinx victims of CSA differed from Black or White with regard to characteristics related to the child, the perpetrator, or the caretaker. For CSA cases involving Latinx children, primary perpetrators were 75.71% male and 21.46% female, which differed significantly from that of perpetrators in cases involving White and Black children. Perpetrators were also primarily Latinx and were more likely to be a parent (45.50%), other relative who was not a foster parent (27.20%), or an unmarried partner of a parent (11.63%). Perpetrators in substantiated CSA cases involving Latinx children were more likely to be caretakers (71.84%) than in cases involving White (67.86%) and Black (70.06%) children.

In the Plummer et al. (2009) study of Latinx youth being seen at a clinic for CSA victims, the majority of reported perpetrators was a known non-relative (47.8%) and 33% were acquaintances. In 15.6% of the cases, children were sexually abused by their biological fathers.

Effects of CSA on Victims

Adults

There is a body of literature that examines the resultant effects of CSA on adults. Symptoms that have commonly been observed in other samples of victims of CSA, have also been found in Latinx victims. Severe CSA has been found to be strongly related to depression among Latinx, especially among Latinx who disclosed their abuse (Sciolla 2011). In their interviews with male survivors of CSA, Payne et al. (2014) found differences in reactions based on ethnicity, with more Latinx men reporting being angry about the abuse and reporting flashbacks and PTSD type symptoms. By contrast, Latinx men did not engage in as many self-hatred statements as the other men (Blacks and non-Latino Whites). Similarly, several studies have found that Latinx women who reported a history of CSA had symptoms of PTSD and depression and substance use (McCabe et al. 2018; Ulibarri et al. 2015). Cuevas et al. (2010) found that CSA was more strongly predictive of psychological distress including anger, depression, dissociation, and anxiety in adulthood among Latinx women. Compared to their African-American, non-Hispanic White, and "Other" counterparts, Latinx women reported less severe psychological distress symptoms due to CSA (Andrés-Hyman et al. 2004). The authors of this study hypothesize that it may be due to the inclusion of a range of Latinx nationalities. These discrepant findings may make drawing conclusions about any differences in the ways in which Latinx experience symptomatology post CSA difficult.

Contrary to these reported findings, Newcomb et al. (2009) found that Latinx adolescents who were victims of CSA did not score any differently than their European peers on measures of trauma symptoms and psychological distress. Similar results were found among college students who were victims of CSA with Latinx students showing no differences in either depressive or PTSD symptoms (Ullman and Filipas 2005).

Factors in Latinx Families That May Affect CSA

Immigration

Heightened stress due to immigration and adjustment to new cultural contexts and roles are experienced by immigrants making their way in a new country. Latinx immigrants currently make up the largest immigrant population in the US. The highest numbers originate from Mexico which accounts for 25% of all US immigrants in 2018, with Central America and South America comprising of 8 and 7%, respectively (Budiman et al. 2020). As immigration from Mexico, and Central and South American countries, are driven by increased economic opportunities in the US, as well as refugee and asylum seeking (Tienda and Sanchez 2013), Latinx immigrants may rely upon support from family who are already in-country as they establish themselves. Poverty and housing instability can exacerbate CSA risk. Dettlaf et al. (2009) found that Latinx children of immigrants in the welfare system were four times as likely to be the subject of a CSA report as compared to non-immigrant counterparts. Latinx children of immigrants were also five times more likely to be a confirmed victim of CSA as compared to Latinx children of native-born parents. Relatedly, Latinx participants in Fontes and colleagues (2001) focus groups spoke about children being exposed to sexual acts by family members inadvertently. Fontes et al. (2001) further explains that due to immigration transition, families may need to share homes and possibly beds. Katerndahl et al. (2005) reported similar findings in their study of CSA experiences between Latinx and White women in that Latinx women reported sharing their living space with extended family members during their childhoods. Sharing such close sleeping quarters may leave children prey to predators or witness to sexual acts. While not all actions should be considered CSA, observing sexual acts may be disturbing to the child. Grest et al. (2021) found that first-generation Latinx adolescents were more likely to report experiencing sexual abuse compared to second and third generation (i.e., twice the odds of reporting CSA compared with second generation). The authors contend that this is likely due to cultural and environmental risk factors including lack of family communication, need to keep a male in the household for financial reasons and authoritarian parenting. They further suggest that in first-generation families, there may be extended family members and unrelated acquaintances having unsupervised access to children at home and a lack of overall awareness of the issue of CSA.

Acculturation

Related to immigration status, other studies have discussed the role of acculturation in CSA reporting rates. It has been found that as families acculturate, they are more likely to discuss CSA. One study reported that Mexican-born US Latinx, reported they were more likely to be aware of CSA than their parents were, causing them to be more vigilant of the risk of CSA to their children (Lira et al. 1999). In other reports, researchers have found that Hispanic women who are more highly acculturated reported higher rates of sexual violence (Cuevas and Sabina 2010). Katerndahl et al. (2005) found that in a study of CSA experience between Hispanic and White adult women, acculturation among Hispanic women was associated with longer periods of CSA. However, higher levels of acculturation were also related to a higher likelihood of reporting CSA to an adult. The authors hypothesize that these women who reported CSA were not believed by the adults they sought help from. Further, they report it may be that although acculturated Hispanics report the abuse they are experiencing, they are not believed perhaps because the perpetrator is a family member. Thus, no action is taken, and the abuse continues adding to an increased duration. This existing literature demonstrates the impact of immigration and acculturation on the incidence of CSA.

Latinx Attitudes Regarding Sexuality/CSA

While there is a lack of consistent literature, it appears that CSA in Latinx may vary from White non-Latinx in part due to differences in attitudes towards sex and sexual behaviours, gender and social norms among Latinx communities and their White counterparts. Culturally based perspectives and beliefs regarding sexuality, and CSA are likely to affect Latinx behaviours related to CSA disclosure, reporting and support for child victims and children at risk for CSA (Graham et al. 2016).

Familismo is a specific aspect of Latinx culture that has been suggested to serve as a protective factor against child abuse (Coohey 2001). Familismo has been described as the high value placed on respect for and loyalty to the family system in Latinx families (Sue and Sue 2012). In Latinx culture, extended family, including cousins, aunts, uncles, grandparents, are considered to be part of the immediate family. These caring family members typically serve as a protective factor, unless one is a perpetrator of CSA (Fontes and Plummer 2012). Given the presence of a large, extended family in the life of the child, there is the opportunity for these individuals to sexually offend. Typically, in Latinx families, there is an emphasis on the family, rather than the individual, with a deep sense of family obligation. Fontes (1995) describes the impact of this value on maintaining family homeostasis in the face of CSA, which may include denial or reluctance to report abuse. Fontes and Plummer (2012) state that the concept of *respecto* (respect) in Latinx culture, emphasizes that children should be respectful of elders, particularly older male relatives. This cultural concept may encourage children to be duped by elderly male family members' sexual requests as well as add to their fear of not being believed if they disclose. Young children may be compliant with sexual requests from older relatives due to the *respecto* they have been taught.

Ligiéro et al. (2009) report on several cultural characteristics in Latinx families that may impact sexual abuse. Specifically, the clear delineation of gender roles, which include *machismo* and *marianismo*. Machismo and marianismo prescribe to cultural norms dictating women be sexually pure, passive, and abstain from any sexual activity except for procreation. *Marianismo* defines the ideal woman as emotional, kind, docile, compliant, vulnerable, and unassertive (Castaneda 2021; Ligiéro et al. 2009). The concept of marianismo for women, promotes the image of women as sexually pure, submissive, and obedient, with a likeness to the Virgin Mary (Terrazas-Carrillo and Sabina 2019). Norms surrounding gender and gender roles for Latinas influence CSA disclosure decisions (Castaneda 2021; Ligiéro et al. 2009; Fontes and Plummer 2010; Dettlaff et al. 2009). The choice to remain silent to protect oneself from the shame of not meeting cultural ideals for women, namely, purity and virginity, have been discussed in the context of CSA (Castaneda 2021). In order to avoid the stigma of "being used goods", and potentially mistreated by family members and others in their community, women chose not to speak out about the abuse that was occurring. Shaw et al. (2001) found that the length of time between CSA onset and report of CSA was shorter among African-American girls as compared to Latinx girls. There are some aspects of marianismo (e.g., subordination to men, self-silencing, chastity) that may contribute to women being vulnerable to CSA because traditional gender roles require they maintain family unity by remaining silent and avoiding conflict (Kelly 2009). The authors hypothesize the role of stigma and shame as a significant barrier to reporting among Latinx girls.

Machismo is a Latinx cultural value emphasizing the man's traditional role of protector and caretaker of the family (Sastre et al. 2015). It is a set of values, attitudes, and beliefs about masculinity, or what it is to be a man. Machismo can be broken down into two forms: traditional machismo and *caballerismo*. Traditional machismo includes hypermasculine characteristics that are valued culturally like physical strength, power over women, and sexual prowess, while caballerismo is nurturing, family-centred, and chivalrous (Arciniega et al. 2008). Fontes (2007) states that in Latinx culture, a boy's masculinity may depend on the number of his sexual conquests, while a girl will be valued for her chastity. Machismo also includes control and aggressiveness. Terrazas-Carrillo and Sabina (2019) discuss the culture of honour for Latinx, which values status and reputation which is enforced by women's subordination to men and men's power over women. This lack of honour by men is associated with shame and there is an expectation that men will use force in order to defend their honour. Fontes (2007) claims fathers of Latinx girls who are sexually abused may be prone to violence against the offender, as the actions have been a direct threat to his role as a man/provider/father.

Ligiéro et al.'s (2009) findings with Latinx women who had been sexually abused confirmed the presence of machismo in all facets of their lives. They emphasized the importance of virginity and that women who have sex before marriage are viewed as "dirty". There was also a general silence around abuse for fear that knowledge by elderly family members may make them ill. Castaneda (2021) found that machismo influenced women's decision not to report CSA. Due to beliefs that their fathers' role is to protect their family, especially the daughters, these women believed disclosing would emasculate their fathers and cause them shame and heartbreak.

Religion

While there is some variability in religion for Latinx groups, the majority identify as Catholic. The Pew Research Center's 2013 National Survey of Latinos and Religion found that 55% of the US Latinx adults identify as Catholic. The largely practised Catholic religion has effects for Latinx who have experienced CSA. The shared Catholicism and patriarchal foundation impacts certain beliefs across these groups including putting extreme value on a woman who makes it to the altar as a virgin (Castaneda 2021; Raffaelli and Ontai 2001). Due to the amount of reverence their families give to the Catholic church and patriarchal norms in Latinx culture, high value is placed on women's virginity, which may affect disclosure rates for CSA. A study using data from the National Survey of Family Growth found that Latinx female adolescents who frequently attended religious services were less likely to have had sex, had fewer sexual partners, and were older at sexual debut (Edwards et al. 2011). It has been suggested that some religious beliefs may heighten victim-blaming responses, which may lower reporting rates and help-seeking by Latina victims, thereby contributing to deleterious psychological effects (Ramos Lira et al. 1999).

Disclosure

Cultural and religious values may also influence the way in which the process of disclosure is experienced and can either facilitate disclosure or act as barriers to reporting CSA (Fontes and Plummer 2010). The desire to not disclose CSA appears strong in Latinx culture due to cultural values regarding virginity, gender ideals, and a general lack of communication regarding sexuality. When studying CSA disclosure among Latinx, Castaneda (2021) warns it is important to note "societal and cultural values related to race, citizenship, and gender heavily influence decisions about privacy issues and create expectations of how people think privacy should be managed" (p. 5). She further reports that a potential risk–benefit calculation could take place by victims as disclosures of CSA can lead to potentially both increased emotional support and necessary interventions, as well as familial estrangement and sociocultural isolation.

In a study of Latinx women and help-seeking behaviour, Sabina et al. (2012) found that 35.5% of women did not seek help after being sexually victimized as children. In her study with adult Latinx women about their CSA, Castaneda (2021) found that the women overwhelmingly reported generational abuse (e.g., mothers and grandmothers with a history of CSA), thus normalizing the abuse they experienced. Several participants reported remaining silent about their abuse due to subtle or overt messages from their mothers to do so. Given the taboo on the discussion of sexual acts, the reporting of sexual abuse may be particularly discouraged by culturally informed gender role beliefs, such as the prohibition against girls losing their virginity before marriage (Castaneda 2021; Kenny and McEachern 2000; Ligiéro et al. 2009) and beliefs about sexual assaults that blame the victim (Ahrens et al. 2010).

Disclosure by male victims may be equally difficult. Williams et al. (2008) posit that Latinx men may not disclose their sexual abuse as the meaning of CSA in their cultures may preclude positive images of strength and prowess. Some of the Latinx men in the Payne et al. (2014) study made statements about how difficult it was to disclose the abuse to others. Boys who are abused by females may be mocked for disclosing with taunts about how disclosing means they did not want sex with a woman (Fontes and Plummer 2010). Alternately, boys may be considered gay if they report victimization by a male, which in Latinx culture is often highly stigmatized (Fontes 2007).

There is limited research on the positive responses Latinx received when disclosing CSA. Ulibarri et al. (2009) found that 56% of the Mexican women who reported some form of CSA told someone about the abuse (e.g., family member, friend, boyfriend), and of those, almost 75% stated they felt supported when they disclosed. In the Plummer et al. (2009) study, 44% of mothers of victims stated there was a time when they suspected something "wasn't quite right", and in the majority of these cases, the mothers would speak to their child or watch them more closely. Almost one-third of these mothers confronted the offender prior to knowing about the abuse (disclosure). When disclosure was made, 53% of the mothers reported completely believing what happened was true, whereas 20% were not at all certain or had very little certainty. The majority of mothers felt guilty about what happened and felt they failed to protect their children. A similar majority reported being more protective and lacking trust in others.

Concerns related to deportation could prevent CSA reporting among undocumented Latinx residing in the US. Gulbas and Zayas (2017) found that secrecy norms and fear of law enforcement within undocumented Mexican families resulted in limited access to necessary services (e.g., medical services). These findings are in line with previous research conducted by Bacigalupe (2009) who described challenges among US Latinx in accessing community or social services due to previous negative experiences with social services providers, experiences of institutionalized racism, and language barriers when seeking services.

Beyond concerns related to citizenship status, navigating the US judicial system due to CSA can be especially difficult for Latinx and other racial/ethnic minority members and a further deterrent to CSA disclosure. In a retrospective study of CSA cases involving Latinx and Black children in the Midwestern US, Powell et al. (2017) highlight the ongoing patriarchal, heteronormative, and racial biases faced by child survivors of CSA. In particular, stereotypes related to Latinx and Black cultures are often emphasized in the court room in order to portray these youths as hypersexual, or deviant (Powell et al. 2017; Stephens and Phillips 2003). For example, in one case of CSA in which the adult perpetrator was the same sex as the victim, jurors speculated that the abuse may have been consensual, but norms around homosexuality in "Latino culture" disallowed for the child to state so (Powell et al. 2017). These racialized and systemic injustices not only perpetuate further harm to marginalized communities but also result in lower rates of child abuse substantiation for racial/ethnic minority children. Specifically, according to Fix and Nair (2020) Latinx youth are significantly less likely to have their CSA case substantiated as comparison to non-Latinx youth despite findings that Black and Latinx children are more likely to be referred for child abuse or neglect (Fix and Nair 2020; Lanier et al. 2014).

Victim Blaming

The notion that the victim is somehow to blame for the CSA, appears to transcend culture. Burt (1980) theorizes that sexual violence is an extension of traditional patriarchal gender roles in general, and previous research has demonstrated strong ties between adherence to traditional gender roles, and victim blaming (Angelone et al. 2012). In a qualitative study exploring the relationship between CSA and domestic violence and familism among Mexican–American women conducted by Marrs Fuchsel (2013), participants experienced adverse outcomes when attempting to report CSA. In particular, a participant was told that she was lying when she reported the abuse to her parents. Many victims reported feeling shame and fear about disclosing abuse. In her work with primarily Mexican–American school children, Clonan-Roy (2019) found that both mothers and school administration had conversations with girls that positioned boys and men as predatory, and girls as (simultaneously) victims of predatory interactions and hypersexual. This included advice from mothers on how girls might protect themselves from boys, as the narrative included boys using girls for sex. This narrative appears to place responsibility on girls for boy's behaviour, as if they can deter offences.

In this same line, Collin-Vézina et al. (2015) found that many of their victims of CSA reported feeling responsible for the abuse, and experienced embarrassment and shame, which were often related to self-blame.

In another study of CSA survivors, Okur et al. (2019) found that a minority of victims blamed themselves. Specifically, victims were more likely to blame themselves for the CSA when they had more conservative attitudes towards gender roles than victims with more liberal attitudes. This may be applicable to Latinx victims, as this culture endorses stereotypical gender roles. Castaneda (2021) also found that Latinx women reported feeling immense shame for their CSA largely because it was contrary to the notion of the ideal Latinx woman who is pure and virginal.

Lack of Sexual Discussions

Given the apparent gender role dichotomies among Latinx men and women, it is important for research to examine the sexual messages that women in this community receive (Aragón and Cooke-Jackson 2021). Strong religious or political beliefs serve as barriers to engaging in constructive familial sex talk in Latinx families. Castaneda (2021) found that the female victims in her sample spoke about not knowing how to speak about anything sexually related with their parents as children because they believed if they did so, they would be viewed as sexual beings and that would be shameful.

Many Latinx women have been subject to negative narratives regarding sex, reproductive health and menstruation which leaves them with little understanding and education about their bodies and reproductive systems (Aragón and Cooke-Jackson 2021). The young women (aged 19–29) in the Aragón and Cooke-Jackson (2021) study reported that communication about sex was not straightforward and that if conversations occurred, they were filled with misinformation, rebukes, or expectations of imminent sexual promiscuity. They represented a range of groups including Mexican, Salvadorian, Mexican and Guatemalan, Puerto Rican, Peruvian/Honduran, Cuban, Mexican–American, and Dominican Republic.

Fontes (2007) reports that questions about the body parts or the acts involved in sexual abuse will be shameful for many victims, who may have been raised to believe that merely discussing these matters is disgraceful. Fontes (2007) states that many Latinx families subscribe to the concept: "*de eso no se habla*", translated to mean "one does not discuss this". Ligério et al. (2009) found that all of the victims of CSA also reported that sex was not something that was openly talked about or taught, especially by women. Castaneda (2021) found that the CSA victims in her study spoke about not knowing how to speak about anything sexually related with their parents as children. This was rooted in their belief that if they did so, they would be seen as sexual beings which is shameful. Many Latinx mothers believe giving their daughters knowledge about sex and sexual health would lead them to promiscuity and sexual deviancy (Aragón and Cooke-Jackson 2021). When children are known victims of CSA, mothers may still have difficulty talking about the abuse due to the cultural emphasis on virginity before marriage and the taboos related to speaking about sexuality (Plummer et al. 2009).

Sanchez et al. (2019) describe healing circles used with Black/Latinx women who were survivors of CSA. For many women, they reported this was the first time they spoke about the abuse. Several were survivors of incest and shared that their families were unaware of the abuse. Luz Marquez Benbow (second author) of the Sanchez paper, shares how her mother never talked to her about her body or sex and encouraged her to stay with her brothers to make sure she was safe. (Ironically, her brother was her abuser.) Fontes and colleagues (2001) found that Latinx women in their focus groups tended to use euphemisms when talking about CSA and they were more reluctant to name specific sexual acts compared to Latino men. One participant mentioned that "good girls don't talk dirty" (p. 109).

In focus groups with primarily Mexican women who had immigrated to the US, Quelopana and Alcalde (2014) found that overall the women reported the quality of sex education in their countries of origin was poor. In general, they reported that sex was viewed as sinful and they mostly learned about it outside of the home. Similarly in a group for middle-school aged Latinx girls at school, Clonan-Roy (2019) was asked questions by them that reflected a lack of knowledge about a range of topics and a curiosity to learn about their bodies, sex, and sexuality. She concludes that they were in need of safe spaces where they could talk and learn about sexuality as they were feeling frustrated with the powerful silence surrounding sexuality in their families, school, and community.

Kenny and Wurtele (2013) found that compared with a sample of Caucasian parents, Latinx parents intended to discuss sexual abuse/molestation at an earlier age, but planned to discuss human reproduction, intercourse, and AIDS at significantly later ages. They also found parents intended to delay discussions of normal sexual development (i.e., genital differences, birth, reproduction). A qualitative study with college students found that Latinx women who experienced CSA reported repressed sexual attitudes in their homes, with no discussions of sexuality (Kenny and McEachern 2007). Research in a previous study comparing Spanish- and English-speaking children's knowledge of genital terminology (Kenny and Wurtele 2008), found that none of the Spanish-speaking children knew the correct terms for breasts, penis, or vulva, suggesting a void in sexuality education in Spanish-speaking homes. Mexican mothers experience shame and embarrassment communicating about sexuality, using the term *cuídate* that translates as "take care of yourself". Children often don't understand that mothers are trying to communicate about sexuality because the terms mothers use are too general and vague (Moncloa et al. 2010). Prikhidko and Kenny (2021) found that Latinx mothers had lower scores than White parents on knowledge of sexual abuse prevention. White non-Latinx parents talked to their children about sexual abuse prevention more than Latinx parents. This is consistent with Jerman and Constantine (2010) who showed that parents expressed views on sexual conversations being a taboo due to family norms and religion.

There may be changes occurring in Latinx families. Recent research found that the majority of Columbian adults believed that sexuality education was necessary and that it should address all aspects of sexuality with both male and female adolescents (Pineda Marin et al. 2019). Among a sample of young Latinx women, Alvarez and Villarruel (2015) found those who believed in more traditional gender norms were less likely to engage in sexual health communication. Thus, as Latinx populations potentially move away from traditional gender beliefs and norms and become more acculturated, they may be more able to engage in discussions regarding sexuality.

Discussion

Ethnic diversity is an important topic to examine in CSA literature, particularly among Latinx, which have been found to a large growing population in the US. Much of the research reviewed in this chapter looked at factors associated with ethnicity and their mediating role in CSA. CSA has some similarities across culture, including secrecy, shame, and effects of trauma (Fontes and Plummer 2012). Ethnically based variables such as religiosity, gender roles, communication about sexuality and family support can all impact CSA. This chapter demonstrates that Latinx youth are experiencing CSA at rates similar to or higher than their peers, but the research indicates several key areas in which the experience of Latinx CSA victims are unique. This chapter sought to examine the intersection of Latinx in the US and CSA.

Latinx cultures tend to hold more traditional values than the US dominant culture, including an emphasis on the role of the family (*familismo*). An environment of familial support may encourage reporting and, in turn, help prevent long-term negative effects for victims of child maltreatment. Past research has shown the importance of maternal support in the recovery of the victim following disclosure. In contrast, the traditional family values noted in many Latino populations may decrease reporting rates and victim support, as failure to protect an abusing relative could be considered a dishonour to the family (Ramos Lira et al. 1999). In addition, the notion of CSA occurring and resulting in a loss of virginity for the female victim as well as possibly bringing dishonour to the family, may impact disclosure and subsequent support. The importance placed on respecting older family members may make young victims easy prey for offenders. Also, the role of extended family, in terms of living together and family cohesion, may allow greater access to young children by potential offenders within the family. In turn, children's lack of understanding and language to discuss the abuse may make disclosure difficult.

Overwhelmingly in the studies cited in this chapter, Latinx women believed culture and religious values play a major role in their sex education, or lack of education. They desired simple, clear body affirming messages that were free from shame or blame (Aragón and Cooke-Jackson 2021). The lack of sexuality discussions and unease parents experience using appropriate sexual language adds to a culture of silence around CSA. Youth are not equipped with the language they need for disclosure. The disclosure process appears difficult for all victims, but particularly those who are Latinx. Given the standards of virginity and the struggle in talking about such matters, it is likely that children will remain silent. Couple this with a potential fear of hurting some family members and causing disgrace to their fathers, victims may suffer in silence for years. As Castaneda (2021) eloquently reports on the dilemma for Latinx victims—there is a desire to gain support from family for the CSA, but also a strong desire to remain silent due to shame and possible isolation by the community. Male victims too struggle with disclosure for fear of being shamed or labelled as gay. The concepts of marianismo and machismo appear to affect the way in which CSA is understood in Latinx communities, and often results in victim blaming.

Latinx communities struggle with a host of issues related to their immigration status. They may experience poverty, language barriers, and limited access to community resources in some areas. This impedes their ability to access services post abuse or receive culturally appropriate interventions. While level of acculturation appears to impact discussions and awareness of CSA, there remains taboos against open, honest discussions of sexuality. Families with intergenerational abuse may be particularly at risk for continued abuse, as they often support a culture of silent acceptance of the fate of CSA.

Alaggia and colleagues (2019) summarizes a body of literature on disclosure of CSA and identified environmental and cultural factors that affect this process. Specifically, they identify lack of discussion about sexuality; passive acceptance that unwanted sexual experiences are inevitable; not wanting to bring shame to the family by admitting sexual abuse; lack of involvement from neighbours, school personnel; and stigma perpetuated by societal perceptions, all of which are present in Latinx families. There are also ways in which culture can impact who is at risk, protection from abuse, and support for victims after CSA.

For practitioners working with these families, there are a number of cultural factors to consider when working with these victims. Cultural mores may affect disclosure and perceived support. As Payne et al. (2014) state, "Practitioners should additionally be aware that men with CSA histories who come for treatment might initially voice specific issues as their presenting problems, based on their cultural background" (p. 241). It may be difficult for Latinx victims to discuss the CSA due to lack of language, feelings of shame and self-blame, and lack of culturally sensitive treatment options. Ideally, practitioners should be matched on ethnicity or at a minimum share culture and language with the victims, as they may feel more comfortable discussing the CSA in their native tongue.

Conclusion: Future Directions

As the US moves to a "minority-majority" country, there is a need for increased attention on the public health issue of CSA in Latinx communities. As Castaneda (2021) states, "the constant fluctuation in evidence highlights the importance of studying CSA among Latinas to gain a better understanding of the scope and impact of this problem" (p. 4). Empirical studies often ignore or fail to report the impact of race/ethnicity or cultural context on victims of CSA. More studies with "larger samples of minority survivors to assess possible ethnic differences and underlying factors explaining these differences" must be conducted (Ullman and Filipas 2005: 82). Analysing separate subgroups of Latinx victims according to nationalities to determine if victims from different groups show varied patterns of CSA in terms of severity, perpetrators and attitude towards discussions of sexuality is warranted to avoid ethnic lumping. Examining levels of acculturation must also occur as inconsistent findings may be related to this construct (Meston and Ahrold 2010). Future research should also examine generational status, making distinctions between first generation, recent immigrants, and other categories. Multigenerational CSA that occurs contributes to a "normalization" of such trauma and prohibits disclosure and supportive responses, as well as limits legal interventions for the perpetrators.

There are also several methodological issues to contend with including definitions of CSA used, severity of CSA, and data collection methods that need to be standardized across studies for comparison. Research remains scant and may suffer from inconsistent definitions of CSA. While retrospective studies provide important information, participants may experience issues with recall bias (Jacobs-Kayam and Lev-Wiesel 2019). The studies examined in this chapter utilized various methodologies, definitions of CSA and groups labelled Latinx. While some conclusions can be drawn, more research is needed in this area. Future studies need to report the definition of CSA used, severity of abuse, perpetrator, family reaction to disclosure (or disclosure process), the sampling methodology, demographic characteristics including level of acculturation and immigration status, language proficiency, location (rural, urban, etc.) of participants. This will allow for greater comparison across studies. As the US continues to become diverse and increase its Latinx populations, there is a need for professionals to recognize culture when planning prevention and education programmes about CSA. Assisting parents in overcoming barriers to sexual discussion and raising awareness about the prevalence of CSA, is paramount in helping our youth. Culturally informed programming that is accessible to Latinx communities is needed.

Summary of Research on CSA in US Latinx Communities

- Latinx youth are at risk for CSA often at higher rates than their White, non-Latinx peers.
- Like other victims, Latinx victims are often sexually abused by family members, friends, and those known to them.
- Gender norms in Latinx culture that polarise males and females with regard to sexuality appear harmful to all victims.
- Disclosure by victims may be impacted by cultural values of virginity for females and cultural norms that identify male victims as gay as a result of victimization.
- Latinx families have difficulty communicating openly about sexuality and awareness of child sexual abuse may be lacking.

- Immigration status and levels of acculturation among families can impact the prevalence and handling of CSA.
- There is a need for culturally sensitive CSA prevention education, with an understanding of the influence of religion, for Latinx families.
- Helping parents create a family environment where sexuality discussion can occur, free from judgement or shame, may assist in potential disclosure of CSA by victims.
- Future research should be conducted with subgroups of Latinx groups to fully inform prevention efforts and treatment planning that is culturally informed.

Note

1. Latinx is defined as "a person of Latin American origin or descent and is used as a gender-neutral alternative to Latino or Latina" (Oxford English online dictionary, n.d.).

References

Ahrens, C. E., Rios-Mandel, L. C., Isas, L., and Carmen Lopez, M. (2010). Talking about interpersonal violence: Cultural influences on Latinas' identification and disclosure of sexual assault and intimate partner violence. *Psychological Trauma: Theory, Research, Practice, and Policy, 2*(4), 284–295. https://doi.org/10.1037/a0018605

Ai, A. L., and Lee, J. (2018). Childhood abuse, religious involvement, and lifetime substance use disorders among Latinas nationwide. *Substance Use & Misuse, 53*(3), 2099–2111. https://doi.org/10.1080/10826084.2018.1455701

Alaggia, R., Collin-Vézina, D., and Lateef, R. (2019). Facilitators and barriers to child sexual abuse (CSA) disclosures: A research update (2000–2016). *Trauma, Violence, & Abuse, 20*(2), 260–283. https://doi.org/10.1177/1524838017697312

Alvarez, C., and Villarruel, A. (2015). Association of gender norms, relationship and intrapersonal variables, and acculturation with sexual communication among young adult Latinos. *Research in Nursing & Health, 38* (2), 121–132. https://doi.org/10.1002/nur.21645

Andrés-Hyman, R. C., Cott, M. A., and Gold, S. N. (2004). Ethnicity and sexual orientation as PTSD mitigators in child sexual abuse survivors. *Journal of Family Violence, 19*(5), 319–325. https://doi.org/10.1023/B:JOFV.0000042081.96997.4e

Angelone, D. J., Mitchell, D., and Lucente, L. (2012). Predicting perceptions of date rape: An examination of perpetrator motivation, relationship length, and gender role beliefs. *Journal of Interpersonal Violence, 27*(13), 2582–2602. https://doi.org/10.1177/0088626051243638 5

Aragón, A., and Cooke-Jackson, A. (2021). The sex talk was taboo…so was wearing a tampon. In A. Cooke-Jackson & V. Rubinksy (Eds.), *Communicating intimate health* (pp. 33–53). Rowman & Littlefield.

Arciniega, G. M., Anderson, T. C., Tovar-Blank, Z. G., and Tracey, T. J. G. (2008). Toward a fuller conception of machismo: Development of a traditional machismo and caballerismo scale. *Journal of Counseling Psychology, 55*(1), 19–33. https://doi.org/10.1037/0022-0167.55.1.19

Arreola, S. G., Neilands, T. B., and Diaz, R. (2009). Childhood sexual abuse and the sociocultural context of sexual risk among adult Latino gay and bisexual men. *American Journal of Public Health, 99*, 432–438. https://doi.org/10.2105/AJPH.2008.138925

Arreola, S. G., Nielands, T. B., Pollack, L. M. Paul, J. P., and Catania, J. A. (2005). Higher prevalence of childhood sexual abuse among Latino men who have sex with men than non-Latino men who have sex with men: Data from an urban men's health study. *Child Abuse & Neglect, 29*(3), 285–290. https://doi.org/10.1016/j.chiabu.2004.09.003

Bacigalupe, G. (2009). Latin@ Sobrevivientes de Abuso Sexual Infantil en los Estados Unidos: Un Acercamiento Relacional al Diagnóstico e Intervención. *Psykhe, 10*(2), 167–180. http://www.redae.uc.cl/index.php/psykhe/article/view/19943

Bowman, K., Rew, L., and Murphey, C. (2009). Childhood maltreatment among community dwelling adult Latinas. *Issues in Mental Health Nursing, 30*(7), 443–450. https://doi.org/10.1080/01612840902722203

Brown, M. J., Jiang, Y., Hung, P., Haider, M. R., and Crouch, E. (2021). Disparities by gender and race/ethnicity in child maltreatment and memory performance. *Journal of Interpersonal Violence*. Advance online publication. https://doi.org/10.1177/08862605211015222

Bruce, D., Harper, G. W., Fernández, M. I., Jamil, O. B., and Adolescent Medicine Trials Network for HIV/AIDS Interventions (2012). Age-concordant and age-discordant sexual behavior among gay and bisexual male adolescents. *Archives of Sexual Behavior, 41*(2), 441–448. https://doi.org/10.1007/s10508-011-9730-8

Budiman, A., Tamir, C., Mora, L., and Noe-Bustamante, L. (2020, August 20). *Facts of U.S. immigrants, 2018: Statistical portrait of the foreign-born population in the United States.* Pew Research Center. https://www.pewresearch.org/hispanic/2020/08/20/facts-on-u-s-immigrants-current-data/

Burt, M. R. (1980). Cultural myths and supports for rape. *Journal of Personality and Social Psychology, 38*(2), 217–230. https://doi.org/10.1037/0022-3514.38.2.217

Camacho, D., Rodriguez, C. V., Moore, K. L., and Lukens, E. P. (2021). Older immigrant Latino gay men and childhood sexual abuse: Findings from the palabras fuertas project. *Qualitative Social Work.* Advanced online publication. https://doi.org/10.1177/14733250211027644

Carballo-Diéguez, A., Balan, I., Dolezal, C., and Mello, M. B. (2012). Recalled sexual experiences in childhood with older partners: A study of Brazilian men who have sex with men and male-to-female transgender persons. *Archives of Sexual Behavior, 41*(2), 363–376. https://doi.org/10.1007/s10508-011-9748-y

Castaneda, N. (2021). "It's in our nature as daughters to protect our familias...you know?": The privacy rules of concealing and revealing Latina child sexual abuse experiences. *Journal of Family Communication, 21*(1), 3–16. https://doi.org/10.1080/15267431.2020.1856851

Child Trends (2018). *Racial and ethnic composition of the child population.* https://www.childtrends.org/indicators/racial-and-ethnic-composition-of-the-child-population.

Clemmons, J. C., DiLillo, D., Martinez, I. G., DeGue, S., and Jeffcott, M. (2003). Co-occurring forms of child maltreatment and adult adjustment reported by Latina college students. *Child Abuse & Neglect, 27*(7), 751–767. https://doi.org/10.1016/S0145-2134(03)00112-1

Clonan-Roy, K. (2019). Latina girls' sexual education in the (new) Latinx diaspora. *Girlhood Studies, 12*(2), 65–81. https://doi.org/10.3167/ghs.2019.120206

Collin-Vézina, D., De La Sablonnière-Griffin, M., Palmer, A. M., and Milne, L. (2015). A preliminary mapping of individual, relational, and social factors that impede disclosure of childhood sexual abuse. *Child Abuse & Neglect, 43*, 123–134. https://doi.org/10.1016/j.chiabu.2015.03.010

Coohey, C. (2001). The relationship between familism and child maltreatment in Latino and Anglo families. *Child Maltreatment, 6*(2), 130-142. https://doi.org/10.1177/1077559501006002005

Cordero, E. D. (2020). Sexual assault and emotional eating among Latino college students. *Psychology of Men & Masculinities, 21*(2), 327–332. https://doi.org/10.1037/men0000244

Crenshaw, K. (1991). Mapping the margins: Intersectionality, identity politics, and violence against women of color. *Stanford Law Review, 43*(6), 1241–1279. https://doi.org/10.2307/1229039

Cuevas, C. A., and Sabina, C. (2010). *Final report: Sexual assault among Latinas (SALAS) study.* Washington, DC: U.S. Department of Justice.

Cuevas, C. A., Sabina, C., and Picard, E. H. (2010). Interpersonal victimization patterns and psychopathology among Latino women: Results from the SALAS study. *Psychological Trauma: Theory, Research, Practice, and Policy, 2*(4), 296–306. https://doi.org/10.1037/a0020099

Dettlaff, A. J., Earner, I., and Phillips, S. D. (2009). Latino children of immigrants in the child welfare system: Prevalence, characteristics, and risk. *Children and Youth Services Review, 31*(7), 775–783. https://doi.org/10.1016/j.childyouth.2009.02.004

Downing, M. J., Benoit, E., Brown, D., Coe, L., Hirshfield, S., Pansulla, L., and Carballo-Diéguez, A. (2020). Early sexual experiences, mental health, and risk behavior among black non-Hispanic and Hispanic/Latino men who have sex with men (MSM). *Journal of Child Sexual Abuse, 29*(1), 41–61. https://doi.org/10.1080/10538712.2019.1685618

Edwards, L. M., Haglund, K., Fehring, R. J., and Pruszynski, J. (2011). Religiosity and sexual risk behavior among Latina adolescents: Trends from 1995 to 2008. *Journal of Women's Health, 20*(6), 871–877. https://doi.org/10.1089/jwh.2010.1949

Ernst, F. A., Salinas, N. I., and Perez, N. (2009). Brief report: Attitudes about responding to survey questions concerning childhood sexual abuse by Hispanic Female College Students. *Journal of Child Sexual Abuse, 18,* 574–581. https://doi.org/10.1080/10538710903182719

Fergusson, D. M., McLeod, G. F., and Horwood, L. J. (2013). Childhood sexual abuse and adult developmental outcomes: Findings from a 30-year longitudinal study in New Zealand. *Child Abuse & Neglect, 37*(9), 664–674. https://doi.org/10.1016/j.chiabu.2013.03.013.Finkelhor

Finkelhor, D., Shattuck, A., Turner, H. A., and Hamby, S. L. (2014). The lifetime prevalence of child sexual abuse and sexual assault assessed in late adolescence. *Journal of Adolescent Health, 55*(3), 329–333. https://doi.org/10.1016/j.jadohealth.2013.12.026

Finkelhor, D., and Shattuck, A. (2012). *Characteristics of crimes against juveniles.* University of New Hampshire. http://www.unh.edu/ccrc/pdf/CV26_Revised%20Characteristics%20of%20Crimes%20against%20Juveniles_5-2-12.pdf

Fix, R. L., and Nair, R. (2020). Racial/ethnic and gender disparities in substantiation of child physical and sexual abuse: Influences of caregiver and child characteristics. *Children and Youth Services Review, 116*, 105186. https://doi.org/10.1016/j.childyouth.2020.105186.

Fontes, L. (1995). *Sexual abuse in nine north American cultures: Treatment and prevention.* SAGE.

Fontes, L. A., Cruz, M., and Tabachnik, J. (2001). Views of child sexual abuse in two cultural communities: An exploratory study among African Americans and Latinos. *Child Maltreatment, 6*(1), 103–117. https://doi.org/10.1177/1077559501006002003

Fontes, L. A. (2007). Sin vergüenza: Addressing shame with Latino victims of child sexual abuse and their families. *Journal of Child Sexual Abuse, 16*(1), 61–83. https://doi.org/10.1300/J070v16n01_04

Fontes L. A., and Plummer, C. (2010). Cultural issues in disclosure of child sexual abuse. *Journal of Child Sexual Abuse, 19*(5), 491–518. https://doi.org/10.1080/10538712.2010.512520

Fontes, L. and Plummer, C. (2012). Cultural issues in child sexual abuse intervention and prevention. In Paris Goodyear-Brown (Ed.) *Handbook of Child Sexual Abuse: Identification, Assessment, and Treatment.* (pp. 487–508). Wiley Press.

Fortier, M.A., DiLillo, D., Messman-Moore, T. L., Peugh, J., DeNardi, K. A., and Gaffey, K. J. (2009). Severity of child sexual abuse and revictimization: The mediating role of coping and trauma symptoms. *Psychology of Women Quarterly, 33*(3), 308–320. https://doi.org/10.1177/0361684309033000306

Gewitz-Meydan, A., and Finkelhor, D. (2020). Sexual abuse and assault in a large national sample of children and adolescents. *Child Maltreatment, 25*(2), 203–214. https://doi.org/10.1177/1077559519873975

Graham, L. M., Lanier, P., and Johnson-Motoyama, M. (2016). National profile of Latino/Latina children reported to the child welfare system for sexual abuse. *Children and Youth Services Review, 66*, 18–27. https://doi.org/10.1016/j.childyouth.2016.04.008

Grest, C. V., Finno-Velasquez. M., Cederbaum, J. A., and Unger, J. B. (2021). Adverse childhood experiences among 3 generations of Latinx youth. *American Journal of Preventative Medicine, 60*(1). https://doi.org/10.1016/j.amepre.2020.07.007

Gulbas, L. E. and Zayas, L. H. (2017). Exploring the effects of U.S. immigration enforcement on the wellbeing of citizen children in Mexican immigrant families. *The Russell Sage Foundation Journal of the Social Sciences, 3*(4), 53–69. https://doi.org/10.7758/RSF.2017.3.4.04

Jacobs-Kayam, A., and Lev-Wiesel, R. (2019). In Limbo: Time perspective and memory deficit among female survivors of sexual abuse. *Frontiers in Psychology, 10*, 912. https://doi.org/10.3389/fpsyg.2019.00912.

Jerman, P., and Constantine, N. A. (2010). Demographic and psychological predictors of parent–adolescent communication about sex: A representative statewide analysis. *Journal of Youth and Adolescence, 39*(10), 1164–1174. https://doi.org/10.1007/s10964-010-9546-1

Katerndahl, D. A., Burge, S. K., Kellogg, N., and Parra, J. M. (2005). Differences in childhood sexual abuse experience between adult Hispanic and Anglo women in a primary care setting. *Journal of Child Sexual Abuse, 14*(2), 85–95. https://doi.org/10.1300/J070v14n02_05

Kelly, U. A. (2009). "I'm a mother first": The influence of mothering in the decision-making processes of battered immigrant Latino women. *Research in Nursing and Health, 32*(3), 286–297. https://doi.org/10.1002/nur.20327

Kenny, M. C., and Wurtele, S. K. (2013). Latino parents' plans to communicate about sexuality with their children. *Journal of Health Communication, 18*(8), 931–942. https://doi.org/10.1080/10810730.2012.757397

Kenny, M. C., and Wurtele, S. K. (2008). Preschoolers' knowledge of genital terminology: A comparison of English and Spanish Speakers. *American Journal of Sexuality Education, 3*(4), 345–354. https://doi.org/10.1080/15546120802372008

Kenny, M. C., and McEachern, A. G. (2007). Family environment in Hispanic college females with a history of childhood sexual abuse. *Journal of Child Sexual Abuse, 16*(3), 19–40. https://doi.org/10/1300/J070v16n03_02

Kenny, M. C., and McEachern, A. G. (2000). Racial, ethnic, and cultural factors of childhood sexual abuse: A selected review of the literature. *Clinical Psychology Review, 20*(7), 905–922. https://doi.org/10.1016/S0272-7358(99)00022-7

Krogstad, J. M., and Noe-Bustamante, L. (2021). *Key facts about U.S. Latinos for National Hispanic Heritage Month.* Pew Research Center. https://www.pewresearch.org/fact-tank/2021/09/09/key-facts-about-u-s-latinos-for-national-hispanic-heritage-month/

Lanier, P., Maguire-Jack, K., Walsh, T., Drake, B., and Hubel, G. (2014). Race and ethnic differences in early childhood maltreatment in the United States. *Journal of Development and Behavioral Pediatrics, 35*(7), 419–426. https://doi.org/10.1097/DBP.0000000000000083

Lee, J. S., Safren, S. A., Bainter, S. A., Rodríguez-Díaz, C. E., Horvath, K. J., and Blashill, A. J. (2020). Examining a Syndemics Network Among Young Latino Men Who Have Sex with Men. *International Journal of Behavioral Medicine, 27*(1), 39–51. https://doi.org/10.1007/s12529-019-09831-1

Leenarts, L. E. W., Diehle, J., Doreleijers, T. A. H., Jansma, E. P., and Lindauer, R. J. L. (2013). Evidence-based treatments for children with trauma related psychopathology as a result of childhood maltreatment: A systematic review. *European Child & Adolescent Psychiatry, 22*(5), 269–283. https://doi.org/10.1007/s00787-012-0367-5

Lefkowitz, E. S., Romo, L. F., Corona, R., Au, T. K., and Sigman, M. (2000). How Latino American and European American adolescents discuss conflicts, sexuality, and AIDS with their mothers. *Developmental Psychology, 36*(3), 315–325. https://doi.org/10.1037/0012-1649.36.3.315

Letourneau, E. J., Brown, D. S., Fang, X., Hassan, A., and Mercy, J. A. (2018). The economic burden of child sexual abuse in the United States. *Child Abuse & Neglect, 79*, 413–422. https://doi.org/10.1016/j.chiabu.2018.02.020.

Levine, E. C., Martinez, O., Mattera, B., Wu, E., Arreola, S., Ruteledge, S. E., Newman, B., Icard, L., Muñoz-Laboy, M., Hausmann-Stabile, C., Welles, S., Rhodes, S. D., Dodge, B. M., Alfonso, S., Fernandez, I., and Carballo-Diéguez, A. (2018). Child sexual abuse and adult mental health, sexual risk behaviors, and drinking patterns among Latino men who have sex with men. *Journal of Child Sexual Abuse, 27*(3), 237–253. https://doi.org/10.1080/10538712.2017.1343885

Ligiéro, D. P., Fassinger, R., McCauley, M., Moore, J., and Lyytinen, N. (2009). Childhood sexual abuse, culture, and coping: A qualitative study of Latinas. *Psychology of Women Quarterly, 33*(1), 67–80. https://doi.org/10.1111/j.1471-6402.2008.01475.x

Lira, L.R., Koss, M.P., and Russo, N.F. (1999) Mexican American women's definitions of rape and sexual abuse. *Hispanic Journal of Behavioral Sciences, 21*(3), 236–265. https://doi.org/10.1177/0739986399213004

Luken, A., Nair, R., and Fix, R. L. (2021). On racial disparities in child abuse reports: Exploratory mapping the 2018 NCANDS. *Child Maltreatment*, 1–15. https://doi.org/10.1177/10775595211001926

Marrs Fuchsel, C. L. (2013). Familism, sexual abuse, and domestic violence among immigrant Mexican women. *Affilia, 28*(4), 379-390. https://doi.org/10.1177/0886109913503265

Mattera, B., Levine, E. C., Martinez, O., Muñoz-Laboy, M., Hausmann-Stabile, C., Bauermeister, J., Fernandez, M. I., Operario, D., and Rodriguez-Diaz, C. (2018). Long-term health outcomes of childhood sexual abuse and peer sexual contact among an urban sample of behaviourally bisexual Latino men. *Culture, Health, & Sexuality, 20*(6), 607–624. https://doi.org/10.1080/13691058.2017.1367420

McCabe, B. E., Lai, B. S., Gonzalez-Guerda, R. M., and Montano, N. P. (2018). Childhood abuse and adulthood IPV, depression, and high-risk drinking in Latinas. *Issues in Mental Health Nursing, 39*(12), 1004–1009. https://doi.org/10.1080/01612840.2018.1505984

Meston, C. M., and Ahrold, T. (2010). Ethnic, gender, and acculturation influences on sexual behaviors. *Archives of Sexual Behavior, 39*(1), 179–189. https://doi.org/10.1007/s10508-008-9415-0

Mimiaga, M. J., Noonan, E., Donnell, D., Safren, S., Koenen, K. C. Gortmaker, S., O'Cleirigh, C., Chesney, M. A., Coates, T. J., Koblin, B. A., and Mayer, K. H. (2009). Childhood sexual abuse is highly associated with HIV risk-taking behavior and infection among MSM in the EXPLORE study. *Journal of Acquired Immunodeficiency Syndrome, 51*(3), 340–348. https://doi.org/10.1097/QAI.0b013e3181a24b38

Moncloa, F., Wilkinson-Lee, A. M., and Russell, S. T. (2010). Cuidate sin Pena: Mexican mother-adolescent sexuality communication. *Journal of Ethnic & Cultural Diversity in Social Work, 19*(3), 217–234. https://doi.org/10.1080/15313204.2010.499325

Murray, L. K., Nguyen, A., Cohen, J. A. (2014). Child sexual abuse. *Child and Adolescent Psychiatric Clinics, 23*(2), 321–337. https://doi.org/10.1016/j.chc.2014.01.003

Myers, H. F., Wyatt, G. E., Ullman, J. B., Loeb, T. B., Chin, D., Prause, N., Zhang, M., Williams, J. K., Slavich, G. M., and Liu, H. (2015). Cumulative burden of lifetime adversities: trauma and mental health in Low SES African Americans and Latino/as. *Psychological Trauma: Theory, Research, Practice, and Policy, 7*(3), 243–251. https://doi.org/10.1037a0039077

Newcomb, M. D., Munoz, D. T., and Carmona, J. V. (2009). Child sexal abuse consequences in community samples of Latino and European American adolescents. *Child Abuse & Neglect, 33*(8), 533–544. https://doi.org/10.1016/j.chiabu.2008.09.014

Niu, L., Brown, J., Hoyt, L. T., Salandy, A., Nucci-Sack, A., Viswanathan, S., Burk, R. D., Schlecht, N. F., and Diaz, A. (2021). Profiles of childhood maltreatment: Associations with sexual risk behaviour during adolescence in a sample of racial/ethnic minority girls. *Child Development, 92*(4), 1421–1438. https://doi.org/10.1111/cdev.13498

Noe-Bustamante, L., Lopez, M. H., and Krogstad, J. M. (2020, July 7). *U.S. Hispanic population surpasses 60 million in 2019, but growth has slowed*. Pew Research Center. https://www.pewresearch.org/fact-tank/2020/07/07/u-s-hispanic-population-surpassed-60-million-in-2019-but-growth-has-slowed/

Okur, P., Pereda, N., Van Der Knaap, L. M., and Bogaerta, S. (2019). Attributions of blame among victims of child sexual abuse: Findings from a community sample. *Journal of Child Sexual Abuse, 28*(3), 301–317. https://doi.org/10.1080/10538712.2018.1546249

Payne, J. S., Galvan, F. H., Williams, J. K., Prusinski, M., Zhang, M., Wyatt, G. E., and Myers, H. F. (2014). Impact of childhood sexual abuse on the emotions and behaviors of adult men from three ethnic groups in the USA. *Culture, Health, & Sexuality, 16*(3), 231–245. https://doi.org/10.1080/13691058.2013.867074

Peragallo, N., Gonzàlez-Guarda, B., McCabe, B. E., and Cianelli, R. (2012). The efficacy of an HIV risk reduction intervention for Hispanic women. *AIDS and Behavior, 16*(5), 1316–1326. https://doi.org/10.1007/s10461-011-0052-6

Pineda Marin, C., Munoz Sastre, T. M., Murcia, A. D., Castaneda, B. M., Hernandez, B. A., and Mullet, E. (2019). Attitudes towards sexuality information for adolescents: What parents should and should not say. *Sex Education, 19*(5), 582–596. https://doi.org/10.1080/14681811.2018.1560254

Plummer, C. A., Eastin, J., and Sylvia, A. (2009). Hispanic mothers of sexually abused children: Experiences, reactions, concerns. *Social Work Forum, 42-43*, 54–74. https://www-proquest-com.ezproxy.fiu.edu/scholarly-journals/hispanic-mothers-sexually-abused-children/docview/741611941/se-2?accountid=10901

Powell, A. J., Hlavka, H. R., and Mulla, S. (2017). Intersectionality and credibility in child sexual assault trials. *Gender & Society, 31*(4), 457–480. https://doi.org/10.1177/0891243217716116

Prikhidko, A. and Kenny, M. (2021). Examination of parents' attitudes toward and efforts to discuss child sexual abuse prevention with their children. *Children and Youth Services Review, 121*, https://doi.org/10.1016/j.childyouth.2020.105810

Quelopana, A. M., and Alcalde, C. (2014). Exploring knowledge, belief and experiences in sexual and reproductive health in immigrant Hispanic women. *Journal of Immigrant Minority Health, 16*(5), 1001–1006. https://doi.org/10.1007/s10903-013-9807-7

Rafaelli, M. and Ontai, L. L. (2001). 'She's 16 years old and there's boys calling over to the house': An exploratory study of sexual socialization in Latino families. *Culture, Health & Sexuality, 3*(3), 295–310. https://doi.org/10.1080/136910501524847 22

Ramos Lira, L. R., Koss, M. P., and Russo, N. F. (1999). Mexican American women's definitions of rape and sexual assault. *Hispanic Journal of Behavioral Sciences, 21*(3), 236–265. https://doi.org/10.1177/07399863992 13004

Sabina, C., Cuevas, C. A., and Schally, J. L. (2012). Help-seeking in a national sample of victimized Latino women: The influence of victimization types. *Journal of Interpersonal Violence, 27*(1), 40–61. https://doi.org/10.1177/0886260511416460

Sanchez, D., Marquéz Benbow, L., Hernandez-Martinez, M., and Serrata, J. V. (2019). Invisible bruises: Theoretical and practical considerations for Black/Afro-Latina survivors of childhood sexual abuse. *Women & Therapy, 42*(3-4), 406–429. https://doi.org/10.1080/02703149.2019.1622903

Santos, A. (2017). The history, struggles, and potential of the term Latinx. *Latina/o Psychology Today, 4*(2), 7–14.

Sastre, F., De La Rosa, M., Ibanez, G. E., Whitt, E., Martin, S. S., and O'Connell, D. J. (2015). Condom use preferences among Latinos in Miami-Dade: Emerging themes concerning men's and women's culturally ascribed attitudes and behaviors. *Culture, Health & Sexuality, 17*(6), 667–681. https://doi.org/10.1080/13691058.2014.989266

Sauceda, J. A., Wiebe, J. S., and Simoni, J. M. (2016). Childhood sexual abuse and depression in Latino men who have sex with men: Does resilience protect against nonadherence to antiretroviral therapy? *Journal of Health Psychology, 21*(6), 1096–1106. https://doi.org/10.1177/1359105314546341

Sciolla, A., Glover, D. A., Loeb, T. B., Zhang, M., Myers, H. F., and Wyatt, G. E. (2011). Childhood sexual abuse severity and disclosure as predictors of depression among adult African American and Latina women. *Journal of Nervous Mental Disoders, 199*(7), 471–477. https://doi.org/10.1097/NMD.0b013e31822142ac

Sedlak, A. J., Mettenburg, J., Basena, M., Petta, I., McPherson, K., Greene, A., and Li, S. (2010). Fourth National Incidence Study of Child Abuse and Neglect (NIS–4): Report to Congress. Washington, DC: U.S. Department of Health and Human Services, Administration for Children and Families

Shaw, J. A., Lewis, J. E., Loeb, A., Rosado, J., Rodriguez, R. A. (2001). A comparison of Hispanic and African-American sexually abused girls and their families. *Child Abuse & Neglect, 25*(1), 1363–1379. https://doi.org/10.1016/S0145-2134(01)00272-1

Stephens, D. P., and Phillips, L. D. (2003). Freaks, gold diggers, divas, and dykes: The sociohistorical development of adolescent African American women's sexual scripts. *Sexuality and Culture, 7*(1), 3–49. https://doi.org/10.1007/BF03159848.

Sue, D. W., and Sue, D. (2012). *Counselling the culturally diverse: Theory and practice.* John Wiley & Sons.

Terrazas-Carrillo, E. and Sabina, C. (2019). Dating violence attitudes among Latino college students: An examination of gender, machismo, and marianismo. *Violence and Victims, 34*(1), 194–210. https://doi.org/10.1891/0886-6708.34.1.194

Tienda, M. and Sanchez, S. M. (2013). Latin American immigration to the United States. *Daedalus, 142*(3), 48–64. https://doi.org/10.1162/DAED_a_00218

Townsend, C. and Rheingold, A. A. (2013). *Estimating a child sexual abuse prevelance rate for practitioners: A review of child sexual abuse prevelance studies.* Darkness to Light. www.D2L.org/1in10

Ulibarri, M. D., Ulloa, E. C., and Camacho, L. (2009). Prevalence of sexually abusive experiences in childhood and adolescence among a community sample of Latinas: A descriptive study. *Journal of Child Sexual Abuse, 18*(4), 405–421. https://doi.org/10.1080/10538710903051088

Ulibarri, M. D., Ulloa, E. C. and Salazar, M. (2015). Prevention and outcomes for victims of childhood sexual abuse: Associations between mental health, substance use, and sexual abuse experiences among Latinas. *Journal of Child Sexual Abuse, 24*(1), 35–54. https://doi.org/10.1080/10538712.2015.976303

Ullman, S. E., and Filipas, H. H. (2005). Ethnicity and child sexual abuse experiences of female college students. *Journal of Child Sexual Abuse, 14*(3), 67–89. https://doi.org/10.1300/j070v14n03_04

U.S. Department of Health & Human Services, Administration for Children and Families, Administration on Children, Youth and Families, Children's Bureau. (2021). *Child Maltreatment 2019.* https://www.acf.hhs.gov/cb/research-data-technology/statistics-research/childmaltreatment

Wang, K., White Hughto, J. M., Biello, K. B., O'Cleirigh, C., Mayer, K. H., Rosenberger, J. G., Novak, D. S., and Mimiaga, M. J. (2017). The role of distress intolerance in the relationship between childhood sexual abuse and problematic alcohol use among Latin MSM. *Drug and Alcohol Dependence, 175*, 151–156. https://doi.org/10.1016/j.drugalcdep.2017.02.004

Welles, S. L., Baker, A. C., Miner, M. H., Brennan, D. J., Jacoby, S., and Rosser, B.R.S. (2009). History of child sexual abuse and unsafe anal intercourse in a 6-city study of HIV positive men who have sex with men. *American Journal of Public Health, 99*, 1079–1086. https://doi.org/10.2105/AJPH.2007.133280

Williams, J. K., Wyatt, G. E., Rivkin, I. Ramamurthi, H. C., Li, X., and Liu, H. (2008). Risk reduction for HIV-positive African American and Latino men with histories of childhood sexual abuse. *Archives of Sexual Behavior, 37*(5), 763–772. https://doi.org/10.1007/s10508-008-9366-5

11

Truth, Trauma and Healing: Stories of Aboriginal Survivors of Child Sexual Abuse in Out-of-Home Care

Carlina Black, Muriel Bamblett, and Margarita Frederico

Introduction

This chapter highlights the importance of the voices and expertise of Aboriginal survivors of institutional child sexual abuse and explores their insights into healing including their healing needs, opportunities for healing and barriers and enablers for healing. The chapter presents themes developed from a phenomenological thematic analysis of 51

C. Black (✉) · M. Frederico
La Trobe University, Bundoora, VIC, Australia
e-mail: c.black@latrobe.edu.au

M. Frederico
e-mail: m.frederico@latrobe.edu.au

M. Bamblett
Victorian Aboriginal Child Care Agency (VACCA), Preston, VIC, Australia
e-mail: m.bamblett@vacca.org

narratives provided via private sessions at the Australian Royal Commission into Institutional Responses to Child Sexual Abuse, conducted between 2012 and 2017. The narratives were provided by adult Aboriginal survivors who were abused in out-of-home care between the 1940s and the 1990s. Findings from the analysis of the narratives highlight that institutional child sexual abuse occurred in the context of cultural abuse and collective trauma. Avenues accessed for healing by Aboriginal survivors included mainstream services, Aboriginal-specific programmes as well as support and healing from engagement in art and creative pursuits, culture and relationships. Survivors' experiences of abuse and trauma and the lifelong and intergenerational impacts of abuse are presented as are their hopes for themselves and their insights for policy and practice needed for a responsive and effective healing response.

The Royal Commission private sessions highlight the importance of this truth-telling approach to counter the silencing of the voices of marginalised and discriminated communities. Whether it be Indigenous populations, people of colour or minority communities more broadly, these are voices research needs to seek out to ensure policy and practice is informed by lived experience evidence and is meaningful to those it seeks to benefit.

Colonisation and the Beginning of Institutional Sexual Abuse for Aboriginal Children

Institutional child sexual abuse in Australia dates back to the invasion and colonisation of Australia. The British invaded in 1788 and declared Australia part of the British colony. The land was stolen through the lie of terra *nullius*, meaning empty land, denying the sovereignty of Aboriginal peoples (Blackstock et al. 2020). This invasion marked the beginning of the violence, dispossession, genocide, colonisation and attempted eradication of Aboriginal people. The Frontier Wars, the massacres, wars and resistance, began in 1788 and continued until the 1930s.[1] Sexual abuse of Aboriginal women and children was a part of these wars (Libesman and McGlade 2019). The first church missions were established in the 1820s. From the 1850s onwards, Aboriginal people were forcibly removed from their lands and placed on reserves and stations, where government 'protectors' controlled all aspects of Aboriginal peoples' lives (Human Rights and Equal Opportunity Commission 1997). The Stolen Generations period began from the mid-1800s. Between 1910 and the 1970s, between one in ten and one in three Aboriginal children were forcibly removed from their families (HREOC 1997). Initially, the Stolen Generations occurred under 'protectionism' policy and was based on the assumption Aboriginal people were a dying race (HREOC 1997). Later, forced removal happened under assimilation policy, with its stated intent being assimilation into white society (HREOC 1997). Assimilation became formal government policy in the 1930s but was already influential well before then. Both policies reflected the ideology of white superiority.

In Australia, both historical and contemporary child welfare legislation is the domain of the colonies, later states and territories. In 1869, Victoria became the first colony to pass laws authorising Aboriginal children's removal from their parents, with the passing of the *Aborigines Protection Act 1869* (Parliament of Victoria 1869). The Act legislated that government regulated the lives of Aboriginal people, including the power to make arrangements 'for the care custody and education of the children of aborigines' (Parliament of Victoria 1869: 2). This Act established the Board for the Protection of Aborigines, and imbued the board with the power to order the removal of any Aboriginal child from their family (Broome 2005). The legislation was amended with the introduction of the *Aborigines Protection Act 1886*, which changed the definition of Aboriginal to exclude those who were 'half-caste' (the offensive term used when one parent was Aboriginal). This commenced the policy of forcibly removing 'half-caste' Aboriginal people from missions and reserves and continued the removal of Aboriginal children from their families (Broome 2005; HREOC 1997).

The racist legislation no longer exists. By 1969, all states had repealed Aboriginal child removal legislation. Policy, including the Aboriginal Child Placement Principle, has been introduced to prioritise keeping children with families as the first priority and when removal is deemed necessary, that placement with Aboriginal family or carers is prioritised (SNAICC—National Voice for our Children 2016). However, contemporary child welfare practice has not abated Aboriginal children being removed from their parents. The over-representation of Aboriginal children in out-of-home care occurs throughout Australia and is most pronounced in Victoria (Australian Institute of Health and Welfare 2022). Current figures reveal Aboriginal children in Victoria are 22 times more likely to be in out-of-home care than non-Aboriginal children. Other Australian jurisdictions range from Aboriginal children being 5–19 times more likely to be in out-of-home care, while the national figure is Aboriginal children are 12 times more likely to be in out-of-home care (AIHW 2022).

Importance of Aboriginal Survivor Voices and Expertise in Understanding Trauma and Healing

The Stolen Generations occurred because of the racist beliefs upon which the relevant policies and legislation were created and enacted. The continued legacy of the Stolen Generations is ongoing trauma impacting Aboriginal peoples (Atkinson 2002, 2019), continuing systemic racism and discrimination and current systems continuing to perpetuate harms on Aboriginal children, families and communities (Anderson et al. 2017). In recognition of this history and the continuing contemporary failures, a national inquiry into the removal of Aboriginal children was conducted from 1995 to 1997. For the first time mainstream Australia learnt of the horror of the Stolen Generations; the extent of forced removal of children, the genocide and the ongoing trauma (HREOC 1997). The process of truth-telling is ongoing and in many instances is in its infancy.

Hearing the voices of Aboriginal survivors is critical if the ramifications of previous racist policies are to be eradicated. Their lived experience provides insight into the actions that are required at policy and practice levels. The silencing and ignoring of Aboriginal expertise including lived experience expertise is part of an ongoing failure to listen to Aboriginal communities, particularly women and children (Libesman and McGlade 2019). This silencing can be understood from an intersectional approach. Bamblett and colleagues reflect: 'The system includes different actors with varying degrees of power as well as resources. In this matrix the Indigenous community have the least control, power and resourcing' (Bamblett et al. 2018: 97). White, Western perspectives determine mental health practice and policy development. This is detrimental to Aboriginal people and other marginalised communities (State of Victoria 2021). Aboriginal knowledge and world views are also too often absent in research, with Western research models excluding Aboriginal voice and knowledge (Ryder et al. 2020). Without an intersectional focus, the distinct experiences and healing needs of Aboriginal survivors of institutional child sexual abuse can be overlooked.

Aboriginal survivors of institutional child sexual abuse in Australia represent the multiple traumas of complex childhood trauma in the context of cultural abuse and collective trauma. The extent of harm and wide-ranging impact of cultural abuse is highlighted in the following statement, developed by Stolen Generations survivors who were sexually abused in out-of-home care and were supported by an Aboriginal support service to explain cultural abuse in this context:

> The loss of cultural identity and sense of belonging in one's community; the loss of connection to family and kin; the loss of connection to spirituality and land; the denial of one's sovereign rights; the loss of connection to one's Elders and all of the knowledge and cultural systems of learning that are passed on through them; and the loss of parenting skills, cultural beliefs and values that could have been passed on to survivors' descendants if not for the cultural abuse.
> (Victorian Aboriginal Child Care Agency 2018: 9)

Collective trauma involves the shared and ongoing wounding across generations derived from mass group trauma experiences (Atkinson 2002; Menzies; 2019; Royal Commission into Institutional Responses to Child Sexual Abuse 2017). As Aboriginal researcher Emeritus Professor

Atkinson explains: 'it needs to be understood that, for Aboriginal peoples, trauma is both individual and collective wounding at multiple levels' (Atkinson 2019: 137).

About the Australian Royal Commission into Institutional Responses to Child Sexual Abuse

Australia's Royal Commission into Institutional Responses to Child Sexual Abuse was conducted between 2012 and 2017. The Commission followed numerous state inquires and significant survivor advocacy over decades (Parliament of Victoria 2013). There were three aspects to the Royal Commission; public hearings, research and policy; and private sessions. The private sessions were a unique aspect to an Australian Royal Commission and represented a truth-telling exercise, hearing directly from survivors. Survivors told their story to one of the six Commissioners and Royal Commission support staff and were welcome to bring a support person with them. Fifteen per cent of survivors who shared their story in a private session were Aboriginal (Royal Commission into Institutional Responses to Child Sexual Abuse 2017). This is in the context of Aboriginal adults making up 3% of the Australian population (Australian Bureau of Statistics 2021). This representation would not have been achieved without the advocacy and culturally safe support from the Aboriginal community controlled sector (Black et al. 2019). Forty-one per cent of survivors who told their story were sexually abused in out-of-home care, making it by far the largest institution type represented (Royal Commission into Institutional Responses to Child Sexual Abuse 2017).

Method and Approach to Analysis

As part of the process of telling their story at a private session, survivors were asked if they agreed to their stories being made publicly available. Royal Commission staff developed narratives based on the survivors' stories, relying heavily on direct quotes from survivors. In 2017, at the conclusion of the Royal Commission, the narratives were made available on the Commission website,[2] with survivors' names changed to maintain confidentiality. The authors analysed these publicly available narratives, rather than seeking to re-interview survivors, as retelling their stories would risk increasing survivors' trauma (Black et al. 2019). This approach allows the rich data of the narratives to progress research without the risk of re-traumatisation of survivors and thus is a trauma-aware approach. This is particularly pertinent in Australia, where Aboriginal people have been an over-researched population (Bainbridge et al. 2015; Ryder et al. 2020). This research was often unethical and immoral, as highlighted by Bamblett et al. (2012) and Raeburn et al. (2021).

Using the inclusion criteria of narratives of Aboriginal survivors who experienced sexual abuse in out-of-home care (residential care, foster care and adoption) and within the state of Victoria, resulted in 51 narratives being included (see Table 11.1 for demographics of survivors). A phenomenological approach to thematic analysis (Braun and Clarke 2022; Creswell and Poth 2018; Sundler et al. 2019) of the narratives of survivors was undertaken. This approach also involved descriptive interpretation and placing the narratives in context, both historical and current. The foundation of this approach is respecting and honouring Aboriginal knowledge and lived experience of Aboriginal survivors in order to amplify the voices of Aboriginal survivors of institutional child sexual abuse. The rational for a phenomenological approach is to generate knowledge about Aboriginal survivors' experience and their views on action required by describing and understanding survivors' healing journeys. Having this understanding allows survivors' healing needs to be contextualised and amplified and to inform practice and policy.

The narratives were mined for themes of healing, hopes for self, and the survivors' insights for policy and practice. Four broad categories

Table 11.1 Demographics of Aboriginal survivors abused in OOHC in Victoria, Australia

Survivors (N = 51) %		
Female	(25)	49%
Male	(26)	51%
Abuse in OOHC		
Foster care & adoption	(12)	24%[a]
Residential care	(36)	71%[a]
Both	(3)	6%[a]
Decade abuse began		
1940s	(1)	2% — Stolen
1950s	(8)	16% — Generations
1960s	(17)	33% / period
1970s	(9)	18%
1980s	(9)	18%
1990s	(4)	8%
unknown	(3)	6%
OOHC management		
Government	(26)	51%
Non-government	(24)	47%
unknown	(1)	2%

[a]Equals more than 100% due to rounding up

were developed from the narratives; removal from parents, institutional child sexual abuse, range of institutional abuses and impacts. The coding of data was focused on categorising the different types of institutional abuses, impacts, hopes and healing accessed and healing needs. Quotes from survivors are included throughout the Discussion and Analysis section to illustrate common and shared experiences and to amplify the voices of survivors directly.

Discussion and Analysis

Narrative Categories

Removal from Parents

All 51 survivors were placed in out-of-home care between the 1940s and the 1990s. The majority of the survivors were part of the Stolen Generations (see Table 11.1). Being placed in out-of-home care represented not only removal from parents, siblings and other family, but also removal from culture. All survivors had either been adopted by white families, fostered with white families or placed in mainstream residential facilities. The age the children were removed ranged from at birth to early teenage years. A recurring theme was the deception involved in being removed from their parents and a lack of information and understanding of why they were being removed. A common experience shared was of being removed with siblings but not placed with siblings. Rosemarie, Gordo, Robina and Jarrod share their experiences of removal:

> Rosemarie was taken from her teenage Aboriginal mother as a newborn baby. 'She [Rosemarie's mother] didn't sign any papers and she was actually breastfeeding me. And she went up there one night to feed me and I was gone'.
> Gordo was two years old when he was removed from his parents, along with his brother. 'I got taken out of the pram... They just grabbed us... I remember a black car with balloons hanging out and they said we was going to a party. That was welfare in the car'.
> Robina was four years old when she and her siblings were taken. 'We didn't know what was going on. We were just shoved in the police car and off we went... I remember Nan's house getting smaller and smaller'.
> Jarrod, removed at aged 10, shared: 'I remember it [life pre-removal] fondly. I also remember not so fondly being taken from that', as he described it, of being 'kidnapped'.

Survivors' descriptions of their removal from parents highlight the extreme vulnerability of these children as they entered out-of-home care. They felt, and they were, completely isolated from family and culture.

This removal, this kidnapping, as Jarrod described it, represents the beginning of the institutional abuse and institutional trauma for the children. Descriptions from survivors highlight the racism embedded within the removal and placement in out-of-home care:

> *Jan:* My mum was white and Dad was black and they said "that man couldn't look after his kids".
> *Marjorie Denise:* 'We had a grandmother that just so much wanted us, but they [child welfare] just wouldn't give us to her, and she wanted to bring some of our culture ... I believe she died of a broken heart. That's the stories we get from our people'.

Institutional Child Sexual Abuse

The majority of survivors reported sexual abuse over a period of several years, by several perpetrators and for some at more than one out-of-home care setting, as well as in a school setting or youth detention. Being sexually abused on one occasion, by one perpetrator at a single institution was the exception. Perpetrators were most often male carers, but also included female carers either directly or complicit in the abuse. There were also narratives of children being sexually abused by young people with whom they were placed in out-of-home care. There were examples of non-penetrative abuse but most commonly the sexual abuse was penetrative. Several survivors shared that at the time of the abuse, they did not understand it as sexual abuse. Bec shared: 'I didn't know what it was. I didn't know it was rape... I'd never heard of rape in my life'.

Range of Institutional Abuses

Survivors' narratives reflected a childhood of abuse and trauma while in out-of-home care. The range of institutional abuses included neglect, emotional abuse, cultural abuse and racism, forced labour, physical punishment and physical abuse and witnessing other children being abused. The neglect included children's basic physical needs being denied and frequent emotional neglect. Anabel shared: 'For punishment then

11 Truth, Trauma and Healing: Stories of Aboriginal ... 351

I'd be starved. I wasn't getting fed meals'. Shauna Beth shared: 'I would rather have been living with a poor family that actually gave a shit about me and still be loved and belonged somewhere'. Much of the cultural abuse was related to carers' denigrating the child's family and denying and dismissing their culture. Table 11.2 provides examples of the sexual abuse, cultural abuse and racism being inextricably linked.

Physical abuse and torture were described in detail. Bridgit Ann shared that her carer would make her 'lie spread-eagle naked on the floor tied to the bed and she would stand over me with a belt'. Then the carer would put her 'on display outside the bedroom… I would put my hand over my breasts and vagina – she would smack my hands away and make me stand like a soldier'. Sometimes the carer would 'whip the dog into a frenzy so he would be attacking and biting me'. For some, the abuse was so severe as to cause lifelong damage, including not being able to have children. The trauma also included witnessing abuse, violence and suicide. Doug Warren, shared that his roommate 'hung himself in front of me. He was too heavy for me to lift down'.

Table 11.2 Connections between racism, cultural abuse and sexual abuse

Survivor	Quote
Gordo	'Get over there, you little black bastard… go and hide in the bush till these white people go' [said by Gordo's foster carer on the rare occasions welfare visited]
Hilda	'You're probably a whore like the rest of them' [stated by a male worker at the children's home following a medical examination that revealed Hilda had internal injuries and a sexually transmitted infection from the sexual abuse]
Anabel	'She [adoptive mother] wrote me a letter, said "You'll be a slut like the rest of the blacks… You'll just be in the gutter like the rest, you'll never move on"'
Meggie	'They [carers] blamed me [for multiple sexual assaults] because I was Aboriginal and I was "looking for it"'
Heidi	'They [foster family] didn't want anything to do with me because I was black'
Harvey Martin	'I'd cop it badder than other kids being the colour I are… They mentally abuse you by doing stuff like that… They try and take the black out of you to make you white'
Euan Frank	'I became a bit of a pet for older kids [who regularly sexually abused Euan Frank] because they always wanted to see the colour of my funk'

The trauma went beyond institutional child abuse and neglect. Also shared were examples of systems abuse and institutional betrayal. Annabel shared: 'No-one believed us. I mean who would've believed us, you know, being Aboriginal... And they [foster carers] were so well known in the society'. Phrases such as 'I was called a liar' and 'I was scared to tell' were common, as were 'I hardly seen the welfare' and 'no one come and visited me'. The abuse went beyond the out-of-home care setting and included child welfare, school and police, who did not believe, did not protect, did not listen, did not visit the children. Venessa tried to tell welfare workers about the abuse but 'nothing was done... I gave up on welfare because I felt like I was just talking to brick walls'. Ken Peter shared: 'You couldn't say anything to the cops because they used to take us Aboriginal children'. The systems abuse continued in adulthood and included frequent accounts of the distress of not being allowed to access their records and for those who tried to gain redress, receiving no compensation or grossly inadequate compensation. The systems abuse included the lack of leaving care support provided. Shauna Beth shared: 'It took years when I got dumped out of the home to actually try to even find a space in this world to belong'.

Impacts of Multiple Abuse

The impacts of the multiple abuse and traumas were evident in all aspects of life. These included education disruption, homelessness, reliance on alcohol and drugs, exposure to further abuse, trauma and violence in adulthood, prison sentences, strained relationships, abusive relationships, disconnection from family, struggling with parenting and mental health challenges. Survivors spoke of the pathway of childhood sexual abuse leading to drug and alcohol abuse, leading to contact with the criminal justice system. Hilda's story highlights the far-ranging impacts of the institutional abuse:

> Hilda's teenage mother was raped by a white man. Because Hilda was the only one of her siblings who was light-skinned she was the only one removed as part of the Stolen Generations. This happened when she was

five, the day before she was to start school. Up until then she remembered a happy family life. She was sent to a boarding house and into forced labour: 'I used to have to chop the wood, make the bread and dig the vegetables. I didn't get to go to school'. Then the emotional abuse began: 'your mother didn't want you'. Then the sexual abuse, by multiple perpetrators. In her 40s her mother found her and asked for forgiveness. Hilda rejected her mother, still believing the lies she was told in out-of-home care. By the time Hilda learnt the truth (of her forced removal) her mother had died. 'It's too late to say I know it's not her fault. She was left powerless. She wasn't an alcoholic, she wasn't a drug addict - she was black'.

Survivors shared a range of mental health impacts, including: anger, shame, guilt, lack of trust, isolating self, sexual identity confusion, depression, anxiety, fears, phobias, flashbacks, intrusive memories, sleep difficulties, suicidal ideation, suicide attempts and mental health diagnoses. Prior research has also demonstrated the negative mental health impacts of out-of-home care for Aboriginal children (HREOC 1997; Jackson et al. 2013; Mendes et al. 2020) and for Aboriginal children who have suffered institutional child sexual abuse (Royal Commission into Institutional Responses to Child Sexual Abuse 2017). Almost all survivors experienced alcohol or drug issues in adulthood, and for some this started while in out-of-home care. Survivors explicitly explained their use of drugs and/or alcohol as a way of coping with mental health symptoms of childhood abuse and trauma and of this being an attempt at psychological pain relief. Lauren shared: 'I was drinking and smoking back then [as an adolescent living between the streets and out-of-home care] just to like, to block out all the bad things that had happened. And then – I think I was 17 – I started using heroin because the alcohol wasn't helping and that blocked it out. But then once I'd come down the memories would come back so it was like an on-going process'. The insights shared of mental health challenges and reliance on alcohol and other drugs to self-medicate highlight the lack of accessibility of appropriate mental health services for Aboriginal clients.

Relationship difficulties with children, partners and parents were common among survivors. There were also stories shared of relationship absences, of not having children or partners due to the fear of intimacy and inability to trust others. Intergenerational impacts were prevalent demonstrating the transmission of intergenerational trauma (Dudgeon 2020; Gee et al. 2014; Krakouer et al. 2018). Survivors' narratives evidenced intergenerational trauma, with many survivors sharing that their own children had been removed from them and placed in out-of-home care, with examples of these children also being sexually abused in out-of-home care. For some, their grandchildren were also in out-of-home care. Some survivors spoke of their own parents being in out-of-home care. Sabrina May shared: 'My children are now put in the system. So it's ... my mother, myself and now my kids are in the [out-of-home care] system'. The negative impacts on cultural connection, identity and belonging were shared and included survivors sharing that they did not discover they were Aboriginal until adulthood (see Table 11.3).

Access to Healing

The narratives revealed an absence of therapeutic support being provided during childhood. Exceptions were five survivors who spoke of having access to counselling in childhood. These survivors were in out-of-home care in relatively more recent decades; one in the 1990s, two in the 1980s and two in the 1970s. Of these five survivors, only Frances was able to speak of the abuse during counselling. Frances shared that while in out-of-home care, she was taught how to speak about the abuse and went to groups where children from other children's homes were encouraged to talk about their sexual abuse. Frances believes that it is because she addressed the sexual abuse when she was young, by talking about it to others, that she does not need counselling now, as an adult. For the other four, they never disclosed the sexual abuse:

> Michael John saw several youth workers but never disclosed because 'it was personal and a shame job'. Caleb was concerned about saying too much: 'I used to tell him [youth worker] a little bit, but not the extent of it. I was always worried because I had nowhere else to go... I was always worried that obviously it [sexual abuse] would get worse and I'd get hurt more'.

Table 11.3 Cultural impacts of abuses

Survivor	Quote
Evelyn Grace	'From 23 to 30, 35, I think were my pretty vicious years. I call them vicious years because I was not only turning Aboriginal but my parents were old. I was starting to lose them'. [Evelyn Grace did not learn that she was Aboriginal until leaving out-of-home care.]
Hilda	'I never got to learn the stories of my culture. I never got to learn about my people. I didn't get any of that... I can remember slashing my arms and peeling bits off my skin because I thought I was black underneath. They took everything from me, that welfare'
Robina	'They'd look at me funny or someone would comment, "Wow, who's the little white girl?"... It wasn't my fault that I was taken away. It wasn't my fault that I speak the way I speak'
Harvey Martin	'When I got out... I didn't know any blackfellas, I didn't even know my own sister... Because you never lived there it's like you're not part of their family thing... Us people who have been taken and try and get back, then getting door shut in your face by your own mob'
Digby Williams	'Yes, I can speak some of my language, but not fluent. I speak in English, it's an embarrassment – I'll say this to the young ones – that I can't speak my language... I didn't know who I was, where I was, who I belonged to, and to this day now I still don't know who I am properly'
Ken Peter	'They took my culture off of me... I reckon I'm still shutdown with me brothers'

Bec and Dallas also spoke of not being able to disclose abuse yet still reflected on clinicians that 'stuck by' as Bec described. Dallas shared: 'Even though I was getting moved he [youth worker at an Aboriginal Community Controlled Organisation] made sure I was still seeing him [for over seven years as Dallas moved between foster carers, group homes and homelessness].' Dallas was grateful for the commitment but acknowledged 'I wouldn't talk, I wouldn't say nothing. I didn't know how.'

The powerlessness of children to disclose abuse in therapy was evident. This was due to the common experience of misplaced shame of child sexual abuse survivors. Shame is a particular issue in Aboriginal communities where the shame of experiencing child sexual abuse, reinforced by the silencing and secrecy strategies of perpetrators, can be intertwined with the shame of being Aboriginal, created through racism, cultural abuse and the process of colonisation (Anderson et al. 2017; Child Wise and the Victorian Aboriginal Child Care Agency 2015). A related theme is the limitations of therapy prior to safety being established (Frederico et al. 2019). An additional theme was the value of continuity in the therapeutic relationship, in disrupted childhoods, which was the reality for these children.

In adulthood, many survivors had no access to psychological support. For some counselling only occurred while they were in prison; a positive experience for some, and not for others. Kane shared that he was having ongoing counselling in prison, which he found beneficial, but there was no support when he was to be released. Caleb had accessed counselling in prison but felt as if he is 'just another number in here... They don't really seem very helpful'. For Michael John, he was upset that access to prison mental health support was limited to people with serious mental illness: 'I want my time to serve me... so I'm screaming at these people now that I want to do programs. I want to become a better person. I don't want to be the same person 'cause when I get out I'm going to be angrier and then it escalates to the next level'.

Survivors discussed barriers to accessing and benefiting from psychological support. Experiences shared by survivors in childhood were shared by others in adulthood; of going to counselling but not disclosing the sexual abuse. As Anabel shared: 'To a lot of us, particularly Indigenous, it can be shameful to be talking about'. Robina shared that she never discussed her childhood abuse as she was scared she may not be able to cope with revisiting her traumatic past. Ann Meredith believes there needs to be lifetime counselling offered to survivors of childhood sexual abuse, reflecting that healing is a journey and survivors may need access to therapy at different life stages (Black et al. 2019). Having to re-tell their story and re-engage was experienced as a barrier. Doug Warren shared: 'Those counsellors aren't there forever. They're only there for three or four months... then you've got to repeat and tell your story again... It re-traumatises'. Survivors spoke of current services being fractured and insufficient: 'When one door opens, another door shuts, another one opens, another one shuts. It's a constant thing. And then one day, you get trapped in the middle. Both doors are shut and you're trapped. The next thing is, you go back into old habits'. Some survivors spoke about healing in the context of it being something they could never attain. Hilda and Gordo shared, respectively, 'I'll die with that hurt' and 'I'll never heal'. Both were not believed when they disclosed the abuses and did not receive any access to healing when they were children.

Survivors shared helpful elements to accessing psychological support. Anabel shared: 'It helps to just talk about things and not bottle it up. Because if I bottle it up I'll get stressed and then I'll have a panic attack and I'll end up back in hospital'. Giles David shared that counselling had helped with his lack of confidence, for Ryan. it helped with his anger. Motivation for accessing psychological support was shared by survivors. The motivation for Amelia was experiencing crippling flashbacks in adulthood. For Bridget Ann, it was becoming a mother and experiencing positive feelings and affection for the first time and being confused: 'I couldn't understand the feelings that I was getting, because I had no positive feelings in the past… I hadn't received any love, hugs or whatever'. Of those who had not accessed psychological care, some spoke of wanting to access support in the future.

Linking Survivors Hopes with Policy and Practice Recommendations for Healing

The legacy of the Stolen Generations looms large and the impact of systemic racism and discrimination is evident in the growing overrepresentation of Aboriginal children in out-of-home care, abuse in care and the lack of accessible and culturally safe healing. For the first time, and in response to recommendations from the Royal Commission into Institutional Responses to Child Sexual Abuse, data has been made public about the abuse of children in out-of-home care. In 2020–2021, almost half of the children abused in out-of-home care were Aboriginal (AIHW 2021). Several recent inquiries provide evidence of the damage of out-of-home care for Aboriginal children (Victorian Commission for Children and Young People 2019, 2020). Learning from the lived experience expertise shared in the survivor narratives can assist in designing and developing trauma-informed and culturally safe healing models that target the entirety of social and emotional well-being (SEWB). An Aboriginal perspective of SEWB is a much broader concept than the Western conceptualisation of mental health. Dr. Graham Gee, Aboriginal clinical psychologist and researcher, has led the development of a much utilised and highly regarded model of Aboriginal SEWB. Importantly, the model has also been refined and endorsed by community involvement (Gee et al. 2014). Table 11.4 presents the seven interconnected elements of the model, including a conceptualisation of connection to culture.

The hopes and aspirations of survivors can be categorised into the different domains of Gee's model of Aboriginal SEWB, as illustrated in Table 11.5. Survivors' hopes for themselves were overwhelmingly

Table 11.4 An Aboriginal model of Social and Emotional Well-being (SEWB)[a]

Element of SEWB
Connection to Body, Mind and Emotions Connection to body is about physical health Connection to mind and emotions refers to experiences of mental well-being, safety and security, a sense of belonging, control or mastery, self-esteem, meaning-making, values and motivation and the need for secure relationships **Connection to Family, Kinship and Community** Connection to family and kinship systems maintains interconnectedness through relationships of caring, sharing, obligation and reciprocity Connection to Community refers to a collective space where building a sense of identity and participating in family and kinship networks occurs, and where personal connections and sociocultural norms are maintained **Connection to Spirituality, Country and Culture** Connection to Spirituality includes traditional systems of knowledge left by the ancestral beings that typically include all the stories, rituals, ceremonies and cultural practices that connect person, land and place Connection to Land or Country—an area to which people have a traditional or spiritual association, and the sense of connection as a deep experience, belief or feeling of belonging to Country Connection to Culture—capacity and opportunity to sustain and (re)create a healthy, strong relationship to Aboriginal heritage. This includes systems of knowledge, law and practices; a secure sense of cultural identity and cultural values, and to participate in cultural practices that allow Aboriginal people to exercise their cultural rights and responsibilities

[a]Gee et al. (2014)

about family and kinship relationships. Many talked of aspirations they had for their children which included that their children should not experience the abuse and disconnection from culture that they experienced. Survivors wanted to connect to their culture both for themselves and their children. Many spoke of the importance of being able to contribute to community. Utilising Gee's model of Aboriginal SEWB helps design healing responses that are holistic and meaningful for Aboriginal survivors. It also helps to understand why it may be that mainstream therapeutic approaches are incomplete and inappropriate; they do not address the entirety of Aboriginal SEWB. Black and colleagues (2019) identified that not feeling culturally safe is an additional reason why Aboriginal survivors do not benefit from mainstream therapy. Cultural safety is more than the absence of racism and discrimination and more than cultural awareness, cultural sensitivity (Commonwealth of Australia 2021) and cultural competency. It includes the positive recognition and celebration of culture, it empowers, it ensures cultural respect, it enables feelings of safety (Commonwealth of Australia 2021) and thus leads to the experience of culturally safe care. If Aboriginal survivors cannot access culturally safe services, they are being disadvantaged and harmed (Black et al. 2019) and this represents profound social injustice.

Aboriginal-Specific Healing Approaches

Cultural connection contributes to positive social and emotional well-being for Aboriginal children, families and communities (Bourke et al. 2018; Dudgeon et al. 2021). This is understood when conceptualising social and emotional well-being from an Aboriginal perspective (see Table 11.4) where connection to community, spirituality, Country and culture is central (Gee et al. 2014). Survivors shared the value of cultural connection and cultural strengthening, specifically connecting or reconnecting with family, community and Elders and giving back to community. Survivors shared that they were provided with practical assistance, (such as food vouchers and cleaning), as well as mental health and other

Table 11.5 Survivors' hopes for self, categorised using Gee's model of Aboriginal SEWB

Survivor	Quote
Connection to Body, Mind and Emotions	
Evelyn Grace	'get to the bottom of all this crap… I wanna give up the grog if I can'
Ann Meredith	'You don't want to live in the past… You've got to move on, somehow, you've got to find a way… You've got to have that spirit otherwise you just fall into a heap'
Marjorie Denise	'sort of go and get hypnotised and forget … clean my whole mind out'
Connection to Family, Kinship and Community	
Venessa	'I just want my babies home with me. I want to protect them, you know. I don't want them going through what I had to go through, 'cause I had a fucked up life'
Meggie	'It's [childhood trauma] a pain in my heart that I carry all the time. I can only hope that sharing my story will stop this from happening to my grandchildren and future generations'
Sabrina May	'[To be] the person that breaks this cycle [of three generations of her family in out-of-home care]. I would love to be'
Robina	'I've protected all of my children from people like that. I saw that was my goal in life, to protect my children. Children should be safe, no matter where they are. Children are so vulnerable. And precious'
Harvey Martin	'That's one thing I wanted to do for my children… Show 'em the things what I didn't have, and just show them that you got a family, always stay together and be strong and respect each other, and don't abuse people… We [Harvey Martin and his wife] didn't want our kids to go through what we went through in our lives'
Connection to Spirituality, Country and Culture	
Venessa	'I want my kids to be proud of who they are and know who their clan is'

medical support, through Aboriginal Community Controlled Organisations (ACCO), demonstrating the benefit of the holistic approach of ACCOs. Sabrina May shared: 'I went and got myself into therapist counselling through [an Aboriginal organisation]. I undertake anger management courses, loss and grief courses, and drug and alcohol courses… I've worked like fucking hell to get these little babies back [her children were removed by Child Protection]'.

Aboriginal culture has a collective outlook where both rights and responsibilities are critical (Gee et al. 2014). Multiple survivors shared that contributing to community is part of their healing. Survivors related that they had embraced their Aboriginal culture in adulthood and were proud of now being well regarded in community. Lewis Paul shared that he now works with Aboriginal young people as a mentor: 'we try to give them healing from the inside'. Gordo shared that he has been able to help others by sharing his story: 'When we go on healing camps with Link Up [Aboriginal support service for Stolen Generations], I'm the first one up to tell my story because I can see them [other survivors] hurting so much... I'll get up straight away because I know it was never, ever my fault'.

Role of art in Healing for Aboriginal Survivors

Engaging in art and creative pursuits, including visual art and the performing arts, were described as assisting in survivors' healing journeys. Survivors described art as a way to connect to culture, including connection to ancestors. Survivors spoke of not being able to put their feelings into words, but being able to express their feelings in art and of gaining strength from the practice of art. Some survivors shared that engaging in the arts had changed their life for the better and helped them to cope.

Importance of Relationships in Healing

Some survivors acknowledged their own strengths and these included their resilience, their spirit, their sense of humour and strength of relationships. A significant theme was of the power of relationships both in providing motivation and support in survivors' healing journeys. The healing power of relationships was discussed in many contexts; support provided by partners. wanting to be a better version of themselves for their children and grandchildren, and reconnecting with parents, family, community and Elders. Importantly, relationships were also mentioned in enabling connection to culture. This reflects that connection to culture is predicated on relationships (Gee 2014; Dudgeon et al. 2021; Krakouer et al. 2018). Connection to culture cannot happen in isolation, cannot be learnt from a book or Google, rather connecting to culture is all about immersion in relationships.

Effective Healing Elements

Survivors' stories need to be placed in the context of social justice and intersectionality. Social justice has been described as the objective of intersectionality (Levac et al. 2018). Addressing intersectionality in research aims to redress inequality by identifying inequalities associated with the intersection of people's multiple oppressions and privileges, and analysing what this means for individuals, the collective and for systems and structures (Levac et al. 2018; Manuel 2018). An intersectional approach considers the entirety of Aboriginal survivors' lived experience and recognises the complex intersection of structural and systemic forms of discrimination, inequality and disadvantage. An intersectional approach thus assists in amplifying the voices of this multiply marginalised group, and highlights the need for specifically designed therapeutic interventions to counter discrimination, support social and emotional well-being and advocate for system change.

Survivors' narratives highlighted practice and policy actions which are required to address Aboriginal survivors' healing needs. These include the need for healing services to address the entirety of the traumas and impacts experienced by Aboriginal survivors. Survivors' stories illustrate that complex childhood trauma, including but not limited to the institutional child sexual abuse, occurs in the context of collective trauma and cultural abuse (Table 11.2) and impacts on all aspects of survivors' lives, including cultural disconnection (Table 11.3). Across all areas analysed, racism was evident; from children's removal from parents, examples of differential abuse experienced, the ongoing impacts experienced and survivors' healing needs.

Historic and current racism needs to be understood when designing responsive mental health models, programmes and service systems, as does the unique culturally specific needs of Aboriginal survivors.

Systemic racism and the culturally specific unmet needs of Aboriginal survivors explain why Aboriginal healing solutions cannot simply replicate a mainstream approach. Aboriginal-specific healing needs to differ from mainstream therapeutic interventions in important ways. These include cultural safety, addressing shame, the importance of cultural connection and the centrality of relationships. Services need to be accessible, holistic, relationally based and address all domains of Aboriginal SEWB (Gee et al. 2014). These policy and practice insights are relevant to services in prevention and early intervention, out-of-home care, leaving care and child and adult mental health systems. It is likely that these policy and practice measures can benefit beyond Aboriginal survivors to include other Indigenous populations, people of colour or minority communities more broadly. Healing approaches designed and developed specifically for the survivor group, with the survivor group, incorporating art in healing and privileging the importance of relationships in therapeutic support are touchstones that can benefit many minority communities.

Intersectionality provides a framework to understand how systems and structures can undermine Aboriginal survivors' access to equitable therapeutic services. The cumulative disadvantages underpinning survivors' lived experience demonstrate the intersectional complexity. An intersectional focus also allows a space for Indigenous ways of knowing to be incorporated (Levac et al. 2018). Understanding the impact of ongoing processes of colonisation, the power of cultural connection and equally the devastation of cultural disconnection helps understand Aboriginal survivors' experience. Recommendations reflect elements of intersectionality including the importance of addressing all aspects of healing from the entirety of abuse and traumas.

Conclusion

The multiple, intersecting traumas experienced by the survivors whose stories have been analysed in this chapter, highlight the wide-ranging, traumatic, lifelong and intergenerational impacts. Today, the harm continues. The escalating over-representation of Aboriginal children in out-of-home care is one of the most shameful impacts of past and present racism and discrimination and is a key reason why truth-telling and recognition of history and ongoing colonisation must be a part of system reform. Providing meaningful healing is an issue of social justice. There needs to be Aboriginal informed and led healing responses for Aboriginal survivors, now adults, such as those who shared their stories at the Royal Commission. Survivors' stories showed the damage and devastation of disconnection from culture. Also shared was that healing came from being able to reconnect with culture, and draw on their experiences to contribute to community. Children today, also need to receive contemporaneous healing, something survivors, in the majority, did not receive.

Having a voice to share their experiences and knowledge was denied to survivors as children in out-of-home care, where the power differential was vast due to the intersection of vulnerabilities. 'I had no voice', Bridget Ann shared in her Royal Commission private session. Many survivors expressed a similar sentiment. These survivors, as children, had no voice, were not listened too and were not believed. No longer can it be considered legitimate or valid to research the experiences of Aboriginal people and communities without being informed by their voices, knowledge, lived experience and Aboriginal expertise centring and leading the research. Aboriginal survivors' voices and expertise are essential in developing policies and designing services that are holistic, anti-racist and accessible at all stages of the journey towards healing. Survivors have shown bravery in coming forward to tell their story. We must also find courage to listen deeply, to learn and to respond. We must respect the expertise of lived experience, and act on it.

Summary Box: Implications of the Key Issues Discussed for Practice, Policy and Research

- The impacts of invasion, colonisation and systematic racism and discrimination need to inform models of healing for Aboriginal survivors.
- The breadth of traumatic experiences and impacts must be accommodated in treatment models.

- Individual, collective and intergenerational trauma are interrelated and all need to be addressed in healing for Aboriginal survivors.
- Connection to culture, engaging in art and relationships are described as important to healing and positive SEWB and can be successfully incorporated in healing models.
- Listening to and learning from lived experience experts informs healing models that are culturally informed and culturally safe. This is critical to developing a culturally responsive service system.

Notes

1. The University of Newcastle has an ongoing research project updating all massacre sites and the data is available at https://c21ch.newcastle.edu.au/colonialmassacres/map.php.
2. Source: https://www.childabuseroyalcommission.gov.au/private-sessions.

References

Anderson, P., Bamblett, M., Bessarab, D., Bromfield, L., Chan, S., Maddock, G., Menzies, K., O'Connell, M., Pearson, G., Walker, R., and Wright, M. (2017). *Aboriginal and Torres Strait Islander children and child sexual abuse in institutional settings. Report for the Royal Commission into Institutional Responses to Child Sexual Abuse*. Sydney: Commonwealth of Australia.

Atkinson, J. (2002). *Trauma trails, recreating song lines: The trigenerational effects of trauma in Indigenous Australia*. Spinifex Press.

Atkinson, J. (2019). Aboriginal Australia—Trauma stories can become healing stories if we work with therapeutic intent. In R. Benjamin, J. Haliburn, and S. King (Eds.), *Humanising mental health care in Australia: A guide to trauma-informed approaches* (pp. 133–142). Routledge.

Australian Bureau of Statistics (2021), Aboriginal and Torres Strait Islander people: Census, ABS Website, accessed 1 October 2022.

Australian Institute of Health and Welfare. (2022). *Child Protection Australia 2020–21*. https://www.aihw.gov.au/reports/child-protection/child-protection-australia-2020-21/contents/about

Australian Institute of Health and Welfare. (2021). *Safety of children in care 2020–21* (cat. no. CWS 86). https://www.aihw.gov.au/getmedia/c2c0f5b9-f376-40f3-b2da-c2a9fdf9cf01/Safety-of-children-in-care-2020-21.pdf.aspx?inline=true

Bainbridge, R., Tsey, K., McCalman, J., Kinchin, I., Saunders, V., Lui, F. W., Cadet-James, Y., Miller, A., and Lawson, K. (2015). No one's discussing the elephant in the room: Contemplating questions of research impact and benefit in Aboriginal and Torres Strait islander Australian health research. *BMC Public Health, 15*(1), 1–10.

Bamblett, M., Blackstock, C., Black, C., and Salamone, C. (2018). Culturally respectful leadership: Indigenous staff and clients. In M. Frederico, M. Long, and N. Cameron (Eds.), *Leadership in child and family practice*. Routledge.

Bamblett, M., Frederico, M., Harrison, J., Jackson, A., and Lewis, P. (2012). *'Not on size fits all': Understanding the social and emotional wellbeing of Aboriginal children*. Melbourne: La Trobe University.

Black, C., Frederico, M., and Bamblett, M. (2019). Healing through connection: An Aboriginal community designed, developed and delivered cultural healing program for Aboriginal survivors of institutional child sexual abuse. *British Journal of Social Work, 49*, 1059–1080.

Blackstock, C., Bamblett, M., and Black. C. (2020). Indigenous ontology, international law and the application of the Convention to the over-representation of Indigenous children in out of home care in Canada and Australia. *Child Abuse and Neglect, 110*, 1–11.

Bourke, S., Wright, A., Guthrie, J., Russell, L., Dunbar, T., and Lovett, R. (2018). Evidence review of Indigenous culture for health and wellbeing. *International Journal of Health, Wellness, and Society, 8*(4), 11–27.

Braun, V., and Clarke, V. (2022). *Thematic analysis: A practical guide*. Los Angeles: Sage.

Broome, R. (2005). *Aboriginal Victorians: A history since 1800*. Sydney: Allen & Unwin.

Child Wise and Victorian Aboriginal Child Care Agency. (2015). *Yarning up about sexual abuse*. Melbourne: Child Wise.

Commission for Children and Young People. (2019). *'In our own words': Systemic inquiry into the lived experience of children and young people in the Victorian out-of-home care system*, Melbourne: Commission for Children and Young People. https://ccyp.vic.gov.au/assets/Publications-inquiries/CCYP-In-Our-Own-Words.pdf

Commission for Children and Young People. (2020). *Keep caring: Systemic inquiry into services for young people transitioning from out-of-home care*, Melbourne: Commission for Children and Young People. https://ccyp.vic.gov.au/assets/Uploads/CCYP-Keep-caring.pdf

Commonwealth of Australia, Department of the Prime Minister and Cabinet. (2021). *Keeping our kids safe: Cultural safety and the national principles for child safe organisations*. Canberra: Commonwealth of Australia, Department of the Prime Minister and Cabinet. https://www.snaicc.org.au/wp-content/uploads/2021/06/SNAICC-VACCA-OCS-ChildSafeReport-LR-with-alt-tags-May2021.pdf

Creswell, J., and Poth, C. (2018). *Qualitative inquiry and research design: Choosing among five approaches* (4th ed.). Sage.

Dudgeon, P. (2020). Decolonising psychology: Self determination and social and emotional wellbeing. In B. Hokowhitu, A. Moreton-Robinson, L. Tuhiwai-Smith, C. Andersen, and S. Larkin (Eds.), *The Routledge handbook of critical indigenous studies* (pp. 100–113). Routledge.

Dudgeon, P., Blustein, S., Bray, A., Calma, T., McPhee, R., and Ring, I. (2021). *Connection between family, kinship and social and emotional wellbeing* (cat. no. IMH 4). Produced for the Indigenous Mental Health and Suicide Prevention Clearinghouse. Canberra, Australian Institute of Health and Welfare. https://www.indigenousmhspc.gov.au/getattachment/e129c621-58a4-4966-8730-dcf6e3a533a8/dudgeon-et-al-2021-family-kinship-20210802.pdf

Gee, G., Dudgeon, P., Schultz, C., Hart, A., and Kelly, K. (2014). Aboriginal and Torres Strait Islander social and emotional wellbeing. In P. Dudgeon, H. Milroy, and R. Walker, (Eds.), *Working together: Aboriginal and Torres Strait Islander mental health and wellbeing principles and practice* (2nd ed.). Canberra: Department of the Prime Minister and Cabinet.

Frederico, M., Jackson, A., Black, C., Pawsey, R., and Cox, A. (2019). Take Two—Implementing a therapeutic service for children who have experienced abuse and neglect: Beyond evidence-informed practice. *Child Abuse Review, 28*(3), 225–239.

Human Rights and Equal Opportunity Commission. (1997). *Bringing them home: National inquiry into the separation of Aboriginal and Torres Strait Islander children from their families*. Sydney: Commonwealth of

Australia. https://humanrights.gov.au/sites/default/files/content/pdf/social_justice/bringing_them_home_report.pdf

Jackson, A., Waters, S., Meehan, T., Hunter, S., and Corlett, L. (2013). *Making tracks: A trauma-informed framework for supporting Aboriginal young people leaving care*. Melbourne: Berry Street.

Krakouer, J., Wise, S., and Connolly, M. (2018). "We live and breath through culture", conceptualising cultural connection for Indigenous Australian children in out-of-home care. *Australian Social Work, 71*(3), 265–276.

Libesman, T., and McGlade, H. (2019). Aboriginal children's lives, sexual violence and the settler state. In. K. Gleeson and C. Lumby (Eds.), *The age of consent: Young people, sexual violence and agency* (pp. 11–30). UWA Publishing.

Levac, L., McMurty, L., Stienstra, D., Baikie, G., Hanson, C., and Mucina, D. (2018). *Learning across Indigenous and western knowledge systems and intersectionality*. Social Sciences and Humanities Research Council of Canada. https://www.criaw-icref.ca/wp-content/uploads/2021/04/Learning-Across-Indigenous-and-Western-KnowledgesFINAL.pdf

Manuel, T. (2018). How does one live the good life?: Assessing the state of intersectionality in public policy. In O. Hankivsky and J. S. Jordan-Zachery (Eds.), *The Palgrave handbook of intersectionality in public policy* (pp. 31–58). Palgrave. https://link.springer.com/content/pdf/10.1007%2F978-3-319-98473-5.pdf

Mendes, P., Standfield, R., Saunders, B., McCurdy, S., Walsh, J., Turnbull, L., and Armstrong, E. (2020). *Indigenous care leavers in Australia: A National scoping study*. Melbourne: Monash University.

Menzies, K. (2019). Understanding the Australian Aboriginal experience of collective, historical and intergenerational trauma, *International Social Work*, 1–13.

Parliament of Victoria. (1869). *Aborigines Protection Act 1869*. Melbourne: Parliament of Victoria.

Parliament of Victoria. (1886). *Aborigines Protection Act 188*. Melbourne: Parliament of Victoria.

Parliament of Victoria. (2013). *Betrayal of Trust: Inquiry into the handling of child abuse by religious and other non-government organisations*. Melbourne: Family and Community Development Committee.

Raeburn, T., Sale, K., Saunders, P., and Doyle, K. (2021). Aboriginal Australian mental health during the first 100 years of colonization, 1788–1888: A historical review of nineteenth-century documents. *History of Psychiatry*, 1–18.

Royal Commission into Institutional Responses to Child Sexual Abuse. (2017). *Royal Commission into Institutional Responses to Child Sexual Abuse Final Report*. Sydney: Commonwealth of Australia.

Ryder, C., Mackean, T., Coombs, J., Williams, H., Hunter, K., Andrew, J., Holland, A., and Ivers, R. Q. (2020) Indigenous research methodology—Weaving a research interface. *International Journal of Social Research Methodology, 23*(3), 255–267.

SNAICC—National Voice for our Children. (2016). *Understanding Aboriginal and Torres Strait Islander Child placement principle: A resource for legislation, policy, and program development*. Melbourne: SNAICC.

State of Victoria. (2021). Royal Commission into Victoria's Mental Health System, Final report: Summary and recommendations, Parliament Paper No. 202, Session 2018–21.

Sundler, A. J., Lindberg, E., Nilsson, C., and Palmér L. (2019). Qualitative thematic analysis based on descriptive phenomenology. *Nursing Open, 6,* 733–739.

Victorian Aboriginal Child Care Agency (VACCA). (2018). VACCA submission in response to Senate Inquiry Community Affairs Legislation Committee: National Redress Scheme for Institutional Child Sexual Abuse Bill 2018. Melbourne; VACCA. https://www.aph.gov.au/Parliamentary_Business/Committees/Senate/Community_Affairs/NationalRedressScheme/Submissions

12

The Blurred Line: Balancing the Treatment of Personality Disorders, Personal Trauma, and Cultural Trauma Among Individuals Who Have Sexually Offended

Michael P. Lasher

Introduction

Understanding what factors place an individual at greater risk to reoffend, adopting intervention strategies which consider this risk, and targeting intervention to factors which have been empirically identified as changeable and related to a greater likelihood to commit new offense are all elements of the Risk-Need-Responsivity model (RNR) (Andrews and Bonta 1991; Bonta and Andrews 2016). In recent years, RNR has been widely adopted as the prevailing theory guiding the assessment and treatment of individuals in the criminal justice system, and

---

Names and details in the three cases presented in this chapter have been altered to ensure the confidentiality of those discussed.

M. P. Lasher (✉)
Virginia Department of Behavioral Health and Disability Services, Richmond, VA, USA
e-mail: Lasher.Michael.P@gmail.com

© The Author(s), under exclusive license to Springer Nature Switzerland AG 2022
A. K. Gill and H. Begum (eds.), *Child Sexual Abuse in Black and Minoritised Communities*, https://doi.org/10.1007/978-3-031-06337-4_12

this model has also benefited the treatment of sexually abusive behavior problems (Hanson et al. 2009). In short, the RNR model advises the consideration of who is in need of higher or lower intensity intervention (risk), intervening on factors which are specifically relevant to reducing the likelihood of future criminal behavior (need), and tailoring interventions to maximize the benefit an individual receives from treatment (responsivity).

The role of trauma in light of the RNR context is complicated. Trauma is not considered a traditional criminogenic risk factor (compared to criminal history; cf. Andrews and Bonta 1991), which is a factor which is directly related to reducing or exacerbating an individual's likelihood to commit a new offense. On one hand, trauma, or more specifically post-traumatic reactions, has been indirectly connected to aggressive behavior through hypervigilance and increased reactive aggression (Barrett et al. 2011; Fritzon et al. 2021; Orth and Wieland 2006). On the other hand, more direct interventions in justice-involved situations have shown less efficacy when not addressing underlying trauma (Sadeh and McNiel 2015).

While it is tempting to consider trauma from a risk principle perspective, trauma can also be thought of as a responsivity factor. Addressing responsivity can maximize the benefits of interventions after an individual's treatment needs are accounted. Originally, accounting for responsivity focused largely on intellectual ability and scholastic achievements (Andrews and Bonta 1991); more recent studies of responsivity have included factors such as mental health and cultural context as part of this (Bogue et al. 2004; Mattson et al. 2012). Ultimately, addressing responsivity means interventions take into account an individual's barriers to learning and behavior change, and take necessary steps to account for these factors so that interventions can be successful.

Addressing trauma has gained considerable attention in the treatment of sexually abusive behavior (e.g., Fritzon et al. 2021; Levenson 2014; Levenson et al. 2016; Stinson et al. 2016). In recent years, the integration of trauma-informed care into the treatment of sexually abusive behavior problems has become more prevalent (Levenson et al. 2016; Wilson et al. 2020). At the same time, the way in which we define trauma continues to evolve. Psychology generally defines trauma as the response to an unexpected and frightening event that threatens one's safety and challenges one's coping skills (SAMHSA 2014). Less well-defined in the psychological literature, but more so in sociological literature, is also the idea of cultural trauma (Alexander 2004). Cultural trauma can take on many forms, related to climate change (Brulle and Norgaard 2019), major health crises such as COVID-19 (Demertzis and Eyerman 2020), and LGBTQ experiences (Hartal and Misgav 2021). In the context of sexual offending and criminal behavior overall, it is necessary to address the potential for cultural trauma when addressing race-related issues (DeGruy 2017; Rodi-Risberg 2018; Simko 2020). Recently, the relevance of cultural trauma has been theorized as a relevant application of trauma-informed cognitive-behavioral therapy for individuals of historically disadvantaged racial groups; however, most of the literature concerning this focuses on practice-based evidence rather than utilizing evidence-based practices (Metzger et al. 2021; Phipps and Thorne 2019).

Whether considering more typically established forms of trauma such as those in psychological literature or less typical traumatic reactions like cultural trauma, there is similarity with those manifestations to personality disorders. Is a person experiencing relationship disruption, impulsivity, and intermittent dissociative episodes because of their borderline personality traits or because of their experiences with childhood abuse? Is a person exhibiting aggressive and angry outbursts because of antisocial personality disorder or because of ongoing cultural and personal maltreatment? This type of question requires professionals to make assessments of the individuals in their care based on the etiology of the client's specific behavior.

Indeed, it is possible for one individual to have both post-traumatic reactions and dysfunctional personality traits; however, the challenge for professionals working with individuals who have sexually offended (ISOs) is that personality disorders (antisocial personality disorder in particular) have been used to explain many behaviors which defy social norms (Ahlmeyer et al. 2003; Sorrentino et al. 2018). In order to promote improved assessment of the role of trauma as a responsivity factor, this chapter will discuss some major presentations of trauma and the parallels with personality disorders. While this is not meant to be a definitive guide to broadly address the differentiation of these two issues, it can be considered a template for decision-making when professionals are confronted with such situations.

Personality Disorders

The 5th Diagnostic and Statistical Manual of Mental Disorders (DSM-5) defines a personality disorder as "an enduring pattern of inner experience and behavior that deviates markedly from the expectations of the individual's culture, is pervasive and inflexible, has an onset in adolescence or early adulthood, is stable over time, and leads to distress or impairment" (APA 2013a: 645). While the DSM-5 describes 11 primary personality disorders, the context of sexual offending behavior often focuses on the four Cluster B personality disorders: antisocial (ASPD), borderline (BPD), histrionic (HPD), and narcissistic (NPD). These personality types are typically marked by poor emotion regulation, dramatic or erratic behavior, and poor adherence to law or social norms. In studies examining incarcerated ISOs (Chen et al. 2016) civilly committed ISOs (Stinson et al. 2008), more than half met criteria for a Cluster B personality disorder. More than a third met the criteria for ASPD, and another quarter exhibited traits of antisocial personality (note: the presence of personality disorder traits, without meeting the full criteria for a specific personality disorder, may be used in the diagnosis of "other specified personality disorder").

Several treatment options exist for Cluster B personality disorders. Among individuals with ASPD, cognitive-behavioral treatments have shown benefits in reducing aggressive tendencies and contemporary psychodynamic approaches show promise (Meloy and Yakeley 2020). The "gold standard" for the treatment of BPD for several years is Dialectical Behavior therapy (DBT; Linehan 1993). DBT involves the integration of mindfulness, interpersonal effectiveness, emotion regulation, and distress tolerance skills while employing behavioral analysis of problem behaviors associated with personality disorders. The treatment of HPD and NPD are not well supported in the literature; however, there are mixed results documented for employing cognitive-behavioral measures and DBT specifically (Blagov et al. 2007; Caligor et al. 2015; Neacsiu and Tkachuck 2016). Including atypical antipsychotics, medications have also been shown to benefit the treatment of Cluster B personality disorders (Findling 2008; Linehan et al. 2008).

Personality traits are generally stable over time, particularly in adulthood. This presents a fundamental challenge to the treatment of a disordered personality, and given that there are interventions to manage the behavioral manifestations of personality disorders, it is difficult in a modern context to even define these disorders' stability (Morey and Hopwood 2013). However, the ease at which these personality disorders can be used to explain persistent rule-breaking behavior or interpersonal problems (e.g., APA 2013a) make a mindful consideration of how to attribute motivations for behavior crucial.

Trauma

Similar to personality disorders, trauma requires a mindful approach in conceptualization—one must carefully consider the history and stability of an individual's presentation to appropriately attribute behavior as a post-traumatic presentation. As noted above, psychological definition of trauma is the response to an unexpected and frightening event that threatens one's safety and challenges one's coping skills (SAMHSA 2014). Since the 1990s, the understanding of trauma, such as in the cases of childhood abuse and neglect and exposure to violence as an adult, has radically grown in the professional literature (Castellvi et al. 2017; Felitti et al. 1998; Levenson 2014; Stinson et al. 2016). Beginning with DSM-III in 1980, trauma was originally conceptualized as an "event that is generally outside the range of usual human experience" and that "would evoke significant symptoms of distress in most people," and as has been reframed in each edition of the DSM since then (APA 2013b; Weathers and Keane 2007). Factors distinguishing the current DSM-5 (2013) criteria of trauma include the recognition of the impact of recurrent trauma, the role of memory in the experience of trauma, and an acknowledgment that the response to an event need not elicit feelings of fear or anxiety during the event (APA 2013b).

The various editions of the DSM and its accompanying materials have concerned the specific diagnosis of PTSD, with traumatic experience(s) being one of the crucial criteria of this disorder. At the same time, some of the most notable research on trauma relevant to issues of sexual offending (e.g., Hall et al. 2018; Levenson et al. 2016, 2020; Puszkiewicz and Stinson 2019) involves the concept of adverse childhood experiences (ACEs; Felitti et al. 1998). The concept of ACEs originated from a study of nearly 10,000 adults by Kaiser Permanente, a health insurance organization in the United States. The elements which continue to be examined since that study include childhood exposure to emotional, physical, or sexual abuse, emotional or physical neglect, and various forms of domestic disruption (domestic violence, divorce, death of a parent, incarceration of a household member, or the presence of a substance-abuse or mental illness in the home). The presence of each ACE is cumulatively considered one's ACE score. ACE scores have been linked to long-term risks for physical diseases such as cancer, diabetes, and heart disease (Felitti et al. 1998), as well as various psychological conditions such as anxiety, depression, personality disorders, and suicidal ideation (Chapman et al. 2007; Dube et al. 2002; Felitti et al. 1998).

The original Kaiser Permanente study found that about half of respondents experienced at least one ACE. A quarter of the population reported only one ACE and an eighth reported two ACEs; only six percent reported four or more ACEs (Felitti et al. 1998). However, individuals involved in the criminal justice system or involved in forensic psychiatric care have shown a higher prevalence of ACEs. Two more contemporary studies have examined the rate of ACEs in both adult and adolescent males who have sexually offended (Hall et al. 2018; Levenson et al. 2016). To briefly contrast groups exclusively made up of those who have offended with the general public, offending groups skew toward increasing numbers of ACEs, whereas the general population skews toward fewer ACEs (Fig. 12.1).

Although the redefinition of PTSD in the DSM-5 occurred at the same time as much of the recent research on ACEs, the assessment of ACE frequency was not included in updates to the PTSD criteria and the experiential criterion of PTSD is inclusive of adult experiences. Each approach to conceptualizing trauma and its impact has strengths, and the

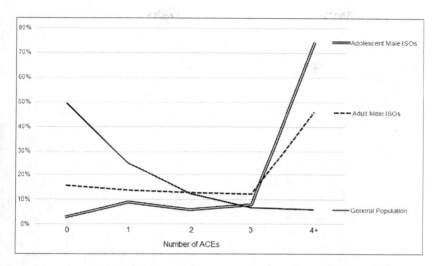

Fig. 12.1 Comparison of ACE rates between the general population, adult male individuals who have sexually offended, and adolescent male individuals who have sexually offended (*Note* General population sample: Felitti et al. [1998]; Adult male ISO sample: Levenson et al. [2016]; Adolescent male IS sample: Hall et al. [2018])

utility of each will depend on the context in which trauma is assessed and addressed. However, the research on ACEs provides a considerable insight to the relationship between trauma and sexual offending behavior. While it is difficult to attribute problem behaviors to causal factors, recently it has been suggested that sexual abuse and other sexually related adverse experiences are directly linked with the early onset of new sexually abusive behavior, and other ACEs related to household dysfunction were statistically linked to the likelihood of engaging in any contact sexual offending behaviors (Puszkiewicz and Stinson 2019).

Cultural Trauma

Until this point, we have discussed trauma from the typical psychological perspective, largely influenced by the criteria for trauma in the DSM-5: directly experiencing the traumatic event, witnessing the event as it occurred to others, learning that the traumatic event occurred to a close family member or friend, or experiencing repeated or extreme details of a traumatic event. This perspective is largely reflective of the bias toward trauma as an individually experienced phenomenon, and the use of this individualistic or experiential conceptualization of trauma has influenced our research on trauma, such as in the case of ACEs (e.g., Felitti et al. 1998; Levenson et al. 2016) to the criteria for PTSD (APA 2013a).

"When members of a collectivity feel they have been subjected to a horrendous event that leaves indelible marks upon their group consciousness, marking their memories forever and change their future identity in fundamental and irrevocable ways" (Alexander 2004). In recent years, the social and cultural discussions of trauma have considered how social disadvantage, historical oppression, and pervasive stigma have cumulative negative effects. There is no shortage of sociological sins in the story of America, often in the context of how people of European origin maintain their dominant sociocultural presence. This includes the treatment of the first peoples of North America, to the increasing restrictions on immigration in the late twentieth and early twenty-first centuries. In many ways, there are opportunities for cultural assimilation: when a minority group takes on the values, beliefs, or behaviors of the dominant group. In some cases, minority groups have succeeded in their assimilation into the dominant group so well that the distinction between the two are at most marginally noticeable in a contemporary context. For other groups, though, the line dividing them from the dominant group is virtually inerasable, either due to their physical attributes like the color of their skin or their seemingly irreparable history (Clark 2003; Ignatiev 2009; Waters and Jiménez 2005).

From an American perspective, one of the most salient sociocultural divisions is between people of African origin and those of European origin. This chapter is not meant to be a comprehensive review of African-American studies; the formal study of African-American culture has warranted the publication of libraries. Instead, we will briefly discuss here the psychological impact of the sociocultural experience of being of African descent in America for the context of its impact on case conceptualization in assessment and psychotherapy.

One readily accessible theory of cultural trauma in the African-American experience is Post Traumatic Slave Syndrome (PTSS) (DeGruy 2017). This phenomenon is described as "trans-generational adaptations associated with traumas, past and present, from slavery and ongoing oppression" (p. 8). While slavery was not unique to people of African origin, it has become primarily associated with the narrative of African-American experience as opposed to other sociocultural groups. In the PTSS perspective, the salience of this dual historical and contemporary context reinforces the experience of multigenerational trauma which began with the process of enslavement, continued with institutional discrimination following emancipation (such as in the case of Jim Crow laws), and sustains with sociocultural narratives today with imagery of subordination and objectification correlated with the origins of the cultural maltreatment.

The foundation of PTSS includes three primary components. First is the idea of vacant esteem. Here, esteem concerns the idea of how one values his or her worth as a member of a cultural group. The idea of having vacant esteem suggests that one's value is seen as empty, and in the context of cultural identity, one sees himself or herself as being inferior due to a combination family, community, and societal messages. Familial influence includes how one's primary messages about how to function and views of one's self are internalized as a function of learning; if parents (or parental figures) do not see their close social network as having values, then they risk teaching this to their children as an implicit message. One's community reinforces this issue of undervaluation, including under-representing positive role models in the media (Richardson-Stovall 2012), diverting fewer resources to schools where these children learn, and decreased opportunity to rise out of socioeconomic disadvantage (Saegert et al. 2011).

A second component of PTSS is "racist socialization." Similar to the issue of vacant esteem, there is the concern of how the identity or characteristics of the dominant sociocultural group—people of European origin—is internalized as of greater value than one's own group identity (e.g., people of African origin). This may include the idea that having physical attributes more closely associated with European features is more desirable. It may also manifest as seeing stereotypical or historically defined qualities of one's own sociocultural group as being inferior or less affluent when compared to the stereotypical attributes of the dominant group. For example, one might endorse the act of "code-switching," or adapting one's speech or presentation to better integrate into a variety of contexts. The act of code-switching has been proposed as a perceived requirement of socioeconomic mobility, from academic achievement to success in politics (Morton 2014). The process of socialization associated with these factors risks the presence of significant cognitive dissonance. It is not surprising that the third component of PTSS is that of "ever-present anger." In this context, anger is defined as "a response to the frustration of blocked goals and the fear of failure" (DeGruy 2017: 115). In the context of PTSS, this anger is not limited to a single situation, a single encounter, or a single family story. It is the cumulative anger resulting from intergeneration disadvantage, devaluation, institutional or societal marginalization, and within-group conflict regarding how the collective identity should be determined separate from or in step with the dominant sociocultural group. All of this is tied together by the power of belief: belief that one's opportunities are limited, belief that what they have learned about their subordinate role in society is appropriate, correct, or real, and even the people of European origin actually wish them harm.

To conclude this discussion of cultural trauma within the African-American community, let us consider the Black Lives Matter movement, and the counter-movement to Black Lives Matter is the idea of "All Lives Matter." As told within the context of some voices, the idea of "all lives" includes the subset of "black lives." However, this assumes that the movement focuses on the preservation of life, which has deep cultural and religious significance to the sacredness of all life. Instead, one should look at this through the context that one's identity as a person of African origin has value, that one's Afrocentric attributes are not inferior to European culture or genetics, and that individuals of African origin are as entitled to the same opportunity as the dominant sociocultural group (Carney 2016; Gallagher et al. 2018). In this sense, the Black Lives Matter movement serves as a call to overcome the cultural trauma endured by the African-American community.

Beyond the experience of African Americans, cultural trauma has been correlated with increased health disparities due to increased stress, stigma, and both material and social barriers to health resources (Phelan and Link 2015; Subica and Link 2022). It is an effect which has practical implications for the individual, but is both underrepresented in our understanding of the etiology of disruptive behavior as well as underemphasized in our interventions. While it may be easy to draw some direct lines from cultural trauma to overt protest, it has been repeatedly (if not loudly) theorized that cultural trauma plays a role in crime and delinquency either as a covert protest, a survival strategy, or maladaptive coping (Phipps and Thorne 2019; Tatum 2002). Indeed, maladaptive coping has been much attended to in the literature about intervening on sexually abusive behavior (e.g., Stinson et al. 2008, 2016). In this sense, accounting for one's trauma, cultural or otherwise, becomes a key component in understanding the etiology of sexually dysregulated behavior and developing interventions tailored to the individual's specific, intersecting needs.

Trauma-Informed Care

In response to the increased understanding of trauma in our society, the greater community of mental health service providers has begun to move toward integrating an improved awareness of trauma's impact on individuals, and the need to consider trauma both when intervening and be aware of its relevance when intervening. In this sense, addressing trauma becomes more than reducing symptoms, but it is also relevant in conceptualizing the way an individual has developed and responds to people and situations.

Taking this into consideration when providing mental health services reflects the contemporary concept of trauma-informed care (TIC). SAMHSA's (2014) approach to TIC considers four major pillars: a realization of the impact of trauma and paths for recovery, recognition of signs and symptoms of trauma, responding by integrating knowledge and understanding of trauma into both practice and policy, and reducing the chance of re-traumatization within the context of treatment and beyond treatment as much as is reasonably possible. TIC does not explicitly advocate for the categorization of trauma or the diagnosis of a specific disorder, instead it is taking into consideration those factors which a person has learned to avoid threats, consciously or not, in response to generalized historical experiences.

As TIC has become more widely embraced, there are now a variety of options to learn about applying this concept to treatment. Several experts in the field provide conference and other continuing education options, and for the treatment of ISOs specifically Levenson and colleagues (2020) have provided an entire book on the subject. TIC has been shown to benefit in general treatment (Hales et al. 2019), and shows promise for the treatment of ISOs (Janssen 2018).

The Intersection of Personality and Trauma, and the Relevance to Addressing Sexually Offending Behavior

Among individuals who have sexually offended, there are four domains to consider in the identification of trauma: one's history of child sexual abuse, one's history of child non-sexual abuse and neglect, one's cultural factors contributing maladaptive behavior, and one's experience with incarceration and the criminal justice system. The manner in which these trauma factors manifest can be highly specific depending on the individual, and the manifestation of these trauma factors can either run parallel to or intersect with maladaptive personality factors.

Consider the impact of child sexual abuse. While there is not a guaranteed pathway from a history of child sexual abuse to engaging in child sexual abuse, one's history of abuse does create a greater risk of perpetuating sexual abuse against more children, either related or unrelated. Sexual trauma may result in having distorted beliefs about healthy sexuality (Ricci and Clayton 2016); children may not have the ability to fully comprehend the sexual abuse perpetrated upon them because of their ongoing psychological development. This may include conflicting feelings related to their sexual abuse due to reacting against the abusive behavior and yet having a positive physiological response during the course of the abuse. Consider the case of Adam:

> Adam was convicted of sexually abusing multiple prepubescent and pubescent boys in the United States. His criminal history included a number of non-sexual juvenile offenses, such as shoplifting and underage drinking, as well as having issues with truancy and eventually dropping out of school. As an adult, he had difficulty maintaining employment, both because of his difficulty following direction from authority figures and because of a lack of opportunity for stable jobs due to his lack of a high school diploma. He considered himself charismatic and clever, though, and was able to make supportive friendships in the community fairly easily. This was generally accomplished by offering to do "odd jobs" for people in the community when between jobs. However, he was vulnerable to sexual attraction to children and becoming more familiar with the family both allowed him to gain the confidence of the family and build trust with the children. Adam's initial psychosexual evaluation focused on his history behavior problems as a child and parasitic tendencies as an adult as evidence of the presence of antisocial personality disorder, but due to the bias at the time of evaluation, the role of trauma was not significantly considered in the case conceptualization. While the core components of Adam's treatment program were generally effective in addressing the development of a basic risk management plan, he continued to express resistance to addressing offense-supportive attitudes. Through the process of participating in group therapy, his hold on these attitudes was reframed less as a reflection of antisocial traits and more a developmental consequence of his own abuse. This shift in perspective allowed for a different approach to Adam's treatment, and allowed him over time to more successfully work through his resistance.

In the case of Adam, the bias toward his history of manipulation failed to address the underlying etiological underpinning of his behavior. The targets in treatment assumed that his antisocial personality in of itself drove the behavior, and because of the immutable nature of personality disorders, the foci focused on how he could achieve his goals without risk of legal consequences. The conceptualization of his treatment failed to consider that his response to having been abused himself played a greater role that he was able to volitionally express. He was in treatment as an adult, but never was provided an opportunity to process the experience of his abuse outside of his concrete operational perspective. While Adam was still vulnerable to some of the emotional and social instability associated with having developed antisocial beliefs, addressing the sexual trauma of his childhood allowed him to tackle his sexual-related risk issues more effectively. In this sense, one could consider his history of trauma as intersecting with his personality disorder.

Trauma in treatment can manifest in other ways, though. For Adam, it manifested as a treatment target concerning how his trauma reinforced his maladaptive beliefs about child sexual abuse while simultaneously supporting maladaptive coping strategies. In the context of personality disorders, Adam's case might be as close as possible to the definition of a "rational actor" with the desire to relieve one's suffering. Many people experiencing personality disorders do not function as rational recipients of treatment (Samar et al. 2013). They may have different priorities or goals than the treatment provider, regardless of their explicitly expressed interest. The case of Ben is presented to consider this issue.

> Ben was returned to a secure custody in the United States following a violation of his community supervision. A previous psychological assessment diagnosed Ben with Antisocial Personality Disorder, along with other substance-related, paraphilic, and mood-related disorders. During this period of detainment, he began to disclose a history of physical and sexual trauma through his life which has previously not been a treatment priority; previous treatment focused on addressing relapse preventionprevention-related targets. He was referred to specialized trauma treatment when available, but this required a considerable delay due to a waiting list for this treatment and limitations on facility resources. During this wait period, Ben became increasingly argumentative about facility rules. Of particular note, Ben would regularly attempt to propose that due to his history of abuse, he should be granted a single room. Space was at a premium and he did not meet the criteria for special accommodations based on his reports of post-traumatic reactions alone. Ben began to report that he was having thoughts of preemptively assaulting his current roommate. His treatment providers discussed augmenting his treatment plan with prazosin to address his nightmares and he was offered less-specialized narrative therapy as an alternative to

waiting for more specialized trauma services. Although he reported benefits from prazosin therapy, he ceased all participation in psychotherapy and began to refocus himself on legal action against the facility. He continued to assert thoughts of harming his roommate and he was reclassified for single-room status due to safety concerns. He continued to refuse participating in therapy despite the consequences against his ongoing assessments of progress.

Ben's story involves a number of other dynamics that are not relevant to the present discussion. However, his psychological assessment highlighted his experiences with the criminal justice system, difficulty with consistent adherence to rules and supervisory expectations, pervasive patterns of impulsivity, and concerns about his attempts to manipulate others to achieve personal gains. His history of trauma did not significantly factor into the diagnostic conceptualization during his previous assessment. When he finally did begin to discuss his history of abuse, unsuccessful attempts were made by treatment providers to validate his reports of abuse and assault while detained at other facilities to ensure the veracity of his self-report (N.B.: such records are not considered definitive as many institutional assaults go unreported or underreported; Saum et al. 1995).

In institutional settings, space is often at a premium (Edgemon and Clay-Warner 2019; Rosenfeld and Kempf 1991). Facilities must develop policies about assigning residents to space balancing the demands of the population (including safety and security) and the needs of the individual (such as medical issues). While it has long been argued that there are many benefits to not placing residents in shared rooms (e.g., Adwell 1991), the populations of inmates and psychiatric inpatients in their respective facilities do not always allow for this opportunity. Having a single room can be reasonably seen as a measure of relief in an otherwise stressful environment, and when facilities make exceptions to undesirable policies, some ISOs may request exceptions based more on personal preference than clinical need (Mallinger 1991; Worley 2016). One of the hallmarks of Antisocial Personality Disorder is the propensity to manipulate others, and the lack of empathy for those effected by that manipulation.

The concern in Ben's case is at what point accommodations should be made based on one's self-report of trauma. Attempts were made to reasonably accommodate his needs through psychiatric and psychotherapeutic means. While he took advantage of some options (prazosin treatment), he elected to pursue his legal efforts instead of utilizing available resources to address his trauma symptoms. This raises the question of secondary gain. While some of his assigned treatment providers made an argument that his warnings of aggression and impulsivity were a manifestation of trauma reaction there were multiple factors leading the majority of clinical staff to interpret this as a manifestation of his personality disorder. First, as noted above, there is the issue of secondary gain: it was known within the facility that making threats against one's roommate increased the probability of being placed on temporary single-room status (although not without long-term consequences). Second: reasonable interventions were available, but despite efforts to work through his resistance, emphasizing motivational interviewing strategies, he continued to refuse available treatment. This was primarily viewed through the perspective of his self-report that it would draw him away from his efforts to pursue legal action, but it was also considered that he may have had the insight that improving his psychiatric status would draw away from the justification for a single room. Finally, the impact of his recently reported history of sexual and physical abuse was weighed against his life history of antisocial behavior. Considering the potential for reinforcing this behavior, as well as providing a blueprint for manipulating the facility to other residents, it was decided to focus on the management of his antisocial tendencies given the earlier mentioned considerations.

Ultimately, Ben was able to make progress addressing his trauma history. He benefited from a change in his primary treatment providers, although it was not definitively determined if this reflected an issue on Ben's behalf (such as transference toward a member of, or his entire treatment team), a better therapeutic relationship fostered by his new therapist, or some other factor. Whatever the reason, Ben was able to begin specialized trauma therapy session after being on a waiting list for this, and shortly thereafter began again participating in core sexually abusive behavior groups. This portion of his history with treatment describes a major contrast from the case of Adam in how individuals with both Cluster B personality disorders and trauma present. The line between these two needs is not clearly drawn. Both can manifest in abusive or aggressive tendencies. Addressing both can provide improvements in quality of life (Black et al. 2010; Morrill et al. 2008). However, the skilled clinician or assessor cannot consider these unilaterally. It is necessary to consider one's own biases when considering case conceptualization (Bottoms et al. 2015), and these include one's expectations regarding available information at the time of assessment (Falvey et al. 2005). At this time, there is no measure to discriminate between trauma and personality manifestations, but the key difference between Adam and Ben is that the advantage in expressing trauma for Adam was that it allowed him to move forward toward his prosocial objective, whereas for Ben it facilitated gaining an advantage that he was not otherwise entitled. If there was one question to begin the examination of this issue, then it could be, "Why is this manifesting (now)?".

These examples presume individuals have the ability to effectively express themselves. Unfortunately, it is not always so easy for individuals to express their history of trauma. This brings us to one final case to discuss the challenges in conceptualizing trauma reactions and personality disorders, with an emphasis on cultural trauma.

Charlie, a man of African origin in the United States, was under detention following his conviction for sexually abusing an adolescent female. His long history of criminal convictions influenced his receiving a considerably longer sentence than others with comparable offenses. His institutional record included a variety of rule infractions, including assaultive behavior and possessing or manufacturing intoxicants. The results of his ongoing rule-breaking behavior is that limited his opportunities to participate in specialized treatment programs and he delayed his opportunity to gain supervised community re-entry. Charlie was referred to a treatment program specifically designed to address ineffective decision-making and resistanceresistance to adhering to institutional and supervisory rules. When he began working with his therapist, it was noted that Charlie had adorned his property and clothing with the initials B.L.M. (Black Lives Matter). Charlie's intervention focused heavily on employing motivational interviewing strategies to identify pathways toward greater rule adherence of treatment amenability. To exemplify this, Charlie was asked to identify what was important to him and what personally relevant goals he had. To summarize the theme of his response, Charlie continually expressed concern for supporting and helping his family and community, and to teach the "younger generation" how to live their lives in a way that both empowers them and reduces the chances of making decisions that result in legal consequences. Charlie was never diagnosed with PTSD or other trauma-related disorders, but his presentation and statement of values encouraged his therapist to view Charlie's presentation through the lens of cultural traumacultural trauma. Charlie was encouraged to consider what was needed for other detainees to improve their chances of community re-entry, rather than focus on what was (perceived as) dictated from administration. It appeared that Charlie was developing more openness to how he could use his experience to benefit himself and his fellow detainees; however, he continued to be cited for rule-breaking behaviors which appeared to reinforce his antagonistic view of the facility. While he was not diagnosed with a trauma-related disorder, he was assigned the diagnosis of Antisocial Personality Disorder. Despite the apparent gains in appealing to his desire to improve the quality of his community's identity and support others in the facility, his behaviors reflected a primary interest in meeting one's own self-interests, whether that be in opposition to the facility or at the expense of other detainees.

The story of Charlie highlights the complicated nature of trauma. In contrast to the stories of Adam (whose trauma history appeared to have a direct impact on his offending history and his ability to successfully return to the community) and Ben (whose trauma did not appear to directly influence his offending behavior but prevented him from fully engaging in treatment), Charlie's story highlights how TIC can provide an avenue toward improved engagement in treatment and improving one's opportunity to demonstrating prosocial personality traits. In addition to their specific and unique trauma histories, each of the men here had behavioral histories which warranted assigning a personality disorder diagnosis as well. Each demonstrated a unique manner in which the manifestation of their trauma history intersected with their unhealthy personality traits. This suggests that case conceptualization goes beyond just diagnosis and theoretical orientation, but can also benefit from having a trauma-informed perspective.

Practical Suggestions for Case Conceptualization

Under the RNR model (Bonta and Andrews 2016), issues of personality disorders most often fall in the realm of needs. For example, when considering individuals with Antisocial Personality Disorder, a major treatment target could be addressing the offense-supportive attitudes and beliefs of the individual. Issues of trauma are not so clearly defined.

One's history of trauma could be related to treatment needs. This is illustrated above in the case of Adam, if in a somewhat simple manner. Adam's history of trauma directly influenced his offense-supportive attitudes, specifically when it came to his beliefs about sexual behavior with children. His history of trauma also blunted his ability to develop healthy coping strategies; another treatment target included building a healthy repertoire of coping strategies to reduce the likelihood of exhibiting with illicit behaviors. Trauma could also be conceptualized as a responsivity factor, though. While responsivity factors are often myopically limited to intellectual ability and learning disabilities, they can also include factors such as gender, age, ethnicity, and mental health concerns (Bogue et al. 2004). For Ben, his trauma history was a factor in treating his general mental health needs, but did not seem to meaningfully influence his history of sexual offending behavior. Not addressing his trauma did become a factor in his ability to benefit in therapeutic options which would target his specific offense-related treatment needs. In this case, unaddressed trauma was a therapy-interfering factor. Not accounting for Ben's trauma history interfered with his ability to self-regulate and, in turn, benefit from the interpersonal dynamics necessary in effective psychotherapy. In a metaphorical sense, Ben could not "hear" what his treatment provider was saying, much as a patient cannot interpret what a treatment provider is saying if the treatment provider is not communicating in a language that the patient understands or utilizing concepts beyond the patient's capacity for comprehension.

Ben's case shows how one's trauma being explicit and definitive is actually an advantage: he could verbalize the etiology of his trauma-related issues even if appropriate accommodations were debated. Charlie's situation demonstrates that while a trauma-informed perspective can provide different insights into responsivity factors, cultural trauma issues do not provide clear intervention targets. While in ideal psychotherapeutic episodes the trauma event is discreet, the impact of cultural trauma on Charlie is potentially ongoing as cultural disadvantages for individuals of minority sociocultural groups continue at this time. As described in the PTSS theory, anger plays a dominant role in a person's coping response. Consider the difference between destructive and constructive anger, though (Tangney et al. 1996). If left to manifest destructively, then it is strongly possible that this anger can result in a treatment-interfering or impeding factor. However, constructive anger can be thought of as a means to bring about change; in the case of Charlie, tapping into his socioculturally driven anger helped focus him on a pathway toward participating in risk-reducing therapy (Table 12.1).

Considering the potential for trauma's impact in the treatment of sexually abusive behavior among individuals with personality disorders, SAMHSA's (2014) key principles remain relevant. Considering the environment in which this treatment occurs, there are some additional considerations to contextualize TIC.

1. On an organizational level, develop (or amend) policies to allow for accommodating trauma-related issues where possible, but first employ policies consistently and with compassion. Policies should balance the implementation of TIC with the practical demands of an environment to promote personal growth and population safety.
2. When working with individuals who have experienced trauma but also manifest personality disorders, objectively consider the motivation for their behaviors. While there are a variety of different models to examine the etiology of behavior, an example of this is to consider the motivation for a behavior, the willingness to engage in a behavior (particularly in cases of rule-breaking or boundary violations), and how much effort is expended in creating the opportunity for the

Table 12.1 Six key principles for trauma-informed care

Key principle	Description
Safety	Ensure that both individuals being served and those providing services feel physically and psychologically safe
Trustworthiness and Transparency	Decisions should be made with transparency with the goal of building and maintaining trust
Peer Support	Peer support can provide a culture and environment of safety, hope, trust, collaboration, and recovery
Collaboration and Mutualit:	Understanding that both the treatment provider and recipient have a role to play in treatment success, and that all aspects of the treatment environment can contribute to therapeutic progress
Empowerment, Voice, and Choice	Organizations should strive to empower those who receive services, as well as support those who directly provide services
Cultural, Historical, and Gender Issues	Systems should be aware of, and responsive to racial, ethnic, cultural, and gender needs of those receiving services, including historical and cultural trauma

Note Adapted from SAMHSA (2014)

behavior. All of these factors can be examined objectively in the context of either personality disorders or trauma.

3. Consider the cultural context of the individual when developing one's conceptualization of their behavior. In this sense, cultural competence and TIC go hand in hand.
4. Do not mandate trauma-specific interventions (such as EMDR). An individual must be ready to address his/her trauma, but engaging in strategies such as those consistent with motivational interviewing may improve openness to addressing trauma-related issues. This is addressed in the context of justice or corrections-motivated treatment; while addressing trauma may be a risk-related need, it should not be

externally motivated through privilege or opportunity. Motivational interview strategies are highly encouraged, though.

In summary, the manifestations of personality disorders and trauma reactions present with a variety of similarities. Trauma and personality may intersect (having an influence on one another), or run parallel (impact the individual virtually independent of each other). This makes the process of case conceptualization as much of an art as it is a science. It may be tempting to view behavior through the lens of a diagnosis such as a personality disorder, but effective case conceptualization requires repeated, objective reassessment as new information comes to light. This requires an individualized approach to each patient. We must not define ISOs solely on their experience committing sexual offenses, but also how their history of being justice-involved intersects with their experience as a person with a gender identity, a racial and/or ethnic identity, and any other relevant social dynamics to create a lived experience. This includes considering the setting that an individual learned to live in as well as the setting they exist in today. While examples and issues are discussed here from an American point of view, understanding the individualized intersectionality of an individual transcends boundaries.

Skilled treatment providers are also aware of their own countertransference as a result of both individual experiences and societal dynamics—in a therapeutic relationship, intersectionality is relevant for both the treatment provider and the treatment recipient. Thus, whether it is a discrete event, repeated occurrences, or a cultural context, a skilled treatment provider working either with the victims of sexual abuse, those who have sexually abused others, or in many cases both, the consideration of trauma is an ongoing process. This makes the employment of a trauma-informed perspective ever necessary, and with the extant opportunities for training and continuing education today, there is little reason to avoid this.

References

Adwell, S. T. (1991). A case for single-cell occupancy in America's prisons. *Federal Probation, 55,* 64.

Ahlmeyer, S., Kleinsasser, D., Stoner, J., and Retzlaff, P. (2003). Psychopathology of incarcerated sex offenders. *Journal of Personality Disorders, 17*(4), 306–318. https://doi.org/10.1521/pedi.17.4.306.23969

Alexander, J. (2004). Toward a theory of cultural trauma. Cultural trauma and collective identity. In J. Alexander, R. Eyerman, B. Giesen, N. Smelser, and P. Sztompko (Eds.) *Cultural trauma and collective identity* (pp. 620–639). University of California Press.

American Psychiatric Association. (2013a). *Diagnostic and statistical manual of mental disorders* (5th ed.). American Psychiatric Publishing.

American Psychiatric Association. (2013b). *Posttraumatic stress disorder.* American Psychiatric Publishing.

Andrews, D. A., and Bonta, J. (1991). *The psychology of criminal conduct.* Routledge.

Barrett, E. L., Mills, K. L., & Teesson, M. (2011). Hurt people who hurt people: Violence amongst individuals with comorbid substance use disorder and post traumatic stress disorder. *Addictive Behaviors, 36*(7), 721–728. https://doi.org/10.1016/j.addbeh.2011.02.005

Beck, J. C. (2010). Dangerous severe personality disorder: The controversy continues. *Behavioral Sciences & the Law, 28*(2), 277–288. https://doi.org/10.1002/bsl.931

Black, D. W., Gunter, T., Loveless, P., Allen, J., and Sieleni, B. (2010). Antisocial personality disorder in incarcerated offenders: Psychiatric comorbidity and quality of life. *Annals of Clinical Psychiatry, 22*(2), 113–120. https://doi.org/10.4135/9781483392240.n23

Blagov, P. S., Fowler, K. A., and Lilienfeld, S. O. (2007). Histrionic personality disorder. In W. O'Donohue, K. A. Fowler, and S. O. Lilienfeld (Eds.), *Personality disorders: Toward the DSM-V* (pp. 203–232). Sage.

Bogue, B., Woodward, B., Campbell, N. M., Clawson, E., and Faust, D. (2004). *Implementing evidenced-based principles in community corrections: The principles of effective intervention.* Washington, DC: National Institute of Corrections

Bonta, J., and Andrews, D. A. (2016). *The psychology of criminal conduct.* Routledge.

Bottoms, H. C., Treichler, E. B., Davidson, C. A., and Spaulding, W. D. (2015). Cognitive characteristics in "difficult-to-discharge" inpatients with serious mental illness: attribution biases are associated with suspiciousness only for those with lower levels of insight. *American Journal of Psychiatric Rehabilitation, 18*(2), 152–172. https://doi.org/10.1080/15487768.2014.954157

Brulle, R. J., and Norgaard, K. M. (2019). Avoiding cultural trauma: Climate change and social inertia. *Environmental Politics.* https://doi.org/10.1080/09644016.2018.1562138

Caligor, E., Levy, K. N., & Yeomans, F. E. (2015). Narcissistic personality disorder: Diagnostic and clinical challenges. *American Journal of Psychiatry, 172*(5), 415–422. https://doi.org/10.1176/appi.ajp.2014.14060723

Carney, N. (2016). All lives matter, but so does race: Black lives matter and the evolving role of social media. *Humanity & Society, 40*(2), 180–199. https://doi.org/10.1177/0160597616643868

Castellví, P., Miranda-Mendizábal, A., Parés-Badell, O., Almenara, J., Alonso, I., Blasco, M. J., ... Alonso, J. (2017). Exposure to violence, a risk for suicide in youths and young adults. A meta-analysis of longitudinal studies. *Acta Psychiatrica Scandinavica, 135*(3), 195–211. https://doi.org/10.1111/acps.12679

Chapman, D. P., Dube, S. R., & Anda, R. F. (2007). Adverse childhood events as risk factors for negative mental health outcomes. *Psychiatric Annals, 37*(5), 359–364.

Chen, Y. Y., Chen, C. Y., & Hung, D. L. (2016). Assessment of psychiatric disorders among sex offenders: Prevalence and associations with criminal history. *Criminal Behaviour and Mental Health, 26*(1), 30–37. https://doi.org/10.1002/cbm.1926

Clark, W. (2003). *Immigrants and the American Dream: Remaking the Middle Class.* Guilford Press.

DeGruy, J. (2017). *Post traumatic slave syndrome* (2nd ed.). Joy DeGruy Publications Inc.

Demertzis, N., & Eyerman, R. (2020). Covid-19 as cultural trauma. *American Journal of Cultural Sociology, 8*(3), 428–450. https://doi.org/10.1057/s41290-020-00112-z

Dube, S. R., Anda, R. F., Felitti, V. J., Edwards, V. J., & Croft, J. B. (2002). Averse childhood experiences and personal alcohol abuse as an adult. *Addictive Behaviors, 27*, 713–725. https://doi.org/10.1016/S0306-4603(01)00204-0

Edgemon, T. G., & Clay-Warner, J. (2019). Inmate mental health and the pains of imprisonment. *Society and Mental Health, 9*(1), 33–50. https://doi.org/10.1177/2156869318785424

Falvey, J. E., Bray, T. E., and Hebert, D. J. (2005). Case conceptualization and treatment planning: Investigation of problem-solving and clinical judgment. *Journal of Mental Health Counseling, 27*(4), 348–372. https://doi.org/10.17744/mehc.27.4.cw8uyjum3w4dnfmn

Felitti, V. J., Anda, R. F., Nordenberg, D., Williamson, D. F., Spitz, A. M., Edwards, V., and Marks, J. S. (1998). Relationship of childhood abuse and household dysfunction to many of the leading causes of death in adults: The Adverse Childhood Experiences (ACE) Study. *American Journal of Preventive Medicine, 14*(4), 245–258. https://doi.org/10.1016/S0749-3797(98)00017-8

Findling, R. L. (2008). Atypical antipsychotic treatment of disruptive behavior disorders in children and adolescents. *Journal of Clinical Psychiatry, 69,* 9–14.

Fritzon, K., Miller, S., Bargh, D., Hollows, K., Osborne, A., and Howlett, A. (2021). Understanding the relationships between trauma and criminogenic risk using the Risk-Need-Responsivity model. *Journal of Aggression, Maltreatment & Trauma, 30*(3), 294–323. https://doi.org/10.1080/10926771.2020.1806972

Gallagher, R. J., Reagan, A. J., Danforth, C. M., and Dodds, P. S. (2018). Divergent discourse between protests and counter-protests: #BlackLivesMatter and #AllLivesMatter. *PloS One, 13*(4), 1–23. https://doi.org/10.1371/journal.pone.0195644

Hales, T. W., Green, S. A., Bissonette, S., Warden, A., Diebold, J., Koury, S. P., and Nochajski, T. H. (2019). Trauma-informed care outcome study. *Research on Social Work Practice, 29*(5), 529–539. https://doi.org/10.1177/1049731518766618

Hall, K. L., Stinson, J. D., and Moser, M. R. (2018). Impact of childhood adversity and out-of-home placement for male adolescents who have engaged in sexually abusive behavior. *Child Maltreatment, 23*(1), 63–73. https://doi.org/10.1177/1077559517720726

Hanson, R. K., Bourgon, G., Helmus, L., and Hodgson, S. (2009). The principles of effective correctional treatment also apply to sexual offenders a meta-analysis. *Criminal Justice and Behavior, 36*(9), 865–891. https://doi.org/10.1177/0093854809338545

Hartal, G., and Misgav, C. (2021). Queer urban trauma and its spatial politics: A lesson from social movements in Tel Aviv and Jerusalem. *Urban Studies, 58*(7), 1463–1483. https://doi.org/10.1177/0042098020918839

Ignatiev, N. (2009). *How the Irish became white* (2nd ed.). Routlege.

Janssen, E. (2018). *Integrating trauma informed care into the treatment of adult male sex offenders: A systematic review* [Master's thesis, St. Catherine University].

Levenson, J. (2014). Incorporating trauma-informed care into evidence-based sex offender treatment. *Journal of Sexual Aggression, 20*(1), 9–22. https://doi.org/10.1080/13552600.2013.861523

Levenson, J. S., Willis, G. M., and Prescott, D. S. (2016). Adverse childhood experiences in the lives of male sex offenders: Implications for trauma-informed care. *Sexual Abuse, 28*(4), 340–359. https://doi.org/10.1177/1079063214535819

Levenson, J. S., Willis, G. M., and Prescott, D. S. (2020). *Trauma-informed care: Transforming treatment for people who have sexually abused.* Brandon, VT: Safer Society Press.

Linehan, M. M. (1993). *Cognitive-behavioral treatment of borderline personality disorder.* Guildford Press.

Linehan, M. M., McDavid, J. D., Brown, M. Z., Sayrs, J. H., and Gallop, R. J. (2008). Olanzapine plus dialectical behavior therapy for women with high irritability who meet criteria for borderline personality disorder: A double-blind, placebo-controlled pilot study. *Journal of Clinical Psychiatry, 69*(6), 999–1005. https://doi.org/10.4088/jcp.v69n0617

Mallinger, S. (1991). Games inmates play. *Corrections Today, 53*(7), 188–190.

Mattson, B., Esposito, M. C., and Eggleston, C. (2012). Assessing educational needs in correctional settings. In B. D. Fitch and A. H. Normore (Eds.) *Education-based incarceration and recidivism: The ultimate social justice crime-fighting tool* (pp. 41–58). Information Age Publishing, Inc.

Meloy, J. R., and Yakeley, J. (2020). Antisocial personality disorder. In V. Zeigler-Hill and T. K. Shackelford (Eds.), *Encyclopedia of personality and individual differences* (pp. 206–215). Springer.

Metzger, I. W., Anderson, R. E., Are, F., and Ritchwood, T. (2021). Healing interpersonal and racial trauma: Integrating racial socialization into trauma-focused cognitive behavioral therapy for African American youth. *Child Maltreatment, 26*(1), 17–27. https://doi.org/10.1177/1077559520921457

Morey, L. C., and Hopwood, C. J. (2013). Stability and change in personality disorders. *Annual Review of Clinical Psychology, 9*, 499–528. https://doi.org/10.1111/j.1467-8721.2009.01600.x

Morrill, E. F., Brewer, N. T., O'Neill, S. C., Lillie, S. E., Dees, E. C., Carey, L. A., and Rimer, B. K. (2008). The interaction of post-traumatic growth and post-traumatic stress symptoms in predicting depressive symptoms and quality of life. *Psycho-Oncology: Journal of the Psychological, Social and Behavioral Dimensions of Cancer, 17*(9), 948–953. https://doi.org/10.1002/pon.1313

Morton, J. M. (2014). Cultural code-switching: Straddling the achievement gap. *Journal of Political Philosophy, 22*(3), 259–281. https://doi.org/10.1111/jopp.12019

Neacsiu, A. D., and Tkachuck, M. A. (2016). Dialectical behavior therapy skills use and emotion dysregulation in personality disorders and psychopathy: A community self-report study. *Borderline Personality Disorder and Emotion Dysregulation, 3*(1), 1–12. https://doi.org/10.1186/s40479-016-0041-5

Orth, U., & Wieland, E. (2006). Anger, hostility, and posttraumatic stress disorder in trauma-exposed adults: a meta-analysis. *Journal of Consulting and Clinical Psychology, 74*(4), 698–706. https://doi.org/10.1037/0022-006X.74.4.698

Phelan, J. C., and Link, B. G. (2015). Is racism a fundamental cause of inequalities in health? *Annual Review of Sociology, 41*, 311–330. https://doi.org/10.1016/j.socscimed.2014.10.023

Phipps, R., and Thorne, S. (2019). Utilizing trauma-focused cognitive behavioral therapy as a framework for addressing cultural trauma in African American children and adolescents: A proposal. *Professional Counselor, 9*(1), 35–50. https://doi.org/10.15241/rp.9.1.35

Puszkiewicz, K. L., and Stinson, J. D. (2019). Pathways to delinquent and sex offending behavior: The role of childhood adversity and environmental context in a treatment sample of male adolescents. *Child Abuse & Neglect, 98*. https://doi.org/10.1016/j.chiabu.2019.104184

Ricci, R. J., and Clayton, C. A. (2016). EMDR with sex offenders: Using offense drivers to guide conceptualization and treatment. *Journal of EMDR Practice and Research, 10*(2), 104–118. https://doi.org/10.1891/1933-3196.10.2.104

Richardson-Stovall, J. (2012). Image slavery and mass-media pollution: Popular media, beauty, and the lives of black women. *Berkeley Journal of Sociology, 56*, 73–100.

Rodi-Risberg, M. (2018). Problems in representing trauma. In J. R. Kurtz (Ed.), *Trauma and literature* (pp. 110–123). Cambridge University Press.

Rosenfeld, R., and Kempf, K. (1991). The scope and purposes of corrections: Exploring alternative responses to crowding. *Crime & Delinquency, 37*(4), 481–505. https://doi.org/10.1177/0011128791037004005

Sadeh, N., and McNiel, D. E. (2015). Posttraumatic stress disorder increases risk of criminal recidivism among justice-involved persons with mental disorders. *Criminal Justice and Behavior, 42*(6), 573–586. https://doi.org/10.1177/0093854814556880

Saegert, S., Fields, D., and Libman, K. (2011). Mortgage foreclosure and health disparities: Serial displacement as asset extraction in African American populations. *Journal of Urban Health, 88*(3), 390–402. https://doi.org/10.1007/d11524-011-9584-3

Samar, S. M., Walton, K. E., and McDermut, W. (2013). Personality traits predict irrational beliefs. *Journal of Rational-Emotive & Cognitive-Behavior Therapy, 31*(4), 231–242. https://doi.org/10.1007/d10942-013-0172-1

Saum, C. A., Surratt, H. L., Inciardi, J. A., and Bennett, R. E. (1995). Sex in prison: Exploring the myths and realities. *The Prison Journal, 75*(4), 413–430. https://doi.org/10.1177/0032855595075004002

Simko, C. (2020). Marking time in memorials and museums of terror: Temporality and cultural trauma. *Sociological Theory, 38*(1), 51–77. https://doi.org/10.1177/0735275120906430

Sorrentino, R., Brown, A., Berard, B., and Peretti, K. (2018). Sex offenders: General information and treatment. *Psychiatric Annals, 48*(2), 120–128. https://doi.org/10.3928/00485713-20171220-01

Stinson, J. D., Becker, J. V., and Sales, B. D. (2008). Self-regulation and the etiology of sexual deviance: Evaluating causal theory. *Violence and Victims, 23*(1), 35–51. https://doi.org/10.1891/0886-6708.23.1.35

Stinson, J. D., Quinn, M. A., and Levenson, J. S. (2016). The impact of trauma on the onset of mental health symptoms, aggression, and criminal behavior in an inpatient psychiatric sample. *Child Abuse & Neglect, 61*, 13–22. https://doi.org/10.1016/j.chiabu.2016.09.005

Subica, A. M., and Link, B. G. (2022). Cultural trauma as a fundamental cause of health disparities. *Social Science & Medicine, 292*. https://doi.org/10.1016/j.socscimed.2021.114574

Substance Abuse and Mental Health Services Administration. (2014). *SAMHSA's concept of trauma and guidance for a trauma-informed approach.* Washington, DC: U.S. Department of Health and Human Services.

Tangney, J. P., Hill-Barlow, D., Wagner, P. E., Marschall, D. E., Borenstein, J. K., Sanftner, J., ... Gramzow, R. (1996). Assessing individual differences in constructive versus destructive responses to anger across the lifespan.

Journal of Personality and Social Psychology, 70(4), 780–796. https://doi.org/ 10.1037/0022-3514.70.4.780

Tatum, B. (2002). The colonial model as a theoretical explanation of crime and delinquency. In S. L. Gabbidon, H. Taylor Greene, and V. D. Young (Eds.), *African American classics in criminology and criminal justice* (pp. 307–322). Sage.

Waters, M. C., and Jiménez, T. R. (2005). Assessing immigrant assimilation: New empirical and theoretical challenges. *Annual Review of Sociology, 31*(1), 105–125. https://doi.org/10.1146/annurev.soc.29.010202.100026

Weathers, F. W., and Keane, T. M. (2007). The Criterion A problem revisited: Controversies and challenges in defining and measuring psychological trauma. *Journal of Traumatic Stress, 20*(2), 107–121. https://doi.org/10.1002/jts.20210

Wilson, R. J., Fernandez, Y., and Prescott, D. S. (2020). Ensuring responsive treatment options for male adults who have sexually offended. In J. Proulx, F. Cortoni, L. Craig, and E. J. Letourneau (Eds.), *The Wiley handbook of what works with sexual offenders: Contemporary perspectives in theory, assessment, treatment, and prevention* (pp. 201–216). Wiley.

Worley, R. M. (2016). Memoirs of a guard-researcher: Deconstructing the games inmates play behind the prison walls. *Deviant Behavior, 37*(11), 1215–1226. https://doi.org/10.1080/01639625.2016.1170541

13

"Pussy Power"? Reflecting on Research Practice with Aboriginal and/or Torres Strait Islander Men Who Have Offended Sexually

Jodi Death and Kelly Richards

Introduction

In Australia, Aboriginal and/or Torres Strait Islander individuals and communities have long been the focus of social research on a broad range of topics. (In line with accepted practice, in this chapter we adopt the terms "Aboriginal and/or Torres Strait Islander" and "Indigenous" interchangeably to refer to Australia's First Peoples. The former recognises that Indigenous individuals may have Aboriginal, Torres Strait Islander or both Aboriginal and Torres Strait Islander heritage). Indeed, it is commonly accepted that Indigenous Australians are the most researched people in the world (Benveniste and King 2018; Dew et al. 2019).

Critically, however, Indigenous individuals and communities have typically been positioned by non-Indigenous researchers as the *subjects*

J. Death · K. Richards (✉)
Queensland University of Technology, Brisbane, QLD, Australia
e-mail: k1.richards@qut.edu.au

© The Author(s), under exclusive license to Springer Nature Switzerland AG 2022
A. K. Gill and H. Begum (eds.), *Child Sexual Abuse in Black and Minoritised Communities*, https://doi.org/10.1007/978-3-031-06337-4_13

of inquiry; research has been conducted *on* rather than *with* Indigenous peoples (Benveniste and King 2018). Research has been conducted according to what Blagg (2011) calls "white fella priorities"—that is, on those issues deemed important by the colonial state. Moreover, despite this vast volume of research, few positive outcomes have resulted for Indigenous people and communities (Blagg 2011; Benveniste and King 2018; Dew et al. 2019). As a consequence, non-Indigenous researchers are often understandably regarded with distrust by these communities (Guillemin et al. 2016). For example, Sherwood's (2010) work documents the belief, commonly held by Indigenous people that researchers do not listen properly and fail to get the story "right". More pointedly, Bond et al. (2021) note that not only does research infrequently result in positive outcomes for Indigenous communities, but that it can be actively harmful. Against this background, this chapter explores some of the epistemological and methodological questions we encountered as non-Indigenous feminist researchers undertaking research on a perpetrator intervention program for Aboriginal and/or Torres Strait Islander men convicted of serious sexual offending (including against children) in Queensland, Australia.

Researching the topic of gendered and/or sexual violence in Aboriginal and/or Torres Strait Islander communities can be especially fraught. It has been well-documented that rates of child abuse, including child sexual abuse, and gendered violence more broadly are often higher in Indigenous than non-Indigenous communities (Cripps and McGlade 2008; Mace et al. 2015; Willis 2011). (For Indigenous Australians, domestic and family violence, sexual violence and child maltreatment are not always differentiated into these separate Western categories but seen as fundamentally interlinked [Cripps and McGlade 2008; Stanley et al. 2002]). It is impossible to say with certainty how widespread child sexual abuse is in Indigenous families and communities. As has been well-documented, reporting rates of sexual violence, including child sexual abuse, are low across the board (Bouhours and Daly 2008; Fraser-Barbour et al. 2018). However, for Aboriginal and/or Torres Strait Islander people, a number of additional barriers exist to reporting child sexual abuse (e.g. language barriers), resulting in lower levels of reporting than are common in non-Indigenous communities (Mace et al. 2015;

Mullighan 2008; Taylor and Putt 2007; Willis 2011). In particular, a lack of trust in the police and formal criminal justice system responses—the result of more than two centuries of state policies with catastrophic impacts on Indigenous families and communities—prevent Aboriginal and/or Torres Strait Islander people from reporting child sexual abuse to the authorities. Nonetheless, a range of sources indicate that child sexual abuse, perpetrated by both Indigenous and non-Indigenous men, may be more common for Indigenous than non-Indigenous children in Australia. The Australian Institute of Health and Welfare (2021) has documented that Aboriginal and/or Torres Strait Islander children are 8 times as likely as non-Aboriginal and/or Torres Strait Islander children to receive state child protection services in response to emotional, physical or sexual abuse and/or parental neglect. A range of formal state inquiries have also documented high levels of child sexual abuse in some Aboriginal and/or Torres Strait Islander communities (for a recent review see Cripps 2021), reaching disastrous levels in some remote communities (O'Brien 2010; Smallbone et al. 2013). For example, Mullighan's (2008) inquiry used a wide variety of evidentiary sources (including court and medical records and evidence of sexually transmitted infections) to investigate child sexual abuse in the Anangu Pitjantjatjara Yankunytjatjara (APY) lands, and concluded that child sexual abuse was a matter of grave concern in these communities (see further Aboriginal Child Sexual Assault Taskforce 2006; Northern Territory Board of Inquiry into the Protection of Aboriginal Children from Sexual Abuse 2007; O'Brien 2010; Smallbone et al. 2013). Rates of child sexual abuse are likely to vary significantly across communities. While the Aboriginal Child Sexual Assault Taskforce (2006) estimated that Indigenous girls were two-and-a-half times more likely to experience child sexual abuse than non-Indigenous girls, Mace et al. (2015) estimate that Indigenous children are 6 times as likely to experience child sexual abuse than non-Indigenous children. In general terms, it is important to recognise that violence occurs in Indigenous communities—indeed, all communities—at highly varied rates (see generally Lawrence 2007).

Research has, however, documented social "problems", including child sexual abuse, without providing culturally appropriate supports or solutions (Northern Territory Board of Inquiry into the Protection of

Aboriginal Children from Sexual Abuse 2007), and has thus resulted in the pathologisation of Indigenous people and communities (Bryant et al. 2021; Sherwood 2010). Rather than positioning violence in Indigenous communities as a consequence of colonisation, dispossession and racism, such research has cast gendered violence as "cultural"—a "normal" or "traditional" component of Aboriginal and/or Torres Strait Islander cultures, despite historical evidence to the contrary (Blagg et al. 2020; Cripps and Adams 2014; Stanley et al. 2002; Watson 2009). The *Ampe Akelyernnemane Mekarle* (*Little Children Are Sacred*) report, for example, documented that media and political commentary often claims that Aboriginal law is used as an excuse to justify child sexual abuse, but ultimately concluded that it had been "unable to find any case where Aboriginal law has been used and accepted as a defence (in that it would exonerate an accused from any criminal responsibility) for an offence of violence against a woman or a child" (Northern Territory Board of Inquiry into the Protection of Aboriginal Children from Sexual Abuse 2007: 58).

The "Northern Territory Emergency Response" (NTER), which began in 2007, is a case in point. What began as a forceful extension of policing in Indigenous communities, under the guise of protecting children from sexual violence following the release of the *Ampe Akelyernnemane Mekarle* (*Little Children Are Sacred*) report (Northern Territory Board of Inquiry into the Protection of Aboriginal Children from Sexual Abuse 2007), ultimately resulted in the dramatic over-criminalisation of Indigenous men for minor offences—primarily driving offences (Anthony 2009)—and a raft of other adverse outcomes for the Indigenous communities targeted (Watson 2009). The NTER—or "Intervention" as it came to be called by Indigenous people—has been criticised on multiple grounds (see especially Watson 2009), including violations of human rights, increasing trauma in communities, failure to protect children, and as reliant on constructions of Indigenous communities and peoples as inherently dangerous and unable to govern themselves (Coram 2009; Howe 2009; Macoun 2011).

Crucially in light of the current chapter, Western understandings of gendered violence as caused by patriarchal power structures are often rejected by Indigenous women, who instead view gendered violence in its diverse manifestations as stemming from complex interwoven processes of colonisation, trauma and racism (Blagg 2011; Stanley et al. 2002). As Cripps and McGlade (2008) point out, rates of violent victimisation are higher among those Aboriginal and/or Torres Strait Islander people who have been removed from their natural families—clearly illustrating the role of discriminatory state policies on individuals' experiences of violence. Moreover, Indigenous women may reject Western solutions to the problem of gendered violence, which inevitably involve the criminalisation of male perpetrators (Cripps and McGlade 2008). Given that Aboriginal and/or Torres Strait Islander individuals are the most over-represented people in the world's prison systems (Anthony 2017), criminalisation may only exacerbate the difficulties already faced by Indigenous women and children, perpetuating cycles of intergenerational incarceration and the dislocation of families and communities: "Indigenous community members have consistently criticised this approach as being irrelevant, discriminatory, and a repeat of the kinds of violence inherent in policies and practises of colonisation" (Cripps and McGlade 2008: 243). Importantly, in light of this discussion, the evidence is clear that Aboriginal and/or Torres Strait Islander perpetrators of sexual violence are far more likely to be apprehended by police than their non-Aboriginal and/or Torres Strait Islander counterparts (Hunter and Onnis 2015).

Against this backdrop, our purpose in this chapter is to critically discuss the tensions raised for us as non-Indigenous feminists researching a program that responds to Indigenous men convicted of sexual offending. We discuss the ways in which we attempted to navigate intersections of culturally sensitive practice when considering constructions of gender that challenged our perspectives as white feminist researchers. It is important to note that we don't propose solutions here but seek to exemplify our own struggle. We have drawn on literature to help us reflect on our experiences, in particular the work of settler colonial theory (SCT) and critiques of feminisms (Macoun 2016; Maddison et al. 2016). The chapter begins by providing an overview of the research project and its findings. Next, we discuss the ways in which our own positions conflicted with those of research participants and the ways in which we engaged in sense-making as researchers. Throughout, we discuss the epistemological, methodological and ethical tensions we encountered as non-Indigenous feminists researching an intervention for Indigenous male perpetrators of sexual violence.

Background to the Research Project

The broader research project discussed in this chapter involved an exploratory study of the Cultural Mentoring Program (hereafter CMP) delivered in Townsville in far north Queensland, Australia. Our research (Richards et al. 2020a, b) was funded via a grant from Australia's National Research Organisation for Women's Safety and was approved by both Queensland University of Technology's Human Research Ethics Committee (approval #1600001093) and by the Queensland Corrective Services Research Committee. It set out to examine how participating in the CMP could reduce sexual reoffending against women and children and to make recommendations about reintegration programs of this nature. Our study asked how the CMP aims to reduce sexual reoffending, and which of its tenets might be applied more strategically to support this aim. We were especially dedicated to documenting the work of the CMP given the lack of evaluation of Indigenous criminal justice programs, which has been identified as a key reason for the lack of recognition, and even discontinuation, of programs of this nature (Cripps and McGlade 2008).

In Queensland, under the *Dangerous Prisoners (Sexual Offenders) Act* (*DPSOA*), a person convicted in relation to serious sexual offences can be subject to indefinite detention or very strict conditions upon their release from prison into the community (Queensland Department of Justice and Attorney-General 2020). These latter conditions include frequent and intensive parole supervision, electronic monitoring, police surveillance and participation in intensive mandated therapeutic programming (Keyzer and Coyle 2009; Keyzer and O'Toole 2006; Queensland Department of Justice and Attorney-General 2020. Those subject to these conditions face extreme marginalisation and stigmatisation, having been designated dangerous sexual offenders under the *Act*. For Aboriginal and/or Torres Strait Islander men, who also face racial discrimination, this stigmatisation is no doubt greatly exacerbated. (To our knowledge, only men (i.e. no women) have been subject to these conditions of release under the *DPSOA* [Richards et al. 2020a].)

In this context, the CMP emerged with the aim of supporting Aboriginal and/or Torres Strait Islander men released under the *DPSOA*, on a voluntary basis, to "reintegrate" into the community and thus to reduce their likelihood of recidivism. We have problematised the notion of "reintegration" here because Townsville is not the home community of most of the men involved in the CMP. Instead, the men are usually from remote island or mainland communities and are relocated to Townsville as a condition of their release. While this is done to preclude the men having contact with their victims or victims' families, and to ensure that support services are available to assist them, it can have the effect of making "reintegration" even more challenging. The CMP is thus designed to alleviate the challenges associated with "reintegration" for this cohort of extremely marginalised men.

The program involves an Indigenous Elder (supported by a small number of other local male Elders and a range of relevant community agencies) providing support to the men on a one-on-one basis. All Aboriginal and/or Torres Strait Islander men released under the *DPSOA* to the Townsville area are informed about the CMP and invited to take part. The one-on-one support provided focuses on spiritual and cultural mentorship, and on (re)connecting the men with aspects of their traditional cultures. Men who opt to take part are encouraged to engage in a range of activities to enhance their ties to culture, such as participation in traditional ceremonies, Indigenous community events, and activities designed to (re)connect the men to Country (e.g. traditional fishing practices). Elders in the program also pass on cultural knowledge to CMP participants (e.g. family histories and traditional arts and crafts (Richards et al. 2020a, 2020b; Richards et al. 2020).

In administrative terms, the state government department responsible for managing prisons and the rehabilitation of prisoners in Queensland (Queensland Corrective Services) is not involved in the delivery of the CMP but supports the program by identifying suitable offenders and connecting them to the program. The Elders who deliver the program are paid on a fee-for-service basis. Participants are offered six two-hour one-on-one individual mentoring sessions with an Elder in the first instance, followed by a further six sessions if requested by the participant and approved by Queensland Corrective Services.

Methodological Approach

A qualitative methodological approach was deemed most suitable for the study for two reasons: first, the CMP works intensively with a small number of offenders (only a very small minority of all Aboriginal and/or Torres Strait Islander perpetrators of sexual violence released from prison each year), making an experimental or quantitative research design a poor fit; and second, Aboriginal and/or Torres Strait Islander scholars have noted that the latter are usually not appropriate for research with Aboriginal and/or Torres Strait Islander people (Blagg 2011; Katz et al. 2016). There are a range of reasons for this. As Aboriginal and/or Torres Strait Islander people comprise only approximately three per cent of Australia's population, there are often too few Aboriginal and/or Torres Strait Islander participants for rigorous statistical analysis of programs to be conducted (McCausland 2019). As a corollary, the quantitative paradigm can fail to "ascribe worth to anything culturally distinct or specific to Indigenous peoples as it cannot be reduced to a comparative statistic with non-Indigenous Australians" (McCausland 2019: 67). Quantitative methods can also fail to account for historical context or capture measures of social, emotional and cultural well-being that are central to Aboriginal and/or Torres Strait Islander world views (Williams 2018).

Qualitative methods are not without limitations in research with Aboriginal and/or Torres Strait Islander people. For example, as McCausland (2019) notes, qualitative methods require relationships of trust to be developed and community protocols to be identified and followed; they may be most useful in assisting non-Indigenous researchers to gain an understanding of the contexts in which they are researching (Putt 2013). Nonetheless, qualitative methods are useful for generating knowledge about whether and how criminal justice programs reflect existing evidence, and for informing recommendations about how they could do so more effectively. Our study thus adopted a qualitative methodological approach, exploring the beliefs, experiences and knowledges of CMP participants in order to produce a "sympathetic understanding and explanation of reality" (Weber in Bayens and Roberson 2011 p. 24). More specifically, the study adopted the tenets of phenomenology, as it sought to privilege CMP participants' own understandings and views (Chamberlain 2009) of the role of the CMP in their journeys of "reintegration" and desistance. The research was especially interested in investigating how (re)connecting with Aboriginal and/or Torres Strait Islander cultures via the CMP shaped the development of participants' narratives about their own identities in the post-prison context, and thus contributed to the sexual safety of women and children.

To that end, we conducted semi-structured qualitative interviews with members of three key participant groups: Aboriginal and/or Torres Strait Islander men who were currently participating in or had participated in the CMP within the preceding three years ($n = 11$ interviews with 14 individuals); the three Indigenous Elders responsible for delivering the program and staff from Queensland Corrective Services who had supported its development or delivery ($n = 6$); and key stakeholders (both Indigenous and non-Indigenous) from government, nongovernment and private agencies who work in parallel with the CMP and/or deliver related services (e.g. therapeutic interventions) to men involved in the CMP ($n = 12$). A combination of purposive and snowball sampling was employed to recruit from these three groups. Prospective participants were informed about the research verbally and provided with a copy of the Participant Information and Consent Form to inform their decision about whether to participate in an interview.

Interviews with CMP participants were undertaken either by Richards or by an Indigenous male Research Assistant who was specifically recruited and trained to conduct interviews. The men were thus able to choose whether to be interviewed by an Indigenous or non-Indigenous researcher. Three participants opted to be interviewed by both Richards and then, separately, by the Indigenous Research Assistant. Interviews with the men were conducted in-person and ranged in length from 20 minutes to an hour (with an average of 45 minutes). The men were asked a loosely structured series of questions designed to elicit whether and how the CMP assisted their processes of "reintegration" and desistance. For example, CMP participants were asked: Has being in the CMP brought about a change in the way you view your past behaviour? How? (For a copy of the interview schedules, see Richards et al. 2020a).

We were committed to privileging Aboriginal and/or Torres Strait Islander voices and perspectives throughout the project, and cognisant that as white academics, we are privileged in our capacity to do so. The broader project was guided by a project Steering Committee that included Aboriginal and/or Torres Strait Islander representation to ensure cultural safety. We also sought advice and input from the Indigenous Elders who deliver the CMP about the interview questions to ensure their appropriateness. In addition, we sought guidance on our findings as they emerged via our contact with the Elders, the Steering Committee and a dedicated roundtable, compered by an Indigenous facilitator, which included diverse Indigenous and non-Indigenous representatives from a wide range of relevant service providers and stakeholder groups.

The Sample

CMP participants were aged between 34 and 53 years, with an average age of 42. Not all interview participants were comfortable discussing their offending and incarceration histories; however, most revealed having served multiple and/or lengthy prison sentences and 5–18 years imprisonment following their most recent conviction for sexual offending (average = approx. 10 years). Many had been incarcerated on previous occasions, either as young people or adults, for other violent and non-violent crimes (but typically not sexual crimes). Most participants had completed the CMP 1–3 years previously. Crucially for our study, the men reported very varying connections to their traditional cultures. Some of the men reported engagement in cultural activities as children or young people in their home communities, while others reported learning about culture for the first time while incarcerated. Still others reported that they connected to culture for the first time only during their participation in the CMP.

Challenging Our Own Understanding

Our research documented, for the first time, the ways in which the CMP supports participants to "reintegrate" into the community in culturally safe ways, and develop identities and lifestyles incompatible with continued offending (Richards et al. 2020a, 2020b). To this end, it identified myriad strengths of the CMP, including: supporting participants to avoid behaviours that contributed to their offending; supporting participants in culturally appropriate ways to accept the value of adhering to the rules that govern their lives in the post-prison context; and supporting participants to avoid breaching the conditions of their release. In particular, our research highlighted that the CMP fostered "redemption scripts" (i.e. narratives that ex-offenders adopt to make sense of their criminal past and subsequent shift away from crime [Maruna 2001]) among participants, supporting the development of desistant identities (Richards et al. 2020b). Our research thus concluded that many of the CMP's activities reflect the extant knowledge about reducing sexual reoffending, and to that end, that it makes a vital contribution to the safety of women and children in the community (Richards 2020; Richards et al. 2020a, b, c).

However, during the course of the research, we became somewhat discomforted by the program's characterisation of victim/survivors of the men's sexual violence, and of women more broadly. This was borne out in both comments made by the Elders who delivered the program and by the men participating in the program. While a small number of the men in the CMP recounted in their interviews that the program focuses on developing respect for women, far more commonly, their narratives seemed to instead blame victim/survivors for the sexual violence they had experienced. This was communicated both generally (i.e. that women generally are responsible for violence perpetrated against them) and specifically (i.e. that individual victims of the men's violence were responsible for the violence perpetrated against them). One CMP participant maintained he had been falsely convicted of a sexual offence and that his then girlfriend (the victim of the offence) "put me in prison—she was playing games…She did it for compensation". A number of the men reported that the CMP taught them about "pussy power"—a term that refers to "a woman's use of her sexual allure or femininity in order to exert influence over men" (www.lexico.com). For example, participants claimed that the CMP had taught them that "[if] you talk to a woman, she will put you inside [prison]", and about the importance of exercising caution in intimate relationships with women: "if she's drunk and you're sober...".

Expressions of denial, minimisation and justification of harm such as these are not uncommon among men who have sexually offended against women and/or children (Ware et al. 2020). Indeed, the literature on sexual offending predominantly understands sexual violence as stemming from perpetrators' "cognitive distortions" (i.e. false beliefs about sexual violence; e.g. that sexual activity does not harm children) (see for example Burn and Brown 2006; O Ciardha and Ward 2013). These "distortions" often serve as self-protective mechanisms that allow perpetrators to deflect stigma, manage shame and minimise the repercussions of their offending as well as maintain a positive sense of self (Blagden et al. 2014). However, this is not to say that perpetrator programs ought to support victim-blaming narratives among participants, much less actively instil them. Some staff and stakeholders we interviewed for the study were, like us, uneasy about the potential for victim-blaming narratives to be permitted or even actively fostered in the CMP, and one had previously raised the issue and believed it had been addressed by the program.

Our research suggested, however, that if it had not. Indeed, the Elders currently delivering the program openly adopted the term "pussy power" when interviewed for the study. One commented:

> They [the men] go back and sleep with the same woman and they find out he's slept with another woman and they put them up on rape charges. They're on these [Correctional] Orders not to see their woman...They come out [of prison] and the first thing they do is go home. That's what we call the PP, the pussy power. They say they're going to Cairns or seeing someone else and their woman calls the police and says, "Hey Billy's here and he's not meant to be." They've been threatened by the woman - "If you don't come see me I'm going out with someone else." And they go back.

This discovery put us in a very uncomfortable position as non-Indigenous feminist researchers. As feminist sexual violence researchers, we felt these narratives of victim-blame at a visceral level. We are only too aware of the damage that such beliefs have created for individual victim/survivors of sexual violence and for social policy efforts to prevent and respond to sexual violence. Such "rape myths" stubbornly endure. The most recent *Community Attitudes towards Violence Against Women* survey in Australia (Webster et al. 2018) found that nearly one-third of the representative sample of more than 17,500 respondents agreed with the statement that "A lot of times, women who say they were raped had led the man on and then had regrets". Sixteen per cent believe that "many allegations of sexual assault made by women are false" (Webster et al. 2018). Forty-three per cent agreed with the statement that "Women going through custody battles often make up or exaggerate claims of domestic violence in order to improve their case" (Webster et al. 2018), further demonstrating widespread mistrust of women's reports of violence. (For an analysis of Aboriginal and/or Torres Strait Islander participants' responses specifically, see Cripps et al. 2019).

Such rape myths endure not only when victims are adult women, but also when they are children. Moreover, these narratives do not only shape perpetrators' explanations for their offending (which we might reasonably expect), but—even more disturbingly—those of criminal justice authorities. By way of a recent local example, Deputy State Coroner Jane Bentley's findings in the case of murdered Queensland schoolgirl Tiahleigh Palmer repeatedly refer to the sexual abuse of the 12-year-old by her 18-year-old foster brother as "sexual activity", "sexual contact" and a "sexual relationship" (Coroners Court of Queensland 2021). In discussing the possibility that the child's foster father (who was convicted of her murder) was also sexually abusing her, Bentley even queries whether the foster father "was himself *having a sexual relationship* with Tiahleigh" (Coroners Court of Queensland 2021: para 191; italics added). Cripps, Davis and Taylor's (2008) research similarly documents what they consider a failure of the justice system in a case involving the sentencing of 9 Indigenous men and boys for repeated gang-rapes committed against a 10-year-old Indigenous girl. In this case, Cripps et al. (2008) highlight that not only the Defence barrister, but *also the*

Crown Prosecutor, appear to have placed at least partial blame on the 10-year-old victim, describing the perpetrators' actions as "naughty" and stating that "although she [the victim] was very young, she knew what was going on and she had agreed to meet the children at this place and it was all by arrangement" (see Cripps et al. 2008: 14).

Simultaneously, however, we did not want our research to replicate the very problems we identified at the outset of this chapter. We did not want to cast gendered and/or sexual violence (and the beliefs and attitudes that may underpin it) as "cultural", or to highlight "problems" (defined in Western terms) in Indigenous programs, or to uncritically adopt Western feminist understandings of gendered and/or sexual violence against women and children in Indigenous communities. We were especially reluctant in this regard given that Western feminism has largely failed Aboriginal and/or Torres Strait Islander women and children and that Western responses to gendered violence (e.g. women's refuges) have been heavily criticised by Indigenous women as culturally inappropriate (Blagg 2011; Cripps and McGlade 2008). Moreover, we were cognisant that Aboriginal and/or Torres Strait Islander women may not identify as feminist, or with our own brand of Western feminism, instead situating gendered and sexual violence in an intersectional framework encompassing a richer and more nuanced understanding of gender, "race" and class disparity (Clark et al. 2021). As Palawa scholar Cripps (2021) has argued, understanding sexual violence in Indigenous communities and against Indigenous women and girls must involve a focus not only on racism and sexism, but also explicitly on colonialism. She draws on the work of Razack (1998), who argues that when Indigenous women and girls speak out about sexual violence, they are "naming something infinitely broader than what men do to women" (in Cripps 2021: 303). In short, we were aware that the "feminist" agenda, which purported to advance women's rights, actually addressed only white feminist concerns (Moreton-Robinson 2006, 2000). As Trask (2003) and Moreton-Robinson (2006, 2000) argue, Indigenous women have little common ground with white feminists (despite white feminist attempts to cast all women's struggles as equal, and to privilege gender over "race" as the predominant category of social organisation). As Moreton-Robinson (2006) argues:

For Indigenous women, all white feminists benefit from colonisation; they are overwhelmingly represented and disproportionately predominant, have the key roles and constitute the norm, the ordinary and the standard of womanhood in Australia. White women are not represented to themselves as being white; instead, they position themselves as variously classed, sexualised, aged and abled. The disjuncture between representation and self-presentation of both Indigenous women and white feminists means that the involvement of Indigenous women in Australian feminism is, and will remain, partial. (see further McQuire 2018)

We began to question whether we ought to have been conducting the research at all. We asked ourselves: who are we to question the knowledge and practices of Indigenous Elders? As Benveniste and King (2018: 53) argue, however, avoiding the uncomfortable and reconsidering research with Indigenous people and communities due to feelings of guilt or uncertainty can have the effect of perpetuating the past. Herring, Spangaro, Lauw and McNamara (in Benveniste and King 2018: 53) argue instead that engaging with the work of Aboriginal and/or Torres Strait Islander leaders and scholars and with Aboriginal and/or Torres Strait Islander people and communities may be a more productive way forward. To be able to step back from a situation that made us uncomfortable is an exercise of privilege we wanted to avoid as another way of perpetuating colonising structures.

From Settler Colonial Theory (SCT), we take an understanding that as descendants of people who arrived in Australia as colonisers, we benefit in an ongoing way from the colonising process, the dispossession of Indigenous Australians and the denial of their sovereignty (Maddison 2019; Maddison et al. 2016). Although there may be growing recognition of the historical harms of colonisation in Australia and the ongoing legacy of these harms, SCT critiques the often accepted notion that politics and institutions are now benevolent and that the solution to the marginalisation of Indigenous peoples lies in policy development (Maddison 2019). The result of this is that institutions used to govern, including the criminal justice system, are often assumed to be conceptually sound even if they may need adjusting to "accommodate" Indigenous people (Strakosch and Macoun 2020). The result of this has been what

Macoun (2016) views as the colonising of white guilt whereby non-Indigenous activists can claim benevolence while remaining invested in the benefits of colonialism. Macoun and Strakosch (2013) argue that "non-Indigenous scholars should challenge the politically convenient conflation of settler desires and reality, and of the political present, and the future".

Activism has always been an essential component of feminisms but the history of assumed benevolence in feminisms should also not be ignored (Griffin 2019). In a salient example of how "race" often becomes obscured and subsumed in feminisms, concern quickly arose that the #metoo movement—founded by African-American woman Tarana Burke—replicated the dominance of white middle-class feminists and neglected the nuanced experiences of women and children (and men) of colour (Griffin 2019; Phipps 2020). Narratives of Indigenous women as dangerous, or women more widely as dangerous, are not new to feminist debate or colonising discourse (Konishi 2008; Ransley and Marchetti 2021). Particularly after the rise of the #metoo movement, however, a wider concern about men's vulnerability to complaints of sexual violence arose. Entrenched in these complaints of male vulnerability were long rehearsed discourses of the ways in which accusations of sexual violence ruined men's—primarily white men's—lives (Banet-Weiser 2021; Phipps 2020). Alongside this, there is a much lesser recognition that sexual violence has, and is, weaponised against men of colour internationally (Phipps 2020).

Responding to the complexities that are evident here, in the first instance, we sought guidance from the scholarship of Indigenous women working on issues of gendered and/or sexual violence and discovered that concerns of a similar nature have been raised previously by Aboriginal and/or Torres Strait Islander and Canadian First Nations women in relation to Indigenous-specific programs that seek to address sexual violence. Stewart et al.'s (2001) research, designed to investigate Canadian Aboriginal women's views of restorative justice measures, found that while participants understood gendered and sexual violence to be the result of colonisation, they nonetheless identified that women and children bear the greatest burden in this regard. They urge the adoption of an intersectional lens, arguing that such programs can miss their mark and re-victimise victim/survivors if gender inequality and victim-blaming attitudes remain unaddressed. They argued that:

> Focus group participants expressed tremendous concern with the diversion of cases of violence against women and children [from the criminal justice system] because they felt that the majority of support goes to offenders along with a prevalence of victim-blaming mentalities. A lack of concern for the safety needs of women and children, particularly in isolated communities was also cited as a major concern in processes such as "Victim-Offender Mediation". (Stewart et al. 2001: 39)

In a critical assessment of Canada's Hollow Water Community Holistic Circle Healing process—a response to endemic rates of sexual violence in one Canadian Aboriginal community—Palawa scholar Cripps and Noongar scholar McGlade critique Western criminal justice measures in which "sexual assault is positioned as a crime against the state and in which victimisers are easily able (even encouraged in some respects) to maintain 'denial' and lack of responsibility for their actions" (Cripps and McGlade 2008: 245; see further LaRocque 1997). They conclude that "we must ensure that community processes adopt precautions that also recognise the power imbalances that often exist within Indigenous communities to the detriment of women and children victims of violence" (Cripps and McGlade 2008: 252). In the Canadian context, LaRocque (1997) offers a scathing critique of criminal justice processes that ignore the needs of victim/survivors of sexual violence in an attempt to stem the tide of criminal justice intervention in Indigenous men's lives, arguing that gender domination in Canadian Aboriginal communities has been "routinely whitewashed under the rubric of cultural differences" (LaRocque 1997: 89). These scholars operationalise intersectionality in varied ways (and do not uniformly use the terminology of "intersectionality") but ultimately assert that gendered and/or sexual violence must not be understood independently of colonisation and dispossession of Indigenous peoples. This perspective has important implications for advancing explanations of child sexual abuse perpetration. Existing dominant explanations (e.g. cognitive distortions explanations (for example O Ciardha and Ward 2013) and situational/environmental explanations [for example LeClerc et al. 2015]) largely eschew intersectional understandings and implicitly disavow the relevance of the colonisation and dispossession of Indigenous peoples. Crucially, even feminist explanations, which assert that child sexual abuse reflects men's sociopolitical privilege (for example Cossins and Plummer 2016) also marginalise the role that colonisation as an ongoing project has in shaping the nature and extent of child sexual abuse in Indigenous communities.

Against this backdrop, we slowly gained confidence in our unwillingness to accept the responsibilisation of Aboriginal and/or Torres Strait Islander women and children for sexual violence perpetrated against them, even if that meant questioning an Elder's perspective. In LaRocque's (1997: 88) terms, we were leery of accepting "culturally appropriate" criminal justice measures at the expense of advocating for victim/survivors of sexual violence (see more broadly Cripps et al. 2008). Indeed, we came to view the notion that Aboriginal and/or Torres Strait Islander men have no control over their own actions—falling prey to "pussy power"—as racist. The notion that Aboriginal and/or Torres Strait Islander women trick or manipulate Aboriginal and/or Torres Strait Islander men for their own nefarious ends or use the mainstream criminal justice system as a tool to wreak revenge against these men, is both sexist (as it relies on tired stereotypes about women and women's sexuality) and, critically, racist (as it positions Indigenous women as responsible for Indigenous men's over-representation in the criminal justice system). Indeed, holding Aboriginal and/or Torres Strait Islander women responsible for Aboriginal and/or Torres Strait Islander men's over-incarceration marginalises vital critiques of the role of the colonial state as a key catalyst of Indigenous over-representation.

As white feminist researchers, we brought knowledge of the complexities of sexual violence discourses and masculinity to this project yet still were not prepared for the discomfort in confronting what we perceived to be sexist discourses in the program. This discomfort was reflected in the voices of female practitioners from Queensland Corrective Services who challenged program leaders around constructions of gender that undermined the aim of the CMP to reduce sexual violence through "investment in Indigenous knowledge and practice". As illustrated above, practitioners were aware that narratives of "pussy power" had persisted despite having been challenged previously and felt the tension that arose from this. This raised a further area of tension in recognising the role of the State as "enablers" of Indigenous programming. This is discussed below.

Questioning Benevolence

The use of the CMP in the "reintegration" of sexual offenders in many ways, but not all ways, challenges the coercive powers of the state. The management of offenders through embedding and upholding Indigenous knowledges as central to responding to Indigenous men who have offended sexually, as well as the need for this knowledge to be delivered by male Indigenous Elders, potentially challenges the expertise of the state. This challenge is conditional, however. The CMP is a voluntary program that is offered in addition to remaining engaged with the state through parole processes and is limited in its delivery. While the CMP may be a small step towards Indigenous management of criminal offending and desistance from it, it is highly dependent on the ongoing support of the state through funding and referral. This is an apt illustration of the benevolent and coercive state at work. This in no way undermines the individual or collective best intention of workers within Queensland Corrective Services so much as it highlights an existing tension whereby state agencies retain control and Indigenous programming maintains dependence on the state's benevolence—a benevolence that, like our own, should be questioned rather than assumed.

Some of the tension evident here is the exercise of power in relationships between the CMP run by male Indigenous leaders and a government department that cannot, and should not, separate itself from a colonial history that continues in the over-policing and incarceration of Indigenous peoples (Dawes et al. 2017; McKinnon 2019). This tension was evident to us as researchers and caused us to question our own role in the ongoing colonial project. Reflecting on her own work as a settler academic, Macoun (2016: 94) encourages us to critically interrogate assumptions that we and our work are fundamentally benevolent and whether we are even capable, as beneficiaries of the enduring colonial project, of "transcending the power relationships we critique and describe".

As feminist researchers, we do not assume impartiality in the research process. We are critically aware of our own ongoing benefit from colonialism. We acknowledge that we benefit as voices in this process including through the professional recognition and benefit of, and by being in receipt of, funding to conduct the research (Macoun 2016). We recognise our vested power in that we are employed, with tenure, in academia—an institution that has perpetuated colonisation, over-researched, and co-opted the voices of Indigenous peoples as the "other". In short, we are aware of our settler status (Macoun and Miller 2014; Macoun and Strakosch 2013). Through the process of this research, we became unsure of what that awareness means in critiquing our own assumptions that our work would benefit the CMP and Indigenous women and children with whom we sought to be allies. In short, we questioned our own benevolence (Macoun 2016).

In designing the research project, we had been careful to include Indigenous voices, to recognise that documenting the CMP could have beneficial outcomes because of the weight academic assessment brings in legitimising programs, to include Indigenous voices on the project Steering Committee, and to train and employ an Indigenous researcher to provide options to Indigenous participants. These are all strategies we perceived, and continue to consider, important in research design. One of the most telling impacts of this research was, for us, our prompts to continue to examine ourselves as settler researchers. To address Macoun's (2016) second point about assuming neutrality in this process, we had not assumed neutrality and were still uncomfortable when we found our own embodiment of settler privilege reflected back to us. This led to questions and discussions about how and what to report in the project and how to proceed knowing we did not hold the knowledge necessary to report in a way that did not inherently reflect our privilege or impose a critical perspective informed by that privilege. Due to the constraints of the project, we were also not able to pursue this knowledge directly from female Indigenous participants. Returning to literature and engaging with Indigenous scholars was an important step in reconciling these tensions. It also highlighted, again, the need to engage in decolonisation in ways that are deeply engaged with, and are led by, Indigenous knowledges (Blagg and Anthony 2019). There is no simple answer to this situation, and we continue to struggle to understand and deconstruct what this means for us as researchers who want to remain engaged in research that decolonises.

Conclusion

Our purpose here has been to discuss some of the ways in which we were challenged as white, female, non-Indigenous researchers investigating a program targeted at Indigenous males who had offended sexually. The research caused us to question deeply our own role and assumptions as settler researchers. These assumptions were revealed as a need to reconsider multiple aspects of the research project from design to interpretation and presentation of results. Issues of concern included: who held power in defining sexual violence, including in Indigenous communities, and rejecting an assumed neutrality in definitions; the potentially diverse impacts of sexual violence on members of Indigenous communities and management of impacts, including by services provided by a colonial state but delivered by Indigenous peoples; the assumed benevolence of a coercive colonial state, and academic research; and how we were situated as non-Indigenous feminist researchers in relation to narratives that conflicted with our own positionality (Macoun 2016; Macoun and Strakosch 2013; Maddison et al. 2016). Despite what we perceived to be reflective and considered approaches to research design and a specific intent to ally with Indigenous research partners, we experienced difficulty in reconciling our own privilege and what this meant for the project. In forcing us to reconsider whether, as settler researchers, we should be undertaking sensitive research in vulnerable Indigenous communities, we came to recognise that in future projects, we should expect to be uncomfortable in confronting and challenging our own preconceived benevolence and that this was an important part of respectfully conducting research in solidarity with Indigenous people (Benveniste and King 2018). This project was an apt reminder of the feminist position that the "personal is political" and as researchers we need to act as if that is true, not only for participants, but for researchers also. Critiquing our own political position includes recognising and challenging our positionality even when it is deeply uncomfortable (Griffin 2019; Macoun 2016). We also recognise that, in a colonial context of forced child removal, dispossession and the pathologising of Indigenous men, Indigenous women have actively resisted sexual violence in their communities. Sexual violence against Indigenous women and children cannot be explained outside of colonisation and the continual colonising project (Howe 2009). In part, we hope this chapter contributes towards discussions about further decolonising research and that it is of relevance to criminal justice practitioners and academics who share this important aim.

Summary

- As non-Indigenous, feminist, and settler researchers there is a need for sensitivity to assumptions of our own benevolence and helpfulness as researchers, alongside sensitivity to the diverse ongoing impacts of the colonial project on Indigenous communities and ourselves as researchers.
- As researchers we should be cognisant that what is defined as gendered and sexualised violence (including child sexual abuse)—and how it ought to be responded to—may not be value-neutral but shaped by the ongoing effects of the colonial project.
- As non-Indigenous feminist researchers we must find ways to act in solidarity with Indigenous people—including victim/survivors of sexual violence—without furthering the harmful effects of colonisation, such as the overrepresentation of Indigenous men in prison. In part, this means exercising caution about supporting state-sponsored Indigenisation programs, even when state-based services are research partners.
- Our experience of attempting to adopt decolonising research practices led to questions for which there are often complex and incomplete answers, and this should be expected.

References

Aboriginal Child Sexual Assault Taskforce. (2006). *Breaking the silence: Creating the future. Addressing child sexual assault in Aboriginal communities in NSW.* Sydney: New South Wales Attorney General's Department.

Anthony, Thalia (2009) Governing crime in the intervention. *Law In Context, 27*(2), 90–113.

Anthony, T. (2017, June 6). FactCheck: Are first Australians the most imprisoned people on Earth? *The Conversation.* https://theconversation.com/factcheck-are-first-australians-the-most-imprisoned-people-on-earth-78528

Australian Institute of Health and Welfare. (2021). *Child protection Australia 2019–20.* Canberra: Australian Institute of Health and Welfare.

Banet-Weiser, S. (2021). 'Ruined' lives: Mediated white male victimhood. *European Journal of Cultural Studies, 24*(1), 60–80. https://doi.org/10.1177/1367549420985840

Bayens, G., and Roberson, C. (2011). *Criminal justice research methods: Theory and practice* (2nd ed.). Boca Raton: Taylor & Marilyncis.

Benveniste, T., and King, L. (2018). Researching together: Reflections on ethical research in remote Aboriginal communities. *Learning Communities, 23,* 52–63.

Blagden, N., Winder, B., Gregson, M., and Thorne, K. (2014). Making sense of denial in sexual offenders: A qualitative phenomenological and repertory grid analysis. *Journal of Interpersonal Violence, 29*(9), 1698–1731. https://doi.org/10.1177/0886260513511530

Blagg, H. (2011). Journeys outside the comfort zone: Doing research in the Aboriginal domain. In L. Bartels and K. Richards (Eds.), *Qualitative criminology: Stories from the field* (pp. 140–152). Federation Press.

Blagg, Harry & Anthony, Thalia (2019). *Decolonising criminology : Imagining justice in a postcolonial world.* London: Palgrave Macmillan

Blagg, H., Tulich, T., Hovane, V., Raye, D., Worrigal, T., and May, S. (2020). *Understanding the role of law and culture in Aboriginal and Torres Strait Islander communities in responding to and preventing family violence.* Sydney: Australia's National Research Organisation for Women's Safety.

Bond, C., Singh, D., and Tyson, S. (2021). Black bodies and bioethics: Debunking mythologies of benevolence and beneficence in contemporary Indigenous health research in colonial Australia. *Journal of Bioethical Inquiry, 18,* 83–92.

Bouhours, B., and Daly, K. (2008). *Rape and attrition in the legal process: A comparative analysis of five countries*. Brisbane: Griffith University School of Criminology and Criminal Justice.

Bryant, J., Bolt, R., Botfield, J., Martin, K., Doyle, M., Murphy, D., Graham, S., Newman, C., Bell, S., Treloar, C., Browne, A., and Aggleton, P. (2021). Beyond deficit: 'Strengths-based approaches' in Indigenous health research. *Sociology of Health & Illness, 43*(6), 1405–1421. https://doi.org/10.1111/1467-9566.13311

Burn, M., and Brown, S. (2006). A review of the cognitive distortions in child sex offenders: An examination of the motivations and mechanisms that undrelie the justification for abuse. *Aggression and Violent Behavior, 11*, 225–236. https://doi.org/10.1016/j.avb.2005.08.002

Chamberlain, B. (2009). Phenomenology: A qualitative method. *Clinical Nurse Specialist, 23*(2), 52–53. https://doi.org/10.1097/NUR.0b013e3181996ae5

Clark, T., Dodson, S., Guivarra, N., and Widders Hunt, Y. (2021). "We're not treated equally as Indigenous people or as women": The perspectives and experiences of Indigenous women in Australian public relations. *Public Relations Inquiry, 10*(2), 163–183. https://doi.org/10.1177/2046147X2110 05358

Coram, S. (2009). Intervention or inversion: Australian Indigenous justice and the politics of cultural incompatibility: A section devoted to issues in applied anthropology. *Anthropological Forum, 19*(2), 195–216. https://doi.org/10.1080/00664670902980421

Coroners Court of Queensland. (2021). *Inquest into the death of Tiahleigh Alyssa-Rose Palmer*. Brisbane: Coroners Court of Queensland.

Cossins, A., and Plummer, M. (2016). Masculinity and sexual abuse: Explaining the transition from victim to offender. *Men and Masculinities, 21*(2), 163–188. http://journals.sagepub.com/doi/abs/10.1177/1097184X1 6652655

Cripps, K. (2021). Media constructions of Indigenous women in sexual assault cases: Reflections from Australia and Canada. *Current Issues in Criminal Justice, 33*(3), 300–321. https://doi.org/10.1080/10345329.2020.1867039

Cripps, K., and Adams, M. (2014). Family violence: Pathways forward. In P. Dudgeon, H. Milroy, and R. Walker (Eds.), *Working together: Aboriginal and Torres Strait Islander mental health and wellbeing principles and practice* (pp. 399–416). Canberra: Commonwealth of Australia.

Cripps, K., Davis, M., and Taylor, C. (2008). Sexual violence in Aurukun: The Queen V BP, DK, MY, PA, Koowarta, Wikmunea, Woolla 2007. *Indigenous Law Bulletin, 7*(9), 14–17.

Cripps, K., Diemer, K., Honey, N., Mickle, J., Morgan, J., Parkes, A., Politoff, V., Powell, A., Stubbs, J., Ward, A., and Webster, K. (2019). *Attitudes towards violence against women and gender equality among Aboriginal people and Torres Strait Islanders: Findings from the 2017 National Community Attitudes towards Violence against Women Survey*. Sydney: Australia's National Organisation for Women's Safety.

Cripps, K., and McGlade, H. (2008). Indigenous family violence and sexual abuse: Considering pathways forward. *Journal of Family Violence, 14*(2–3), 240–253. https://doi.org/10.5172/jfs.327.14.2-3.240

Dawes, G., Davidson, A., Walden, E., and Isaacs, S. (2017). Keeping on country: Understanding and responding to crime and recidivism in remote indigenous communities. *Australian Psychologist, 52*(4), 306–315. https://doi.org/10.1111/ap.12296

Dew, A., McEntyre, E., and Vaughan, P. (2019). Taking the research journey together: The insider and outsider experiences of Aboriginal and non-Aboriginal researchers. *Forum Qualitative Sozialforschung, 20*(1). https://doi.org/10.17169/fqs-20.1.3156

Fraser-Barbour, E., Crocker, R., and Walker, R. (2018). Barriers and facilitators in supporting people with intellectual disability to report sexual violence: Perspectives of Australian disability and mainstream support providers. *The Journal of Adult Protection, 20*(1), 5–16. http://doi.org/10.1108/JAP-08-2017-0031/full/html

Griffin, P. (2019). MeToo, white feminism and taking everyday politics seriously in the global political economy. *Australian Journal of Political Science, 54*(4), 556–572. https://doi.org/10.1080/10361146.2019.1663399

Guillemin, M., Gillam, L., Barnard, E., Stewart, P., Walker, H., and Rosenthal, D. (2016). "We're checking them out": Indigenous and non-Indigenous research participants' accounts of deciding to be involved in research. *International Journal for Equity in Health, 15*(8), 1–10. https://doi.org/10.1186/s12939-016-0301-4

Howe, A. (2009). Addressing child sexual assault in Australian Aboriginal communities: The politics of white voice. *Australian Feminist Law Journal, 30*(1), 41–61. https://doi.org/10.1080/13200968.2009.10854415

Hunter, E., and Onnis, L.-A. (2015). 'This is where a seed is sown': Aboriginal violence—Continuities or contexts? In J. Lindert and I. Levav (Eds.), *Violence and mental health: Its manifold faces* (pp. 221–241). Springer.

Katz, I., Newton, B., Bates, S., and Raven, M. (2016). *Evaluation theories and approaches: Relevance for Aboriginal contexts*. Sydney: University of New South Wales Social Policy Research Centre.

Keyzer, P., and Coyle, I. (2009). Reintegrating sex offenders into the community: Queensland's proposed reforms. *Alternative Law Journal, 34*(1), 27–31. https://doi.org/10.1177/1037969X0903400105

Keyzer, P., and O'Toole, S. (2006). Time, delay and nonfeasance: The Dangerous Prisoners (Sexual Offenders) Act 2003 (Queensland). *Alternative Law Journal, 31*(4), 198–202. https://doi.org/10.1177/1037969X0603100403

Konishi, S. (2008). 'Wanton with plenty' questioning ethno-historical constructions of sexual savagery in Aboriginal societies, 1788–1803. *Australian Historical Studies, 39*(3), 356–372. https://doi.org/10.1080/10314610802263331

LaRocque, E. (1997). Re-examining culturally appropriate models in criminal justice applications. In M. Asch (Ed.), *Aboriginal and treaty rights in Canada* (pp. 75–96). University of British Columbia.

Lawrence, R. (2007). *Research on strong Indigenous communities*. Sydney: Indigenous Justice Clearinghouse.

Leclerc, B., Smallbone, S., and Wortley, R. (2015). Prevention nearby: The influence of the presence of a potential guardian on the severity of child sexual abuse. *Sexual Abuse, 27*(2), 189–204. https://doi.org/10.1177/1079063213504594

Mace, G., Powell, M., and Benson, M. (2015). Evaluation of Operation RESET: An initiative for addressing child sexual abuse in Aboriginal communities. *Journal of Crminology, 48*(1), 82–103. https://doi.org/10.1177/0004865814524217

Macoun, A. (2011). Aboriginality and the Northern Territory intervention. *Australian Journal of Political Science, 46*(3), 519–534. https://doi.org/10.1080/10361146.2011.595700

Macoun, A. (2016). Colonising white innocence: Complicity and critical encounters. In S. Maddison, T. Clark, and R. de Costa (Eds.), *The limits of settler colonial reconciliation: Non-indigenous people and the responsibility to engage* (pp. 85–102). Springer Singapore. https://doi.org/10.1007/978-981-10-2654-6

Macoun, A., and Miller, D. (2014). Surviving (thriving) in academia: Feminist support networks and women ECRs. *Journal of Gender Studies, 23*(3), 287–301. https://doi.org/10.1080/09589236.2014.909718

Macoun, A., and Strakosch, E. (2013). The ethical demands of settler colonial theory. *Settler Colonial Studies, 3*(3–4), 426–443. https://doi.org/10.1080/2201473X.2013.810695

Maddison, S. (2019). *The colonial fantasy: Why White Australia can't solve Black problems*. Allen & Unwin.
Maddison, S., Clark, T., and De Costa, R. (Eds.). (2016). *The limits of settler colonial reconciliation: Non-indigenous people and the responsibility to engage.* Singapore: Springer Singapore. https://doi.org/10.1007/978-981-10-2654-6
Maruna, S. (2001). *Making good: How ex-convicts reform and rebuild their lives.* Washington, DC: American Psychological Association.
McCausland, R. (2019). 'I'm sorry but I can't take a photo of someone's capacity being built': Reflections on evaluation of Indigenous policy and programmes. *Evaluation Journal of Australasia, 19*(2), 64–78. https://doi.org/10.1177/1035719X19848529
McKinnon, C. (2019). The lives behind the statistics: Policing practices in Aboriginal literature. *The Australian Feminist Law Journal, 45*(2), 207–223. https://doi.org/10.1080/13200968.2020.1800931
McQuire, A. (2018, March 6). Mainstream feminism still blind to its racism. *IndigenousX*. https://indigenousx.com.au/amy-mcquire-mainstream-feminism-still-blind-to-its-racism/
Moreton-Robinson, A. (2000). *Talkin' up to the white woman: Indigenous women and feminism.* University of Queensland Press.
Moreton-Robinson, A. (2006). Whiteness matters: Implications of Talkin' up to the White Woman. *Australian Feminist Studies, 21*(50), 245–256. https://doi.org/10.1080/08164640600731788
Mullighan, E. (2008). *Commission of Inquiry Report (Children on the APY Lands): A report into sexual abuse.* Adelaide: Government of South Australia.
Northern Territory Board of Inquiry into the Protection of Aboriginal Children from Sexual Abuse. (2007). *Ampe Akelyernnemane Mekarle (Little children are sacred).* Darwin: Northern Territory Government.
O'Brien, W. (2010). *Australia's response to sexualised or sexually abusive behaviours in children and young people.* Canberra: Australian Crime Commission.
O Ciardha, C., and Ward, T. (2013). Theories of cognitive distortions in sexual offending: What the current research tells us. *Trauma, Violence, & Abuse, 14*(1), 5–21. https://doi.org/10.1177/1524838012467856
Phipps, A. (2020). *Me, not you: The trouble with mainstream feminism.* University of Manchester.
Putt, J. (2013). *Conducting research with Indigenous people and communities.* Indigenous Justice Clearinghouse.

Queensland Department of Justice and Attorney-General. (2020). *Annual report 2019–20*. Brisbane: Queensland Department of Justice and Attorney-General.

Ransley, J., and Marchetti, E. (2021). Medicalizing the detention of Aboriginal people in the Northern Territory: A new/old regime of control? *Social & Legal Studies, 30*(1), 104–122. https://doi.org/10.1177/0964663918779652

Razack, S. (1998). *Looking white people in the eye: Gender, race, and culture in courtrooms and classrooms*. University of Toronto Press.

Richards, K. (2020). *Post-prison programs for Indigenous sex offenders*. Indigenous Justice Clearinghouse.

Richards, K., Death, J., and McCartan, K. (2020a). *Community-based approaches to sexual offender reintegration*. Sydney: Australia's National Research Organisation for Women's Safety.

Richards, K., Death, J., and McCartan, K. (2020b). Toward redemption: Aboriginal and/or Torres Strait Islander men's narratives of desistance from sexual offending. *Victims & Offenders, 15*(6), 810–833. https://www.tandfonline.com/doi/full/10.1080/15564886.2020.1754311

Richards, K., Death, J., McCartan, K., and Australia's National Research Organisation for Women's Safety. (2020). *Research to policy and practice issue 07: Community-based approaches to sexual offender reintegration: Key findings and future directions*. Sydney: Australia's National Research Organisation for Women's Safety.

Sherwood, J. (2010). *Do No Harm: Decolonising Aboriginal health research*. Sydney: University of New South Wales.

Smallbone, S., Rayment-McHugh, S., and Smith, D. (2013). *Preventing youth sexual violence*. Brisbane: Queensland Department of Premier and Cabinet.

Stanley, J., Kovacs, K., Tomison, A., and Cripps, K. (2002). *Child abuse and family violence in Aboriginal communities—Exploring child sexual abuse in Western Australia*. Melbourne: Australian Institute of Family Studies.

Stewart, W., Huntley, A., and Blaney, F. (2001). *The implications of restorative justice for Aboriginal women and children survivors of violence: A comparative overview of five communities in British Columbia*. Ottawa: Law Commission of Canada.

Strakosch, E., and Macoun, A. (2020). The violence of analogy: Abstraction, neoliberalism and settler colonial possession. *Postcolonial Studies, 23*(4), 505–526. https://doi.org/10.1080/13688790.2020.1834930

Taylor, N., and Putt, J. (2007). *Trends & issues in crime and criminal justice no. 345: Adult sexual violence in Indigenous and culturally and linguistically diverse communities in Australia.* Canberra: Australian Institute of Criminology.

Trask, H.-K. (2003). Review of: Talkin' up to the white woman: Indigenous women and feminism. *Contemporary Pacific, 15*(2), 474–475.

Ware, J., Blagden, N., and Harper, C. (2020). Are categorical deniers different? Understanding demographic, personality, and psychological differences between denying and admitting sex offenders. *Deviant Behavior: An Interdisciplinary Journal, 41*(4), 399–412. https://doi.org/10.1080/01639625.2018.1558944

Watson, I. (2009). In the Northern Territory intervention: What is saved or rescued and at what cost? *Cultural Studies Review, 15,* 45–60.

Webster, K., Diemer, K., Honey, N., Mannix, S., Mickle, J., Morgan, J., Parkes, A., Politoff, V., Powell, A., Stubbs, J., and Ward, A. (2018). *Australians' attitudes to violence against women and gender equality: Findings from the 2017 National Community Attitudes Towards Violence Against Women Survey.* Sydney: Australia's National Research Organisation for Women's Safety.

Williams, M. (2018). Ngaa-bi-nya Aboriginal and Torres Strait Islander program evaluation framework. *Evaluation Journal of Australasia, 18*(1), 6–20. https://doi.org/10.1177/1035719X18760141

Willis, M. (2011). *Trends & issues in crime and criminal justice no. 405: Non-disclosure of violence in Australian Indigenous communities.* Canberra: Australian Institute of Criminology.

Index

A

Aboriginal and/or Torres Strait Islander men 17, 402, 406, 407, 409, 418
Aboriginal community 346, 360, 417
Aboriginal-specific healing approaches 359
Aboriginal survivors 15, 16, 20, 341, 342, 344, 345, 347, 359, 362–364
abuse
  disclosure 12, 17, 63, 82, 86, 93, 102, 304
  fear 63, 71, 99, 189, 222, 318
  sexual 3, 5, 10–13, 15, 16, 21, 32, 33, 43, 45, 52, 61, 69, 85, 92, 95, 116, 125, 134, 148, 171, 187, 188, 195, 207, 211, 218, 220, 224, 226, 227, 236, 239, 240, 244, 251, 256, 273, 281, 294, 308, 382, 402, 417
acculturation 315, 326–328
African American women 122
African-Caribbean British families 136
African-Caribbean British women 11, 123, 128–131, 148
African descent 12, 116, 118, 120, 123, 125, 128–131, 133, 138, 378
aftermath of disclosure 100, 101
agency 65, 116, 118–124, 128, 131, 135, 137, 139, 143, 148, 149, 260, 292
alterity 11, 116, 131, 132, 138
American racism 288
Anna Mae 117, 118, 120–123, 125, 138, 139, 150
art in healing 361, 363

Index

Asian family structures 87, 99
asymmetrical power relation 278
attitudes and beliefs 260, 389
Australian courts 403, 413
Australian Royal Commission 15, 342, 346

B

backward communities 359
barriers to reporting 319
beatings 12, 132, 140
becoming 35, 116, 131–133, 150, 209, 238
behaviour 34, 35, 46, 51, 62, 65–67, 77, 79, 161, 166, 208, 227, 228, 252, 253, 255, 262–264, 319, 321
behavioural beliefs 258, 319
behaviours that constitute CSA 4
benevolence 416, 419–421
Black/Afro-Latina victims 9
black and racially minoritised women 122
Black boys 15, 19, 273–277, 279–287, 289, 292–296
Black females 122, 129
Black Lives Matter 130, 380
Black male identity 275
Black maleness 14, 292
Black masculinity 275, 280, 284, 291
black minority ethnic women 41
  violence against 10
Black-on-Black rape 129
Black womanhood 118, 129
Blind Eye 134, 135, 137, 143
British South Asian men 11, 60, 61, 64, 66, 102

Brixton Black Women's Group (BBWG) 130

C

Catholic communities 305
characteristics of Abuse 311
chastity 317
childhood exposure 376
child protection 8, 13, 157–160, 167, 169–173, 195, 253, 256, 261, 403
child sexual abuse
  control and powerlessness issue 355
  culturalist discourses 251, 252
  fear 63, 222, 295
  nullity 342
  othered culture discourse 230
  victim credibility 210
  victims 48, 50
child sexual exploitation 8, 33, 34, 192, 220, 222
Chile 8
'clash of culture' 231
  immigrants 160
code-switching 380
coercion
  conception of 266, 274, 277, 278
  family members 277, 280
  pressure 260
coercion/consent 250, 259
coercive control 42, 51, 135, 143
collective trauma 15, 342, 345, 362
colonisation 20, 342, 356, 363, 364, 404, 405, 415–418, 420, 421
colonising structures 415
community 12, 13, 15, 17, 32–34, 36, 39, 41, 42, 45, 52, 61,

Index

70–73, 80, 89, 99–101, 138, 156, 161, 162, 186, 191, 195, 202, 222, 227, 238, 242, 322, 359, 379, 383, 407
community attitudes 5
community honour 34, 198
community reputation 92, 222
concealing CSA 18
concept of honour 98
consent
    conception 278
    parental 267
continuum
    violence against women 10, 254, 265
control 45, 102, 254, 262, 317
counselling 60, 70–74, 76, 78, 79, 354, 356, 357, 360
Crenshaw, K. 11, 38, 119, 121, 128, 304
    theory of intersectionality 115, 131
criminal justice responses 10
criminal justice system 12, 18, 44, 45, 51, 130, 190, 191, 209–212, 225, 226, 238, 253, 352, 371, 376, 382, 385, 403, 415, 417, 418
Crown Prosecution Service (CPS) 192
CSA and substance abuse 310
CSA disclosure 7, 9, 13, 63, 67, 81, 83, 85, 161, 169, 173, 309, 316, 317, 319, 320
cultural and religious values 319
cultural background 234, 327
cultural bias and discrimination 309
cultural competency 170, 221, 240, 359

cultural context 10, 21, 43, 101, 211, 314, 327, 372, 391, 392
cultural differences 4, 62, 91, 290, 417
cultural inhibitors 18, 262
culturalised violence 21, 289, 404
culturally appropriate support 234, 403
Cultural Mentoring Program 406–412, 419, 420
cultural norms 3, 5, 9, 11, 15, 82, 156, 160, 161, 303, 316
cultural sexualisation 256
cultural specificities 13
cultural stereotypes 13, 32, 33
cultural trauma 373, 377, 379–381, 387, 390
culture
    and domestic violence 92
    and human rights 6
    and masculinity 8, 11, 60, 64, 92, 289
    and multiculturalism 63, 221
    and religion 7, 18, 41
    and violence against women 275, 292
    as excusing violence 404
culture and honour 210
culture clash 231
culture of silence 5, 287, 326

D

daughters 12, 51, 115, 116, 118–120, 125, 128, 132, 138, 140, 147, 148, 150, 318, 323
decolonising research 422
definition
    child sexual abuse 2

digital communication 256
disclosures or 'tellings' 11, 115, 149
dishonour 9, 13, 163, 172, 191, 210, 325
domestic violence 10, 32, 41, 61, 85, 92, 121, 189, 280, 321, 376, 413
dominant culture 325
duty and honour 68

E

education 20, 39, 51, 61, 73, 238, 252, 253, 267, 275, 280, 305, 322–325, 328, 343, 352, 382, 392
effects of CSA 118, 304, 313
environmental risk factors 315
epistemic injustice 11, 31, 36, 37, 41, 48, 50–52
ethnicity 6, 10, 13, 17, 19, 36, 41, 43, 61, 100, 102, 143, 157, 160, 161, 170, 171, 188, 220, 225, 231, 232, 235, 241, 242, 306, 308, 311, 313, 325, 327, 389
ethnic minority communities 13, 19, 217–220, 222, 223, 230, 234–241, 243, 244
expectations 11, 60, 64–67, 72, 82, 87, 94, 119, 164, 172, 258, 317, 319, 322, 374, 385, 387
'explorative' and 'exploitative' sexual behaviours 261, 262

F

families
 conflict 266, 273
 extended 70, 74, 75, 91, 163, 164, 168, 312, 314, 316, 325
 power 82, 324
 resolution 100
 violence in 61, 102
Familismo 316, 325
family 5, 12, 15, 32, 35, 45, 50, 62, 71, 72, 75, 77, 80, 81, 87, 91, 99, 118, 135, 161, 191, 228, 277
family honour 99, 169
family (ies) coercion within
 power relations in 262
'family life' 72, 136, 160, 164, 169, 170
 respect for 316
family violence 402
female genital mutilation 9, 12, 42, 186, 211
female homicide offenders 121, 122
Female-perpetrated CSA 156, 161
females 2, 5, 6, 9, 165, 251, 255, 260, 264, 284, 319
Female sexual autonomy 62
femininity 64, 97, 151, 412
 gendered scripts 65
feminism 6, 279, 405, 414–416
forced marriage 10, 12, 32, 186, 197, 211
'free' and 'informed' consent 262

G

gang-associated sexual violence 258
gender 6, 15, 19, 20, 37, 38, 41, 50, 103, 116, 118, 120, 121, 131, 135, 143, 149, 157, 188, 210, 220, 230, 240, 250, 254, 291, 304, 316

gender based violence 18, 20, 38, 41, 44, 51
  and masculinity 418
gendered sexual stereotypes 259
gender role conflicts 64
gender socialising 65, 94, 260
Global North 305
Global South 7, 8
guilt and shame 7, 8

H

Halo Project 12, 185–187, 189–191, 195, 208, 209, 211, 212
harmful behaviour 261, 264
harmful cultural practices 101
harmful sexual behaviour (HSB) 13, 14, 250–253, 256, 259, 261, 263, 264, 266, 267
healing 16, 20, 52, 71, 73, 81, 100, 101, 241, 242, 323, 341, 345, 347, 348, 354, 357, 358, 361, 363, 364
'healthy' sexual behaviour 14, 263
hegemonic masculinities 37
  behaviour 66
  manifestation of 67
hermeneutical injustice 37
Hispanic women 315
historical narratives 230
history of trauma 384, 385, 387, 389
homophobic attitudes 96, 97
homosexuality 95–97, 321
'honour'
  codes of 69
  community 61
  concept 98
  power 69
  violence 101
  women 61
honour and gay men/LGBTQI+ 97
honour and self-harm 51
honour-based violence 12, 186, 187
honour cultures 210
How to Get Away with Murder 12, 116, 117, 120, 121, 148
hyper-masculinity 66, 102, 280, 293
hyper-sexuality 10, 136, 275, 276, 284, 293

I

'ideal victim' 65
identification and treatment efforts 4
immigration 18, 38, 41, 51, 52, 130, 135, 314, 315, 378
immigration status 43, 220, 304, 315, 326, 328, 329
implications for practitioners 10
implicit/explicit 11, 115, 132, 143, 146, 234
inclusive, intersectional interventions 17, 18
Independent Inquiry into Child Sexual Abuse 32, 171, 218
India 3, 71, 79, 156
Indigenous communities 402–404, 414, 417, 418, 421
Indigenous Elder 17, 407, 409, 410, 415, 419
Indigenous men 17, 404, 405, 413, 417–419, 422
Indonesia 8
informal support 189, 221, 223, 235
institution 221, 227, 346, 350, 420
institutional assaults 385
institutional barriers 13

institutional child sexual abuse 341, 342, 345, 347, 348, 350, 353, 362
institutional CSA 15
institutional racism 188, 197, 221, 222, 237
institutional responses 19, 218, 225
intention and honour 38
intergenerational abuse 326
intergeneration disadvantage 380
intersecting socio-cultural forces 7
intersecting traumas 363
intersectional abuse 12, 115, 116, 118–120, 122, 124, 128–130, 137, 143, 149
intersectional feminist theories 280
intersectionality 6, 10, 21, 36, 38, 41, 52, 96, 132, 157, 274, 303, 304, 362, 363, 392, 417
intra-generational victim-survivors 150
Izzat (concept of honour) 61, 62, 80, 88, 97–99, 102, 161, 162, 165, 166, 197

lack of diversity 229
Latinx 10, 303, 305–309, 311, 313, 314, 316, 318, 320, 323, 325
Latinx community 15, 303
Latinx cultures 15, 305, 316–320, 325
Latinx populations 15, 303–306, 324, 328
Left in the Dark 209
legal professionals 14, 157
LGBTQ+ 251, 309
losing honour 97

M
machismo 316–318, 326
'macho' culture 8
maladaptive coping 310, 381, 384
Malaysia 8
male familial control 419
males 2, 8, 14, 15, 64, 87, 92, 123, 125, 139, 156, 157, 161, 232, 255, 256, 261, 273, 274, 276, 280, 282, 285, 288, 289, 295, 376, 421
male sexual vulnerability 274, 276, 277, 293
male survivors 11, 59, 60, 64, 65, 68, 93, 101, 295, 313
male victimisation 9
male victims 8, 65, 67, 122, 187, 188, 280, 287, 296, 304, 319, 326
male violence 64, 67
Mama 117, 120–123, 125, 150
manhood 64, 101, 274, 276, 288, 291, 293, 294
marianismo 316, 326
masculinities theory 11, 60, 64, 67, 96
masculinity 8, 60, 64–66, 80, 92–95, 97, 102, 221, 250, 258, 418
masculinity and homophobia 64, 97
masculinity and sexuality 11, 60, 92
mass incarceration 285
maternal mimesis 11, 116, 118–121, 123, 126, 130, 133, 134, 147–149
mental health impacts 353
#metoo 416
Mexican and Mexican American women 307

Middle East 7, 8
mimetic performance 132, 133, 148
mimicry 116, 120, 131, 132
minimisation 412
minoritised communities 2, 5, 7, 12, 17–19, 32–35, 37, 52, 61, 63, 65, 101, 118, 157, 162, 166, 170, 171, 186–191, 207, 208, 210, 211
misogynist violence 260
mother-daughter relationship 116, 120, 131, 138, 149
mothers 11, 12, 35, 51, 86, 92, 115, 116, 118, 119, 124–126, 128, 130, 132, 134, 138, 139, 143, 148–150, 279, 319–321, 324
motivation and honour 250
multi-agency cooperation 5
multi-generational households 61
Multiple 'Tellings' 139
multiple identities 6

N

National Society for the Prevention of Cruelty to Children (NSPCC) 4, 39, 44, 49
new media 249, 256, 257
NGO 221
non-Indigenous feminists 405, 406
non-Indigenous women 17
normalised settings 262
North Africa 8

O

offenders 16, 263, 267, 325, 406, 417

oppression 6, 10, 19, 38, 115, 131, 286, 287, 291, 362, 378
ostracism 100, 101, 197
out-of-home care 15, 342, 344–347, 349, 350, 352–354, 357, 363, 364
overcomer 147

P

Pakistani communities 12, 156
patriarchal culture 7, 92
patriarchal societies 67
patriarchy 66, 128, 284
peer-based HSB 14, 256, 264, 266
peer pressure 259
peer support 235, 236, 239, 242, 391
perpetrator intervention 17, 402
perpetrators 15, 37, 65–67, 99, 169, 187, 189–191, 195, 198, 199, 203–205, 209, 220, 250, 251, 259, 274, 277, 285, 292, 295, 296, 304, 311, 312, 327, 356, 405, 406, 412, 414
  brothers 194, 202, 312
  brothers and sisters 194
  cousins 194, 312
  family 15, 41
  father 34, 312
  husband 44
  parents 295
  relatives 205, 312
  sons 195
personality disorders 16, 373–376, 383, 384, 386–389, 392
physical punishment 142, 350
police 4, 12, 18, 32–34, 39, 44, 49, 70, 77, 86, 136, 186–190,

192, 195, 196, 201, 203–205, 208, 226, 287, 405
police homicide 286
police response failures 189
policing responses to CSA 12
polyvictimisation 10, 35, 36, 50
pornography online 259
'postcode lottery' 13
post-traumatic reactions 16, 372, 373
Post Traumatic Slave Syndrome (PTSS) 379, 380, 390
poverty 17, 119, 131, 135, 149, 280, 314, 326
power 1, 6, 18, 20, 36, 38, 42, 50, 52, 65, 82, 83, 102, 123, 131, 133, 138, 150, 190, 196, 208, 262, 278, 294, 343, 361, 404, 417
powerlessness 123, 355
prevalence of child sexual abuse 237, 255
prevalence rates of CSA 309
prevention 2, 4, 9, 13, 14, 21, 38, 239, 266, 324, 328
privilege 6, 38, 123, 129, 362, 392, 409, 410, 414, 415, 418, 420, 421
process of disclosing 81
psychological support 357
public health implications 14
public health practitioners 296
punitive maternal responses 140

R

race and gender theory 292
racial/cultural solidarity 129
racialized males 284, 289

racially minoritised communities 2, 5, 7, 12, 17–19, 32, 34, 35, 37, 52, 185–191, 207, 208, 210, 211
racial scripts 287
racism 5, 13, 19, 20, 32, 33, 45, 59, 60, 116, 119, 123, 128, 131, 135, 138, 148–150, 222, 223, 237, 239, 243, 274, 276, 280, 286, 320, 344, 350, 356, 357, 359, 362, 364, 404, 405, 414
racism and systemic oppression 286
racist stereotyping 230, 238
rape
  culture 10
  victim blaming 45, 321, 326
  victims 33, 65, 186, 188
rape myths 413
redemption scripts 411
religion 7, 18, 41, 42, 50, 51, 61, 70, 220, 224, 305, 318, 324
  honour 42
religious communities 35
religious leaders 34
religious norms 18, 41, 49, 52
remaining silent 119, 136, 317, 319
removal from parents 348, 349, 362
reputation 92, 160, 222, 317
resilience 11, 116, 119, 120, 122, 128, 134, 148, 151, 361
resistance 48, 51, 52, 116, 119, 120, 147, 149, 221, 222, 295, 342, 383, 386
respecto (respect) 316
Risk-Need-Responsivity model (RNR) 371, 372, 389
risky sexual scripts 284
Roman Catholic Church 309, 318
Rotherham 33, 192

Rotherham effect 199

S

safeguarding 13, 19, 20, 157, 158, 170, 172, 198, 205, 224, 242, 252
safe spaces 17, 52, 323
secrecy 4, 12, 139, 166, 195, 320, 325, 356
self-silencing 317
settler colonial theory (SCT) 405, 415
Sex
  honour 61
sexism 119, 123, 284, 414
sexting 14, 250–252, 254, 255, 259, 263–266
sexual behaviours
  'abusive' 14, 20, 249, 254, 259, 267
  'exploitative' 20, 249, 254, 259, 261, 262
  'explorative' 20, 261, 262
  'healthy' 14, 20, 257, 263
sexual health 323, 324
sexualised violence 20
sexuality 9, 37, 38, 67, 75, 92, 95–97, 116, 120, 121, 136, 149, 256, 258, 260, 263, 264, 275, 288, 290, 323. *See also* women's sexuality
  human rights 186, 404
  social construction 6
sexually offended (ISOs) 16, 373, 376, 382, 412
sexual messaging 258
Sexual Offences Act 2003 3, 264
sexual permissiveness 289

sexual relations 61, 230, 256, 259, 413
sexual violation 275, 278, 285, 292, 294
shame 4, 11, 13, 50, 61, 63, 82, 100, 150, 155, 168, 191, 326
sharam 61–63, 161, 163
Shelters
  refuges 414
  women's protection 253, 256, 258, 279, 326
siblings 71, 73, 74, 194, 201–203, 205, 209, 349
silence and shame 239
silencing 50, 129, 342, 344, 345, 356
socialisation 9, 64, 94, 260
social mobility 122
social pressures 64
social workers 231, 286, 287, 295
socio-cultural contexts 10
South Asian male survivors 11, 59, 68, 101
Southeast Asia 7, 8
speaking out 50–52, 142, 149
speak out 42, 43, 45–47, 51, 67, 122, 130, 317, 414
state
  failure 211, 228
  lack of 188, 193, 403
  limitations 159, 220
  protection 160, 403
  responsibility 18, 77
statutory institutions 221, 223, 224
statutory rape laws 275, 279
stereotyping 5, 228, 234, 239, 243
Stolen Generations 343–345, 349, 357, 361

'strong black woman' (SBW) 11, 116, 119–123, 126, 128, 132–134, 138, 147, 148, 150, 151
subculture of violence 275, 289
suicide
  domestic violence escape 51
  honour killing 99, 166
  pressured 259
super-complaint 12, 13, 34, 185–187, 189, 193, 201, 208, 211, 212
survivor 4, 5, 7, 10–13, 15, 18, 19, 32, 33, 38, 39, 44, 51, 59, 60, 62, 63, 69, 82, 83, 90, 95, 97, 100, 102, 132, 150, 163, 169, 186, 201, 212, 231, 238, 243, 327, 346, 349, 361
systematic racism 20
systemic police failures 207

teachers 47
telling 11, 33, 73, 79, 115, 128, 132, 139, 140, 143, 159
testimonial injustice 37, 41
testimonies 11, 36–38, 41, 42, 51, 52, 277, 285, 292
Torres Strait Islander 17, 401–403, 405, 408–410, 414, 416
trauma 11, 14, 60, 68, 89, 233, 241, 276, 280, 303, 353, 375, 392
trauma-informed care (TIC) 16, 372, 381, 391
trauma reactions 386, 387, 392
Turkey 7, 9
turning a blind eye 134, 135, 137, 139, 143

underreporting 4, 256, 261, 263, 307
UNICEF 3, 7
United Kingdom (UK) 3–5, 32, 44, 60, 65, 78, 116, 125, 131, 135, 166, 186, 210, 218, 251
United States 14, 15, 273, 274, 277, 281, 282, 284, 285, 290, 292–294, 296, 303, 304, 376, 383

victim blaming 45, 321, 326
victim(s) 4, 7–10, 12, 13, 17–19, 43, 51, 61, 151, 185, 193, 207, 210, 221, 232, 240, 252, 274, 294, 304, 322, 411
Victims' Code 191, 193, 196, 204, 205, 212
Victim Support 209, 252, 325
victim-survivors 32, 115, 118, 119, 121, 126, 131, 132, 134, 139, 141–143, 148, 149
violence 5, 6, 8, 9, 19, 32, 39, 51, 64, 67, 102, 120, 126, 161, 166, 186, 249, 262, 273, 274, 276, 278, 281, 295, 342, 402, 411, 414
violence against women 274, 275, 292, 414, 417
  commonalities 19, 21
  continuum 10, 254, 265
  domestic. See domestic violence
violence against women in South Asian communities 50
virginity 9, 317–319, 325, 326

voluntary suspect interviews 187, 190, 195, 208, 212

W

Western feminism 414
White females 122
white feminist researchers' 17, 405, 418
white feminists 414, 415
whiteness 288

women
   British Muslim 43, 46, 208
   gender-based myths 260
   policing women 12, 20
women of African descent 12, 116, 118, 120, 123, 125, 128–131, 133, 138
women's sexuality, fear of/regulation 291, 418
World Health Organisation 263

Printed in the United States
by Baker & Taylor Publisher Services